P9-AFM-341

MYSTIC CHEMIST

The Life of
Albert Hofmann
and His Discovery of LSD

Dieter Hagenbach and Lucius Werthmüller

Foreword by Stanislav Grof

 Synergetic Press
Santa Fe, New Mexico

Copyright © 2011 by AT Verlag Aarau und München
Text Copyright © 2011 Dieter Hagenbach and Lucius Werthmüller
English translation copyright © 2013 by Synergetic Press
Foreword copyright © 2011 by Stanislav Grof
All rights reserved.

No part of this publication may be reproduced, stored in any retrieval system, or transmitted, in any form or by any means, electronic, mechanical, photocopying, recording, or otherwise without the prior permission of the publisher.

Published by Synergetic Press
1 Bluebird Court, Santa Fe, NM 87508

Library of Congress Cataloging-in-Publication Data

Hagenbach, Dieter A.
   [Albert Hofmann und sein LSD. English]
  Mystic chemist : the life of Albert Hofman and his discovery of LSD /
Dieter Hagenbach and Lucius Werthmüller ; foreword by Stanislav Grof.
      pages cm
  Translation of: Albert Hofmann und sein LSD.
  Includes bibliographical references and index.
  ISBN-13: 978-0-907791-46-1 (hardcover)
  ISBN-13: 978-0-907791-44-7 (pbk.)
  ISBN-10: 0-907791-44-1
  1. Hofmann, Albert, 1906-2008. 2. LSD (Drug)--History. 3.
Chemists--Biography. I. Werthmüller, Lucius, 1958- II. Title.
  BF209.L9H34 2013
  615.7'883092--dc23
  [B]
                                          2013003308

Editor: Linda Sperling
Translation: William Geuss and Linda Sperling
Interior book design: John Cole Graphic Design
Cover design: Lakshmi Narayan, Awake Media
Cover photo: François Lagarde
Cover artwork: Richard Toelanie
Typeface: Optima and Formata
Printed in China by Global PSD

Contents

Light Painting by Dean Chamberlain, 1997

Introduction

This book is dedicated to all whose lives were changed by Albert Hofmann's discoveries.

"Not I, LSD was chosen" succinctly said Albert Hofmann in 2007 when, at the age of 101, he was selected as the most important living genius by a jury from the renowned British newspaper the *Daily Telegraph*. Hardly any other discovery in the twentieth century has exercised greater influence on science, society, and culture than the mysterious, incomparably potent substance that in doses of a mere millionth of a gram profoundly alters consciousness. The chemist discovered its psychedelic effect on April 19, 1943, during a self-experiment on his legendary bicycle ride. This first LSD trip fundamentally changed his life as it later would lead millions of people throughout the world into new directions.

Albert Hofmann's biography takes us on a journey through the twentieth century: From his mystical experiences of nature as a child in Baden, to his study of chemistry with Nobel Prize winner Paul Karrer in Zurich, his discovery of LSD and of psilocybin at Sandoz in Basel, his adventurous expe-

ditions and journeys and the many years of retirement devoted to natural philosophy and an extremely rich social life.

His research into ergot alkaloids led to several drugs that he developed virtually by himself and these earned and continue to earn his former employer billions in sales. Even though Albert Hofmann never earned the Nobel Prize due to the controversy surrounding LSD, he is the best known twentieth-century chemist and the only one with pop star status—as the storm of flashbulbs at his frenetically celebrated appearances on his 100th birthday at the LSD Symposium in Basel clearly demonstrated.

After its fateful discovery, LSD became the subject of thousands of clinical studies for decades as well as obscure experiments by Secret Services and the Military. In the 1960s it left the laboratory and fueled the emerging youth and Hippie movements in the USA that ultimately changed the world—a mass phenomenon that unleashed downright hysteria about LSD, which was described as the devil's work. The creativity-enhancing effect of this psychedelic substance influenced the development of computer technology just as significantly as it led to pioneering scientific discoveries and a holistic relationship of humans to their environment.

Albert Hofmann remained linked to this molecule for the rest of his life, which prepared the ground for innovative therapy approaches and a new estimation of mystic states, and brought him into contact with such thinkers as Aldous Huxley, Ernst Jünger and Karl Kerényi, as well as countless scientists, artists and counter-culture proponents. He never lost faith in his "problem child" to which he attested the potential of a wonder drug, and he was pleased when he had the experience in his later years of LSD once more gaining acceptance. The Swiss Federal president of the time, Moritz Leuenberger wrote, "Through your research and writings, Dr. Hofmann, you have helped keep artistic, philosophical and religious questions alive in scientific discussions," as he congratulated him on his 100th birthday.

Albert Hofmann—an extraordinary person, researcher and mystic, maintained his openness, curiosity and love of the living creation up to his last breath at the age of 102.

Dieter Hagenbach and
Lucius Werthmüller

Foreword by Stanislav Grof

Stanislav Grof,
Basel 2008

It is an extraordinary privilege and pleasure for me to write a foreword for this book honoring the life and work of Albert Hofmann, a brilliant researcher and scientist whom I consider my spiritual father. Words can hardly describe my deep gratitude for everything that his discoveries brought into my personal and professional life and into the lives of countless other people, who used the substances he had synthesized responsibly and with the respect that these extraordinary tools deserve.

I first heard Albert's name in 1954 when I worked as a medical student volunteer at the Psychiatric Department of the School of Medicine of Charles University in Prague. My preceptor, Docent George Roubiček, had a good working relationship with Sandoz Pharmaceutical Company in Basel and regularly received complimentary samples of new Sandoz products as they were brought to market. As part of this cooperation, he received a supply of diethylamide of lysergic acid, or LSD-25, a new experimental substance with unprecedented psychoactive power. The package arrived with a letter describing the discovery of LSD—Albert's accidental intoxication during the synthesis of this substance, his subsequent self-experiment, and Werner Stoll's pilot study with a group of normal volunteers and psychiatric patients.

Werner Stoll's paper "LSD, ein Phantastikum aus der Mutterkorngruppe" (Stoll 1947) became an overnight sensation in the scientific world. His pilot study showed that miniscule dosages of this new substance (in the range of millionths of a gram—micrograms or gammas) were able to induce a state in experimental subjects that in many ways resembled naturally occurring psychoses; Stoll also mentioned in his paper that LSD might have interesting therapeutic potential. Sandoz was now sending samples of the new substance to psychiatric research institutes, university departments, and individual therapists asking them if they would be interested in experimenting with LSD and exploring if this substance had any legitimate uses in psychiatry and psychology. The letter gave two suggestions for possible use of LSD: As an agent inducing "experimental psychosis" that might provide insights into biochemical causes of schizophrenia and as an unconventional therapeutic tool that would make it possible for mental health professionals to spend a few hours in a state resembling the experiential world of psychotic patients.

Docent Roubiček was very interested in conducting research with LSD, but his busy schedule did not allow him to spend six to eight hours in sessions with experimental subjects. He asked me and a few other students to be guides for these people, observe them, and keep records about their experiences. This gave me a unique opportunity to be present in psychedelic sessions of many volunteers, including psychiatrists, psychologists, and artists. I was fascinated by what I saw and heard and was eager to volunteer for a session myself. Unfortunately, to my great dismay, the faculty board decided that students should not be used as experimental subjects. I could not wait to experience LSD personally and as soon as I graduated from the medical school, I volunteered for a session. Docent Roubiček was interested in electroencephalography and, more specifically, in a process called "driving" or "entraining" brainwaves. He exposed his subjects to a powerful stroboscopic light and studied the effect of various frequencies on the brainwaves in their suboccipital cortexes.

He was curious how this process would be influenced by administration of LSD;

participation in this research was thus a necessary prerequisite for having an LSD session under his aegis. The combined effect of LSD and the stroboscopic light triggered within me an experience of cosmic consciousness of extraordinary proportions.

Albert Hofmann and Stanislav Grof

(Grof 2006) Although it lasted only a few hours—and its most significant part only about ten minutes—it resulted in a profound personal transformation and spiritual awakening that sent me professionally on a radically different course than the one for which I had been trained and prepared. I have, in fact, been following that trajectory with great determination to this very day. The research of non-ordinary states of consciousness has been my passion, vocation, and profession ever since.

Now, more than fifty years later, I look at this experience as an initiation similar to that of participants in ancient mysteries of death and rebirth. I could not agree more with Albert, who saw deep similarity between LSD and the sacramental drink *kykeon* used in the Eleusinian mysteries (Wasson, Hofmann, Ruck 1978) and hoped that responsible ritual use of LSD would one day be integrated into Western civilization. He believed that this New Eleusis would bring to modern humanity spiritual and cultural benefits similar to those that its ancient antecedent bestowed on ancient Greece and her neighboring city states.

After my first LSD session, I became deeply involved in psychedelic research and in the study of all related literature. Albert Hofmann's "wonder child" engendered a wave of scientific enthusiasm and optimism and spawned a new discipline—the science of consciousness. Never before in the history of science had a single substance held so much promise in such a wide variety of fields. For neuropharmacologists and neurophysiologists, the discovery of LSD meant the beginning of a golden era of research that could potentially lead to major advances concerning neuroreceptors, synaptic transmitters, chemical antagonisms, the role of serotonin in the brain, and the intricate biochemical interactions underlying cerebral processes.

Experimental psychiatrists saw LSD as a unique means for creating a laboratory model for naturally occurring functional, or endogenous, psychoses. They hoped that the "experimental psychosis," induced by miniscule dosages of this substance, could provide unparalleled insights into the nature of these mysterious disorders and open up new avenues for their treatment. It was suddenly conceivable that the brain or other parts of the body could, under certain circumstances, produce small quantities of a substance with effects similar to those of LSD. This meant that disorders like schizophrenia would not be mental diseases, but metabolic aberrations that could be counteracted and neutralized by specific chemical intervention. The potential of this research was nothing less than the fulfillment of the dream of biologically oriented clinicians, the Holy Grail of psychiatry—a test-tube cure for schizophrenia.

LSD was also highly recommended as an extraordinary unconventional teaching device that would make it possible for clinical psychiatrists, psychologists, medical students, and nurses to spend a few hours in a world resembling that of their patients and as a result be able to better understand them, communicate with them more effectively, and be more successful in their treatment. Thousands of mental health professionals took advantage of this opportunity. These experiments brought surprising and astonishing results. They not only provided deep insights into the inner world of psychiatric patients, but also revolutionized our understanding of the nature and dimensions of the human psyche.

As result of their experiences, many professionals found that the current model, limiting the psyche to postnatal biography and the Freudian individual unconscious, was superficial and inadequate. The new map of the psyche that emerged from this research added two large transbiographical domains—the perinatal level, closely related to the memory of biological birth, and the transpersonal level, harboring among others the historical and archetypal domains of the collective unconscious as envisioned by C.G. Jung. Early experiments with LSD showed that the roots of emotional and psychosomatic disorders were not limited to traumatic memories from childhood and infancy, as traditional psychiatrists assumed, but reached much deeper into the psyche, into the perinatal and transpersonal regions.

Reports from psychedelic psychotherapists revealed LSD's rare potential as a powerful tool that could deepen and accelerate the psychotherapeutic process. With LSD as a catalyst, psychotherapy could now be useful with patients who previously had been difficult to reach—sexual deviants, alcoholics, narcotic drug addicts, and criminal recidivists. Particularly valuable and promising were early efforts to use LSD psychotherapy in working with terminal cancer patients. With this population, administration of LSD could relieve severe pain, often even for patients who had not responded to medication with narcotics. In a large percentage of these patients, it was also possible to ease or even eliminate difficult emotional and psychosomatic symptoms, including depression, general tension, insomnia, and the fear of death. With this kind of relief for patients, the quality of their lives was significantly improved during their remaining days and their experience of dying was positively transformed.

For historians and critics of art, the LSD experiments provided extraordinary new insights into the psychology and psychopathology of art, particularly various modern movements, such as abstractionism, cubism, surrealism, fantastic realism, and

into paintings and sculptures of various native, so-called "primitive" cultures. Professional painters who participated in LSD research often found that their psychedelic sessions marked a radical change in their artistic expression. Their imaginations became much richer, their colors more vivid, and their styles considerably freer. They could also often reach into deep recesses of their unconscious psyche and tap archetypal sources of inspiration. On occasion, people who had never painted before were able to produce extraordinary works of art.

LSD experimentation brought also fascinating observations of great interest to spiritual teachers and scholars of comparative religion. The mystical experiences frequently observed in LSD sessions offered a radically new understanding of a wide variety of phenomena from the world of religion, including shamanism, the rites of passage, the ancient mysteries of death and rebirth, the Eastern spiritual philosophies, and the mystical traditions of the world. The fact that LSD and other psychedelic substances could trigger a broad range of spiritual experiences became the subject of heated scientific discussions revolving around the fascinating problem concerning the nature and value of this "instant" or "chemical mysticism."

LSD research seemed to be well on its way to fulfill all these promises and expectations when it was suddenly interrupted by the infamous Harvard affair, as a result of which Timothy Leary and Richard Alpert lost their academic posts, and the subsequent unsupervised mass experimentation of the young generation. In addition, the problems associated with this development were blown out of proportion by sensation-hunting journalists. The ensuing repressive measures of administrative, legal, and political nature had very little effect on street use of LSD and other psychedelics, but they drastically terminated legitimate clinical research.

Those of us privileged to have personal experiences with psychedelics and to use them in our work, saw the great promise that these they represented not only for psychiatry, psychology, and psychotherapy, but also for modern society in general. We were deeply saddened by the mass hysteria that pervaded not only the lay population, but also clinical and academic circles. It tragically compromised and criminalized tools with extraordinary therapeutic potential that properly understood and used had the power to counteract the destructive and self-destructive tendencies of the industrial civilization.

It was particularly heart-breaking to see the reaction of Albert Hofmann, the father of LSD and other psychedelics, as he watched his prodigious "wonder child" turn into a "problem child." (Hofmann 2005) I had the great privilege to know Albert personally and met him repeatedly on various occasions. Over the years, I developed great affection and deep admiration for him, not only for his outstanding and genuine scientific achievements but also for his extraordinary humanity which radiated astonishing vitality, curiosity, and love for all creation. I would like to briefly describe several of our meetings that made a particularly deep impression on me.

I first met Albert in the late 1960s when he visited the newly built Maryland Psychiatric Research Center where we were conducting extensive research on psychedelic therapy. After spending some time with the members of our staff, Albert expressed interest in sightseeing Washington, D.C. and I offered to be his guide. We visited the Capitol, Washington and Lincoln Monuments, the Reflecting Pool, and the tomb of J.F. Kennedy at Arlington Cemetery. It was April, the time of the National Cherry Blossom festival, and Albert, a passionate lover of nature, immensely enjoyed the beauty of the blossoming trees.

Before we returned to Baltimore, he said he would like to see the White House. At that time, pedestrians and cars were still permitted in the immediate proximity of the White House. I pulled to the curb and stopped the car. Albert rolled down the window, laid his hands on the edge of the glass panel, and looked for a while at the majestic building towering over the flower-decorated lawn. Then he turned to me and said with an almost child-like expression in his face: "So this is the great White House where important people like Richard Nixon and Spiro Agnew make the decisions that change the course of the world!" Albert's comment and his humility astonished me. Nixon certainly was not one of the most admirable American presidents and Spiro Agnew, Nixon's Vice-President, was a third-rate politician who was later forced to resign because of charges of extortion, tax fraud, bribery, and conspiracy. I said to Albert: "Do you realize what impact you have had on the world as compared to Spiro Agnew?" In his modesty, Albert clearly did not realize and appreciate how his own discoveries had affected the lives of millions of people.

Albert Hofmann, Stanislav and Christina Grof, Anita Hofmann

In 1988, my wife Christina and I had the chance to invite Albert to be the keynote speaker at the Tenth International Transpersonal Conference in Santa Rosa, CA, entitled *The Transpersonal Vision: Past, Present, and Future*. There is hardly any part of the world where Albert was and still is more appreciated than in California. A large number of Californians have experimented with LSD and other psychedelics as part of their spiritual journey and feel deeply grateful for the profound contribution it made to their lives. Albert received enthusiastic welcome from conference participants and had the status of a rock star throughout this meeting.

Another of my memorable meetings with Albert occurred in the late years of his life when I was teaching an advanced training module for practitioners of Holotropic Breathwork entitled *Fantastic Art*. It was held in the HR Giger Museum

in Gruyères and we had invited Albert to come and spend a day with our group as the guest of honor. After lunch, Hansruedi Giger—extraordinary fantastic realist painter, sculptor, and interior architect who in 1980 had received the Oscar for the otherworldly creatures and environments he had created for the movie *Alien*—took us for a guided tour through his remarkable museum. We all were curious to see how Albert, a man of fine discriminating esthetic taste, would respond to Hansruedi's large-scale biomechanoid paintings, abounding with brutally realistic images of biological birth, explicit sexual imagery, and dark satanic and scatological motifs. (Giger 1977) Albert's reaction was unequivocal—not only did he admire Hansruedi's artistic genius, but also the extraordinary power and authenticity with which his art portrayed the dark recesses of the human psyche that could be revealed during our inner journeys in the depth of the unconscious.

After his tour of the museum, Albert sat down with our group for a lecture and panel discussion. One of the most striking aspects of his personality was his passionate love of nature. As a child, Albert had a powerful mystical experience while walking in a meadow and his favorite pastime was spending time in nature, including his beautiful garden. During his professional life, his main interest was the chemistry of plants and animals. He conducted important research regarding the chemical structure of chitin, the main component of the cell walls of fungi and the exoskeletons of arthropods such as crustaceans (crabs, lobsters, and shrimp) and insects, for which he received his doctorate in

xvii

1930. Later, he studied the Mediterranean medicinal plant squill (Scilla glycosides) and elucidated the chemical structure of its common nucleus as part of a program to purify and synthesize active constituents of plants for use as pharmaceuticals. And, of course, he became world-famous for his research on ergot and lysergic acid derivatives that led to the discovery of LSD, and for chemical identification of the active alkaloids of Psilocybin mushrooms (teonanacatl) and morning glory seeds (ololiuqui).

Albert talked about LSD in a way that was reminiscent of native cultures where psychedelic plants are seen as having certain characteristics of conscious beings. He shared with us his conviction that his discovery of psychedelic effects of LSD-25 was not an accident or even "serendipity" as he used to call it in his public lectures. In 1938, when he first synthesized LSD, he found it difficult to accept the conclusion of the pharmacological department of Sandoz that this substance did not have any properties warranting further research. As he continued to synthesize additional derivatives of lysergic acid, he could not get LSD-25 off his mind; he had a strong sense that the pharmacologists must have overlooked something when they were testing this particular substance.

By April 1943, this feeling became so compelling that he decided to synthesize another sample of LSD-25. This was very unusual as a rule, experimental substances were definitely eliminated from the research program if they were found to be of no pharmacological interest. While working on this synthesis, Albert experienced the nonordinary state of consciousness

("accidental intoxication") that led him to his famous self experiment with 250 mcg of LSD. (Hofmann 2005) His strong conviction that there was something special about LSD, finally culminating in the urge to synthesize another sample for deeper investigation, was difficult to

Albert Hofmann and Stanislav Grof

explain rationally. Describing this sequence of events, Albert said: "I did not discover LSD; LSD found and called me."

Albert's presentation to our group in Gruyères turned into a passionate apotheosis of the beauty and mystery of nature and creation in general. He spoke about the miraculous chemistry that gives rise to the pigments responsible for the gorgeous colors of flowers and butterfly wings. He saw the intricacy of the chemical formulas responsible for the colors in nature as unmistakable proof that the universe had a master blueprint and was created by superior cosmic intelligence. Studying this remarkable alchemy of nature, he could sense the thoughts and the hand of the Creator. According to him, those who believe that atoms can do such things all by themselves do not know what they are talking about.

Albert also spoke at some length about the gratitude he felt for being alive and participating in the miracle of consciousness. He emphasized the need to embrace creation in its totality—including its shadow side—because without polarity, the universe in which we live could not have been created. When he left, we all felt that we just had attended a darshan with a spiritual teacher. It was clear that Albert had joined the group of great scientists—like Albert Einstein and Isaac Newton—whom rigorous pursuit of their disciplines had brought to the recognition of a miraculous divine order underlying the world of matter and the natural phenomena.

Several months after the Gruyères event, I returned to Switzerland to celebrate Albert's hundredth birthday. The morning celebration, in the Museum of Natural History in Basel, was a very official event, attended by many people from the psychedelic world, public figures, and Albert's friends. Swiss Bundespresident Moritz Leuenberger wrote a special letter for this occasion; he called Albert "a great figure in the exploration of human consciousness." In the evening, I was invited, along with my two friends and colleagues, Sonia and Juraj Styk, to a very different kind of celebration of Albert's birthday held in an old inn in Berg, a small village on the Swiss-French border, where the Hofmanns lived. Children brought Albert flowers, recited poems, and sang songs. In this moving ceremony, we did not hear LSD mentioned once; we were not sure if the villagers in Berg even knew what Albert had contributed

to the world. They were just celebrating a wonderful neighbor who had reached the very respectable age of one hundred years.

The last time I had the chance to spend some time with Albert was two years later during the World Psychedelic Forum in Basel. His name was among the presenters, but he felt too weak to come and lecture. Hansruedi and Carmen Giger, their assistant Stephan Stucki, and I were invited to visit Albert in his home in Berg. Although Albert's intellect was still very clear, his physical condition was rapidly deteriorating. We spent several precious hours with Albert revisiting old memories and listening to him as he shared with us his most recent philosophical and metaphysical ideas. I was very moved to hear that he had been reading daily passages from my book *The Ultimate Journey: Consciousness and the Mystery of Death* (Grof 2006), which he kept on his bedside table.

As we watched a beautiful sunset from the living room window, we were all very much aware that this was our last meeting and the end of an era. In view of Albert's long and productive life, we were experiencing very mixed feelings—deep sadness in anticipation of Albert's impending passing as well as celebration of a full and blessed life well spent. Albert died peacefully of heart failure four weeks later.

However harsh and irrational were the administrative and legal measures against the personal and professional use of psychedelics, Albert never lost his faith in their therapeutic and spiritual potential and always hoped that scientific evidence would eventually prevail over mass hysteria. He continued to believe that one day these valuable tools would be again used with great benefit to human society. Thanks to his extraordinary vitality and longevity along with the determination and persistence of Rick Doblin and the Multidisciplinary Association for Psychedelic Research (MAPS), Albert was able to see toward the end of his life the beginning of a remarkable global renaissance of academic interest in psychedelic substances that included the resumption of LSD-assisted psychotherapy research.

In the United States, several major universities have returned to psychedelic research: Harvard University, University of California Los Angeles (UCLA), Johns Hopkins University, New York University, University of California San Francisco (UCSF), University of Chicago, and University of Arizona Tucson. In Charleston, South Carolina, Dr. Michael Mithoefer and his wife Annie have reported positive results with the use of the entheogen MDMA (Ecstasy) in the treatment of post-traumatic stress disorder (PTSD). (Mithoefer et al. 2010) Their work could have important implications for solving the formidable problem of emotional disturbances in war veterans. And important psychedelic research is currently being conducted in Switzerland, Germany, Spain, England, Holland, Israel, Brazil, Peru, and many other countries of the world. The Seventeenth International Transpersonal Conference that took place in June 2010 in Moscow included a special track featuring the presentations of a new generation of psychedelic researchers.

While the renaissance of psychedelic research is very exciting, most of the new studies repeat , albeit with more rigorous scientific methodology, the studies done in the past, including Walter Pahnke's

Stanislav Grof, Albert Hofmann, and H.R. Giger in front of the HR Giger Museum

Good Friday experiment that showed the entheogenic effects of psilocybin (Pahnke 1963), psychedelic therapy with cancer patients (Grof 2006), and administration of psychedelics to neurotic and alcoholic patients. (Pahnke et al. 1970) Among the notable exceptions to the revisiting of past studies are the uses of the new imaging techniques in basic research exploring the effects of psychedelics on the brain and the pioneering and groundbreaking work with individuals suffering from PTSD. (Mithoefer et al. 2010) The promising results in the last category have the best chance to inspire clinicians worldwide and make this therapy mainstream. The problems with American soldiers returning from the Korean War, Vietnam War, Persian Gulf War, Afghanistan War, and Iraq War, have been truly formidable: Insomnia, terrifying nightmares, depression, high rates of suicide, and outbursts of violence. Traditional therapies have proved to be painfully ineffective for these recalcitrant disorders. The challenge posed by PTSD for the Soviet and Russian Armies—although less publicized—has been equally enormous. If the therapeutic effects of LSD and other psychedelics withstand the test of these new studies, the research will hopefully move into new exciting areas presently lacking scientific data but abounding with anecdotal evidence.

The capacity of psychedelics to facilitate creativity is one of the most promising areas of investigation. In the 1960s, Willis Harman, Robert McKim, Robert Mogar, James Fadiman, and Myron Stolaroff conducted a pilot study of the effects of psychedelics on the creative process. They administered LSD-25 and mescaline to a group of highly talented individuals and studied the effects of these substances on inspiration and problem-solving. (Harman et al. 1966) In their book *Higher Creativity: Liberating the Unconscious for Breakthrough Insights,* Willis Harman and Howard Rheingold gave scores of examples of scientific and artistic breakthroughs that were facilitated by non-ordinary states of consciousness. (Harman and Rheingold 1984) A program offering supervised psychedelic sessions to prominent researchers facing an impasse in their work on important projects and to prominent artists could significantly advance scientific progress and foster unique contributions to our cultural life.

LSD has already facilitated discoveries that subsequently received the highest scientific awards. In 1993, molecular biologist and DNA chemist Kary Mullis received a Nobel Prize for his development of the Polymerase Chain Reaction (PCR), a central technique in biochemistry and molecular biology that allows the amplification of specific DNA sequences. During a symposium in Basel celebrating Albert Hofmann's 100th anniversary, Albert revealed that Kary Mullis attributed his accomplishment to insights from his experience with LSD. Francis Crick, the father of modern genetics, was under the influence of LSD when he discovered the double-helix structure of DNA. He told a fellow scientist that he often used small doses of LSD to boost his power of thought. He said it was LSD that helped him to unravel the structure of DNA, the discovery that won him the Nobel Prize.

In his book *What the Dormouse Said: How the Sixties Counterculture Shaped the Personal Computer Industry,* John Markoff described the history of the personal computer. (Markoff 2005) He showed the direct connection between the use of psychedelics in the American counterculture of the 1950s and 1960s and the development of the computer industry. Steve Jobs said that taking LSD was among the "two or three most important things" he had done in his life. He noted

Albert and Anita Hofmann, Stanislav Grof

that people on his staff, who did not share his countercultural roots, could not fully relate to his thinking. Douglas Engelbart, who invented the computer mouse, also explored and experimented with psychedelic drugs. Kevin Herbert, who worked for Cisco Systems in the early days, once said: "When I'm on LSD and hearing something that's pure rhythm, it takes me to another world and into another brain state where I've stopped thinking and started knowing." Mark Pesce, the co-inventor of virtual reality's coding language, VRML, agreed that there is a definite relationship between chemical mind expansion and advances in computer technology: "To a man and a woman, the people behind virtual reality were acidheads."

Albert Hofmann's "wonder child" thus helped other scientists solve challenging problems. Those scientists, who are not blinded by the stormy cultural controversy surrounding LSD-25, have no doubt that Albert Hofmann himself deserved the Nobel Prize for his brilliant and important

discoveries. Unfortunately the sad irony—if not blunder—in the history of science is that the only Nobel Prize of relevance for psychiatry was awarded in 1949 to the Portuguese neurologist Antonio Edgar Moniz for the development of prefrontal lobotomy—a massive mutilating surgical intervention of questionable value and with serious side effects. This procedure was used especially from the early 1940s to the mid-1950s for a wide range of conditions—psychosis, obsessive compulsive disorder, depression, criminality, and aggressive behavior.

The most infamous example of the use of lobotomy was Rosemary Kennedy, sister to John, Robert, and Edward Kennedy, who was given a lobotomy when her father complained to doctors about the mildly retarded girl's "embarrassing new interest in boys." Even in its greatly mitigated form (prefrontal or "icepick" lobotomy), this procedure was abandoned within a decade by the psychiatric profession. Because of the unfortunate historical developments during the second half of the 20th century, mainstream academic circles have not recognized and acknowledged the importance of Albert's extraordinary and influential discoveries. And instead of honors and praise from his employer for his extraordinary achievements, he was blamed because the controversy associated with his discoveries had tarnished the reputation of Sandoz Pharmaceutical Company.

Human history features many great individuals—ground-breaking pioneers of various eras—who were not appreciated by their contemporaries, both the lay population and the scientific authorities of their time. Just to give a salient example: the heliocentric system of Nicolas Copernicus was not generally accepted until one hundred years after his epoch-making discovery. It is my firm belief that future generations will see Albert Hofmann as one the most influential scientists of the twentieth century, a Promethean visionary whose discoveries helped to chart a new trajectory not only for psychiatry, psychology, and neuroscience, but also for the evolution of the human species.

References:

Giger, H.R. *Necronomicon* (text in French). Paris: Les Humanoïdes Associés, 1977.

Grof, Stanislav. *LSD Psychotherapy*. Sarasota, Florida: Multidisciplinary Association for Psychedelic Studies, 2001.

Grof, Stanislav. *The Ultimate Journey: Consciousness and the Mystery of Death*. Ben Lomond, California: MAPS, 2006.

Grof, Stanislav. *When the Impossible Happens: Adventures in Non-Ordinary Realities*. Boulder, Colorado: Sounds True, 2006.

Harman, W.W., R.H. McKim, R.E. Mogar, J. Fadiman, and M. J. Stolaroff. "Psychedelic Agents in Creative Problem-Solving: A Pilot Study." *Psychological reports* 19, no. 1 (1966): 211-27.

Harman, Willis W., and Howard Rheingold. *Higher Creativity: Liberating the Unconscious for Breakthrough Insights*. Los Angeles; Boston: J.P. Tarcher, 1984.

Hofmann, Albert. *LSD - My Problem Child: Reflections on Sacred Drugs, Mysticism, and Science*. Los Angeles: J.P. Tarcher, 1983.

Markoff, John. *What the Dormouse Said: How the Sixties Counterculture Shaped the Personal Computer Industry*. New York: Viking, 2005.

Mithoefer, M.C. "The Safety and Efficacy of ±3,4-Methylenedioxy-Methamphetamine-Assisted Psychotherapy in Subjects with Chronic Treatment-Resistant Posttraumatic Stress Disorder: The First Randomized Controlled Pilot Study." *Journal of Psychopharmacology*, 25 , no.4 (July 19 2010).

Pahnke, W.N., A.A. Kurland, S. Unger, C. Savage, and S. Grof. "The Experimental Use of Psychedelic (LSD) Psychotherapy." *JAMA: the journal of the American Medical Association* 212, no. 11 (1970): 1856-63.

Pahnke, Walter Norman. *Drugs and Mysticism: An Analysis of the Relationship between Psychedelic Drugs and the Mystical Consciousness: A Thesis*. Harvard University, 1963.

Stoll, W.A. "LSD, Ein Phantastikum aus der Mutterkorngruppe." *Schweizer Archiv für Neurologie und Psychiatrie* 60 (1947) 279.

Wasson, R. Gordon, Albert Hofmann, and Carl A.P. Ruck. *The Road to Eleusis: Unveiling the Secret of the Mysteries*. New York: Harcourt, Brace, Jovanovich, 1978.

The only constant is change. *Heraclitus of Ephesus*

The Beginnings of the Modern Era

A new century had dawned when the long life of Albert Hofmann began in the heart of Europe. He was born at a time of drastic political, social and cultural upheaval and meteoric technological and scientific advances. No prior period had gone through as many changes in so short a time as "La Belle Époque." Hardly anyone then had any idea of the dramatic transitions in all areas of life and knowledge that were to come in the following decades. No one could have anticipated that, after the destructive madness of two world wars, a discovery would be made by this new-born citizen of the world which would significantly affect the development of mankind.

Rooted in Great Britain's colonial hegemony, the second phase of the industrial revolution opened in the mid-nineteenth century, inaugurating the triumph of world capitalism. A new era of technological advances was ushered in. The growing number of railway lines brought new mobility. The War of Currents was won by the Serb Tesla's utilization of alternating electric current which competed with Edison's discovery of direct current whereupon electrification started in the cities of the United States. Let there be light: At first electricity came only to the factories, to public buildings and the streets, but ultimately to people who enjoyed the blaze of light in their homes from "incandescent bulbs." Journalists, fascinated by the new technology, spoke of the "magical spell" of the enchanting "electric flame." Electricity changed the rhythms of life and work. In 1895, Wilhelm Röntgen discovered the rays named after him and immediately thereafter, Antoine Henri Becquerel found radioactivity. Around the same time, Guglielmo Marconi patented the radio. In 1905, Albert Einstein, previously a complete unknown, published three decisive papers in the *Annals of Physics*.

Physicists such as Max Planck uncovered the secrets of the atom and puzzled over quantum mechanics. The spread of pocket watches, together with the worldwide telegraph network, introduced a new

First photo of Albert Hofmann

1

Baden in 1881

Baden train station, postcard ca. 1910

awareness of time. The advent of the auto-mobile heralded the emergence of a mobile society. Sigmund Freud conceived of a new image of the human psyche. Art and architecture moved away from his-toricism. Increasing industrialization brought functionality to the fore: Thus, form follows function

The transition from the *Gründerzeit* (rapid industrialization) to the modern age opened another chapter of world history. The monumental character of the Paris 1900 World Exposition documented the technological progress and cultural spirit of optimism in Europe. Concurrent with these early signs of globalization, Europe's nobility, who had played a determining role in political affairs, began to come under pressure from the lower classes. First trade unions arose, political opposition forces such as social democratic parties, and private and state social service institutions followed. Women won the right to participate in public life in many countries.

These upheavals in society were met by threatening political gestures and nationalistic claims to dominance from the great powers and cast a shadow over a seemingly peaceful Europe. The *Entente Cordiale* after the Franco-Prussian War of 1870/71 did little to lessen the cen-turies-old antagonism between Germany and France. Designed to resolve conflicts of interest in their African colonies, it did not succeed, let alone usher in friendly relations between the two countries. The idea of the nation state became a dominant principle in Europe. When France allied itself with Russia, which in turn warmed to England, the German Empire felt threat-ened and hemmed in. Political unrest also prevailed in the Balkans. Although Ottoman sovereignty was slowly eroding, the Turkish minorities in southeastern Europe fueled political conflicts. Europe turned into a powder keg characterized by nationalism and patriotism, especially in intellectual circles where latent enthu-siasm for war was spreading.

As a neutral nation, the Swiss Confeder-ation remained aloof from the quarrels of its neighbors. In 1904 it concluded treaties with various European countries that com-mitted both parties to any dispute, should

Factory building at Brown & Boveri Ltd. ca.1910

Noon hour at BBC ca.1910

direct negotiations fail, to acknowledge the International Court of Justice in The Hague for arbitration. Although counter to the longstanding principle of the Confederation to tolerate no foreign judges, it was urgently expedient, given the imbalance of power between tiny Switzerland and its powerful European neighbors.

As did many other European countries, Switzerland shifted from an agricultural to an industrial economy at the beginning of the twentieth century. An economic upsurge and increasing exports from the textile and machinery branches opened up this landlocked country to new ties to the rest of the world. By 1910, the earlier construction of hydroelectric plants had made Switzerland, like the USA, a leading producer of electricity. For most Swiss citizens, working conditions and the standard of living improved appreciably.

From Health Resort
to Industrial Town

The first rail line in Switzerland inaugurated in the summer of 1847 ran between Zurich and Baden. The railway shortened the thirty mile drive which took a half-day by horse-drawn carriage to just forty-five minutes by train. People named it the "Spanish Brötli Bahn" after a pastry baked in Zurich that was popular with wealthy Zurich visitors to the spas in Baden. Thanks to the general prosperity and substantial investment in casinos, grand hotels, new treatment centers, and renovated Roman thermal baths, Baden flourished around 1900 to become the "capital of lust,"[1] a popular destination for spa guests from all of Europe.

The transformation of this placid little town is typical of the course of industrialization throughout Switzerland. In 1891, Charles Brown and Walter Boveri founded the corporation Brown & Boveri Ltd. (BBC) in Baden. The company built extensive manufacturing plants on the flat terrain known as the Haselfeld. Their first project was to build a power plant for Baden and manufacture generators for the municipal electrical utility. Within five years, the first street cars rolled

Incidentally, everything in Switzerland is prettier and better.
Adolf Muschg

out of BBC's plant. That year also saw the start of collaboration with the Swiss Locomotive and Machine Works in the manufacture of rail cars. Plants in Milan and Vienna made BBC (today's ABB) a global concern. It is a market leader in the production of steam turbines, generators and electric locomotives. "Every available factory space is filled with machine parts despite continual expansion of the plant. At this point, the world-wide reputation of Brown & Boveri Ltd. is uncontested" observed the *Badener Kalender* in 1902. BBC was the largest company in Switzerland and the most important employer in the region, making it possible for Baden to remain a stable seat of industry. The disappearance of foreign competition during the First World War benefited Swiss industry. In 1900, BBC employed 1,500; by 1920 there were 5,500 employees and the population of Baden had grown to nearly 10,000.

Founding a Family

This was the context into which Albert Hofmann was born in Baden on January 11, 1906 at three o'clock in the afternoon—much to the joy of his German-born father Adolf Hofmann and his mother Elisabeth (née Schenk), who was from the Canton of Basel-Land. They had met while working in Münchenstein, a suburb of Basel, for a subsidiary of Brown, Boveri, he as a metal worker and she as a secretary. They married in August of 1902. Their first son was born in March of 1903, but died at birth. Soon after

The house at
1 Martinsbergstrasse

their marriage, Adolf Hofmann was transferred to the company's main metal works in Baden where he was quickly promoted to foreman and later put in charge of the metal working equipment plant. Despite the promotions, his wages were low and the family's circumstances modest. They lived in a multifamily dwelling on the edge of Baden on Schönaustrasse and led a contented life.

In 1906, Ludwig Forrer was President of the Swiss Confederation and Theodore Roosevelt served as President of the United States. The writer Hannah Arendt, the dancer Josephine Baker, the writer Klaus Mann, the shipping magnate Aristotle Onassis, and film directors Luchino Visconti and Billy Wilder were born that year. News of the San Francisco earthquake, which shook the coast of northern California, quickly circled the globe, thanks to new communication technology.

Looking back at his birth one hundred years later, Albert Hofmann commented that, "The constellation of the comets or whatever governs human fate must have been pointing to happiness." And history was to prove him right.

The first event of Albert's life that is documented was his baptism on March 31, 1907, in the Reformed Church in Baden. Two friends from the family's time in Basel, Hans Küeni and Lina Ritter served as godparents. Although Albert no longer recalled any details about his family's small apartment, he did remember the lively household of which his devoted mother was the center. Due to an arduous six-day work week, Albert saw his father less often. The family's routine involved a simple evening meal followed by an early bedtime to enable them to be off to school or the factory on time the next morning. On Sundays, the head of the family joined his colleagues at the regulars' table at the local tavern for a welcome break from his daily routine at the factory and at home. Albert's brother Walter was born in 1908.

One of Albert's earliest memories was the image of "large red strawberries" as his mother carried him in her arms through the garden. He also remembered quite clearly when he was four, seeing a crowd gathered in the street pointing excitedly at the sky. Looking up, he saw Halley's Comet. It was April 21st, 1910, the day Mark Twain died and at whose birth in 1835 the brilliant comet also had been visible. Seventy-six years later, Albert would see the comet pass again for a second time and remember his childhood in Baden.

One year later, the family moved to Martinsbergstrasse, which was on a hill above town. There, his sister Gertrud was born in 1913 and in 1915 Margareta, who died before her second birthday. Albert remembered the move well: "I stood in front of the house holding my little brother

Adolf and Elisabeth Hofmann in 1903

Albert's baptismal certificate

by the hand and looked around at our new neighborhood; the Rowan trees were shining golden in the autumn sunlight." That was home for Albert from age five through age ten—again, in a small apartment in a multifamily dwelling. To help supplement his father's meager income for the growing family, Albert's mother worked part-time as a laundress. For Albert it was self-evident to do his part helping out at home and be a caring brother to his younger siblings.

Their house lay below the crest of the mountain upon which the ruin of Stein Castle sat, surrounded by meadows and forest. To Albert it was paradise. He quickly found new friends to play with and explored the area as often as possible. The labyrinthine ruins made an enthralling playground: "I can still hear my mother call us to dinner from the kitchen window when we lost track of the time up there." Across the street was a wainwright's and the Rymann family's farm where Albert made friends with the children. They played together in the big barn and watched as the famer milked the cows. Nearby was a farrier and Albert often watched him, fascinated, as he saw horses shoed. At the wainwright's, he was amazed at how easily the man fit glowing iron hoops onto wooden wheels of commercial and farm vehicles and private carriages. Although the streets of the small town of Baden were mostly filled with the bicycles of factory workers and with pedestrians, an increasing number of carriages were seen.

View of Baden's industrial zone from Martinsberg

From September 3rd to 6th of 1912, Germany's Kaiser Wilhelm II made a second state visit to Switzerland—deemed by him to be one of his "most faithful provinces." The monarch wished to form his own opinion about the military capability of the Swiss army as it held fall maneuvers in Eastern Switzerland. He sought reassurance that his empire's southern border could be protected by the Swiss confederates against a French counter attack, since war plans for attacking Belgium and France cached in his drawer had been prepared long ago. Later, Albert Hofmann often spoke of having spotted the Kaiser when his special train stopped at the Baden train station. When he told this story at his 95th birthday party, one of his childhood schoolmates expressed doubt. He himself had been present when the official town delegation met the train, and he couldn't catch a glimpse of the Kaiser because the blinds were lowered and the doors remained closed. Hofmann replied slyly, "That's because you all were standing on the wrong side of the train. I saw him and recognized him. In fact, he even waved at me!"

Many of Albert's memories were linked to the route he took to school which led below the castle hill and through the old town gate; something always caught his or his friends' eyes. One day, he was fascinated to see for the first time an automobile as it clattered noisily through the narrow streets of Baden's old town. At a friend's house, he experienced the advent of radio and of the telephone "where you heard the voice of a person who wasn't even there." These technical achievements were seen by many older persons as the devil's work. Two years later, as Albert rode along with neighboring farmers on their hay wagon drawn by oxen or horses to the fields high above the town to mow and make hay, they heard the sound of cannon fire from distant Alsace. On July 28, 1914, Germany and Austria-Hungary declared war on Serbia and, soon after, on France and Russia, both allied with Serbia: The First World War had begun.

The Mystical Wonders of Nature

The distant battlefields had little effect on eight-year old Albert. Despite the horrors of war, those years spent with his parents and siblings on Martinsberg were happy ones for him. His primary school teacher was impressed by this attentive and diligent pupil. His love of nature was reinforced by the plants and animals surrounding him. Nothing pleased him more than to wander through the fields and forests, alone or with his pals, and look out over the valley below through which the Limmat river wound its way to Zurich. Albert was a keen observer of the changing seasons, the greening of spring, the long summer days, the withering foliage in fall, and the winter snow that magically blanketed the fields and meadows in white. "Back then, I promised myself that one day I would again live in a countryside like the Jura."

Like many young children, Albert was interested in philosophical questions. Decades later, he recalled a conversation he'd had on the way to school as a ten-year old with a friend who asked him, "Do you still believe in God? I don't—not since I found out they've been fooling me about the Christ Child [bringing presents] and that St. Nicholas was no one other than my Uncle Fritz." Albert answered that it was different with God than with the Christ Child and St. Nicholas because only God could have made the world and people."

Each spring, Albert returned to wander through the forest on Martinsberg. There, he felt free yet secure and forgot all worries. One sunny morning he would remember the rest of his days, his perceptions rose to unexpected dimensions and he experienced a spontaneous mystical vision of the unity of all being that would shape his life ever after. He could vividly recall every detail: "It was these experiences that shaped the main outlines of my world view and convinced me of the existence of a miraculous, powerful, unfathomable reality that was hidden from everyday sight." He could not recall the year but knew it was on a May morning and the particular place it happened. As he walked through the forest, he began

Albert (l.) on his first bicycle

to hear birdsong more clearly, the fresh green of the trees and the sparkling of sun through the leaves seemed more intense. Everything shone with incredibly clear light. He wondered if he hadn't looked or listened carefully until then or whether, on that particular morning, the springtime forest first revealed itself in actuality. He felt his heart surge and was filled with bliss more profound than at any time before in his life, a sense of affinity with his surroundings, absolute emotional security as part of creation. As these overwhelming impressions slowly ebbed, he regretted their passing. And Albert wasn't sure if he could report these marvels to grownups since he had never heard them speak of such things.

Later in his youth, this happened several more times—exhilarating experiences of nature, "enchanting" moments that granted him a glimpse behind the veil of the everyday world. He began to reflect upon the nature of the material world and wondered if as an adult he would still be able to have similar experiences and communicate them to others.

These experiences prepared him to follow the path that led to his career: "It was unexpected, but hardly fortuitous that, in midlife, my professional activity converged with the visionary intuition of my boyhood."

> How long will this last, this delicious feeling of being alive, of having penetrated the veil which hides beauty and the wonders of celestial vistas? It doesn't matter, as there can be nothing but gratitude for even a glimpse of what exists for those who can become open to it.
>
> *Alexander Shulgin*

With a Clear Goal

The aimless suffers his fate; the purposeful shapes his destiny. *Immanuel Kant*

Illness and Social Poverty

For some time, Albert's father had been suffering from consumption, which was what pulmonary tuberculosis was called at the time. The majority of the medical profession considered it to be an ailment, not a serious disease—especially not among the poorer working classes where tuberculosis was rampant. As his condition worsened, Albert's father found even the short trip from Martinsbergstrasse to his workplace was too difficult. In view of the circumstances, the family decided to move once again and found an apartment in an unappealing housing block on Dynamostrasse. It had the advantage of being directly at the factory entrance, opposite the gatehouse and the "Glogge-hüsli" (bell house), the hallmark of BBC. For Albert this meant "expulsion from his childhood paradise." Whenever school, his daily homework, or household duties permitted, he fled the drab factory quarter, hurried up to join his friends, into nature, to the meadows and fields he had come to love during the past years, and to the

forest on Martinsberg which was so meaningful to him.

The war being waged in the surrounding European countries had little impact on Albert's life. Switzerland remained neutral and was spared. Nevertheless, the land-locked country suffered extreme shortages of food and raw materials.

In addition, the economy faltered, inflation was high, and military service took many men from their jobs. Large swaths of the population sank into poverty, posing challenging socio-political problems for Switzerland. Many factories and firms had to let people go, swelling the ranks of the unemployed. International Socialist Congresses were held in the country. In April 1917, revolutionary Vladimir Ilyich Lenin left his exile in Switzerland, where he had dabbled in vegetarianism, theosophy, and naturism on Monte Verità near Ascona and had stirred up enthusiasm for revolution in Russia amongst artists and writers of the Dada movement in Zurich's old town. Upon Lenin's return to Moscow, he and

his comrades successfully started the October Revolution.

In Baden, where BBC had dismissed over half its work force, social unrest began to grow. Up until the middle of the twentieth century, the company fought employee absenteeism and loafing with "scientific management methods." Rigid policies were meant to 'fill every moment of the workday with production quotas to boost output.'[2] For the general public in Baden, the BBC grounds were "the forbidden city" where access was permitted only to bona fide employees.

What happened in Baden spread throughout Switzerland. Conflicts between workers and the middle class and between town and rural populations led to a general strike in November 1918. The government considered the nationwide action might be the beginning of a revolution similar to the Russian model. To prevent this possibility, the army was called up and, soon, 100,000 troops faced around 400,000 strikers. Baden was affected as well and occupied by the army for several days. Albert and a few buddies watched from a wall at the entrance to the BBC grounds as locked-out workers angrily sought to gain entrance to the closed factory. What impressed the youngsters most was the determined appearance of the armed troops. Like the adults, they sensed the confrontation could escalate into violence. While there were dead and injured reported in other parts of Switzerland, Baden remained calm and the troops left

1919 class photo with Albert in back row, right

BBC plant entrance showing the Gloggehüsli (bell house) around 1910

town after a short time.

Towards the end of 1918, peace treaties were signed between states, monarchies were abolished, borders were newly drawn, and, in response to the civilian casualties and combat atrocities, the League of Nations was founded with the noble intention of preventing future wars.

A Model Student

At the age of twelve, Albert finished the regional primary school. With his native curiosity and thirst for knowledge, and since learning was a pleasure for him, he yearned to transfer to high school which would allow him to attend university. He recalled that, "Mr. Speidel, our teacher in the regional secondary school, asked who wanted to move into the Latin program, but my family's circumstances were simply too poor." With his father still seriously ill, the weak economic outlook, and continuing social and political turmoil, his parents decided that Albert should go out on his own as soon as possible. They thought he should be prepared to contribute to the maintenance of the household when conditions required. This seemed all the more likely at the time, since Albert's youngest sister Anni in 1918 would add a sixth person to the family.

Thus, shortly after finishing school, Albert began a commercial apprenticeship with BBC, his father's employer, but with little enthusiasm. Albert's teacher, convinced of

11

his talent, was sorry that this was necessary. Consequently, he continued to supply Albert during his apprenticeship with the most important textbooks for subjects in natural sciences such as botany and Latin, which were necessary for the university qualifying certificate. Secretly he translated works of Tacitus using a typewriter. Albert never lost sight of his goal—the school diploma and university studies.

The apprentice in 1921

BBC office ca.1910

Brighter Horizons

More out of a sense of duty than of desire, Albert completed his apprenticeship. Meanwhile, he happily dedicated whatever free time remained to high school subjects. He received his diploma after three years and for financial reasons decided to continue working at BBC as a commercial clerk. During this time, he was confirmed. On Palm Sunday of 1922, Albert and forty-eight other boys and fifty-three girls entered the world of adults, and he proudly received a pocket watch, the traditional gift for boys at this rite of passage.

His stint as a business clerk did not last long because his sympathetic godfather, Hans Küeni, the founder and owner of a tool factory bearing his name in Allschwil near Basel, had noticed Albert's ambition for greater things and his zeal and unfailing thirst for knowledge. One day, he surprised Albert with the news that he was prepared to pay the tuition to Minerva, a private school in Zurich. With that diploma, Albert would be able to fulfill his longing to attend university.

> Nothing great was ever achieved without enthusiasm.
> *Ralph Waldo Emerson*

Albert's apprenticeship contract from 1924

Albert Hofmann in the mountains

The teachers at Minerva, a school mostly attended by the sons and daughters of the upper class, quickly noticed Albert Hofmann's outstanding diligence and exceptional desire to learn. His teachers, who were more used to lazy, spoiled students, encouraged him as a praiseworthy exception to the average private school student because "I soaked up the material like a sponge and, after just a year, passed the federal high school diploma which was known for its difficulty." Despite the three years he had spent in his apprenticeship, he qualified for university entrance earlier than most of his peers from Baden who had gone directly to the gymnasium in Baden.

Albert Hofmann applied his determination and discipline to training his body as well as his mind. He took up a vigorous program of swimming and running, along with other track and field activities. Although he trained regularly, he never saw athletics as a potential career, but as a welcome change from the rigor of long hours spent studying. He joined the *Wandervogel* youth movement which started at the end of the nineteenth century. Inspired by earlier figures from the Romantic period, young people enthusiastically sought freedom from the narrow strictures of a society marked by increasing industrialization. They believed that a healthier life style should include time in the great outdoors. This philosophy appealed to Hofmann as well, and he became a member in the mid-1920s. He also had a creative vein, artistic talent, and aesthetic sensibility, and he enthusiastically took evening classes in drawing, painting and sculpture. Art history fascinated him and, for a time, he considered a course of study in the arts. But this was not to be.

From Clerk to Chemist

Inspired by indelible memories of his mystical experience in the forest on Martinsberg, Albert Hofmann felt compelled to uncover

With sister Gertrud

Professor Paul Karrer in 1927

the nature and structure of living matter: What lay unseen behind it? What lay beyond his visionary insights into the material world? He was aware of how deeply these early and extraordinary experiences affected him and how importantly they figured in his decision to study chemistry. It was not an easy choice because his diploma from the Latin school qualified him for advanced study leading to a profession in the arts or humanities, and his considerable talent qualified him to study at a fine arts academy. Hence, his choice of chemistry astounded both teachers and friends. The curriculum at the pri-

> Without a goal, there is no path.
>
> *Lao Tse*

vate school had not included chemistry and at one point, Hofmann had briefly flirted with the idea of studying architecture. One of his teachers was dismayed to the point of asking, "You aren't thinking about developing another toxin for the next war, are you?" In retrospect, Hofmann viewed his decision as pragmatic and profound: "I became a chemist and devoted myself to plant chemistry precisely because I was drawn to the puzzles posed by matter and by the marvels of the plant world. My profession gave me insight into the structure of things, into the chemical structure of flower pigments and other components and deepened my amazement about nature and

With fellow students (front row, 3rd from left) and Professor Paul Karrer in 1927

its processes, its forces and laws. In addition to perceiving the form and color of things on their surface, we learn about their inner structure and life processes. This yields a more complete picture of reality, a more comprehensive truth."

Once he had chosen, Hofmann focused solely on the scientific aspect. He was convinced that chemistry would play an important role in the future and his education would earn him a decent living. He told himself that, in contrast with the humanities, he can count on the natural sciences because nature doesn't change as quickly and unexpectedly.

Albert Hofmann began studying organic chemistry at the University of Zurich in the spring of 1925 under the renowned professor Paul Karrer. Karrer had received his doctorate in Zurich in 1911 and worked from 1912 to 1918 in the laboratory of Paul Ehrlich, the Nobel Prize laureate in Medicine of 1908. Subsequently, Karrer returned to the University of Zurich as a Professor Extraordinarius for Organic Chemistry where he served until his retirement in 1956. In 1937, Karrer and Walter Norman Haworth were awarded the Nobel Prize in Chemistry for their work on the structure of carotenoids, flavins and vitamins A and B. According to Hofmann, despite Karrer's formality, he was unassuming and did not play up his authority; rather he earned respect and great esteem just from his work.

Albert Hofmann's German father had taken up residency in Weiningen in the Canton of Zurich for work-related reasons and acquired Swiss citizenship. This enabled his son to receive a scholarship from the cantonal university and apply for tuition exemption. Hofmann still lived with his parents and siblings in Baden since money barely stretched to cover his commute by train to and from Zurich. He pursued his studies as ever with customary enthusiasm and plunged into the marvelous world of chemistry, the "mystery of matter." It was not long before the Director of the Chemical Institute, Paul Karrer, got Hofmann a job as Assistant, making him manager of the chemistry curriculum for medical students. This step up the ladder provided the young student with welcome additional income to help support his family. His goal was to complete his studies in the shortest time possible—and he did so.

During Christmas of 1928, Albert Hofmann finished his doctoral thesis on the structural clarification and enzymatic decomposition of chitin and chitosan. Chitin is an important component in the exoskeleton of crayfish, lobsters, and other crustaceans. Its purest form is found in the wings of May bugs. Chitin also is present in the skeletons of insects and arachnids, and in the cell walls of plants and lower fungi. It can be broken down by the gastrointestinal fluid of snails. For his work, Hofmann mixed this fluid with chitin from lobster shell. His highly regarded dissertation *Über den enzymatischen Abbau des Chitins und Chitosans* (Hofmann 1929) corrected the structural formula previously published by his thesis

On the roof of the University of Zurich

supervisor Paul Karrer, who praised it as a work of distinction. Albert Hofmann completed the eight semester program in chemistry at the age of twenty-three and received his doctorate in the spring of 1929. Completing his doctorate under an internationally renowned chemist helped Albert Hofmann in his search for a suitable position in the chemical industry. His choice of workplace turned out to be as crucial as his earlier decision to become a chemist.

Three months before finishing his studies, Albert Hofmann's father Adolf died on January 25, 1929. His eldest son was still able to tell him that he had agreed to take a position with Sandoz, a chemical company, and would soon sign the employment contract.

The mourning family

After the death of her husband, Albert's mother received a widow's pension and soon purchased a house, in Baden at No. 1 Schellenackerstrasse for thirty-two thousand Swiss francs resulting in a large mortgage. Her husband had known the house, but refrained from buying it because it lay in a shady hollow. Albert Hofmann's three siblings moved into their new home and his sister Gertrud continued to live there after her marriage. Since this house was also located near the factory site, Hofmann's mother began by renting out first one, then two rooms to BBC workers for whom she also maintained a luncheon table. Even though Hofmann never lived there, he felt strong ties to the home of his mother and siblings; it was a kind of parental home to him which he visited often. Over the next decades, he always saw them on Christmas Eve to eat traditional pea soup. His mother was thoughtful and calm, but firm and straightforward. Though she never said much, her grandchildren remembered her as a loving person. She lived in that house until the end of her life in 1964, when she died without warning at her dining table.

Do you strive for the highest and the sublime?
The plants can instruct you. *Friedrich Schiller*

The Chemistry is Right in Basel

Basel nestles at the southern end of the Upper Rhine Valley, between the Black Forest, the Vosges and the Jura in the tri-border region, where Germany, France and Switzerland meet. Each of the mountain ranges features one named "Belchen" after *Belenos*, the Celtic god of light. Together with other peaks, the three form an archaic astronomical calendar system. On the solstices and equinoxes, observation of the sun from one of the three peaks as it rises over a second one can be used to calculate the eight stations of the Celtic annual cycle and the lunistices or standstills of the moon. The Celts first settled the Basel region around 500 BCE. Shortly after the turn of the eras, the Romans founded Augusta Raurica a few kilometers upstream from Basel, which is first documented as Basilia in 374 CE. The town's coat of arms features the Basilisk or cockatrice, a mythical creature part rooster, part dragon. By the time the Romans left in 500 CE, Basel was largely populated by Alemannic peoples and gradually grew into a small city. Its

selection as an episcopal town and the construction of a bridge over the Rhine further enhanced its importance. For a few years, from 1331 to 1348, the Council of Basel made it the intellectual center of the Christian world. Hard times followed: In 1356, a mighty earthquake destroyed large portions of the city. The plague killed half its inhabitants. Then in 1460, Pope Pius II endowed the city's first university which drew humanists such as Erasmus of Rotterdam. With the introduction of printing, Basel became one of the earliest and most important centers of publishing in the fifteenth century. In 1501, Basel joined the Swiss Confederation; a few decades later, the Reformation was adopted and the bishop forced to resign.

During this period, Philippus Theophrastus Aureolus Bombast von Hohenheim, called Paracelsus, was the city physician and lectured at the faculty of medicine. He continually challenged Basel's officials and conservative citizens with new ideas. He sharply criticized the prevailing four-humor

Albert Hofmann in his laboratory in 1936

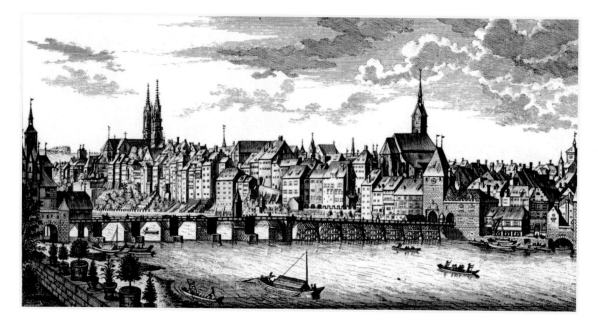

Basel in 1761

theory of the Greek physician Galen and publicly burned his works. Instead of lecturing in the customary Latin, Paracelsus used German and opened his lectures to everyone. He summarized his revolutionary ideas about medicine with the legendary saying: "Sola dosis facit venenum" (The dose makes the poison). His success at healing and his unorthodox methods of teaching attracted students from far and wide to Basel. After he also severely criticized the city's pharmacists and medical faculty, he was subpoenaed to appear in court. Ultimately, he had to flee to Alsace to escape trial.

By the middle of the sixteenth century, religious refugees from Italy and France began to exert significant influence over commerce and the silk trade. Basel's silk ribbon industry arose around 1670 and the city became an important center of commerce; exports flourished. The influx of Protestant immigrants from throughout Europe after 1685 brought new manufacturing techniques. In 1758, Johann Rudolf Geigy founded a trading company for "Materials, Chemicals, Dyes and Medicaments of All Kinds," thereby laying the cornerstone for the chemical industry in Basel. With the "Elsässerbahn" (Alsatian railroad) from Strasbourg to Basel in 1844, the first train rolled into Switzerland. In 1869, Friedrich Nietzsche was appointed professor of philosophy at the university. During his ten-year stay, his radical thinking enlivened the city's intellectual life.

In the Footsteps of Paracelsus

Even before completing his studies, Albert

A physician should and must start with nature and read from and learn from her; beyond her, there is nothing; everything is from and in nature.

Paracelsus

20

Hofmann was encouraged by his highly esteemed doctoral advisor Paul Karrer to explore opportunities in Basel which was at that time the second largest city in Switzerland and had long been a stronghold of the chemical industry in Europe. While Karrer would have gladly retained Hofmann as an assistant in his institute, he was aware of the financial circumstances of his candidate and urged him to "Go out quickly and earn money." Karrer then wrote a letter of recommendation for him to Arthur Stoll, the Director of the pharmaceutical research division at Sandoz, in January of 1929. It read, "One of my current assistants, Mr. A. Hofmann, will complete his dissertation in April and wishes to find work in industry. He is extraordinarily capable, very serious, and conscientious so that I believe he would do well in your factory. If you are interested in him, it might be best if Mr. Hofmann could arrange for an interview with you in the near future. Although he has an offer from another company, I would prefer to see him work for Sandoz and would so advise him, should you make him an offer. I would appreciate it if you would let me know as soon as possible."

Hofmann's applications brought three offers of employment: Hoffmann-La Roche and Durand & Huguenin offered him 650 Swiss francs starting monthly salary with three weeks' vacation, whereas Sandoz offered only 450 Swiss francs and two

Arthur Stoll

weeks vacaton. Karrer wrote again to Stoll and told him that Hofmann would prefer to work for him, but asked whether they could improve their offer to make Hofmann's decision easier. Sandoz stood by the original offer, but held out the opportunity of a monthly salary increase of twenty-five francs in each of the next two years. Hofmann chose to work for Sandoz in their pharmaceutical-chemical research laboratories. On January 31, 1929, six days after his father's death and barely a month following his professor's recommendation, Albert Hofmann signed the contract to begin work for Sandoz on May 1, 1929. Decisive for him was the opportunity to work in the department for pharmaceutical research founded by Stoll on the chemistry of natural products and do research on the makeup of medicinal plants. This job matched his well-developed love of the plant world, whereas the offers from the other two companies dealt with inorganic chemistry.

Sandoz was founded in Basel in 1886 by Dr. Alfred Kern and Edouard Sandoz under the name of Kern & Sandoz as a factory for the production of basic dye components. The first dyes produced by Sandoz were alizarin blue and auramine. The first pharmaceutical substance, antipyrine for fever reduction,

> Belief and conduct, knowledge and doing are one and the same thing.
>
> *Paracelsus*

View of the Sandoz facilities in 1927

Production area in 1925

Lunch break

followed in 1895. Prior to WWI, the production of drugs was a niche business—the big money was in dyes which were bought for the most part by the English textile industry for their production of military uniforms. With the outbreak of the war and England's boycott of German products, the Basel chemical industry boomed as it gladly filled the gap left by German firms. As a consequence, in 1917, Arthur Stoll was engaged to expand Sandoz operations with the development of a pharmaceutical research department, which gradually grew, and numbered forty subsidiaries worldwide by the end of the 1960's.

Arthur Stoll was born on January 8, 1887, in the village of Schinznach. He studied chemistry at the Swiss Federal Institute of Technology (ETH) in Zurich where he was awarded a doctorate under Richard Willstätter. When Willstätter received the Nobel Prize for Chemistry in 1915 and left for Berlin, Stoll followed him and became his research assistant. Five years later, Stoll was appointed Pro-

fessor of Chemistry at the Ludwig Maximillian University of Munich and was hired by Sandoz the same year. He served as managing director from 1949 to 1956, then president of the board of directors from 1964. Stoll died in Dornach near Basel on January 13, 1971. His most significant scientific achievement was to first isolate the ergot alkaloids ergotamine and ergobasine. In addition, he succeeded in identifying digitalis glycosides. Even so, as a chemist, Stoll did not appear to match the brilliance of his teacher, Will-

Packaging department in 1930

stätter. Hofmann accepted him as his superior but in later comments let it be known that he did not have a high opinion of him as a chemist.

The research program at Sandoz focused on isolating, preparing in a pure state, and synthesizing the active ingredients of medicinal plants. The prospect of doing multifaceted, basic research towards the production of plant-based medicaments fascinated Hofmann. Once again, his talent and his determination helped him realize his dream of working at the intersection of chemistry and the plant world. The prospect of starting a career in research excited him as it promised to deliver broad professional satisfaction. Early in 1929, Hofmann moved to Basel and first

took a small apartment, then shared an apartment with his sister Anni in a multifamily dwelling on Holeestrasse, which lay in a quiet neighborhood on an unpaved road. Modern for its time, and built in 1932, it was the first flat-roofed building in town. Hofmann later became friends with the architect and student of Bauhaus who designed it, Giovanni Panozzo. Since 2006, the building has been protected as a site of historic interest.

Squill and Foxglove

During his first three years at Sandoz, Albert Hofmann investigated the active substances in *Scilla maritima*, or squill, and concluded his work by clarifying the structure of this

23

class of substances. He succeeded at isolating the highly active glycoside, scilliroside, from squill, also known as the red sea onion; it is noxious to the mucus membranes and a strong emetic. Because rats cannot vomit, it can also be used as a rat poison. Its use was controversial because laying out bait could result in the poisoning of house pets and farm animals. Scilliroside affects heart activity, like the glycoside digitalis, and among its uses, sometimes serves as a treatment for cardiac insufficiency.

The next task Hofmann tackled was to further research various species of foxglove (*Digitalis purpurea, Digitalis lanata,* among others), a plant genus of the plantain family with active ingredients related to those of squill. The active substances in both plants belong to the group cardiac glycosides—sugary substances used in treating heart ailments. The therapeutic and toxic doses of the cardiac glycosides lie dangerously close to each other so exact dosage is crucial and requires pure substances. Hofmann's most significant contributions to squill research con-

Scilla maritima

sisted in elucidating the structure of Scilla glycosides and presenting how they differ from digitalis glycosides. He ended his pioneering research into this class of substances for the time being in 1935.

At that time, the Sandoz laboratories were modestly equipped and, as Hofmann described in a lecture to his colleagues sixty years after he began his work with Sandoz, the procedures used "were subject to limitations that are unimaginable to today's researcher. There had been little change since Liebig's days."[3] The pharmacology research department consisted of just three academics: Dr. Walter Kreis, Dr. Jules Peyer, and Dr. Bruno Brenken. Brenken directed the analytical laboratory which, however, worked more for the factory than for research. Pharmaceutical production was also very limited in scope. It was run by Dr. Burckhardt, who along with the foreman, Schäppi, led the ergot and alkaloid operation. The calcium plant was under Dr. Gadient and the squill and insulin operations under Dr. Kussmaul. I could tell you these names because there were very few people involved and I wanted to give you an idea of how family-like the circumstances were then."

"A year after I was hired, Professor Stoll employed Dr. Erwin Wiedemann who worked with chlorophyll. He joined Dr. Kreis and me in our laboratory. So you had three different chemists working in three different areas in the same lab. We

> It is a joy to be allowed to work in a city with such a rich intellectual and academic history.... From the Bernoullis and Carl Gustav Jung to Albert Hofmann, everyone who researched here was passionate about their subject and enjoyed a worldwide reputation. That's pretty impressive.
>
> *Roderick Lim, Nanobiologist*

Erwin Wiedemann, Walter Kreis, Albert Hofmann

Advertisement
late 1930s

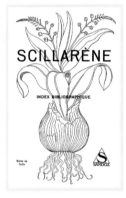

had just one gas jet under the exhaust hood. When we ordered an exhaust fan for the hood, which we badly needed, since colleague Wiedemann's work often involved hydrochloric acid fumes, Professor Stoll said that in Willstätter's lab, where he did his basic research on chlorophyll, the exhaust hoods were similarly equipped with gas jets. But we finally did get our exhaust fan. Only after six years, did I finally get my own lab."[4]

By comparison, Novartis—which resulted from the 1996 fusion of Sandoz and Ciba-Geigy—has nearly one hundred thousand employees today. In 2010, over two thousand people work in research just in Switzerland and are in constant contact with their colleagues worldwide via modern communication technology. The company currently invests approximately eight billion Swiss francs in research and development annually.

Luck is talent for destiny. *Novalis*

Turning Point

In addition to his demanding work, Albert Hofmann continued to pursue his many private interests and apply his talents as he had done earlier. He was a member of the Academic Athletic Club of Basel and also regularly trained at the Boxing Club. An evening course for still life drawing at the Arts and Crafts Department of the General Vocational School led by Theo Eble, a graphic artist and painter in the renowned Group 33, was also part of his weekly routine. While Hofmann found these activities fulfilling and he had a generally positive outlook on life, he was not immune to negative mood swings. When he was completing work on the alkaloids of fox glove and squill, he experienced an existential crisis which he described fifty years later as follows: "The external world seemed to be increasingly devoid of anything substantive and increasingly shadowy. Nothing appeared to be of any value. People acted like marionettes. I was often overcome by a dread of completely dying away and was afraid to go to sleep for fear of never waking again. I felt guilty that it was all entirely my fault without being able to discover concrete evidence of my blame. It was a dreadful state of mind. Since I believed my suffering was spiritual in nature, I attempted to work my way out of it by using my reason and will power to understand and escape this frightening condition. However, the attempt failed and only increased my anxiety.

One day, as I half dozed in my room, I happened to look out the open window and see a green bush in the garden. My increasing fascination with it led me to the possibility of healing, of breaking the spell of confusion I was under. It occurred to me that this tree had the same biochemical structure as I; it consisted of cells with a nucleus that contained genes and was surrounded

> The happy man is he who lives the life of love, not for the honors it may bring, but for the life itself.
> *Lawrence Durrell*

Albert Hofmann, 1931

Body building   At the Boxing Club (standing, third from right) ca. 1930

by protective plasma, just as were the cells of my own body. It too was the result of a female and a male germ cell combining. It developed, grew, and breathed the same air as I and was kept alive as a part of creation. My sudden awareness of the fellow creatureliness of this tree, which clearly lived its life without troubling worries, suddenly filled me with serenity and confidence; confusion and anxiety vanished. If my anxiety should resurface, I merely needed to picture the serenity of my fellow tree in order to feel safe and secure in the hands of a common creator."[5]

Beginning of an Eternal Love

In the winter of 1934, Albert Hofmann and a friend planned a winter vacation to Arosa, which lies at an elevation of 1800 meters (5,900 feet) in the Grisons in southeastern Switzerland. An internationally known health resort, Arosa nestles at the end of a sun-drenched valley and is popular in summer and winter; impressive peaks nearly three thousand meters

(9,800 feet) high offer vacationers unique alpine scenery. The two "Lowlanders" were excellent skiers and thoroughly enjoyed the sunshine and powder snow along with the mountain lodge atmosphere, the noontime fare of local dried beef with a glass of regional Veltliner wine; and in the evening, the *après ski* scene at one of the local traditional bars or rustic taverns. That Saturday night, a popular masked ball, held at Fastnacht (carnival) throughout Switzerland every year, was held in the village's "Kurhaus" (entertainment hall). Naturally, the two bachelors did not miss the opportunity to get acquainted with other costumed guests at this informal dance.

Near the end of the ball, it was customary for a prize to be awarded the woman with the best disguise and the prettiest costume. On one particular evening, the winner was a certain Anita Guanella. When the gracious young woman removed her mask to receive the honor, Albert Hofmann fell hopelessly in love. He knew at once: "She is going to be my wife."

Anita Guanella prepares a pirouette, followed by a secure landing, Arosa in 1934

The very next morning he set out to find the lady of his dreams. His customary determination also served him well in matters of the heart. He quickly learned that Anita was also vacationing in Arosa and arranged to meet her parents. The dashing and dapper bachelor made a good impression and it was not long before the couple was on the ski slopes together. Hofmann later described their first date: "When we met, I wanted to impress her with what an ace skier I was, but she was much better than I and quickly left me far behind."

Anita Guanella was as enthusiastic about sports as Albert Hofmann and was a highly accomplished figure skater. Both of her parents came from Graubünden, her mother from Andeer, her father from Bever. Anita, born on January 31, 1913, in Chur, was a young girl when the family moved to Lucerne where her father began working for the Swiss National Accident Insurance Fund, which is headquartered there.

Cupid had an easy job. Anita's chance meeting with the chemist from Basel resulted in love at first sight for her as well. Thoroughly enamored, both relished the white splendor of their winter surroundings. Just as quickly as they had met, they decided to marry. The civil ceremony took place in Lucerne less than three months later. The wedding followed the next day in Othmarsingen and Brestenberg Castle on idyllic Lake Hallwil to the music of Swiss pianist and composer, Paul Burkhard, whose song "Oh! My Pa-Pa" made him famous the world over years later.

The following day, the newlyweds went on their honeymoon. First they traveled to Munich, then on to Vienna, where they visited one of Austria's most prominent cultural treasures, Schönbrunn Palace. From there, they continued on to Budapest, Hungary's capital. Here, in addition to attending a Sunday service in the Coronation Church, they rode the cog railway to the top of Schwabenberg and also enjoyed a Danube River cruise.

> Love alone endures eternity, because they are of one substance.
>
> *Khalil Gibran*

Bride and groom

Albert and Anita Hofmann

After a brief visit to Venice and its lagoons, they returned home. Albert Hofmann was fully aware that with marriage, a new chapter in his life began. He marked this caesura by burning all of the diaries from his bachelor days. Basel was his workplace, so it was logical to live there, and Anita Hofmann joined her happy spouse in the apartment he still shared with his sister. Nine months after their marriage, on February 10, 1936, their son Dieter, the first of four children, arrived.

War and Peace

Happiness comes naturally in a peaceful family.
Chinese Proverb

As the world slowly recovered from the long, difficult twenties and early thirties, which were marked by poverty and joblessness after the global financial and eco-nomic crises, National Socialism took root in Germany. The majority of those in the stricken nation who had lost all they had were receptive to Adolf Hitler's ideas. After seizing power in 1933, he successfully suppressed political opposition and his job-creation and economic programs brought improved employment statistics and rapid growth. The humiliation of a lost World War, the loss of large areas of the former empire, and subsequent ostracism by the community of nations was hardly forgotten. The "Führer" and his cohorts used unprecedented demagoguery and racist hate campaigns to exploit the nation's wounded psyche. The ever-sharper tone of the campaign and the attacks by marauding bands of SA and SS troops on dissidents, Jews, and Gypsies portended the worst.

Most Swiss loathed the ideas of Nazism and the recent rise of their mighty neighbor to the north into a military superpower. The danger grew for Switzerland when

Lt. Albert Hofmann (center) and his company during military service in Ticino in 1939

Lt. Albert Hofmann in Ticino in 1939

Germany allied with fascist Italy. Consequently, the 1939 Swiss National Exposition focused on "defending the national spirit" —the government used all means to strengthen awareness of the nation's heritage and values to ward off Nazi propaganda. As in other countries, a minority sympathized with Hitler. They saw themselves as the vanguard and joined together into "fronts," earning them the name "Fröntler" (frontists). Although the appeal of right-wing extremist parties grew with increasing unemployment, they never posed a serious threat. With Germany's attack on Poland in the early hours of September 1, 1939, World War II began. Switzerland called for a general mobilization on September 2nd in keeping with its tradition of armed neutrality. Gradually, Swiss troops reported to their mustering stations and barracks to report for the so-called "Aktivdienst" (military service).

As a border city, Basel prepared to defend against a possible attack. The border was fortified, the soldiers stood ready. The deprivations resulting from being landlocked were heightened by the languishing cross-border trade. Near the end of the war, American bombers sometimes strayed over Swiss territory and dropped their deadly cargo on Basel rather than on nearby Freiburg in Germany, destroying the freight station and nearby residential quarters. This happened to Swiss rail lines and cities elsewhere, leaving several dozen dead and wounded. Rumor had it these "accidents" were meant as warnings by the Allied forces. Thanks to air raid alarms and luck, Basel suffered few casualties and relatively little damage.

The Second World War severely hampered Basel's chemical industry with shortages of raw material and coal. All four of the largest chemical companies maintained subsidiaries in Germany, two of

31

Albert Hofmann (in front) on troop maneuvers in Ticino in 1940

Lieutenant Albert Hofmann

these across the border in nearby Grenzach where forced labor was used. In comparison to their competitors abroad, however, the Swiss chemical-pharmaceutical industry benefited; their plants were undamaged and, though on a much smaller scale, were able to maintain their exports worldwide. Research, too, advanced on a broad basis and companies got an early start preparing for the end of the war. This gave them economic advantages and made the chemical industry one of the country's most important industries.

Like any other healthy Swiss, Albert Hofmann did his military duty in the militia. Even before the outbreak of the war, he was stationed in the canton of Ticino in southern Switzerland. During that time, his second son, Andreas was

Sons Dieter and Andreas in Bottmingen, ca. 1942

The family in their garden, ca. 1947

The family shortly after birth of their second son

born on June 12, 1939. Hofmann managed to secure a short leave to visit his wife and newborn. After returning to his unit, the overjoyed father treated his comrades to a big celebration. During the war, Hofmann, who advanced to first lieutenant in the Fortress Artillery Battalion, was called back for several three-month tours of duty "to defend the southern border against Mussolini." He was glad that all his service was in Ticino. The countryside, the people and his experiences in the south influenced Hofmann positively and led the Hofmanns to return on holiday to the so-called "sun chamber" of Switzerland many times after the war.

Midway through the war, the Hofmann family moved from their now cramped quarters into half of a large two-family house in the still rural village of Bottmingen near Basel. The house stood in an open field and the last several hundred meters of road were unpaved. Some friends and relatives commented that it was too remote for regular visiting. At first, they rented it but grew to love their home and, a few years later, when they had the means, they became its proud owners. "During a vacation in May of 1941, we moved to Oberwilerstrasse in Bottmingen and lived in our own home in the countryside with its lovely garden for twenty-seven years." Today, an alley named "Albert-Hofmann-Weglein," dedicated in 2006 to commemorate Hofmann's 100th birthday, serves as a reminder of his time there. A year after the move, daughter Gaby was born on August 23, 1942. Bottmingen became an important

Anita and Albert Hofmann on their honeymoon in Budapest, 1935

place to the family. To this day, they gather to celebrate significant birthdays, wedding anniversaries and other occasions in the restaurant of the impressive Weiher Castle. The surrounding moat often freezes in winter and is ideal for the children to ice skate on. Since Hofmann began to work more during his free time, he set up a study in the attic. A few years later, he remodeled the spacious garden house and moved into his "retreat," as he called it. Here, he could withdraw to prepare lectures and write articles, complete his lab journals and correspond with researchers from around the world. His youngest daughter Beatrix, born October 23, 1948, remembers as a little girl hearing the clatter of her father's typewriter in his retreat and found it comforting when she was falling asleep nearby.

Outside of Switzerland, war still raged. On May 14, 1944, the Hofmann's ninth wedding anniversary, they were arrested and taken into custody briefly by Swiss customs officials during a morning run near the French border. Hofmann's diary entries highlighted the nearness of the war: "On November 20, 1944, we could see the start of the battle for St. Louis-Hüningen between the retreating German occupation force and an advancing Algerian light armored brigade. At three o'clock we had to leave the factory. Alsatian civilians and a few German soldiers crossed the Swiss border at Lysbüchel. November 30 marked the final phase of the fighting between the French at St. Louis and the Germans occupying Hüningen. In those ten days, Hüningen was bombarded by French artillery and tanks, while St. Louis,

Together with sons Andreas (l.) and Dieter (r.), ca. 1942

Father Guanella with godson and daughter in Davos in 1944

especially the barracks, came under attack from German mortars. During the night of December 1, the Germans evacuated Hüningen and retreated across the Rhine. Now, French soldiers once again patrol along the border under my laboratory window, just as they did before 1940."

When Albert Hofmann returned to military duty, his wife and children often visited her parents in Lucerne, where she felt safer. This gave Anita's parents an important role in the lives of the children. Whenever Anita and Albert traveled, grandparents came to Bottmingen to care for the children and supervise homework.

Albert Hofmann managed the longer distance to work by bicycle. His son Andreas rode along on the bike's luggage rack to be dropped at school. Soon after he got his driver's license in 1947, he bought his first car, a Studebaker.

LSD Finds Its Discoverer

Where observation is concerned, chance favors only the prepared mind. *Louis Pasteur*

In the Beginning was the Ergot

Ergot is the name given to the spore, the sclerotium, of the parasitic filamentous fungus *Claviceps purpurea* which attacks various cereal grains and wild grasses, especially rye. The sclerotium is a black-violet, slightly curved, conical body, a few millimeters to up to six centimeters in length that can develop in place of a pollen grain. The name ergot (Mutterkorn in German) derives from its earlier use as an abortifacient and a midwife's aid, since the components trigger labor. The ergot of rye, *Secale cornutum*, is primarily used medically. Depending upon the habitat, host grass, and climate, the fungus contains different ergot alkaloids, for the most part lysergic acid derivatives. It was long used medicinally in many areas of the northern hemisphere.

Ergot first figured in the historical record during the early Middle Ages when it caused the mass poisoning of thousands. The poisoning was caused by consuming bread that, in extreme cases, contained up to twenty percent ergot. Most affected were the poorer classes who ate rye bread in quantity, whereas the wealthier had more wheat at their tables. Epidemics of ergot poisoning occurred in different regions of Europe and North America. St. Anthony was the patron of the sick and the Antonines the order which cared for the afflicted. Because of the terrible effects of ergot poisoning, known as St. Anthony's Fire or Ergotism, it was deemed to be divine punishment until the true cause was discovered in the 17th century. This knowledge, along with improved planting methods, led to the decline of such epidemics.

The healing effect of ergot was discovered quite early. The first written record of its medical use is found in *Herbal*, published in 1582 by Frankfurt's city physician, Adam Lonitzer. He recommends it for labor pains and mentions that ergot extracts have long been used by midwives to promote contraction of the uterus and to speed up birth. In 1907, the English chemists George Barker and Howard Carr

Production of the first larger quantities of dihydroergotamine for clinical trials in 1943

Rye with ergot   Inoculating rye by hand

isolated an ergot alkaloid mixture that affected the uterus. Because of its toxic side effects, it was named ergotoxine and was never used medically. After 1932, the English gynecologist Chassar Moir used aqueous ergot extracts which strongly affected the uterus.

Albert Hofmann's superior, Arthur Stoll, began investigating ergot in 1917 and by the following year had succeeded in isolating pure alkaloids of ergotamine. The compound was brought to market in 1921 as Gynergen®. After that, Stoll ended his research in this area.

In 1935, Hofmann was looking for a new project and suggested to Stoll that he resume investigation of ergot alkaloids. Based on what was known about them so far, Hofmann believed things looked promising. His objective was to continue Stoll's work and develop new medicines out of ergot. Stoll approved, but warned about the difficulty of working with these unstable substances. The required ergot was grown by farmers in the Emmental region as a secondary income and shipped to Sandoz in Basel in one hundred kilogram barrels. There, it would be milled, extracted with benzene, and concentrated. The components would be fractionated[6] and delivered to the experimental laboratory to be tested for purity before further processing. Safety measures in laboratories of the thirties did not compare to present day standards. The workers had no effective protection against highly poisonous chemicals and solvents. Consequently, there were frequent accidents and health hazards, especially with toxic and highly volatile solvents that often led to fainting.

Controls at Sandoz became ever more stringent. Arthur Stoll watched to see that raw materials were treated sparingly and criticized Hofmann for his allegedly wasteful methods. Hofmann recalls: "Once, when I requisitioned 0.5 grams

Sandoz coworkers in a rye field (late 1940s)

of ergotamine from the ergot plant which produced it in batches of several kilograms, Professor Stoll personally came to my lab and reproached me for using so much. I needed to adopt microchemical procedures if I was to work with his costly substances."[7] Hofmann found a way out thereafter by working with the less expensive ergotoxine.

The Synthesis

In 1934, American scientists W.A. Jacobs and L.C. Craig succeeded in determining the chemical structure of lysergic acid, the basic component of many ergot alkaloids. Lysergic acid proved to be a substance that easily decomposed. It was 1938 before Hofmann applied the Curtius Synthesis, a

Transfer of ergot harvest bound for Basel

Special harvester for ergot

Harvesting ergot by hand, Emmental in the 1950's   Harvesting with a sickle

method which enabled him to combine and stabilize lysergic acid with basic groups for further ergot research. From lysergic acid he began synthesizing the indole derivative ergobasine. This gave him a more rational method of producing a substance that is present only in extremely small quantities in ergotamine. Moreover, the synthesis led to the eagerly sought clarification of its structure, which had previously remained unresolved.

Hofmann achieved the first synthesis of a natural ergot alkaloid by combining lysergic acid with propanolamine. After Stoll's isolation of ergotamine, this was a further step in ergot research and proved to be of practical as well as scientific importance. This partial synthesis made it possible to convert the other alkaloids in ergot into ergobasine, which was valuable in obstetrics. Hofmann's method of synthesis became the generally recognized basis for producing a number of related structures from the original ergot alkaloid.

Hofmann subsequently produced many more lysergic acid derivatives, among them the twenty-fifth on November 16, 1938, which was lysergic acid diethylamide; hence the designation LSD-25. He was planning to synthesize an analog to the cardiovascular agent Coramine which was produced by Ciba, a competing pharma-

It is likely that unlikely things should happen.
Aristotle

If there is a remedy that would generally make people more intelligent, we must find it.
René Descartes

40

Albert Hofmann holding an LSD molecule model

ceutical firm on the opposite bank of the Rhine. He recalled that: "I ate lunch that day in the lab rather than the cafeteria and fed myself a slice of bread with honey and butter, and a glass of the milk which was delivered every morning from the Sandoz experimental farm. It was delicious. I had just finished and had begun to pace back and forth and think about my work. Suddenly, I thought of the circulatory stimulant, Coramine, and had the idea of producing an analog compound based on lysergic acid, the building block of ergot alkaloids. Chemically, Coramine is nicotinic acid diethylamide so I decided to produce lysergic acid diethylamide. The chemical and structural relationship of these two compounds led me to suspect they might have similar pharmacological properties.

I hoped that lysergic acid diethylamide would be a new and improved cardiovascular stimulant."[8] The experiments carried out by the pharmacological department at Sandoz with LSD-25 found it had approximately seventy percent of the effect of ergobasine. The trial audit mentioned slight restlessness in lab animals. Because the effects observed were less than expected, the physicians and pharmacologists at Sandoz quickly lost interest in the new substance. For the next five years, nothing more was done with LSD-25.

Potency

However, LSD-25 didn't pass into oblivion; Albert Hofmann could not stop thinking about the substance. "I had a strange premonition that this drug might have additional effects to those exhibited during the first trial. This led me to produce LSD-25 again five years after the first synthesis and pass it on to the pharmacological department for further trials. This was unusual, because test compounds were normally struck from the research program once declared to be of no pharmacological interest." Later, Hofmann could neither find a rational explanation for his hunch nor for the rest of his life reconstruct why it was that he chose to resurrect that particular compound out of the many he had created. "It was more a feeling—the chemical structure appealed to me—that prompted me to take that extraordinary step." (Bröckers, Liggenstorfer 2006) Most chemists would have rejected such a diffuse feeling as irrational fantasy and forgotten the matter, but Hofmann trusted and followed his intuition.

Hofmann's lab scheduled the second synthesis of this compound for April 16, 1943. It was a matter of producing a few tenths of a gram. Again, things were orderly and clean and all the safety measures required for work with poisons were followed. Nonetheless, during the final phase of the synthesis, it seemed that Hofmann unintentionally must have come into contact with the substance: "While we were purifying and crystalliz-

The inquiring eye often found more than it had sought.
Gotthold Ephraim Lessing

Doubt is the beginning of science. Whoever doubts nothing, examines nothing. Whoever examines nothing, discovers nothing. Whoever discovers nothing, is blind and remains blind.
Teilhard de Chardin

ing the lysergic acid diethylamides, I began to feel unusual sensations." For the first time Hofmann became aware of this molecule's potency. He described the sensations in a report to Professor Stoll: "Last Friday, April 16, 1943, I was forced to interrupt my work in the laboratory in the middle of the afternoon and proceed home, being affected by a remarkable restlessness, combined with a slight dizziness. At home I lay down and sank into a not unpleasant intoxicated-like condition, characterized by an extremely stimulated imagination. In a dreamlike state, with eyes closed (I found the daylight to be unpleasantly glaring), I perceived an uninterrupted stream of fantastic pictures, extraordinary shapes with intense, kaleidoscopic play of colors. After some two hours this condition faded away." Hofmann had no idea that the experiment with the chemical compound had anything to do with this surprising effect since he was always so careful about keeping a clean workplace, and he was aware of the toxicity of ergot derivatives. However, the next day he thought that "perhaps some of the LSD solution got on my fingertips during recrystallization and a trace of the substance was absorbed into my skin." He realized at the same time that should his conjecture hold up, this compound had unknown and very strong properties if just a trace could cause such noticeable effects.

The First Trip

Albert Hofmann had to know and decided to undertake a series of experiments, beginning with a test on himself on April 19th, 1943. Again he proceeded with great caution and chose a dosage of 250 micrograms, the smallest amount of ergot alkaloid deemed to have a noticeable effect.

But once again, strange and, initially, decidedly frightening images overcame the chemist, this time more acutely than before. According to his lab journal, his experiment began at four twenty in the afternoon when he ingested "0.5 cc of ½ pro mil tartrate solution of diethylamide per-oral = 0.25 mg tartrate. To be taken thinned with ca. 10 cc water." At five pm he notes: "Beginning dizziness, anxiety, disturbed vision, paralysis, urge to laugh." Two days later he adds: "Cycled home. Severest crisis from six to eight pm" and refers to a special report because he can barely record the last entry. He is at once certain that his experiences on April 16th stemmed from unintentional ingestion of a small amount of LSD-25. The experiences were the same, but this time more intense and profound.

Hofmann with model of an LSD molecule in the early 1950s

During the war, fuel was difficult to find. Gasoline was rationed and available for very few private vehicles. Indispensable commercial vehicles such as tractors and trucks were fitted with wood gasifiers. At that time, even in Switzerland only a few wealthy could afford an automobile and taxis were not available. That is why Hofmann did not have someone drive him home; instead, his lab assistant, Susi Ramstein accompanied him by bicycle. He had the impression that they made little headway, but she later assured him that they cycled very fast and she had to pedal hard to keep up with him. The rows of houses took on threatening forms, the street seemed wavy, and the few persons they met changed into distorted shapes. The distance between the laboratory and his home was ten kilometers, with a few gentle inclines on the way.

Once they reached his house, Hofmann asked Ms. Ramstein to call his doctor and to bring him a glass of milk from the neighbor woman as an antidote: He feared a fatal poisoning. Dizziness and faintness alternated. Exhausted, he went into the living room and lay on the sofa. Just as on the way home, the familiar surroundings in the cozy home looked distorted and eerie. The walls and ceiling appeared to bend and arch, furniture took on grotesque forms and appeared to move. He asked for more milk. He hardly recognized the neighbor who brought him more than two liters of milk. Instead, he perceived her as "a nasty, insidious witch with a colored mask."

Hofmann found the transformation of his inner world at least as unsettling as those in his surroundings: "All my efforts of will seemed in vain; I could not stop the disintegration of the exterior world and the dissolution of my ego. A demon had invaded me and taken possession of my body, my senses, and my soul. A terrible fear that I had lost my mind grabbed me. I had

> I didn't look for LSD.
> LSD came to me.
> *Albert Hofmann*

entered another world, a different dimension, a different time." His body seemed to him without feeling, lifeless and foreign. "Was I dying? Was this the transition?" were the agonizing questions that pressed in upon him and persisted.

He thought of his wife and three children who, precisely on this day, had driven to visit his in-laws in Lucerne. Would he ever see them again? Would he die without being able to say farewell. How would posterity judge him? That a young head of a family had been recklessly careless and risked leaving his young family fatherless? Had his obsession with research driven him too far? Hofmann was certain that he had not acted carelessly, and had always conducted his research prudently. Did this mean the end of the career that had begun with such promise and meant so much to him and promised so much more? "I was struck by the irony that precisely lysergic acid diethyl amide, which I had brought into the world, was now forcing me to leave it prematurely." His situation struck him as a most appalling and terrifying, hardly comprehensible tragedy.

It seemed an eternity had gone by for him before the doctor arrived and Ms. Ramstein could report the self-experiment at the Sandoz laboratory. Although Hofmann believed the worst of his desperate experience was over, he was not able to formulate a coherent sentence. Dr. Beerli, who had come in place of Hofmann's regular physician, Dr. Schilling, found no indications of any abnormal condition or poisoning. Respiration, pulse and blood pressure were normal. He helped Hofmann move to the bedroom to rest, but refrained from prescribing any medicine as none seemed indicated. This reassuring diagnosis had a positive effect. Within a rather short time, the anxieties and terrifying images subsided and gave way to "feelings of happiness and thankfulness." Hofmann began to enjoy his involuntary excursion into unknown and unfamiliar realms of consciousness. With closed eyes, he saw a wonderful play of color and forms: "a kaleidoscopic flood of fantastic images dazzled me; they circled and spiraled, opened and closed again as fountains of color, reorganizing and crisscrossing in constant flux. Particularly remarkable was how any acoustical perception, like the sound of a door handle or a passing car, transformed into optical perceptions. For each sound, there was a corresponding, vividly shifting form and color."

By late that evening, Hofmann had recovered sufficiently to describe his remarkable adventure to his wife, Anita. She had left the children with her parents and returned home after receiving a telephone call about her husband's breakdown. With the return of some tranquility to the Hofmann house, the exhausted chemist went to sleep. The following morning, he felt physically tired, but mentally refreshed and fit. "A feeling of well-being and new life flowed through me. Breakfast tasted marvelous, an extraordinary pleasure. When I went outside, the garden was still damp from a spring rain, and the sun made everything sparkle and gleam in fresh light. The world felt newly created. All my senses vibrated in a state of high sensitivity which lasted throughout the day." All in all, Albert Hofmann's experiment on himself, the first LSD trip in history, ended gently. He had discovered the most potent psychoactive substance yet known.

Hofmann's first experience contains many elements and descriptions that would be found in thousands of later reports of comparable trips. This first self-experiment contained two decisive factors in the course of any psychedelic experience, later designated as "set and setting" by the American psychologist Timothy Leary. "Set" referred to the mental and physical state and expectation of the consumer and "setting" to the atmosphere and surroundings during the session. Hofmann's experience became a positive one after his doctor told him that he need not fear he was on the threshold of death or permanent damage from a life-threatening poisoning. He had no frame of reference for what was happening to him and no certainty that his condition would normalize a few hours afterwards. He at least remained aware the entire time that he had undertaken a self-experiment. "The most frightening thing was that I didn't know if I would regain my normal state of mind. It was only when the world slowly began to look normal again that I felt exhilaration, a kind of rebirth."[9]

Albert Hofmann was impressed by his discovery[10] and by the intensity of his experiences during that first self-experiment with LSD-25 which would long resonate for him. He knew of no other substance with such profound psychological effects at such a low dosage that so dramatically

LSD crystals in polarized light

altered experience of the inner and outer worlds in human consciousness. Hofmann found it remarkable that he was able to recall details of his LSD intoxication and explained it with the hypothesis "that no matter how perturbed someone's worldview was at the height of the trip, the part of consciousness that registers experience was unimpaired." He was equally amazed that he remained aware of it as an experiment on himself yet was unable to voluntarily alter it and banish the "LSD-induced world." Just as surprising and welcome was the absence of any noticeable hangover afterwards; rather he felt left in excellent physical and mental condition.

Three days later, Hofmann presented his detailed report to Arthur Stoll and Professor Rothlin, the director of the pharmacological department. "As might be expected, it met with incredulous astonishment," he recalled. They both immediately asked him whether he had made an error in dosage. It was clear to them that no psychotropic substance was known to be that effective at a micro dosage level. The last doubts were erased only when Rothlin and Stoll both cautiously tried dosages of LSD one-third the strength of Hofmann's trial dose and had nearly as impressive results. In subsequent trials, Hofmann never ingested a comparable dosage again and described 250 micrograms as an "overdose." He was astonished that the "tripping generation" of the sixties considered his first dosage to be the standard measure.

His spectacular bicycle ride from the Sandoz factory through the outskirts of Basel and on beyond the city limits to his house became the stuff of legends. Since 1984, April 19th has been celebrated as "Bicycle Day" among pop-culture LSD fans. It was initiated by Thomas B. Roberts, emeritus professor of educational psychology. Americans in particular found the idea of a bike ride while on LSD amusing and admirable. Back then, hardly anybody in that land of boundless possibilities used bicycles and certainly not in the condition Hofmann was in on his original trip.

Looking back, Hofmann thought about the circumstances and significance of his discovery: "From a personal perspective, without the intervention of chance, I think the psychedelic effects of lysergic acid diethylamide would not have been discovered. It would have joined the tens of thousands of other substances that are produced and tested in pharmaceutical research every year and are relegated to obscurity for lack of effect and there would have been no LSD story.

However, in light of other significant discoveries of the time in medical and technical fields, the discovery of LSD could be considered less a matter of chance than of being called into the world as part of a higher plan.

In the 1940's, tranquilizers were discovered and proved to be a sensation for psychiatry. As their name expresses, tranquilizers cover up emotional problems whereas LSD is at the opposite pole of pharmacology; it reveals problems, making them more accessible to therapeutic intervention.

About the same time, nuclear energy became technically usable and the atomic bomb was developed. A new dimension of threat and destruction had been created compared with earlier energy sources and weapons. That corresponds to the increase in potency in psychotropic drugs such as mescaline to LSD, of a factor of 1:5,000 to 1:10,000.

One might suppose that the discovery of LSD was not a coincidence but drawn to attention by the *Weltgeist*. From this perspective, that would make the discovery of LSD no longer a matter of coincidence. Further reflection might lead one to think that its discovery was predetermined by a higher force and emerged as people began to contemplate prevalence of the materialism of the past century; LSD, an illuminating psychotropic drug, appearing on the way to a new, more spiritual age.

All of this could suggest that my initial decisions leading up to finding LSD were not a product of free will, but were guided by the subconscious mind which links us all to the universal, impersonal consciousness."[11]

The Assistant

Susi Ramstein began her training as a lab assistant at Sandoz research laboratories at the age of seventeen after a year in French-speaking part of Switzerland as an *au pair*. She was born in Basel in 1922, had two brothers, and her father was an optician. Although she was a good student, she did not attend high school because

Chemistry: The New Time, 1940, 55 x 86.6 cm.

Commissioned by Sandoz from the Basel painter Niklaus Stoecklin.

The painting hung for years in the office of Professor Arthur Stoll; today it has a place of honor in the lobby of Novartis headquarters

women were expected to marry early. She was the only female apprentice. She successfully finished her apprenticeship at age twenty and became Albert Hofmann's assistant. Susi Ramstein had deep respect for her superior. When Hofmann made his first conscious self-experiment with LSD and noticed its dramatic effects, she agreed to his request to accompany him home by bicycle.

Everyone on Hofmann's team made at least one self-experiment with LSD. Ms. Ramstein did three, the first on June 12, 1943, at the age of twenty-one. She was the first woman to take LSD and the youngest experimental subject at Sandoz. The dosage of her first trial was 100 micrograms, and she found the effects mild and pleasant. She had beautiful visions in which the surrounding world began to shine and in her own words, it was "a good experience." Unlike her superior, she decided to take a tram home. At that time, the ticket was purchased on board from a ticket agent. She thought his nose overly long and the other passengers looked comical. Ms. Ramstein felt steady, was not confused, and found her way home without problem. To be of help in establishing standards for the medical use of LSD, she repeated the experiment twice. The tests were conducted in the lab—at least they began there. All experiences and observations were noted. Susi Ramstein was intent on contributing to the advancement of science and determining the clinical usefulness of LSD. One year after her last trial, she married and left Sandoz.[12]

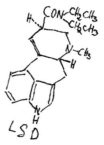

The Dose Makes the Poison

All things are poisonous and nothing is poison-free.
Solely the dosage makes the difference. *Paracelsus*

Successful Drugs

Albert Hofmann's long years of basic research into ergot alkaloids brought his employer, Sandoz, several successful drugs with sales in the billions. One was Methergine® for inducing labor and controlling bleeding after onset of delivery. Hofmann described Methergine® and LSD as his favorite medicaments. As he put it, Methergine®, is an aide during physical birth while LSD is an aide during spiritual birth. Also important was Hydergine® a drug used in geriatrics to dilate blood vessels. During the 1970s, Hydergine® was Sandoz' most lucrative drug with annual sales of 400 to 600 million Swiss francs.

After confirmation of the hallucinatory effect of LSD and the first trials on healthy and psychiatric subjects by the physician Werner Stoll, the son of Arthur Stoll, Sandoz produced LSD under the brand name Delysid® from 1947 to 1966. It was made available to physicians and psychologists for use in research. The package insert mentioned two indications for use: "For disinhibition in analytic psychotherapy, particularly with anxiety and obsessive-compulsive neuroses" and "for experimental investigation of the nature of psychosis: Delysid® gives the physician an opportunity through self-trial to gain insight into the mental state of the psychiatrically disturbed; it also makes it possible to study pathogenetic problems through brief model psychoses induced in normal experimental subjects."

From Phantasticum to Entheogen

There are a number of notations for the class of psychoactive substances such as LSD, mescaline, and psilocybin: Phantastica, psychotomimetics, hallucinogens,

> I am often called the 'father of LSD'. Who, then, was its mother? It was a mushroom, the ergot, Mutterkorn in the German-speaking area. She bore some of my pharmaceutical children. The first was methergine which helps during childbirth. The second child was LSD. Whereas methergine helps bring physical children into the world, LSD proves to be helpful in spiritual childbirth, the child slumbering in each of us.
>
> *Albert Hofmann*

Methergine®

Methylergometrine, the active substance in Methergine®, is a derivative of ergometrine which occurs naturally in ergot and is used in obstetrics. It causes sustained uterine contractions and is used to treat postpartum bleeding, delayed bleeding, excessive post abortion bleeding or delayed involution of the uterus. Methergine® was patented in 1939 and first marketed in 1946.

Hydergine®

Hydergine® primarily improves blood circulation in the brain. Dihydroergotoxine, the active substance, is a vasodilator and used to treat diseases resulting from constriction of blood vessels. Hydergine® enhances the effect of dopamine, has neuroprotective properties, and reduces the response of receptors of adrenaline and noradrenaline. Hydergine® was patented in 1940 and first marketed in 1949.

Dihydergot®

Dihydergot® is used in treating low blood pressure and associated symptoms. It combines two active ingredients, dihydergotamine and etilefrinhydrochloride, in one medicament to act on the veins, arteries, and heart, all of which are involved in abnormal blood pressure. Increasing below-normal blood pressure improves circulation and the blood supply to the brain, hence correcting the deficiency. The combined substances in Dihydergot®, which elevate blood pressure, relieve related symptoms. It was first patented in 1940 and first marketed in 1946.

Bromocriptine®

Bromocriptine® is used in treating Parkinson's disease, amenorrhea, acromegaly[13], and to block secretion of prolactin. It acts as a dopamine D2-receptor agonist and stimulates the postsynaptic dopamine D2-receptors of the central nervous system. Bromocriptine® can also affect the corresponding neurons in peripheral organ systems, particularly in the cardiovascular system and gastrointestinal tract. Chemically, Bromocriptine® is a derivative of the ergot alkaloid ergocryptine sold in Switzerland by Novartis as Parlodel®. The third drug stemming directly from his research was the circulatory and migraine medicine Dihydergot®. Hofmann also succeeded in finding the structural formulae of additional ergot alkaloids which led to further innovative drugs, such as Bromocriptine®. In addition to its use in controlling lactation after birth, it serves as a female fertility drug. Bromocriptine® also leads to a better understanding of the neurotransmitter dopamine.

psychedelics or entheogens.[14] The names say much about the opinions of those who gave them and the context in which they are used.

The respected German physician, pharmacologist and toxicologist Louis Lewin (1850–1929) coined the wonderful term "Phantastica," which is scarcely used any longer. It implies that these substances may lead to an enchantment of everyday reality and under their influence, access to the magical dimensions and visionary aspects may result. Lewin was the first to establish a classification system for the drugs and psychoactive plants known at the beginning of the twentieth century based on their pharmacological action.[15]

After the discovery of LSD, the term psychotomimetics—imitating psychosis—

> Of course, I was able to fish when the pond was full; today that is no longer the case.
> *Albert Hofmann*

was coined by the American psychiatrist Paul Hoch. Psychotropic substances that act upon the central nervous system and the psyche but do not cloud consciousness and induce a condition similar to a psychotic or schizophrenic state are called psychotomimetics. These states comprise feelings of alienation, hallucinations, and, depending upon the dose, ravings and dreamlike ecstasies. The term is based on the view that these substances trigger so-called "model psychoses" and can give the psychiatrist insight into the world of the mentally ill, as could be seen in the original patient information leaflet for Delysid®.

Today, the commonly known term is hallucinogen. This places the emphasis on the substances' properties, such as the ability to cause striking changes in visual, acoustical, or tactile perceptions, but seldom causing cognitive confusion, memory loss or disorientation. This distinction separates hallucinogens from other classes of agents such as deliriants, dissociatives, or oneirogens which all trigger dissociation, meaning the decoupling and loss of coordination of mental and physical functions.[16]

To be more precise, most hallucinogenics produce pseudohallucinations whereby the subject remains aware of the "unreality" of the impressions; the subject's inner observer and the awareness of being under the influence of a drug remain—yet, at times, it is impossible to keep emotional distance. Hence, "genuine" hallucinations are those taken to be real and are indistinguishable from everyday reality.

The writer Aldous Huxley and the psychiatrist Humphry Osmond both recognized the potential for self-awareness and

Package of LSD from the UK Sandoz affiliate in 1964

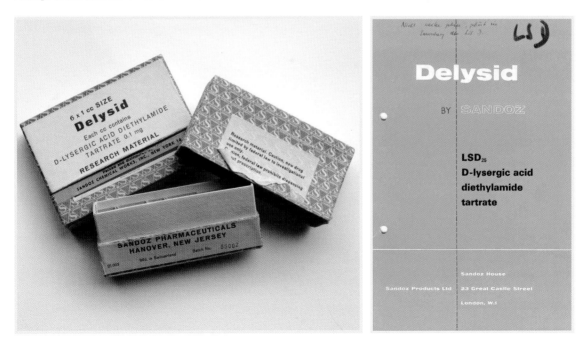

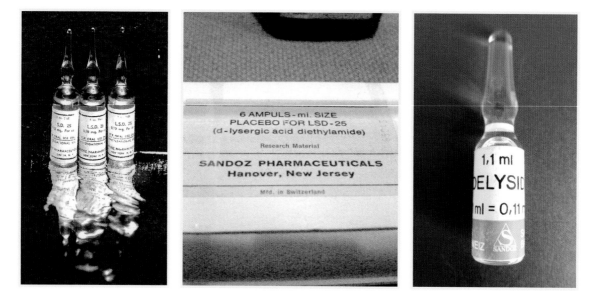

LSD ampoules from the
U.S. Sandoz plant

LSD placebo for research

An original vial of Delysid®

LSD diminishes intellectual
powers in favor of emotional
experience of the world. Our
attention shifts away from ourselves to spiritual dimensions
of being perceivable only
by the heart.

Albert Hofmann

These substances have formed
a bond of union between men
of opposite hemispheres,
between the uncivilized and
the civilized.

Louis Lewin

consciousness expansion presented by this "new" kind of psychoactive substance. They coined the now current term, "psychedelics," in their correspondence in 1956. Huxley wrote to Osmond: "To make this trivial world sublime, take half a Gramme of phanerothyme," whereupon Osmond answered: "To fathom hell or soar angelic just take a pinch of psychedelic." Osmond based his coinage on the Greek words "psyche" (soul) and "delos" (revelation) which describe a condition "in which the soul is revealed;" this term aptly describes the properties of these substances, which both men valued.

The latest term for these substances is "entheogens." The word combines the ancient Greek concepts "en" (in), "theos" (god), and "genesthai" (to effect). The term was introduced by Jonathan Ott in 1970 and specifically describes the experience of the unity of all which imparts the feeling of being at one with God and all that exists.

The Effect of LSD

Hallucinogens such as LSD are not drugs in the usual sense but, according to Albert Hofmann, "rank among the sacred substances rediscovered through LSD as far as their chemical structure and pharmacological action are concerned, being used in ritual context for thousands of years." They differ from other psychoactive substances in many ways: They are rarely poisonous at the effective dosage; they do not lead to psychic or physical dependency, even with repeated use over a long period, and they cause no organ damage. Fears of genetic mutation and other significant physical risks have never been scientifically confirmed. Deaths associated with LSD overdose are virtually unknown as is the dosage expected to be deadly to humans.

Psychedelics show a characteristic set of effects. While the active agents in other groups essentially affect mood insofar as they induce relaxation, sleep or produce stimulation, psychedelics cause profound psychological changes combined with an altered experience of space and time. Also, the perception of one's personality and corporeality is deeply changed. Consciousness is clearly preserved whereas, depending upon dosage, substances such as alcohol and morphine cause a more or less clouded awareness. Psychedelics bring people, while being fully conscious, into other worlds and dimensions which often seem more real and intense than everyday reality. Altered sensory perception is the salient feature of the use of LSD.

The colorless, tasteless LSD crystals are mind-altering at microgram dosages. LSD remains the strongest known hallucinogenic drug to date. The threshold dosage for mild physical and psychic effects for most people lies below 25 micrograms; the typical dosage is between 50 and 150 micrograms; in the 1960s the preference was for 250 micrograms while up to 500 micrograms was administered in therapeutic settings and up to 1500 in extreme cases. It is most widely available on the black market as saturated blotting paper called "blotters" or as microtablets containing between 50 and 250 micrograms. Drug effect receptivity varies widely from person to person. Since users have to buy LSD from black market sources, few know what dosage they are taking. LSD produced by underground sources is often far weaker than claimed. In 1967, Hofmann tested four samples from the USA sent to him by Humphry Osmond and found they contained less than ten percent of the dosage claimed. A further assay done by him after his retirement in the 1970s showed similar results.

The intensity and length of an LSD trip depend upon the dosage. When taken orally, effects are felt within thirty minutes and normally last eight to twelve hours. The body breaks down and assimilates LSD within one hour, and the level of LSD in the blood reaches its maximum after two hours. The strongest effect is most usually felt from the third to the fourth hour. Respiration, pulse, body temperature and blood sugar levels may rise especially in the initial phase; sometimes vertigo and lightheadedness are felt.

Chemically, a hallucinogenic substance is nearly identical with natural serotonin, one of the messenger substances that regulate particular brain activities. And because the hallucinogen's effect is chemically so closely related to serotonin, the effect is so severe!

Franz X. Vollenweider

In a harmonious setting with open expectations, LSD influences our sense of time, our inner processes, tolerance, empathy. It expands our outlook and dissolves aggression; it gives us insight into the concept of spirituality. LSD, used correctly and seriously, revolutionizes our world view, destroys the devastating idea of making comparisons, of competitors, and erases identification per se.

Manuel Schoch

These physical side effects are temporary and seldom detract from the feelings of well-being.

LSD's mechanism of action has not been completely explained. LSD has a great structural similarity with the body's own neurotransmitter serotonin and imitates its effect. LSD binds to particular serotonin receptors and in this way, transmits signals to nerve cells similar to those from strong concentrations of serotonin in the synaptic gaps. Since only a limited portion of the serotonin receptors are activated, the brain must process an uncustomary flow of information which leads to changes in perception.[17]

In general, it can be said that small doses of LSD sharpen the sense of everyday reality: We see more clearly, colors are more intense, noises are more distinct, and the senses of touch, taste and smell are subtler and more differentiated. At higher doses, users feel a heightened relationship and connection with all that is perceived; everything becomes more

The album LSD from 1966 contains experience reports of LSD trips, a selection of psychedelic music, and commentaries from experts, such as Sidney Cohen, Timothy Leary, Aldous Huxley and Allen Ginsberg.

meaningful and we enter a realm of symbols and archetypes. Objects we normally barely notice, whether it be a telephone, a curtain or a spoon, take on symbolic and specific significance. Synesthesia, a coupling of different sensory inputs, occurs—most commonly, sounds are seen as colors. Time awareness can change greatly, a minute seems like an eternity. Although we continue to experience everyday reality, it has a dimension of transcendence.

If the dosage is further increased, we enter another world in which everything is alive and in constant motion, a magical realm. It is the world of *Alice in Wonderland*, of fairy tales. We might reach a stage found in meditative contemplation: The sensation of abundant joy and happiness, deep inner peace, and comprehensive love, feelings of unity with all beings and the world, liberation from all restraints, and knowledge of another reality.

Experienced LSD-users report that recollection of specific events becomes more precise, imagination more vivid, creativity and powers of association enhanced. Many find the experience of LSD so profound and dramatic, that avoidance and repression are almost impossible. We experience ourselves as naked and vulnerable, stripped of all the layers of convention, habit, and self-images accumulated in the process of socialization. The experience of one's essence makes it possible to eliminate old imprints. This releases constructive and

If you concern yourself for weeks with mysticism, then the probability is great that you will have a mystical or spiritual experience if you take LSD in a meditative setting. But, if you do this without preparation and then go to a horror movie, the experience will be quite different. Psychedelic drugs are the only substances from which the effects depend upon the state of the person taking it.

David E. Nichols

I think hallucinogens are extremely dangerous, much more dangerous than heroin.

William S. Burroughs, 1965

Timothy Leary vividly described the LSD experience in a *Playboy* interview:

"… But as the LSD effect takes hold, everything begins to *move,* and this relentless, impersonal, slowly swelling movement will continue through the several hours of the session. It's as though for all of your normal waking life you have been caught in a still photograph, in an awkward, stereotyped posture; suddenly the show comes alive, balloons out to several dimensions and becomes irradiated with color and energy.

The first thing you notice is an incredible enhancement of sensory awareness. Take the sense of sight. LSD vision is to normal vision as normal vision is to the picture on a badly tuned television set. Under LSD, it's as though you have microscopes up to your eyes, in which you see jewel–like, radiant details of anything your eye falls upon. You are really seeing for the first time not static, symbolic perception of learned things, but patterns of light bouncing off the objects around you and hurtling at the speed of light into the mosaic of rods and cones in the retina of your eye. Everything seems alive. Everything is alive, beaming diamond-bright light waves into your retina…. Ordinarily we hear just isolated sounds: the rings of a telephone, the sound of somebody's words. But when you turn on with LSD, the organ of Corti in your inner ear becomes a trembling membrane seething with tattoos of sound waves. The vibrations seem to penetrate deep inside you, swell and burst there. You hear one note of a Bach sonata, and it hangs there, glittering, pulsating, for an endless length of time, while you slowly orbit around it. Then, hundreds of years later, comes the second note of the sonata, and again, for hundreds of years, you slowly drift around the two notes, observing the harmony and the discords, and reflecting on the history of music.

But when your nervous system is turned on with LSD, and all the wires are flashing, the senses begin to overlap and merge. You not only hear but *see* the music emerging from the speaker system–like dancing particles, like squirming curls of toothpaste. You actually *see* the sound, in multicolored patterns, while you're hearing it. At the same time, you *are* the sound, you are the note, you are the string of the violin or the piano. And every one of your organs is pulsating and having orgasms in rhythm with it….

Touch becomes electric as well as erotic. I remember a moment during one session in which my wife leaned over and lightly touched the palm of my hand with her finger. Immediately a hundred thousand end cells in my hand exploded in soft orgasm. Ecstatic energies pulsated up my arms and rocketed into my brain, where another hundred thousand cells softly exploded in pure, delicate pleasure. The distance between my wife's finger and the palm of my hand was about 50 miles of space, filled with cotton candy, infiltrated with thousands of silver wires hurtling energy back and forth. Wave after wave of exquisite energy pulsed from her finger. Wave upon wave of ethereal tissue rapture–delicate, shuddering–coursed back and forth from her finger to my palm."[19]

creative potential that can transform neurotic behavior and enable a lasting connection with natural, vital energy. At even higher doses one might be able to disengage from the context of reality and travel into other dimensions experienced as real or even hyper real.

Not all LSD trips are pleasant or run smoothly. Acute panic reactions triggered by particularly severe shifts in perception,

Classification of Psychoactive Substances According to Their Effect

Analgesics or euphoriants, like the alkaloids of opium (morphine, heroin, and codeine) and methadone, are pain-relieving, intoxicating and tranquilizing.

Anxiolytics, such as diazepam (Valium) or tetrazepam, are anti-anxiety agents.

Dissociatives, such as ketamine, PCP, and salvinorin A, cause feelings of detachment.

Empathogens and entactogens, such as MDMA (Ecstasy), MDA, MMDA and related substances, are stimulants that affect the emotions.

Hallucinogens or psychedelics, such as mescaline, psilocybin, LSD, DMT, 2CB and numerous other synthetic substances, trigger a state of intoxication while remaining fully conscious. Some sources include THC, the agent in hashish and marijuana, in this group; also atropine and scopolamine, the agents in plants of the nightshade family, such as henbane, jimson weed, and belladonna.

Hypnotics, such as barbiturates or chloral hydrate, are soporifics; differentiation from sedatives is a quantitative measure.

Inebriants, such as alcohol, ether, or chloroform, are anesthetics.

Narcotics, such as laughing gas, barbiturates, fentanyl, and ketamine, are anesthetics.

Sedatives or tranquilizers, such as rauwolfia (reserpine), phenothiazine (chlorpromazine, etc.), diazepam (Valium), Tofranil and other drugs, are tranquilizing.

Stimulants, such as amphetamine, caffeine, and cocaine, accelerate physiological activity.

This classification involves overlapping and cross connecting categorization of the effects of the substances enumerated. For instance, some sources list salvinorin A as a psychedelic, others as a dissociative. Ketamine is, at low dosages, a hallucinogen with dissociative effect, at higher dosages a narcotic. Valium is both an anxiolytic and a sedative. THC is a special case and assigned to the hallucinogens by many. Likewise, some experts designate the nightshade drugs atropine and scopolamine as hallucinogens, even though they have significant dissociative effects.

a loss of the accustomed feeling of identity, flashbacks of repressed traumatic experiences, or becoming worked up into a crisis can all happen. Panic attacks, so-called "bummers" can be serious enough to require medical intervention. Those affected normally recover within a matter of hours, but hallucinations can last up to forty-eight hours and psychotic conditions can last several days. The severe side effects often attributed to LSD, such as irrational acts leading to suicide or unintended death, occur extremely rarely. Whether LSD affects someone negatively depends on their personality structure, their prevailing mental health, their momentary mood, and their surroundings—Set and Setting. According to the consensus opinion among experienced users, therapists, and researchers, if general circumstances are favorable, the risks are minimal.

Stanislav Grof's book, *Realms of the Human Unconscious* (Grof 1975), provides a good overview of the worlds of consciousness experienced on LSD. Nonetheless, it should be remembered that these experiences occurred in a therapeutic context with a focus on psychological problems and subjects were often in locked, clinically equipped rooms with eye patches to stimulate perception of internal imagery.

For good reason, a psychedelic experience is called a "trip," or journey. Though it is shorter than one taken in the external world—from a few minutes with DMT (dimethyltryptamine),[18] to around five hours with psilocybin to eight to twelve hours with LSD and mescaline—many impressions remain just like those from an adventurous journey.

Drugs

Public discussion concerning the differences between various drugs is fraught with immense lack of knowledge. Our image of intoxication is determined by alcohol. Even today, substances like LSD, hashish and heroin are often mentioned in the same breath. Misunderstanding terms has nurtured this confusion. What determines the danger of a psychoactive substance is its toxicity, above all the spread between an effective and a poisonous dosage. A further aspect is how quickly and how decisively a substance leads to psychological or physical dependence. Psychedelics present neither danger.

The distinction between "hard" or "soft" drugs is entirely arbitrary. It tells us nothing about the potential for dependency on a substance nor does it in most cases help us reliably determine into which category the drug should be classified. Cocaine ranks as a classical "hard" drug but causes few symptoms of physical withdrawal—hence, the classification is apparently based on its potential for psychological dependency. On the other hand, someone with the same personality traits might risk dependency on "soft" drugs as well. The significance of this distinction between "hard" and "soft" has for the most part been amplified by public discussion and reporting by the media. It is thus not based on the intensity of a drug's effect, which is often greater for soft drugs, but on its toxicity and potential for dependency.

Categorizing psychoactive drugs into different classes is problematic. It would be more exact to classify them according to their chemical structure, but chemically related substances can have divergent effects, making this approach not really useful. Today, these drugs are divided into three main groups according to their action: stimulants, sedatives and hallucinogens.

> Designating nearly all intoxicants (aside from alcohol) as "narcotics" is highly unscientific. For no substance is a toxin per se, rather a particular substance can be toxic to a particular body at a particular dosage. The same substance could be used as either an intoxicant or as a toxin, depending upon the dosage.
>
> *Rudolf Gelpke*

> Antidepressants fit our society's underlying biases. Psychedelics emphatically do not. Is it possible that we have demonized hallucinogens because we fear the contents of our own minds?
>
> *Daniel Pinchbeck*

> Potent brains are not strengthened by milk, but by alkaloids.
>
> *Gottfried Benn*

Researchers Discover LSD

The endlessness of scientific endeavor ever ensures that the two noblest impulses of the inquiring human spirit are kept alive and rekindled, namely enthusiasm and reverence. *Max Planck*

Mescaline

The German physician and pharmacologist Louis Lewin published in 1886 a first analysis of the peyote cactus (*Lophophora williamsii*) which he considered to be highly poisonous. His compatriot and colleague Arthur Heffter first isolated the main psychoactive alkaloid from peyote and confirmed its properties by a self-experiment in 1896, naming it mescaline. In 1919, chemist Ernst Späth succeeded in clarifying its chemical structure and how to synthesize it. In 1927, Lewin published his comprehensive study of psychoactive plants in his pioneering *Phantastica* (Lewin 1927). In contrast to many subsequent researchers, Lewin distinguished between mystic visionary experience and pathological states of consciousness. Up until then, self-experiments with hallucinogenics had been carried out for the most

Lewis Lewin

Kurt Beringer

part by lay people; artists or scientists outside of research assignments, as was the case with sexuality researcher and social reformer Havelock Ellis; in the 1920s, it was largely physicians or psychiatrists who carried out experiments and studies with mescaline. In the following years, several researchers attempted to scientifically systematize the experiences.

The most important publication came from Kurt Beringer (1893–1949), a German psychiatrist and mescaline researcher and confidante of Hermann Hesse, C.G. Jung and Louis Lewin; his work *Der Meskalinrausch* (Beringer 1927) summarized the results of his extensive trials with humans and animals. As a private lecturer, Beringer experimented with mescaline at the psychiatric clinic of the University of Heidelberg and published the results in his professorial dissertation. His

Albert Hofmann by Robert Venosa, oil on canvas, 2006

Peyote cactus

subjects were physicians and medical students, who injected mescaline, and documented their experiences. Beringer considered mescaline intoxication to be a reliable means for exploring and better understanding pathological states of consciousness. In contrast with the criminal drug experiments conducted later by the Nazis on humans in concentration camps, Beringer's subjects were volunteers or self-experimenting physicians. When no evident medical applications emerged, the considerable initial interest in this agent dropped off sharply. Up until the middle of the twentieth century, research and experiments into the therapeutic application of psychoactive substances were infrequent.

Albert Hofmann's discovery of LSD lent unforeseen new momentum to research on hallucinogens. Researchers throughout the world began to investigate the psychological effects of LSD and associated neurological changes in the brain with renewed interest. Although the range of effects from LSD was not completely unknown, corresponding extensively to those of mescaline, its novelty was its unmatched potency—about 5,000 times greater than that of mescaline. LSD research quickly

Normal spider web

Spider web created under the influence of caffeine

Spider web created under the influence of LSD

exceeded the boundaries of chemistry and pharmacology. It became interdisciplinary and influenced medicine, psychology, psychiatry, neurology, anthropology and the history of culture and religion. Between 1950 and 1965, around one hundred scientific articles on LSD appeared. According to several sources, up to 3,000 studies were published.

Experiments on Animals

The first animal experiments with LSD took place following its initial synthesis at Sandoz in 1938. After discovery of its psychological effects, LSD was removed from the category of drugs warranting further testing. Five years later, in 1943, it was again added to the list of experimental compounds. Most of the animal trials were carried out by Aurelio Cerletti, to be regarded according to Hofmann as a "pioneer of pharmacological research on LSD." Sandoz arranged several hundred animal experiments in their laboratories worldwide. In Basel, a small menagerie of animals received doses substantially higher than those effective on humans. The results were contradictory. Mice and rats reacted primarily with impaired mobility, aquarium fish with poor coordination while swimming. Cats showed symptoms implying spells of hallucinations, i.e., anxiety when confronted with small balls. Hofmann remembered, "The animals stare anxiously in the air and, counter to the proverb, the cats do forget to hunt mice; they fear them in fact." Dogs showed comparable reactions. A chimpanzee clan living together in a cage was disturbed over the one member that had been given LSD even though he showed no outward behavioral changes. It was hypothesized that the family was upset because that member no longer behaved according to the family hierarchy.

A famous spider experiment took place in Berne. Pharmacologist Peter Witt had been feeding spiders different drugs and then photographing the webs they wove while intoxicated. The most chaotic web of all was woven under the effects of caffeine, the loveliest under marijuana, the most regular under a low dosage of LSD. Under high dosages of LSD, the spiders wove three-dimensional webs that no longer were effective in catching prey. Under even higher dosages, the spiders did not bother any longer to weave webs. These now famous experiments were conducted under the sponsorship of Sandoz, which also supplied the LSD (Witt 1956).

When a dead whale washed ashore on the Maine coast in 1949, John C. Lilly began his career in dolphin research. Born in 1915, the American neurophysiologist came to the site with several colleagues to dissect the animal's brain. He had previously conducted brainwave measurements on cats and monkeys. From the whale, Lilly went on to dolphins, which have long fascinated humans. These animals were revered in ancient Greece; it was deemed a crime to kill them. According to many personal accounts, dolphins have saved humans from drowning. Lilly found that not only are dolphin brains larger but they are also more complex than human brains. Hence, he wished to investigate these special creatures as living rather than dead specimens to see what their capabilities were.

Lilly invested his entire savings—he came from a wealthy family—to buy a strip of Caribbean coastland on St. Thomas in the Virgin Islands. There he established the Communication Research Institute. In the early 1960's, Lilly and up to thirty coworkers began studying the mental abilities of dolphins, including under the influence of LSD. The experimental animals were kept in a large basin where the researchers could swim with them. Lilly found that a 200 kilogram dolphin on a dosage of 100 micrograms exhibited increased respiratory (by 50%) and pulse (by 20%) rates. These physiological changes interested him less than the experiment carried out with an injured, traumatized female dolphin. When they would approach her, she would immediately swim to the far edge of the basin. Forty minutes after receiving a dosage of 100 micrograms of LSD, she began to exhibit curiosity and approached the edge of the basin where Lilly was observing. That was the first time in two years that the female dolphin approached him this closely. She lay still and, with one eye above the water, observed Lilly for ten minutes. Previously, she had maintained a distance of at least six meters, but when he walked around the basin, she followed him and approached within one meter, astonishing Lilly that LSD could so quickly induce trust in this dolphin. It remained unknown whether similar results would occur with other mammals.[20]

Lilly and his colleagues later abandoned the use of LSD and attempted by means of underwater microphones to communicate with dolphins in English and with symbols on monitors; their success was rudimentary. From this, Lilly concluded that dolphins

Photos from Sandoz report
in 1943

John C. Lilly eye to eye
with his dolphin

communicate in more subtle ways and at other levels of consciousness and intelligence than humans. He became so fond of the animals that he no longer wished to hold them captive and, in 1987, 'the dolphin whisperer' gave the last pair their freedom.

An impetuous researcher does not fear even the largest animals, as was proved by a legendary experiment with an elephant, performed on behalf of a branch of the U.S. Intelligence Services. In 1962, Dr. Louis Jolyon West, known for not being squeamish, was asked by the CIA to conduct an LSD test with an elephant at the University of Oklahoma. The animal which weighed over three tons was injected with a dosage of 297 milligrams. West and two other men conducting the absurd experiment sought to determine whether LSD unleashed the uncontrolled aggressiveness noted in elephants during their rutting season. Five minutes after being injected, the elephant collapsed and went into severe convulsions. To calm the animal, a dosage of 2.8 grams of chlorpromazine was injected in one

ear after an additional fifteen minutes, but to little effect. One hour later, West injected the suffering pachyderm with an unspecified amount of pentobarbital, an anesthetic. The elephant died an hour and forty minutes after the LSD injection. It remained unknown whether death was caused by the enormous dosage of LSD or by the other two substances. Albert Hofmann wrote: "An elephant given 0.297 grams of LSD died within minutes. Assuming a weight of five thousand kilograms, this gives us a fatal dosage at 0.06 thousandth grams per kilogram body weight. Since it was a single case, this value is not useful but from it we can deduce that the sensitivity of the largest land animal to LSD is relatively high since the lethal dosage was one thousand times smaller than that used with a mouse. Most animals die of respiratory failure after a lethal dose of LSD." Hofmann himself never rejected animal experiments as the practice was simply an accepted aspect of pharmacological research at that time.

The most important conclusion from the animal trials was that the fullest effect of LSD is only found in those creatures having the most developed nervous systems and that, compared with humans, higher dosages are necessary with animals to achieve comparable effects.

The First Experiment on Humans

The first report on systematic human experiments with LSD appeared in the *Schweizer Archiv für Neurologie und Psychiatrie* (Stoll 1947), four years after the discovery of its effects. Its author, Werner Stoll, a physician and the son of Arthur Stoll, conducted the test at the psychiatric clinic of the University of Zurich with both mentally ill, (mostly persons with schizophrenia) and healthy subjects. Of the forty-nine administrations of LSD, twenty-nine were with healthy adults (eleven men and five women). The first series consisted of the fifteen self-experiments by LSD's discoverer, his lab assistant, and physicians, as report-ed in their personal notes. Stoll considered the observations gained from these trials of varying dosages to be preliminary trials. They laid the ground-work for a second series of fourteen uniform trials which he personally conducted, monitored and recorded. He endeavored to systematically study the psychological effects

> For neuropharmacologists and neurophysiologists, the discovery of LSD meant the beginning of a golden era of research that could solve many puzzles concerning the intricate biochemical interactions underlying the functioning of the brain.
>
> *Ann Shulgin*

of LSD using psychiatric methodology. The doses used were low, from twenty to one hundred and thirty micrograms. The results describe many of the experiences known today. Once experiments with normal subjects showed LSD to be essentially harmless, twenty clinical trials were conducted at Burghölzli, the Psychiatric University Clinic of Zurich, on six schizophrenic patients who had not responded to the usual treatments. Stoll especially noticed that the symptoms from the action of LSD observed in those patients were weaker and less developed than in normal subjects.

Stoll concluded that "the question of whether there is a therapeutic application is still open." He urged that "experimental testing of LSD be continued. Every trial with an intoxicant poses a host of interesting questions about psychopathology. But above all, the enormous effectiveness of LSD should justify further investigation." (Stoll 1947) He suggested adding a radioactive marker to LSD to permit tracing it through the human body. His report on the experiment was a sensation among experts in the academic world and aroused attention both for the experiences described and for the effect of such minimal dosages of a chemical substance.

The Psychotomimetic Paradigm

In his investigation of mescaline, the psychiatrist, Tayleur Stockings considered the state induced by it to be a kind of pharmacologically controlled schizophrenia: "Mescaline intoxication is indeed a true schizophrenia if we use the word in its literal sense of split mind, for the characteristic effect of Mescaline is a molecular fragmentation of the entire personality, exactly similar to that found in schizophrenic patients. Thus the subject of the mescaline psychosis may believe that he has become transformed into some great personage, such as a god or a legendary character, or a being from another world. This is a well known symptom found in states such as paraphrenia and paranoia." (Stockings 1940) Like Stockings, most physicians and psychotherapists in the 1940's assumed that the state of consciousness triggered by LSD and mescaline was comparable to schizophrenia and that it involves an artificially induced psychosis. They considered LSD to be a proven means for bringing about a "model psychosis," a term coined by Kurt Beringer.

The enormous effectiveness of LSD lent credence to the theory that endogenous psychoses and schizophrenia are biochemically contingent and arise when, under specific circumstances, a person's metabolism produces a substance similar to LSD that, in turn, induces abnormal conditions. Advocates of this theory reason that schizophrenia does not involve mental illness, but is rather the body poisoning itself through pathological changes in biochemical processes. Research initially focused on testing this hypothesis, scrutinizing descriptions of the similarities and differences between descriptions of the phenomena of psychedelic experience and schizophrenia. Of particular interest was the similarity of the chemical structures of psychedelics with those of neurotransmitters, the biochemical substances which send information between nerve cells. It was found that, chemically, mescaline resembles noradrenaline and adrenaline and that psilo-cybin and lysergic acid amides have similarities to the neurotransmitter serotonin. During the 1950's there were several theories about which specific substances or metabolites—waste products of the body's metabolic processes—might trigger schizophrenia. The consensus centered on the explanatory model that LSD interferes with the neurotransmitter serotonin to trigger abnormal psychic processes; this was thought to provide a similar mechanism and yield the biochemical cause for schizophrenia. This reductionist view of schizophrenia was later criticized and eventually most researchers discarded it. Many studies examined the effect of LSD on biochemical and physiological functions, on the organs, on tissue structure, and on enzyme systems.

In the early days of LSD research, monitored self-experiments were seen by many as a reliable and useful exercise when training psychiatrists, psychologists, and other therapeutic professionals to give them a brief and limited glimpse of the world of their schizophrenic patients. In this way, healthy volunteers gained insight and understanding through simulated mental illness. Even though the idea of

> You can say everything imaginable about LSD just as LSD can say everything imaginable about you.
> *Michael Horowitz*

> Psychedelics are extraordinary tools, when used with psychotherapy, because in one day you can let go of so much, and have insight into so much. Sometimes more than in a year of traditional psychotherapy. I think they should be used in psychotherapy. But I don't know who should be entrusted with the toolbox – priests or psychiatrists? That is the difficulty.
> *Laura Archera Huxley*

model psychosis was later widely abandoned, Stanislav Grof found this to be "a unique and valuable learning experience for all clinicians and theoreticians studying abnormal mental states." (Grof 1980)

A Helpful Tool for Psychotherapy

The possibility of using LSD therapeutically was first suggested by Gion Condrau, the Swiss psychiatrist and psychotherapist, in 1949, two years after Werner Stoll's publication. At the time, LSD was beginning to be seen as a purely pharmacological tool with properties that gave it curative power. Condrau himself proposed treating depression with LSD since it had shown euphoric effects in some subjects. Hoping to achieve positive mood shifts in depressive patients, he administered successively greater daily doses of LSD. His results and those of other researchers who followed his procedures of daily dosage were not convincing. Instead, ingestion of LSD led more often to reinforcement of the patient's prevailing mood than to a lasting, positive mood shift. Other attempts at using LSD as a medicament rather than as a therapy support also failed to bring the desired effect. This notion of LSD as a chemotherapeutic agent was eventually dropped altogether. Hofmann emphasized that while hallucinogens fulfill the role of a medicinal tool, they are not therapeutic agents *per se*.

In the early 1950s, several researchers suggested independently the use of LSD to deepen and intensify the psychotherapeutic process. Its use with psychoanalysis is based on the knowledge that patients who are bogged down in their problematic patterns can be more easily jarred loose by shaking up their customary outlook. The resulting relaxed state can improve the patient-therapist relationship and make the patient more receptive to suggestions. Forgotten or repressed experiences become more quickly available for psychotherapeutic treatment. As a consequence of these insights, two main therapeutic approaches emerged.

The approach widely used in Europe was psycholysis or psycholytic therapy, a term coined by the British psychotherapist Ronald Sandison which is still applied today. This psychotherapy uses LSD in low to medium doses at intervals of about a week. The material that resurfaces from the patient's subconscious is usually interpreted from the Freudian psychoanalytic perspective. While generally approached from a depth psychological perspective, LSD-supported psychotherapy has been influenced by humanistic psychotherapies since the 1960s. An extension of the psycholytic approach is anaclitic therapy (from the Greek *anaklinein*—to lean upon) in which the patient and therapist enter into close contact and, during the dramatic phases of the LSD experience, physical contact is permitted. The theoretical framework is expanded by archetypal and mystical elements. These are largely related to experiences of fusion and oneness, hence the synonymous designation as "fusion technique." Two London psychoanalysts, Joyce Martin and Pauline McCririck, developed it during the 1970s and built upon the finding that deep regressions can occur during LSD sessions. In contrast with traditional therapy procedures, Martin and McCririck took on a mothering role and engage in close bodily contact with their patients. This gives the patient an experience of primal symbiotic unity. Patients commonly report experiencing a feeling of oneness with the cosmos.

In the USA, psychedelic therapy was developed during the 1960s. It differed considerably in many points from the psycholytic approach but found little resonance in Europe. In the psychedelic approach, a high dosage of LSD was administered generally once or twice during the therapy after extensive preparation. Analytic aspects play a subordinate role. The decisive factor for a successful therapy was achieving a spiritual peak experience that was supposed to bring about a profound transformation and restructuring of the personality. This approach was born out of the recognition that for many patients who reported mystical experiences in their sessions, their clinical condition improved dramatically and their personality changed positively. In contrast with psycholytic therapy, which continuously seeks to change unconscious structures, here the emphasis is on achieving a radical transformation within a short time. Critics fault insufficient comprehension of the underlying mechanisms of psychedelic therapy in accounting for the frequent attacks on it, despite its great successes.

The strongest indicators for applying LSD therapy are alcoholism and other addictions, depression, neuroses, psychosomatic disorders, and alleviation of mental suffering and physical pain in terminally ill cancer patients.

Realms of Consciousness

The German neurologist Walter Frederking inquired of Albert Hofmann in February 1951 how and where he might obtain LSD. He learned of it from articles which the German writer Ernst Jünger sent him. Hofmann was pleased with the interest and had Professor Rothlin, director of the pharmacological division, send Frederking a sample. In April, Frederking sent his first interim report of the results to Sandoz. He had experimented with mescaline since 1935 and subsequently used it in treatment. He sent Hofmann a report in 1954 on treatment of sixty patients with LSD and forty with mescaline—all involving neurotic, therapy-resistant patients. Frederking judged the treatment effect of LSD to be greater than that with mescaline. He expressly recommended that any physician employing LSD study the effects of a higher dosage on oneself under supervision in order to better interpret a patient's experience under LSD.

Frederking's colleague, Göttingen physician and psychiatrist Hanscarl Leuner, developed the idea of intensifying catharsis through the use of low dosages of LSD. Between 1955 and 1960, he carried out more than thirteen hundred individual sessions with neurotic patients and healthy volunteers, administering different hallucinogens. In 1960, he organized the first European Symposium for Psychotherapy under LSD 25 at the University of Göttingen. It drew experienced colleagues from Denmark, the Netherlands, England, Norway, Czechoslovakia, Italy, and Germany. In 1964, Leuner founded the European Medical Society for Psycholytic Therapy

(EPT). At the time, psycholytic therapy was being practiced in eighteen European treatment centers as well as by many psychotherapists. It appeared to be an effective, scientifically established, and safe treatment method that held great promise. Particularly good re-sults were achieved for patients with severe neuroses. Leuner became the leading proponent of the psycholytic approach in Germany. More than two decades later, in 1985, he and other researchers founded the European College for the Study of Consciousness (ECSC) and he became its president. He conceived of the ECSC as a forum for further research and exchange of knowledge in the area of altered states of consciousness and placed high value on its multi-disciplinary orientation. This ranged from the basic sciences, such as neurochemistry, neurophysiology, and psychopharmacology, to psychopathology, psychiatry, psychotherapy, anthropology, the psychology of religion, and research into creativity. After its founding, the ECSC organized several international symposia and three theme-specific congresses under the heading "Realms of Consciousness." Albert Hofmann and Hanscarl Leuner had enjoyed a collegial relationship since the 1950s and Hofmann was delighted to chair the collegium at Leuner's invitation. Hofmann participated regularly as a presenter at ECSC events between 1985 and 1999.

Hanscarl Leuner and Albert Hofmann at the ECSC Congress in Heidelberg, February 1996

Trauma Therapy

The Dutch psychiatrist Jan Bastiaans began working with psilocybin and LSD in 1961. From 1963 to 1985, he was professor of psychiatry at the State University of Leiden and by 1988 had practiced hallucinogen-assisted psychotherapy with some three hundred patients at the psychiatric clinic in Oegstgeest. His criteria for use of LSD consisted of three categories of patient: Those with psychosomatic disorders and highly rigid defense and coping mechanisms, those with survivor or concentration camp syndrome, and patients who showed no improvement after several years of psychoanalysis. Unfortunately, the state health authorities could provide no systematic and concluding summary of results from his treatment, due to missing patient records.

Bastiaans became internationally known upon the successful LSD-assisted treatment of Israeli writer Yehiel De-Nur. As prisoner number 135633, De-Nur survived two years in Auschwitz. Harrowing memories of what he had experienced and seen haunted him over the next thirty years. He could not sleep or focus on his work. To end his suffering, he sought treatment through LSD-assisted therapy in Jan Bastiaan's clinic. It took three sessions during which he lived through the hell of Auschwitz again before he could speak about it with Bastiaans. The fourth session brought a breakthrough. He saw himself die on a death march at Auschwitz and hover above the camp. In his books, he vowed as a survivor to be the voice of the murdered. But now he is dying and experiences the reunion of his divided self. Although Bastiaans would have preferred to analyze De-Nur's trauma more deeply, his patient stopped therapy. He felt cured and was no longer plagued, either awake or asleep, by his memories. He realized that it wasn't Satan who caused the clouds of smoke above the fiery ovens of Auschwitz, but you and me, us. Humans and not "the devil" were responsible for the Holocaust. The insights from this death and rebirth experience freed De-Nur from his mental concentration camp. As Ka-Tzetnik ("Concentration Camper") number 135 633, he described the stages of his therapeutic process in *Shivitti* (1989).

LSD Comes to England

In September 1952, British physician and psychiatrist Ronald Sandison visited the Sandoz Laboratories in Basel and, with Albert Hofmann, discussed using LSD in treating the mentally ill. In November he returned to Basel and Hofmann gave him ampoules of Delysid® each containing 100 micrograms of LSD. Thus, the first LSD came to Great Britain. In 1953, Sandison began to work with it at Powick Hospital in Worcestershire. He opened the first LSD clinic in 1958. Sandoz supplied him with the substance at no cost until 1964. After he left the clinic, Justin Johanson, a physician, took over and worked with LSD until his retirement in 1972. In all, 638 patients treated in 13,785 sessions had better than average outcomes. Sandison published his results with LSD treatments in the *Journal of Mental Science*

in 1954. His article formed the basis for LSD therapy in Great Britain. In June 1954, the *News Chronicle* published an article with the title "Science has Alice-in-Wonderland-Drug"[21] giving an objective report of Sandison's work. This brought greater understanding of his work and made him more widely known in Britain.

Studies in Saskatchewan

The British psychiatrist Humphry Fortescue Osmond began to study pharmaceutical treatment of psychiatric conditions in 1950 in London. Together with his colleague, John R. Smythies, he compared the symptoms of schizophrenia to the effects of hallucinogenic drugs and studied their similarities and interrelationships. After he had established a similarity in the molecular structures of mescaline and adrenaline, he formulated the hypothesis in 1952 that biochemical substances might be responsible for schizophrenia. Osmond and Smythies moved to Saskatchewan, Canada, and continued their research at Weyburn Mental Hospital where the psychiatrist Abram Hoffer soon joined them. Together they formed a psychotherapeutic research team that carried out different patient studies using LSD and other hallucinogenic drugs. In 1954, Osmond, Smythies, and Hoffer published their theory that the body's own adrenochrome could lead to hallucinations

> We began examining a group of problematic alcoholic patients who were psychopathic. We now have treated sixty, and half of them are no longer alcoholic after just one treatment. It is clear to us that this drug has great potential to bring about behavior change.
>
> *Abram Hoffer*

and trigger schizophrenia, but this was later refuted.

Beginning in 1953, Osmond successfully treated chronic alcoholics using LSD. Nearly half of those treated, volunteers from Alcoholics Anonymous who failed to achieve sobriety using the self-help group alone, no longer drank after one year. As yet, no other treatment has even approached this success rate.

Behind the Iron Curtain

The Polish physician Rostafinski was the first to work with LSD in what were then the Eastern Bloc countries. He treated eight children who suffered from epilepsy with LSD in 1950. Czech physician and psychiatrist Milan Hausner began his study of LSD therapy in the mid-1950s in a sanatorium near Prague. As a consequence, nearly thirty psychologists and psychiatrists received LSD therapy training.

The most comprehensive studies and experiments were done at the Psychiatric Research Institute at Charles University in Prague. In 1956 the brain researcher, Professor George Roubiček, received a package of LSD he had ordered from Sandoz. After reading Werner Stoll's report on his LSD experiments, Roubiček was curious to try the substance on himself and his students. His particular interest was in the effect of LSD on the brain's electrical activity. He administered a strong dose of 250 micrograms LSD to subjects in a dark room and recorded their physiological parameters throughout the trial. Three hours after receiving the drug, the subjects were exposed to a stroboscope emitting alternating frequencies

of oscillating flashes to determine their effect on brain wave activity. In the fall of 1956, Stanislav Grof had his first experience with LSD as a young medical intern. This introduction to the effects of LSD, this "divine thunderbolt," sparked the beginning of Grof's career. He was convinced he had found an extremely elegant shortcut for Freud's "royal road" to the unconscious. "This combination of the light and the drug evoked in me a powerful mystical experience that radically changed my personal and professional life. Research of the heuristic, therapeutic, transformative, and evolutionary potential of non-ordinary states of consciousness became my profession, vocation, and personal passion." (Grof 2006) Stanislav Grof received a two-year research grant from Johns Hopkins University in Baltimore and afterwards he remained in the USA where his work was later to have an important influence.

LSD Conquers America

In 1949, Army psychiatrist Max Rinkel brought the first LSD to the United States after visiting Sandoz in Basel; with his colleague, Robert W. Hyde, he began to use it in the first experiments in the USA at the Psychopathic Hospital in Boston. Hyde is considered to be the first American to have an LSD experience. In the same year, American psychiatrist Nick Bercel procured LSD in Basel and began using it in his therapeutic practice in Los Angeles. As early as May 1950, at a meeting of the American Psychiatric Association (APA), Rinkel and Hyde reported the results of the LSD treatments they had begun a year earlier on one hundred students at the Boston Psychopathic

Hospital. Hyde simultaneously published the first article on LSD to appear in the *American Psychiatric Journal* in which he gave details on inducing a model psychosis. In contrast to those therapists who concentrated on giving their patients a pleasant or mystical experience through LSD, Rinkel and Hyde were focused on temporarily inducing a psychotic state in their students. Another researcher at the conference, psychiatrist Paul Hoch, agreed with Hyde and Rinkel's theory of model psychosis. He believed that such substances could upset a person's mental stability and that LSD gave the clinicians a tool with which to explore model psychoses in the laboratory. Hoch, Hyde, Rinkel and, later, many of their colleagues considered LSD to be a great tool for research into schizophrenia and other mental illnesses. In the eyes of many scientists, the psychotomimetic properties of LSD opened up new possibilities for exploring the biochemistry of the brain and the functions and dysfunctions of the human mind.

Early on it was clear that LSD had fallen upon fruitful ground in the United States, and would have a far greater impact than in Europe. The first international conferences dedicated to LSD and mescaline took place in 1955 in Atlantic City and at Princeton. Around that time, first reports emerged of recreational use of LSD by physicians in Los Angeles. In October of 1952, Carlo Henze of the American branch of Sandoz wrote to Albert Hofmann and asked him to write an article about the discovery of LSD for the periodical *Medical Horizons*. He closed his request with the prophecy: "Sooner or later, LSD will become an important affair in New York." He wrote Hofmann a short time later that, "We are getting cold feet about LSD because of the extreme interest official and unofficial circles have shown. We should therefore should consider whether communications that go beyond the scope of psychiatrists and bona fide scientists are currently in order. I think we will wait a bit until we have a clearer idea about the future development of LSD."

As individuals they may be anything. In their institutional role they are monsters because the institution is monstrous. *Noam Chomsky*

Dividing the World

The capitulation of the German army on May 7, 1945, marked the end of the Second World War in Europe, but behind the scenes, the Cold War had already begun. As soon as it became clear that Germany would be liberated by the Allied Forces from the west and by Russia from the east, the division of Europe into East and West on an ideological and political level loomed ahead. No longer did armies face each other, but occupation forces that defended their political and economic systems. The partition ran through the middle of Europe and corresponded to the territories and countries the victorious powers had conquered and pacified. The Iron Curtain divided Western Europe from the Soviet Union's satellite states of the Eastern Bloc. In 1949, the western part of Germany became the Federal Republic of Germany and the eastern part the German Democratic Republic.

Diplomatic relations were strained by escalating mistrust that triggered a massive arms race. The top priority of the two superpowers, the USA and the Soviet Union, became the stockpiling of atomic weapons. By the mid-1950s, the world faced the threat of atomic overkill. For the first time in its history, humankind was in a position to annihilate itself many times over with one blow. Generals and leaders justified this mutual nuclear threat with the concept of a balance of terror, and businesses profited from the meteoric growth of the arms industry. Planned economies and real socialism ruled in the communist East and modern consumerism in the West. The automobile, refrigerator, and television offered unlimited mobility, abundance, and entertainment. Advertising and marketing served the desires of a mass society geared to immediate satisfaction. A majority of citizens were influenced

You don't easily give up the pride of being an American. And the military and political leaders are only too happy to convince you that America is the "best, biggest, most beautiful and freest of all countries.

Margaret Boveri

and intimidated by the bogeyman orchestrated by the media and politicians; gradually, some of the younger population began to show discontent with the increasingly shallow culture and political manipulation of the economy. They saw through the discrepancy between superficial gratification and the deadly seriousness of the situation.

Experiments without Limits

The multiple scenarios of the Cold War included not only the stockpiling of weapon arsenals, but also the secret services increasing their number of intelligence agents. In the West, the American CIA and in the East, the Russian KGB massively expanded the range of their "set of tools" and their activities. Espionage and counterespionage were their major focus, and the military wanted to know how to neutralize the enemy without armed force. No means were beyond consideration, no measure too horrible to pry secret information from enemy agents or to render hostile soldiers harmless. If thumbscrews, electroshock, psychosurgery or worse failed, agents recalled the fabled truth serum sought since ancient times, a tiny drop of which instantly would release every tongue

> To take a dose of LSD is all right, and you will have the experience of being more or less crazy, but this will make quite good sense because you know you took the dose of LSD. If, on the other hand, you took the LSD by accident, and then find yourself going crazy, not knowing how you got there, this is a terrifying and horrible experience. This is a much more serious and terrible experience, very different from the trip which you can enjoy if you know you took the LSD.
>
> *Gregory Bateson*

and thwart every mental trick for withholding secret information.

Shortly after the end of WWII, the U.S. Army began Operation Paperclip. Over one thousand war criminals and Nazi scientists of the Third Reich were secretly smuggled out of Germany into the USA via the Vatican or South America. Rocket engineers, spies, and concentration camp doctors condemned for murder were granted immunity if they would work on secret projects for the U.S. Army and the CIA. By late 1944, the German Army's military intelligence general, Reinhard Gehlen, had already planned for his future: "The Western powers will turn against their Russian ally. They will need me, my coworkers, and my copies of documents to fight Communist expansion because they don't have any agents there."[22] According to the CIA's Director of Intelligence Operations Harry Rositzke, it was "absolutely necessary that we use every last one of the bastards; the main thing was that he was Anti-Communist."(Hunt 1991, Simpson 1988)

Among the most infamous of these Nazi doctors was Josef Mengele, the "Angel of Death of Auschwitz," who fled to South America after the war. His frequently lethal experiments were carried out on Jews, Sinti, Roma, and prisoners of war and included experiments with pathogens, poisonous and psychotropic substances of all kinds, including mescaline. The American physician Charles Savage heard of experimentation with drugs being done in nearly all of the concentration camps. In the fall of 1947, he began work for the U.S. Navy at its Medical Research Institute near Washington and conducted the first mescaline experiments, code-named

Allen Dulles

Sidney Gottlieb

Chatter. The military officers wanted to know how they could induce people to reveal information against their will without the use of force. Because the experiments brought little success, they were discontinued in 1953.

Meanwhile, the news of Albert Hofmann's discovery of a psychoactive substance had traveled around the world. Moreover, Werner Stoll's publication in 1947 of his first trials on humans generated great interest among professionals internationally. The Viennese physician Otto Kauder discussed Stoll's work in 1949 at a conference held at the Boston Psychopathic Hospital which was affiliated with Harvard University. Among those present was Army psychiatrist Max Rinkel, who then travelled to Basel, visited Sandoz Pharmaceuticals, and returned, bringing the first LSD to the USA. Sandoz was interested in seeing their drug tested internationally and in gathering research results; they gladly provided physicians and clinics around the world with Delysid® at no cost. It was not Rinkel but his more adventuresome colleague Robert W. Hyde who became the first American to have an LSD experience. That same year they began the first LSD trials in the U.S. at Harvard. One hundred volunteer subjects under the influence of LSD were observed for changes in behavior. By May 1950, Rinkel and Hyde were able to present their findings at a meeting of the American Psychiatric Association (APA). At the same time, Hyde published the first article about their LSD experiments which permitted investigating "temporary psychic disturbances" in a controlled setting. Shortly thereafter, the American intelligence service and the army noticed the report and imagined that in LSD they had found the long sought truth serum for counter espionage and for weakening resistance in enemy soldiers. It was rumored that the CIA underwrote additional LSD experiments of Dr. Rinkel and Mister Hyde and fed them ideas for experiments that met the agency's own needs.

On April 20, 1950, the CIA under Allen Dulles gave the green light for the intelligence service to evaluate the use of LSD in the secret operation Bluebird. During WWII, Dulles was chief of the Office of Strategic Services (OSS) and stationed in Berne. From there he visited Sandoz in Basel to gain direct knowledge of the utility and range of effects to be gained from LSD. (Marks 1979) On April 13, 1953, he ordered Richard Helms, head of the Office for Scientific Intelligence, to begin the research program dubbed MK-Ultra. This highly secret program directed by military psychiatrist and chemist Sidney Gottlieb was launched in response to the brain washing employed by the Chinese and Soviets as well as the North Koreans with American prisoners of war during and after the Korean War. MK stood for Mind Control and was derived from the German "Meinungs-Kontrolle" or thought control; "Ultra" indicated that the experiments went to all possible extremes. Quite a few MK-Ultra experiments were modeled after those carried out on humans in German concentration camps; some proved to be deadly in the U.S. as well. Up until the end of the 1960s, they were carried out on thousands of unsuspecting experimental subjects—normal citizens, prisoners, the ill, handicapped and even children. Chemical and biological substances were used and, for the first time, LSD. These experiments were combined with torture methods like electroshock, sensory deprivation, and simulated drowning. Most of the subjects were not informed that drugs had been administered, and the experiments were done without medical and psychological supervision since few agents or superiors were trained professionals. (Koch 2004)

To meet the growing demand for LSD, the American government offered to buy the entire stock held by Sandoz—an informant had erroneously calculated it to be ten kilograms—but the company in Basel declined. They did however contract with the U.S. for weekly deliveries of 100 grams of LSD and promised not to supply any to communist countries. During this time, Albert Hofmann refused repeated invitations from the CIA and the U.S. military to participate in their research projects. To achieve independence from Sandoz and its

> Born with a club foot and a stutter, he compensated by becoming an expert folk dancer and obtaining a PhD from Cal Tech. A pleasant man who lived on a farm with his wife, Gottlieb drank only goat's milk and grew Christmas trees, which he sold at a roadside stand.
>
> *Evan Thomas*

terms of delivery, the CIA contracted with the U.S. pharmaceutical company Eli Lilly & Co. to start production of LSD in mid-1954. To conceal the transactions involved in financing their secret experiments, the CIA cooperated with several charitable organizations and foundations.

The CIA started another secret project which was less dangerous but no less abstruse. Harry Anslinger, the head of the Food and Drug Administration (FDA),[23] charged George Hunter White, a former army officer, with starting Operation Midnight Climax. Consequently, he established a brothel in a Greenwich Village apartment in New York in the summer of 1953. Prostitutes with heroin dependency were to slip LSD in the drinks of their unsuspecting clients and involve them in intimate conversation while White and his agents observed and filmed their talkativeness and sexual behavior through a one-way mirror. In return, the prostitutes received one hundred dollars a night, their daily ration of heroin, and immunity from police interference. Two years later, White set up two more such brothels for the CIA in San Francisco. Their purpose was to find out how to bring spies to divulge secrets under the influence of LSD.

One MK-Ultra program carried out for the military between 1952 and 1974 was coded-named Project 112 and was conducted at the biomedical laboratory north of Washington, DC, at the Army's Edgewood Arsenal, later the headquarters for chemical warfare. Two hundred fifty-four different biological and chemical agents were tested on more than six thousand soldiers. The substances included 3-Quinuclidinyl Benzilate (BZ), a chemical weapon developed in 1952 by the chemical company Hoff-mann-La Roche, and ranged from mustard gas to LSD in extremely high dosages. One of the leading scientists at Edgewood was psychiatrist James Ketchum whose detailed autobiography published in 2006 (Ketchum 2006) broke his silence on the extensive neuro-logical behavioral exper-iments. Among his col-leagues were psychiatrist Sidney Cohen and George Aghajanian, professor of psychiatry at Yale Univer-sity, who investigated the possibility of administering LSD as an aerosol (Ketchum 2006) as well as eight former Nazi scientists. (Hunt 1991)

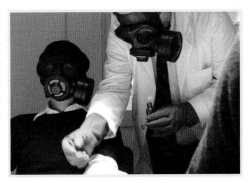

Harris Isbell

The effects of these different substances were tested under hair-raising condi-tions, including realistically simulated life-threatening battle field situations. Among the "volunteer subjects" were pris-oners from Holmesburg Prison in Philadel-phia; in return for their participation, they were promised a shorter sentence. During a later Senate hearing on the human exper-iments, Allan Lawson, a former prisoner and subject, testified that "any claim of voluntary participation…in human exper-imentation is a cruel hoax."[24] Most of the "volunteers" suffered depression, sleep disturbances, and hallucinations during the remainder of their incarceration.

In 1954, Sidney Gottlieb started MK Pilot, another CIA project, at the Lexington Nar-cotics Hospital in Kentucky. Physician Harris Isbell led a team in the research division for addiction at the Department of Health; they experimented on drug dependent

patients with LSD and other chemical sub-stances. Most of the patients were African American and prisoners who were subject to tests around the clock; some were admin-istered LSD for up to seventy-seven days straight. When, after the test period, Isbell could detect no effects injurious to the health of the subjects, he disparag-ingly noted that he had expected nothing different from that kind of patients. After the trials, the subjects were rewarded with the drug of their choice. (Lee, Shlain 1992, 24)

At the end of April 1961, the U.S. Army start-ed Operation Third Chance to test LSD on their troops stationed at West European mil-itary bases, especially in Germany. The trials included psychological and physical torture and focused on interrogation techniques in case of a suspicion of espionage as well as on the behavior of soldiers in battle situations. Similar LSD army experiments were carried out beginning in February 1962 under the code name Derby Hat at a few U.S. bases in Asia and Hawaii.

A particularly refined method of treat-ment was develop-ed by the Scottish-American psychia-trist Donald Ewan Cameron, president of the American Psy-chiatric Association from 1952–1953. It was based on his the-ory that behavior change could be

It is absolutely not something about which we can talk! What we did in Edgewood, was seen by me, as 100% okay. Yes, we sought a weapon that does not kill, but just incapacitates—I said, this was not ethical!

James Ketchum, 2010

achieved once the brain of a mentally ill patient had been "depatterned" and all memories and patterns were erased. The idea stemmed from British psychiatrist William Sargant whom Cameron considered to be the best informed about Soviet brain-washing techniques. He conducted "psychic driving," as he called it, as part of the MK-Ultra program from 1957 to 1964 at the Allain Memorial Institute at McGill University in Montreal, Canada. Treatment began with "sleep therapy" in which patients were continuously under massive sedation for up to several weeks. During that time, loudspeakers under their pillows played a tape loop with simple, brief messages. Some patients were subjected to up to a quarter million repetitions. After this phase which lasted up to three months, the patients were given strong electro-shocks and repeated, strong dosages of LSD meant to clear their minds of all previous patterns. The aim was to completely break a person's spirit in order to provoke behavior change. Journalist Naomi Klein described Cameron's contribution to project MK-Ultra not as thought-control or brainwashing, but as "developing scientifically based systems for extracting information from 'resistant sources.' In other words, "torture."[25]

After more than ten years of abuse of LSD at the hands of intelligence services and the military, more detailed information about their clandestine human experiments continued to surface. Reports in the media were sporadic and cautious. It became apparent that LSD was not the truth serum hoped for and could not be deployed in case of war. It also became evident that the experiments had not contributed to

the security of the nation nor its soldiers. This led the U.S. Congress to establish new security guidelines for hallucinogenic drugs in 1965. Substances like LSD were classified as research drugs and their use restricted to scientific study. In early 1966, the U.S. Senate began the so-called LSD hearings under Senator Robert F. Kennedy. His wife Ethel had undergone LSD therapy in Vancouver, Canada, with Ross McLean. (Lee, Shlain 1985, 93) The Senators discussed the whole spectrum of LSD use, as a sacrament, a therapeutic agent or weapon, ingested by hippies, or administered by physicians, intelligence agents and scientists. Meanwhile, all secret human experiments had been stopped, but the records largely remained sealed. Kennedy asked representatives of the health and drug agencies why all the LSD projects had been suddenly stopped when just shortly before they had been characterized as quite promising. His questions were met with evasiveness and vague apologies.

By the mid-1960s, the youth movement, the spread of hallucinogens like LSD, and their underground production peaked. Politicians realized that the intelligence services and army saw no application for LSD but that many of the young had made it their "love and peace" drug; it strongly influenced their world view, undermining their willingness to serve in the military. The nation found itself in the midst of the Vietnam War with an increasing number of young Americans refusing to serve. This development contributed significantly to LSD's being declared illegal first in California in October of 1966, then in all of the U.S., and before long worldwide.

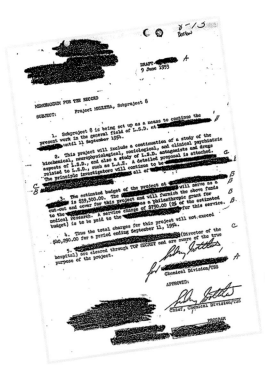

Following the directive of his superior, CIA Director Richard Helms, Sidney Gottlieb destroyed all documents and files from the MK-Ultra project in 1973. Not until December of 1974 did the *New York Times* print a lengthy article about the most extensive and expensive secret project ever conducted by the CIA and U.S. Army. The new CIA director, Admiral Stansfield Turner, surprised the United States Senate Select Committee on Intelligence headed by Senator Edward Kennedy, with the news that apparently not all MK-Ultra files had been destroyed. An employee had turned up a box containing five thousand pages documenting the experiments. Turner informed the senators in detail about these secret human experiments camouflaged as scientific research at around eighty institutions in the U.S. and Canada—among them forty-four universities, various hospitals, psychiatric clinics, prisons, and pharmaceutical companies. The MK-Ultra project enlisted one hundred and eighty-five non-government scientists in one hundred and forty-nine different secret operations, a majority of which involved LSD. Due in part to these and many other disclosures, hundreds of victims of these experiments with hallucinogens have successfully pursued lawsuits claiming abuse and torture and in some cases they have received compensation up to several hundred thousand dollars in damages for their pain and suffering.

> Perhaps to some extent we have lost sight of the fact that LSD can be very, very helpful in our society if used properly.
>
> *Senator Robert Kennedy, 1966*

Understatement

Up until now, few drug experiments on humans have come to light in Great Britain. It is likely that the most extensive trials were carried out between 1953 and 1955 under the psychiatrist William Sargant. They took place in the military research laboratory for biological and chemical weapons at the military base Porton Down. At the request of the British secret service M16, scientists conducted experiments on soldiers with LSD. Participation in the trials was just as "voluntary" as the information policy of the researchers was "straightforward." The thirty-seven servicemen participating in one experiment were told the liquid being administered was a cold remedy. (Roberts 2008, 40) Sargant too drew upon the Nazi experiments with mescaline and other psychoactive drugs and turned to LSD to test the change in behavior of soldiers in combat. One such experiment filmed during a mock troop maneuver showed the humorous consequences: A half hour after ingesting LSD, the first soldiers began to stagger as they marched, then to giggle, lay their rifles down, and roll on the meadow laughing. The commentary from off camera: "Fifty minutes after taking the drug, communication by radio became problematic if not impossible. But the men remained capable of physical activity. However, not all possess the necessary sense of responsibility to carry out logical sequences of action despite their physical symptoms. One hour and ten minutes after ingesting the drug, and after one man had climbed a tree to feed the birds, the commander of the troops admitted that he was unable to keep either his men or himself under control. Then he no longer was able to keep himself from laughing."[26]

Beginning in 1964, additional experiments were carried out under such original code names as Moneybags, Recount, and Small Change—LSD stands for abbreviations of the Latin terms for the British currency of the time—pound, shilling, and pence—namely, *libra, solidus* and *denarius*. This work was done in collaboration with representatives of the American MK-Ultra project, Sydney Gottlieb and biochemist Frank Olson, experts in germ warfare and biological weapons. They were invited to London, and experimental methods used in the USA were then adopted in Great Britain. Not until 2006 was the British government forced to compensate former soldiers who participated in William Sargant's 1953 LSD experiments at Porton Down.

Iron Silence

The KGB, Soviet intelligence, was not idle as Moscow learned of the discovery of a wonder drug in Basel during WWII. In contrast to most Western countries, particularly the USA, scarcely any information or documentation is accessible to the public regarding comparable LSD experiments in the Soviet Union. Unsubstantiated information and reports about equally brutal human trials with psychedelics in Soviet clinics, gulags, and barracks still circulate in different media. By chance, it became known in the early 1990s that the Soviet secret service carried out experiments as early as the 1920s on "enemies of the people," prisoners and soldiers in "Laboratory 12" using psychotropic drugs and lethal poisons.[27]

Documents confirm that the CIA knew the KGB was in possession of LSD. It remains questionable whether Allen Dulles received a 1951 Army report according to which the Soviet Union had bought fifty million doses of a new drug from Sandoz. A supplementary report claimed that Sandoz had ten additional kilograms or around one hundred million doses of the drug ready for sale on the open market. Dulles instantly convened a special commission which ordered the CIA to buy Sandoz' remaining inventory of LSD to keep it from falling into the hands of the KGB. Two agents were immediately dispatched to Basel with a suitcase containing $240,000 in large bills. (Stratton 1994) Even after Glasnost and Perestroika, Russian authorities have kept all documents related to the matter under lock and key. Too many of the persons directly or indirectly involved are still living and there is no incentive for the perpetrators to publically disclose the atrocities committed by them or their family members.

In 1945, the Czechoslovak government established its intelligence agency, the StB, on the Russian model, and Soviet agents helped develop it into one of the world's largest and most active—which remained true up until 1989. The Czechs profited as well from WWII criminal expertise of the Nazis. Gestapo and SS members who fell into their hands were recruited as Czech agents and they applied their knowledge of human experiments. As with the Americans and Russians, hallucinogens were used. The Czechs had been experimenting with mescaline since the 1920s; LSD was added in the 1950s and became the drug of choice in countless experiments that matched the cruelty of American trials. The subjects used by the StB were the spies of all Eastern Bloc countries and hundreds, perhaps thousands, of American prisoners of war who were brought to Czechoslovakia from North Korean concentration camps and later North Vietnamese prisoner of war camps. One of the few witnesses was the Czech general Jan Sejna who defected to the USA in 1968; his testimony is still secret. The U.S. government still remains silent about the fate of nearly ten thousand prisoners captured during the two wars in Asia.[28] The Czechs became the world's largest producer of LSD. From 1962 to 1974 the Czechoslovakian concern Spofa manufactured the LSD compound lysergamide and sold it mainly to Communist countries, including the GDR where it found its way to the West via the underground. In 2002, the government in Prague decided to open most StB files to the public. However, documents relating to questions of national security or whose publication might endanger persons still living remained secrets; this applies to nearly all documents concerning Czech intelligence activities.

Serious Sweden

One of Albert Hofmann's many lecture tours took him to Sweden and Finland from the end of March to the middle of April, 1960. He met with a working group from the Swedish military laboratory in conjunction with a talk he gave in Stockholm on hallucinogens. Over a snack, he answered a variety of questions posed by the three scientists about LSD. According to Hofmann, the Swedish army authorities "knew about experiments in American and Russian army laboratories exploring the use of psychotomimetics like LSD." The Swedish army lab was tasked with "clarifying the likely manner of their use and proposing suitable defensive measures. I answered the questions about whether we might know more details of the American plans and whether we had even stronger or more easily obtainable agents in the negative." As protection in case of their use in warfare, Hofmann suggested chlorinating the water supply. The Swedish experts found his remarks to be valuable and thanked him politely.

The chemist Nils Löfgren also spoke with Hofmann. In 1943, the same year as Hofmann's discovery of LSD, Löfgren discovered the anesthetic Xylocaine, also known as Lidocaine. Löfgren's anesthetic is still used by dentists to spare patients discomfort from drilling. He alerted Hofmann to the alkaloid gelsemicine that, like LSD, was effective in small doses. Otomi Indians used the drug as a poisonous potion called Bebo-sito or "glass coffin." Its curare-like effect renders victims unable to move all the while fully conscious. "The Swedish chemist had recently managed the difficult task of isolating a trace of the alkaloid for a self-experiment with 0.05 mg peroral which severely disrupted his field of vision (scotoma)."

In the Name of the Fatherland

Albert Hofmann received a telephone inquiry regarding psychotropic drugs from Colonel H. Gessner, an NBC (nuclear/biological/chemical) decontamination Officer in the Swiss army.[29] Gessner summarized the reason for the call and his questions at Hofmann's request in his letter of March 15, 1962.[30] It opens with a summary of his views: "In view of both the massive number of atomic bombs presently available on both sides and their effect should they be used in all-out atomic warfare, I think the same thing could happen with atomic weapons as happened with chemical weapons in WWII, namely, they would never be used. In that case, I believe it highly probable that all parties would resort to the chemical weapons they have at the ready." After enumerating the chemical weapons suitable for use in combat, such as phosgene, cyanide, yperite, and others, Gessner focused on psychopharmaceuticals. He mentioned a Captain Dolder, who further divided the latter into psychomimetic and psychotropic chemical warfare agents and asked Hofmann: "As an expert, do you disagree with any particulars?" Then he inquired in detail about production, storage capabilities, costs, and about Hofmann's assessment concerning "the use of the different materials in a war." Of particular interest to the officer were: their toxicity (both lethal and effective doses for humans and animals)," the possibility of delivery as an aerosol to the skin as a contact poison, and whether Hofmann knew of specific substances "that would have to be reckoned with if a war broke out today." Gessner also stated there is the "problem of so-called 'humane warfare' (the term itself is of course sheer nonsense!), in other words, whether substances really exist that only render people unable to fight due to mental confusion and in higher doses do not cause lasting damage."

In conclusion, he asked Hofmann whether "despite your workload (we're all in the same loony bin!) you might be able to give a one or two hour lecture in the next training course for NBC officers in which you summarize your answers to the above questions. I can only pay you a standard honorarium, but you are cordially invited for an aperitif and lunch. I and the other officers would owe you sincere thanks in the name of the fatherland."

Hofmann answered him on April 3rd, politely, but he makes his reluctance clear about considering psychopharmaceuticals as chemical warfare agents when he believes they fall solely in the category of medicinal remedies. "In the following, insofar as I am able, I will answer the questions you asked in your letter of March 15th regarding psychopharmaceuticals.

Beforehand, it should be noted that we have only worked with psychopharmaceuticals with view to be applied in medicine, especially in psychiatry. Hence, we can say very little regarding their military potential. The only compound from our laboratories that might relate to your questions is D-lysergic acid diethylamide. So I will limit my comments to that substance. It is known that U.S. Army laboratories are investigating this compound from the point of view of military technology. In the form of its easily water-soluble tartrate, lysergic acid diethylamide has come to be known in experimental psychiatry and pharmacology as LSD 25. Sandoz supplies it to professional psychiatrists and psychiatric clinics under the trade name of Delysid® for use as a medical adjunct in psychotherapy." Hofmann explained that medical interest was due to its great effectiveness at low dosages making it practical for use in psychoanalysis—and that it was reversible in case of a strong overdose. Hofmann further stated: "LSD is a very expensive substance. It can be synthesized entirely in the lab but only at a price that is economically unfeasible. By contrast, partial lab synthesis is more reasonable whereby a complex fragment, lysergic acid, is produced by ergot fungus. With that process, the price of producing a kilo of LSD still falls in the order of SFr 100,000." And: "In crystalline form, protected from atmospheric nitrogen and oxygen, LSD remains stable for years." Regarding its use in warfare, Hofmann remarked: "In solution, LSD is photosensitive and extremely prone to oxidize; the more dilute the solution, the more this is so. In aqueous solutions used for medicinal purpose, air is entirely displaced by CO_2, and the solutions must be stored in the dark. How stable the substance is in aerosol form would need to be determined experimentally.... Fifty micrograms suffice to achieve noticeable effects, while the effects from 100 to 200 micrograms are profound and last several hours. The lethal dose for humans is not known. A chemist at the Army Chemical Center in Maryland (USA) told me that trials of 2 milligrams, forty to fifty times greater than a 'therapeutic' dose, had been carried out on volunteers who recovered completely.... The most effective medicine discovered for interrupting LSD intoxication is chlorpromazine (Largactyl).... Oxidants, such as chlorinated water destroy and deactivate LSD instantly. Drinking water could be protected by

> People from the U.S. Army labs came to see me three times. They were interested in knowing how to produce LSD in large quantities.
>
> *Albert Hofmann*

chlorination which, to my knowledge, is standard procedure in case of war. Absorption through the skin: As far as I know, no studies are available but as might be expected, in the form of dust, it is readily absorbed through the lungs.

Regarding your question concerning nomenclature of psychopharmaceuticals, I refer you to the classification found in "Psychotomimetika" in the *Svensk Kemisk tidskrift* (see the enclosed reprint). Psychomimetics are a subgroup of the psychotropic agents to which all substances belong that in any way influence psychological states. These terms are thus not used in the sense of expert circles by Captain Dolder in his communication.

I am sorry not to be able to accept your kind invitation to address the NBC officers. I am, however, happy to answer any further questions that fall within my area of expertise as completely as possible."

The Mystery of the Cursed Bread

The summer calm in the little town of Pont-Saint-Esprit on the banks of the Rhone River in southern France was suddenly interrupted in mid-August of 1951 when nearly three hundred inhabitants fell ill suffering extreme hallucinations and exhibiting signs of massive poisoning. Five persons died and twenty-five had to be taken to hospitals or psychiatric clinics; all others were looked after for days and weeks as outpatients by their doctors. Daily newspapers and illustrated magazines reported the dreadful events in great detail: "Patients thrashed around on their beds, screaming that red flowers were growing out of their bodies; a man jumped out of

a window crying 'I am an airplane!;' some jumped from roof tops; an eleven-year old attempted to strangle her mother, gigantic plants and beasts were creeping around the houses, women and men tore their clothes off and ran naked through the streets, someone saw how his heart was bulging out of his foot, while others complained that their stomachs had been attacked by writhing, biting snakes."[31]

It soon became clear that it must be a case of food poisoning. Once it was established that all those who had fallen ill had eaten bread from the local baker, Roch Briand, it was hypothesized that his flour stemmed from grain contaminated with ergot—even though by that time cases of ergot poisoning were rare. Consequently, doctors and authorities turned to Sandoz, the leading researcher of ergot. In response, Albert Hofmann and Werner Stoll were dispatched to Marseille on November 3, 1951. They arrived in a company car accompanied by their wives. The trip required two days, during which they visited Avignon, Orange, and Les Baux. In Marseille they conferred with Professor Henri Ollivier of the institute for forensic medicine to study the chemical analyses done up to that point. Then they continued on to Montpellier where, together with the principal of the medical faculty of the university, Professor Gaston Giraud, they interviewed patients. In the ancient Roman town of Nimes, a psychiatrist, Dr. Pitot, presented some of his patients to them. Finally, they reached the scene of the event, where the local physician Dr. A. Gabbai gathered five of his patients for consultation and the visitors from Basel could learn details of the epidemic caused by the "pain maudit," the cursed bread.

Passport photo of Frank
Olson

Kurt Blome

(l. to r.) Werner Stoll, Anita and Albert Hofmann

The collective chemical analyses and medical diagnoses confirmed bread poisoning; the physical symptoms supported the conclusion of ergot poisoning. When Stoll and Hofmann returned home on November 9th, their luggage held 42 grams of bread from the baker Briand, 1.2 kilograms of the suspect flour, and 600 grams of poisoned bread that had been saved by a victim. Subsequent tests in Basel led to contradictory conclusions. The chemist was of the opinion that the poisoning was due to a mercury-bearing seed treatment, whereas, based on the acute psychological symptoms, the psychiatrist concluded it was "an agent similar to LSD, given the current knowledge about ergot, since only LSD in comparison was both highly potent and psychotropic."[32] In his report to Professor Rothlin on January 15, 1952, entitled "Current State of the Investigations: Test Results on Ergot Alkaloid

Content," Hofmann concluded that "no trace of ergot alkaloid was found in any of the three samples when the corresponding extracts of ergot alkaloid were subjected to a colorimetric[33] test."[34] The events in Pont-Saint-Esprit remained a mystery. Neither LSD nor mercury caused the symptoms and clinical features described. LSD does not cause severe poisoning or organic damage. On the other hand, the intense hallucinations which afflicted many could scarcely have been caused by mercury poisoning.

The incidents at Pont-Saint-Esprit gained international media attention after publication of a book by the American journalist Hank P. Albarelli in 2009. He speculated that the CIA had conducted a highly secret operation with LSD in the small town in southern France under the umbrella of operation MK-Naomi led by biochemist Frank Olson. Olson was with the Special

85

Operations Division of the army for chemical warfare unit in Fort Detrick. LSD was allegedly sprayed into the air, added to tap water, or mixed into the bread dough (Albarelli 2009.) However, LSD quickly disperses in the air, immediately disappears in sunlight due to UV radiation, and quickly loses its effect in chlorinated drinking water as it does when bread bakes. What is more, the effect of LSD fades after twelve hours at the most and never causes the symptoms found at Pont-Saint-Esprit.

During the early 1950s, Frank Olson worked as a CIA agent in the U.S. Army laboratories at Fort Detrick where he was responsible for secret experiments involving the anthrax virus and other biological and chemical warfare agents. It can be proved that he was involved with intelligence agency experiments in England and, according to his son Eric, his passport carried a stamp indicating a trip to France. According to our research, documents regarding an alleged CIA action indicating his participation in Pont-Saint Esprit have not been released as yet. (Albarelli 2009.)

During his later trips to Germany, Olson witnessed dreadful and sometimes death-dealing interrogation methods used on suspected double agents, refugees, and soldiers. In an old villa near Frankfurt, LSD in combination with heroin, hypnosis and torture, was used by the former Nazi doctor in Dachau, Kurt Blome, under the umbrella of Operation Artichoke. Shaken by these discoveries, Olson returned to the U.S. and told a friend: "You would be shocked what techniques they use. They get people to talk. They brainwash their victims. They use all kinds of drugs. And torture. Promise me, that we never talked about this!" (Koch, Wech 2003)

At a secret service retreat in November 1953, MK-Ultra chief Sidney Gottlieb served Olson and other agents an after dinner drink spiked with LSD without their knowledge. While the others enjoyed the effects, Olson found his first LSD trip extremely disturbing. He suffered a nervous breakdown followed by severe depression. He then decided to quit his job, told his wife about his activities, and confessed to her he had "made a terrible mistake." (Albarelli 2009) The CIA sent Olson to Harold Abramson, one of their MK-Ultra psychiatrists in New York. On November 28, 1953, Frank Olson fell from a hotel window in Manhattan under mysterious circumstances. Initially, the talk was of suicide, but later suspicions hardened of a murder carried out by the CIA because Olson had become a risk. In 1975, Olson's family received compensation of $750,000 and his widow and son Eric were invited to the White House to receive a personal apology from President Gerald Ford and CIA Director William Colby. However, this was not because he was murdered, but because another CIA agent was alleged to have met Olson in his New York Hotel and given him an extremely high dose of LSD, which led him to jump from the window. Indemnity and apology served solely to silence the survivors and avoid a lawsuit.[35]

The Olson case is one of the best known among still unsolved cases in the less than admirable chapter of experiments and human trials carried out by the intelligence services and military during the Cold War. Their activities did not completely stop in 1989 with the disintegration of the Soviet Union and the fall of the Berlin

Albert and Anita Hofmann on the road to Pont-Saint-Esprit

wall. Nothing has ever been found implicating Albert Hofmann or Sandoz in the case; Hofmann's diary entries about the trip to Pont-Saint-Esprit make clear beyond a doubt that he and Stoll had no part in a covert CIA operation.

Speculation by the writer John G. Fuller (Fuller 1968) about the cause of the events in Pont-Saint-Esprit caused uncertainty in the mind of the LSD researcher John Beresford. In February 1973, he asked Albert Hofmann for his personal assessment and the response was clear and unequivocal: "The quotations in John G. Fuller's book *The Day of St. Anthony's Fire* are an invention of Mr. Fuller as most what he has written in this book. The whole publication is a scandal. There is conclusive proof that ergot was not involved in the tragedy at Pont-St.-Esprit. Mr. Fuller must have been aware of this fact.... And, in order to mention just one of the arguments, that prove that Mr. Fuller is wrong—LSD is a semi-synthetic product which does not occur in ergot nor in any other part of nature. Mr. Fuller has misused ergot (St. Anthony's Fire) and LSD to make a bestseller of his book."[36]

Flesh of the Gods

He who eats many, many things, sees.
Bernardino de Sahagún (1500-1590)

The Mushrooms Reach Basel

Albert Hofmann first learned of Mexico's magic mushrooms in 1956 from a newspaper. As the director of the Department for Natural Products at Sandoz, he would like to learn more, but the article mentioned no names and places to pursue further information. Nonetheless, these mysterious mushrooms continued to preoccupy him, and he was intrigued to analyze them chemically. Meanwhile, Professor Roger Heim, a mycologist who was director of the Musée National d'Histoire Naturelle in Paris, with the Wasson husband and wife team had discovered the *Psilocybe* mushroom species. He sent samples to different laboratories in the USA and Europe for analysis and determination of their hallucinogenic agent. When none of the results proved to be significant, the director of Sandoz France who knew of their successful work with LSD, referred Heim to Sandoz in Basel. Hofmann noted: "Hence, LSD attracted the mushrooms to my laboratory," but he did not suspect the important insights and friendships that would result from his work with these mushrooms.

The Kingdom of Sacred Plants and Mushrooms

With over one hundred million inhabitants and an area of nearly two million square kilometers, Mexico is the fifth largest country on the American continent. In the north it borders the USA and to the south lie Guatemala and Belize; to the west the Pacific Ocean which stretches to Asia, to the east are the Caribbean islands in the Gulf of Mexico. Until 1519 when the Spanish invaded under Hernán Cortés, various highly developed cultures prevailed in Mexico—the Mayans on the Yucatan peninsula, the Olmecs, the Toltecs, and then the Aztecs on the mainland between the oceans. The Aztecs were known for their rich spirit world, including Huitzilopochtli, the sun god and protective deity of the country; Quetzalcoatl, the feathered serpent god of the arts and knowledge; and his counterpart, Tezcatlipoca, the dark god of annihilation and destruction.

Albert Hofmann and his research team for Psilocybe mushrooms, 1957

Similarly abundant are the varieties of psychoactive plants, mushrooms, and cactuses found in Mexico. For thousands of years, medicine men and priests of the various cultures have used them in healing rituals and religious ceremonies. This is documented by archeological finds, among them the famous mushroom stones. These stone sculptures, approximately fifty centimeters tall and shaped like a cap mushroom, have the head or figure of a god chiseled into their stem. The oldest specimens are more than three thousand years old. While anthropologists initially considered the mushroom stones to be purely phallic symbols, they later recognized their true meaning during the course of examining "magic mushrooms."

In Mexico, such "plants of the gods" remain an integral part of Indian culture and serve as mediators between humans and the cosmos, between the earthly and spirit realms—in expanded states of consciousness, humans connect with the invisible world of magic.

Teonanácatl

The chroniclers of the sixteenth century Spanish conquerors first reported the use of hallucinogenic mushrooms in Mexico. Hernán Cortés landed on the Mexican coast on April 21, 1519. Conquest of the country, including subjugation and partial annihilation of the Indian population and their culture began when natives encountered the foreigners from the east.

The Europeans regarded the Indian mushroom cult as strange and suspect. The intoxicating feasts and rituals devoted to their gods and the welfare of their people met

incomprehension and repugnance. The with Christian missionaries who accompanied the voyages of discovery and conquest regarded the sacred mushrooms as infernal and described the associated ceremonies as the work of Satan. Famous for his comprehensive knowledge of the conquered territories and cultures, the Franciscan monk Bernardino de Sahagún reported in 1569 of the noxiousness of *teonanácatl*: "The brew was indeed intoxicating like wine, but induced supernatural visions and even sexual ecstasy." (Sahagún 1905) The Aztecs and Maya revered the sacred mushrooms as the "flesh of the gods" or *teonanácatl* in the Náhuatl language. The mushroom enabled *curanderos*, women healers and shamans to have visions, make prophecies and to "see" the maladies inside their patients during nighttime ceremonies. Their rituals gave them access to the supernatural world of the gods, to pray for healing, to give thanks for a bountiful harvest, or for victory over enemies. They made the raw, slightly bitter and earthy-flavored mushroom into a pleasanter drink by mixing in *cacuatl* (cacao) or honey. The personal physician of Spanish King Philipp II, Francisco Hernandez, described three different mushrooms, one of which was lethal and the other two "led not to death but occasionally to permanent insanity that expressed itself in uncontrollable laughter." Based on their assessment of the customs and practices of the alien culture, the conquerors summarily decided in 1521 to ban the mushroom drink, along with mescaline-containing peyote, as a "non-alcoholic drink" and to severely punish it's consumption.

It may be due to the categorical prohibition of the use of hallucinogenic mushrooms,

A Mexican mushroom stone

An Aztec god of the underworld speaks through the mushroom as illustrated by a 16th century artist.

A demon hovers above a group of magic mushrooms to illustrate the diabolic character of the Indian's mushroom ritual in the eyes of the Catholic conquerors.

or to the subjugation, missionary activity, and extermination of indigenous cultures that the mushroom cult was forgotten and scarcely mentioned in any chronicle during the following centuries. Only sporadic reports from amateur botanists, a few ethnologists, mycologists and pharmacologists appeared. However, Europeans failed to eliminate completely the magically curative mushroom rituals and religious ceremonies in Mexico; even today, the Indians simply carry them out in secret.

Exploration

In 1915, the American botanist William E. Safford revisited reports from Spanish chroniclers and expressed his hypothesis that they had confused the peyote cactus with a mushroom. Safford's mistake was corrected by the Austrian physician and globetrotter Blas Pablo Reko.[37] His travels took him to the USA, Ecuador, and finally to Mexico in the vicinity of Oaxaca where he settled and practiced as a doctor. Reko was a careful observer and keenly interested in the ritual practices of indigenous people. Once he had been able to witness several shamanic ceremonies and investigate the ingredients used, he rejected Safford's hypothesis in 1919. He noted that the substances inducing intoxication were definitely from mushrooms and not from a cactus. Some twenty years later, he met his countryman Robert Weitlaner who was working as an engineer in Mexico. He was as fascinated as Reko was by Indian customs and had gained access to their rituals. Weitlaner provided a sample of the sacred mushrooms to Reko, who sent them to the anthropologist Henry Wassén, Director of the Ethnographic Museum in Göteborg. However, by the time they arrived in Sweden, the mushrooms were too spoiled to analyze. Nevertheless, Wassén sent them on to Harvard University where they attracted the attention of a young ethnobotanist, Richard Evans Schultes. He was convinced that the sample must be one of the mysterious teonanácatl reported by the Spanish chroniclers. Schultes contacted Robert Weitlaner and traveled with him, his daughter and his son-in-law, the ethnologist Jean Basset Johnson, numerous times to the south of Mexico. They confirmed that native people ingested mushrooms for their magical properties in different regions of Mexico. In July 1938, Johnson himself had the opportunity to participate in a nocturnal mushroom ceremony in the province of Oaxaca and described it in a well-respected report about the Mazatecan magic cult.[38] In that same year, Reko and Schultes sent further samples of teonanácatl for analysis to the pharmacologist and Nobel Prize winner Carl Gustav Santesson in Stockholm. He noted that extracts from the samples caused certain behavior changes, a kind of semi-consciousness, in frogs and mice; however, chemical analysis did not confirm the presence of alkaloids. (Santesson 1939) Shortly after, the outbreak of WWII brought these experiments to a halt for over a decade, and they were not resumed until the early 1950s.

> There are no apt words to characterize your state when you are, shall we say, "bemushroomed."
>
> *Gordon Wasson*

Banker and Mycologist

For much of our knowledge about magic mushrooms, we have to thank Russian-born New York pediatrician Valentina Pavlovna Guercken and the successful American banker R. Gordon Wasson, a member of the board of the New York banking house J.P. Morgan. The two met in London where she had received her medical degree and were married in 1926. To their great surprise, the pair found mushrooms during their honeymoon in New York State that Valentina Pavlovna recognized from her homeland. She inspired enthusiasm in her husband for the study of mushrooms throughout the world. Thanks to his wife and their unexpected find, Gordon Wasson, Wall Street banker with a bachelor's degree in literature, became a passionate amateur mycologist. They called the field of research they founded "ethnomycology." They first read the work of Schultes on the "flesh of the gods" in 1952. At the same time, they also received a detailed letter from their friend, writer and mythology researcher Robert Graves about the longstanding tradition of shamanic use of psychoactive mushrooms which survives in Mexico; his letter included a pencil drawing of a mushroom stone. (Ott 1993) From then on, the Wassons focused their investigations on Mexico and believed they were on the right path to explore an "ancient and sacred mystery." A first expedition led the researching couple to the Mazatec Indians in Huautla de Jiménez. It took two years for them to win the confidence of the natives and finally be initiated into their shamanic secrets. Since their proscription by the Spaniards, public display of the mushrooms had been taboo; spoken of only in whispers and used only in secret nighttime ceremonies. Using the Mazatec language, Wasson confidentially inquired if Cayetano Garcia, a city government employee, one of their informants whom Wasson names "Filemón," knew someone with whom they could take these mushrooms as part of a secret ritual. Looking back, Wasson believed it was his knowledge of the native language that convinced civil servant Garcia of their altruistic motives. Filemón led the gringos to a spot where they found an abundance of mushrooms and could pick enough for a ceremony. He then introduced them to Maria Sabina, a highly respected curandera. To protect her privacy, Wasson called her "Eva Mendez" in his first publications.

The following night, around twenty people gathered in Filemón's house: The Wassons, photographer Alan Richardson, who provided photo documention of the nocturnal ceremony, French anthropologist Guy Stresser-Péan, Filemón with his wife, Maria Sabina and her daughter who assisted her, and other family members and acquaintances. The curandera and her daughter were very pleased with the quality of the mushrooms. With invocations to spirits, saints and invisible helpers, along with prayers, hymns, and the customary cocoa drink, the participants were attuned to the proper mood for the traditional *Velada* ritual. Maria Sabina had carefully washed the mushrooms and distributed them in pairs. Each visitor received twice six mushrooms; she and her daughter each ingested thirteen pairs. "They tasted acidic and bitter and slightly rancid," Wasson noted. After a good half hour, Richardson said, "Gordon, I'm seeing things!" and he answered, "Don't worry, me too." The visions reached their peak around midnight and lasted until nearly four o'clock in the morning. All the participants had stretched

out on their mats but felt no fatigue, never before had they felt more awake. "We saw visions with our eyes open or closed, as if they sprang from a center point, sometimes faster, sometimes slower, in vibrant colors and artistic motifs in complete harmony, geometric figures and patterns as in rugs or carpets; then they changed into palaces adorned with gemstones with interior courtyards, colonnades, and gardens of supernatural splendor," Wasson recalled, "Soft, soothing songs of Señora and her daughter sounded continuously in the background. At other times the mushroom spoke through Maria Sabina with sharp words and answered the participant's questions."[39] After many hours, the effect finally wore off and the participants soon fell into a deep, dreamless sleep. Upon waking, they felt refreshed but still strongly influenced by the powerful nighttime experiences and visions. The hosts served coffee and bread and, after heartfelt thanks, the visitors made their way home. They completed their notes, providing one of the first detailed reports on a Mazatecan ritual ceremony with the "flesh of the gods." Gordon Wasson now had impressive proof from personal experience that the sketchy reports about magic mushrooms were really true, and in his case, exceeded the effects previously described. Three days later in a second *Velada,* he experienced amazing visions a second time. The Wassons told the story of their discovery in their book *Mushrooms, Russia and History* (Wasson 1957) in a print run for bibliophiles of only 512 copies.

Albert Hofmann commented on these events as follows: "It was the destiny of Maria Sabina to come to the attention of this ethnological research project. It was she, who for whatever reasons, revealed the secret of the sacred mushrooms by granting these strangers access to nocturnal mushroom ceremonies. On the night of June 29 to 30, 1955, in Huautla de Jiménez, R. Gordon Wasson and his photographer Alan Richardson received the sacred mushroom from her hand and were most likely the first white men to eat it in the context of such a ceremony." (Estrada 1980)

The Active Substance

In 1956 the Wassons invited French researcher Roger Heim to Oaxaca to scientifically investigate the intoxicating mushrooms; together, they embarked upon a further expedition to investigate the mushrooms' botany. Heim succeeded in identifying fourteen species and several subspecies previously unknown to him. The great interest shown by researchers from Europe and the USA in sacred mushrooms and their cultic ceremonies finally motivated Mexican mycologists to participate. Two young biologists, M.A. Palacios and Gaston Guzmán, joined the German-American mycologist Dr. Rolf Singer in 1957 to classify the various mushrooms found around Oaxaca. That same year Gordon Wasson published the first popular science article about psychoactive mushrooms in *LIFE* magazine. (Wasson 1957) Thanks to this widely read report on his experiences, the general public first learned of the existence and hallucinogenic properties of the sacred mushrooms and ceremonies of the native Mexican people. Because Wasson carried the stigma of being an amateur, it earned him skepticism among those in the scientific guilds. The term "Magic Mushrooms," supposedly first used by Wasson,

trivialized the matter in the minds of many academics. Even more troubling to them was the fact that his report in *Life* had made the mushrooms so popular that some historians saw it as the origin of the psychedelic movement of the 1960s.

After his wife's early death in 1958, Gordon Wasson dedicated himself with even greater zeal to the traditions concerning psychoactive mushrooms around the world. From then on he focused on Russia and fly agaric (*Amanita muscaria*), a widely distributed species held to be sacred in North Asian cultures. He believed it to be "Soma," the intoxicating cultic drink described in the ancient Rig Veda. He published this hypothesis in his book *Soma—Divine Mushroom of Immortality*. (Wasson 1968)

MUSHROOM CEREMONY of the MAZATEC INDIANS of MEXICO

recorded by
V. P. & R. GORDON WASSON
at Huautla de Jiminex

This record will be of interest to everyone who is concerned with psychedelics, despite the fact that the particular ceremony recorded was "unsuccessful". The repetitive incantations of the Mazatec "curandera," Marie Sabina, convey to the listener the form and atmosphere of the Indian mushroom ceremony. An enclosed illustrated booklet contains notes by R. Gordon Wasson and translation of Mazatec text.

$4.95

Please send all orders (pre-paid — no charge for postage) to UNIVERSITY BOOKS, Box 171, New Hyde Park, New York.

Psilocybin and Psilocin

Meanwhile, Roger Heim sent samples of *Psilocybe* species he and the Wassons had discovered to several laboratories in the USA and Europe. When none of the analyses yielded results worth noting, Professor Heim turned to Sandoz in Basel. During a visit to Basel in June 1957, Heim personally handed Hofmann the mushrooms he had cultivated in his Paris lab. Hofmann

Psilocybe mexicana Heim

preferred to assign the analysis of the magic mushrooms to one of his colleagues, but he politely declined the offer. The policy of the head office at Sandoz was to avoid any activity that had even the remotest connection to LSD, therefore doing such research was not career-enhancing. Consequently, Hofmann refrained from delegating as he assumed a minimum of motivation from his colleagues, and he took it on himself. In the summer of 1957 he and his lab assistant Hans Tscherer began the extraction and isolation experiments with 100 grams of dried mushrooms of the species *Psilocybe mexicana Heim*. Since the chemical contents were completely unknown and tests on mice and dogs showed no particular pharmacological effects, a human experiment was the only remaining possibility. Despite his dramatic

experiences with LSD, Hofmann once again decided on a self-experiment. As a conscientious researcher, he was unwilling to submit a colleague to an uncertain fate and potential risk. In any case, he was favorably disposed towards the mushrooms and prepared for his first experiment with thirty[40] medium-sized dried *Psilocybe mexicana* having a total weight of 2.4 grams. At 3:40 pm on July 1, 1957, Hofmann carried out the self-experiment, as he had done earlier, at his workplace. According to information from Heim and Wasson, that amount corresponded to an average dose like those taken during ritual shamanic ceremonies in Mexico. However, the mushrooms had a "strong psychological impact" on Hofmann as he described it in his experimental protocol: "After one half hour, the external world became unfamiliar. Everything took on a Mexican flavor. Since I was fully aware that my knowledge of the Mexican origin of the mushrooms might lead me to imagine scenes from Mexico, I consciously tried to see my surroundings as I normally did. These efforts to see things in their familiar shapes and colors were in vain. Whether my eyes were open or closed, I saw only Indian motifs and colors. When the physician supervising the trial bent over me to check my blood pressure, he became an Aztec sacrificial priest and it would not have surprised me if he had drawn an obsidian knife. Despite the seriousness of the situation, it exhilarated me to see how the Alemannic face of my colleague had taken on purely Indian features. At the height of my intoxication, about one and one-half hours after ingesting the mushrooms, the onrushing images—mostly abstract motifs that rapidly shifted in form and color—became so intense that I feared being swept away and drawn into them and losing myself. Around six hours later, the dream ended. Subjectively, I was unable to say how long this timeless state had lasted. Reentry into familiar reality was a welcome return home from a strange world that had seemed so real."

Seeing images specific to Mexican culture while under the influence of psilocybin is not unusual and had also struck Gordon Wasson who conjectured that ancient Mexican art had been influenced by images and visions resulting from psilocybin intoxication. Li Gelpke, the wife of the Basel orientalist Rudolf Gelpke, undertook three trials with psilocybin and recorded her visions in brush sketches. She wrote: "Weeks later, I happened upon books

Albert Hofmann and Gordon Wasson

about Mexican art and found the motifs from my visions there—which truly startled me." This same phenomenon occurred with other psychoactive substances. Klaus Thomas documented examples in his book *Die künstlich gesteuerte Seele (The Artificially Steered Mind)* and concluded: "An art historical comparison would convince an unbiased observer of ancient and modern creations of Indian art ... of the correspondence of the images, shapes and colors to a psilocybin intoxication." (Thomas 1970) The question remains as to what extent the images seen while intoxicated are influenced by the subject's knowledge of the origin of the active substance. In the late 1950s, the only mushrooms known to contain psilocybin were from Mexico. Today, we know that they occur on every continent; it seems illogical that psilocybin *per se* should evoke only imagery specific to Mexico.

As with LSD, chemists were unable to rely on animal trials because of their lack of response to the corresponding active agents. Hence, numerous human self-experiments with the various extracts remained the only means of determining

Gordon Wasson looking for spores, surrounded by Albert Hofmann and coworkers, 1959

the effective fraction of the active agent. After initial reluctance, Hofmann's coworkers and colleagues in the "psychedelic lab" at Sandoz participated in the experiments with him. These self-experiments quickly brought the desired success. By the beginning of 1958, Hofmann had succeeded in isolating and transferring the active agent in a pure chemical state. On January 10, 1958, he conducted his first experiment with two milligrams of the effective fraction. He named the new colorless, crystalline substance "psilocybin" after its genus *Psilocybe* and the second psychoactive substance discovered shortly thereafter "psilocin." Together with his colleagues, Dr. A. Brack, Dr. H. Kobel,

and Professor Heim, who had been responsible for providing the mushroom samples, Hofmann published the results in March 1958 in the periodical *Experientia*. (Hofmann, Kobel, et al 1958)

Motivated by their unexpected and rapid success, Hofmann and his coworkers[41] continued their experiments and began to investigate the chemical structure of the two substances they had discovered. Their goal was to synthesize them. On September 4, 1958, Hofmann noted in his diary, "Last night in my retreat, I recognized the correct structural formula for psilocybin. The next day, synthesis of this psychoactive agent was achieved. It is a new indole derivative."

Like LSD, psilocybin and psilocin are indole compounds and, according to Hofmann, "closely related not only regarding their psychological effects but also in their chemical structure.... Structurally, psilocybin and psilocin are quite similar to the neurotransmitter, serotonin.... Serotonin is extremely important in brain chemistry. Like LSD, both mushroom derivatives block the effects of serotonin in different organs in pharmacological tests. They resemble LSD in other pharmacological properties as well; the main difference lies in the quantity required for efficacy. A medium strength dose of psilocybin or psilocin in humans is 10 milligrams; hence, the two substances are over 100 times less potent than LSD for which 0.1 milligram constitutes a strong dose. Moreover, the duration of the mushroom derivatives' effect is briefer, namely four to six hours versus eight to twelve for LSD."

With that, their discoverer had "fulfilled the demystification of magic mushrooms. The chemical structure of the substances which have such wondrous effects and for thousands of years have led the Indians to believe a god lives in the mushroom, now have been determined and can be produced artificially in glass vials." Hofmann asked himself what gain in scientific knowledge the research had brought: "It consisted only in the knowledge that the mystery of the effects of teonanácatl had been reduced to the puzzle of two crystallized

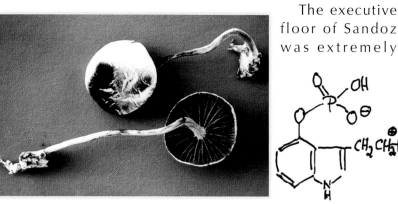

Psilocybe mexicana Heim

substances—but their effects cannot be explained by science, rather only described." Hofmann speaks as a classical natural scientist here; the term "demystifying" refers only to decipherment of the active agents and not to their effect, for as a chemically pure substance, psilocybin causes "enchantment" of external reality.

The executive floor of Sandoz was extremely pleased with these accomplishments and decided to promote further intensive research on mushrooms despite the company's ambivalence about its experiments with LSD. The pharmaceutically manufactured psilocybin was given the brand name "Indocybin." Hofmann's work on the structure of psilocybin established a milestone in the medical chemistry of indole structures. From then on, Sandoz assumed a leading role in indole chemistry. F. Troxler's synthesis of 4-hydroxindole, the starting product for psilocybin, came back into the public eye at the beginning of the 1960s when British pharmacologist James Black described the first highly effective beta-blocker, propranolol. This class of compounds for regulating heart function later achieved great therapeutic significance for lowering blood pressure. By combining the side chain of a propranolol molecule with 4-hydroxindole. Pindolol was developed in 1965. It was mainly used to treat hypertension and marketed under the trade name Visken®.

The Magic Vine

Compared to Hofmann's dramatic experience with LSD, the "demystification" of psychoactive mushrooms was comparatively easy. For a creative scientist working for a profit-oriented pharmaceutical company, such circumstances were desirable and highly welcome. All the more motivated now, Hofmann turned to investigating another magical Mexican drug waiting to be chemically deciphered, namely the seed of a member of the morning glory family (*Convolvulaceae*); its secret psychoactive properties interested him. It was known by its Aztec name "ololiuqui"— round thing—and like teonanácatl and peyote cactus, Central American and particularly Mexican cultures had been using it in their ceremonies and healing rituals since pre-Columbian times.

Once again, it was Sahagún's chronicle that

Ipomoea violacea

This wall relief in Teotihuácan, Mexico, shows the great mother goddess and her female servants, protected by an artfully stylized vine, the sacred ololiuqui of the Aztecs, approx. 500 CE

first mentioned ololiuqui and the remarkable vine's magical effects: "There is an herb called *coatl xoxouhqui*—green snake— that produces a seed called ololiuqui. This seed numbs and confuses the senses; it is administered as a magical potion." (Sahagún 1905) The Spanish physician Francisco Hernández who had been sent to Mexico by his king to study the healing plants of the natives gave us the first botanical description of ololiuqui. In his major work, *Nova Plantarum, Animalium, Mineralium Mexicanorum Historia* published in Rome in 1651 he wrote in the chapter "De Ololiuqui seu planta foliorum," that priests ate the ololiuqui and became in-toxicated and receptive to supernatural messages enabling them to communicate with the gods. The drug caused visions and induced a state filled with frightening hallucinations. Indian cultures, particularly the Aztec and Mayan, soak-ed the seeds in milk and honey for a ritual drink called *balche* which put them into trance and en-abled them to get in touch with good spirits and the deceased. The custom still exists in many parts of Central America to protect house and home from witches and evil spirits with a sprig of the magic vine.

Centuries later, the ololiuqui plant was given the botanical name *Turbina corymbosa* or *Rivea corymbosa*. It is known colloquially in English-speaking countries as morning glory. The Swedish pharmacologist C.G. Santesson published a first summary of the seed's chemistry in 1937, but failed to find a psychoactive agent. Ethnobotanist Richard Evans Schultes summed up the complete botanical, ethnological and historical aspects of ololiuqui in a monograph. (Schultes 1941) Psychiatrist Humphry Osmond, who already had some experience with mescaline and LSD, became interested in the magical vine's effect and began various self-experiments with morning glory seeds in 1955. He reported dosages of between fifty and one hundred seeds caused apathy, emptiness and relaxation accompanied by increased visual sensitivity.

After his initiation into the secrets of teonanácatl, Gordon Wasson investigated peyote cactus and ololiuqui. Since he already knew Albert Hofmann through Heim and Schultes, he sent the chemist in Basel two samples of ololiuqui seeds. His cover letter from Mexico City of August 6, 1959, says: "I am sending you herewith a small package with seeds which I believe are *Rivea corymbosa*, also known as ololiuqui, the proverbial Aztec intoxicant. In Huautla they are known as "semilla de la Virgen" (seeds of the Virgin). As you will see, the packet contains two small bottles with seeds I got in Huautla and a larger container with seeds which Francesco Ortega, a Zacotecan Indian, gave me that he himself gathered from plants near the Zapotecan town of San Bartolo Yautepec."

Hofmann's lab confirmed Wasson's sup-position at least in part and identified the sample of light-brown, round seeds correctly as *Rivea corymbosa*, respectively *Turbina corymbosa*, while the black, angular seeds of the second sample from San Bartolo Yautepec were *Ipomoea violacea*. The funnel-shaped vine *Ipomoea violacea*, respectively *Ipomoea tricolor*, with its sky blue, velvety blossoms, is similar to ololiuqui, but is found not only in tropical or subtropical climates like ololiuqui is, but also in temperate zones; it is the ornamental plant found in our gardens known as morning glory. Hofmann received a second delivery of *Ipomoea violacea* from Don Thomas MacDougall who investigated its ceremonial use by the Zapotecans; they call the seeds "badoh negro."

Albert Hofmann focused on chemical analyses of ololiuqui assisted by "my capable assistant Hans Tscherter with whom I had already isolated the active ingredients of the mushrooms." Based on the reports of different experiences, he hypothesized that the active ingredients in ololiuqui seeds, like LSD, psilocybin and psilocin, were indole compounds. Hofmann's hunch quickly led to success. He knew that indole compounds could easily and quickly be determined by colorimetric reactions and that with the appropriate reagent even slight traces immediately yielded a blue solution. "We were fortunate with our hypothesis," Hofmann said when extracts from the ololiuqui seed samples did in fact show typical blue coloring for indole compounds. This enabled the researchers "to isolate these substances from the seeds and obtain them in a chemically pure form." Identifying them was a surprise and exceeded all early expectations and speculation: "At first, we could scarcely believe what we found. Only after repeated and careful examination of our procedures did we completely trust our findings. The active ingredients of ololiuqui, the ancient magical drug from Mexico, turned out to be identical with substances already present in my laboratory, namely alkaloids, which had been isolated in part during the course of decades of analyses from ergot and derived in part from chemical treatment of substances won from ergot substances." Among them were the major agents lysergic acid amide and lysergic acid hydroxyethyl amide and a few closely related alkaloids such as ergobasine, the starting point for Hofmann's ergot research. Structurally, lysergic acid amide is related to lysergic acid diethylamide or LSD. Lysergic acid amide had first been mentioned in the 1930s by English chemists Sydney Smith and Geoffrey Millward Timmis. No one could have imagined that two decades later the same synthetically produced substance would be found in a traditional Mexican shaman's drug. The startling chemical similarity up to that point and the congruity of the psychological experiences with both LSD and the mushrooms containing psilocybin suggested that the lysergic acid amide of the ololiuqui seed would yield comparable hallucinogenic effects. Almost as a matter of routine, Hofmann decided on a further self-experiment and established that it took a dosage of lysergic acid amide ten to twenty times greater than with LSD and mushrooms to achieve a state he described as dreamlike and characterized "by a feeling of mental emptiness and the unreality and senselessness of the external world, by heightened

sensitivity of hearing and not unpleasant physical fatigue which finally ended in sleep." Humphry Osmond also undertook several self-experiments with the lysergic acid amide Hofmann made available. He came to the same negative judgment as eight years earlier with the morning glory seeds and wrote to him: "I can't see why anyone would ever want to take Morning Glories for either kicks or therapy—its effect on all three of us was just plain negative and I don't mean in a constructive way."[42] The Indians of Central America use the ololiuqui seeds for their anti-inflammatory and analgesic properties as Hofmann explained a few years later to Osmond. "Meanwhile our labs have been working mainly in areas other than psychotropic substances. Nonetheless, we found a few new lysergic acid derivatives with strong analgesic and apparently also anti-depressive effects. "[43] Since all of the alkaloids contained in ololiuqui had already been tested in the course of ergot research, no new drugs resulted from the work with morning glory seeds.

Distrust

Hofmann finished his research on ololiuqui in the summer of 1960 and was glad to be able to present his remarkable results to experts at the International Symposium on the Chemistry of Natural Products of the IUPAC (International Union of Pure and Applied Chemistry)[44] held in the fall of that year in Australia. His journal entry on July 24, 1960, reads:" Statement that the active ingredients of ololiuqui are lysergic acid alkaloids....That result is remarkable because up until now these

Albert Hofmann with a BBC reporter, 1959

highly active alkaloids have only been found in the lower mushrooms of the genus *Claviceps*. Now I have material for an interesting original communication at the chemical congress in Melbourne." However, his colleagues viewed his remarks with great skepticism and during the following discussion even ventured the opinion that in his "laboratory that has worked so much with lysergic acid derivatives, the ololiuqui extracts could have inadvertently become contaminated."

These misgivings were based on the then-current state of knowledge that ergot alkaloids were only found in the lower mushrooms. Chemotaxonomy postulated that particular alkaloids or specific agents occurred only in one genus and were characteristic for the corresponding mushroom family. Even today, it is rare that a specific group of materials such as lysergic acid derivatives can be found in two so divergent families. This was a surprising discovery for Hofmann too and as a

chemist, he found it difficult to explain how a lower mushroom and a bindweed produced the same specific active agents. Even though other laboratories in Europe and the USA checked Hofmann's investigations and confirmed his results, there was still skepticism in professional circles. Hofmann commented: "That the seeds could have been infected with alkaloid-producing mushrooms has now been experimentally excluded."

In contrast with Gordon Wasson, whose article on hallucinogenic mushrooms appeared in *LIFE*, Albert Hofmann published his findings on ololiuqui only in relevant professional journals. Nevertheless, the information about the psychedelic effect of morning glory seeds spread like wildfire among those who cared little about scientific research. Hofmann noted that "two Dutch seed wholesalers told us that sales of *Ipomoea violacea* seeds, the ornamental garden vine, have boomed recently. And a different kind of customer has appeared. They heard that this great demand had something to do with experiments done in our labs with these seeds and they would like more information."

As might be suspected, behind the subdued correspondence between the companies were: Hippies! Youth bent on intoxication had learned quickly. Instead of the proven high from LSD, which had in the meantime become harder to obtain, it was both simpler and legal to get a handful of seeds from the plant with the evocative name "morning glory." Hofmann explained the fad which quickly passed as follows: "The morning glory seed boom was short-lived in the drug scene because the results from this new yet ancient intox-

Gordon Wasson and a BBC Reporter in a Sandoz office prepare for a television documentary on researching the psilocybin mushroom, 1959

icant were just not very good. Ololiuqui seeds taken crushed with water, milk or some other drink taste terrible and are hard for the stomach to digest. Furthermore, the psychological effects of ololiuqui are different from those of LSD because the euphoric and hallucinogenic components are less pronounced, and feelings of emptiness, anxiety and depression predominate. Listlessness and fatigue are not what people want from an intoxicant. Those are all reasons why interest in morning glory seeds decreased in the drug scene."

The Magic Circle

This ended a great voyage of discovery through the realm of psychoactive plants and substances for Albert Hofmann. "These experiments with ololiuqui rounded off my work in the area of hallucinogenic drugs

nicely. They formed a circle, you could say a magic circle: It began with the experiments on production of lysergic acid amides from the naturally occurring ergot alkaloid ergobasine. They led to synthesis of lysergic acid diethyl amide, LSD. The work with the hallucinogenic agent LSD led to experiments with the hallucinogenic magic mushroom teonanácatl from which psilocybin and psilocin were isolated. The study with the Mexican magic drug teonanácatl led to a second Mexican magical drug, ololiuqui. In ololiuqui we again found as hallucinogenic agents lysergic acid amides, among them ergobasine, which closed the magic circle."

> I have always had a special fondness for morning glories. They were the first flowers I grew in my little garden as a child. The blue and red funnel-shaped calyxes are among my first childhood memories.
>
> *Albert Hofmann*

Nothing the mushrooms reveal should be feared.
Maria Sabina

In the Land of the Mazatecs

Albert Hofmann's investigation of ololiuqui had closed the "magic circle" of three active substances that were closely related chemically, but another Mexican plant with remarkable hallucinogenic properties soon caught his interest. Meanwhile, his exchange with Gordon Wasson about psychoactive plants and mushrooms had deepened and their friendship had grown. Once again, it was Wasson who described his travels in southern Mexico and mentioned a plant the natives called *Hojas de la Pastora* or *Hojas de Maria Pastora*—Leaves of the Shepherdess Maria. The extracted juice was used in shamanic ceremonies comparable to those with *teonanácatl* mushrooms and ololiuqui seeds. Wasson invited Hofmann to accompany him on an expedition to find and identify this as yet unknown plant. Hofmann quickly accepted and was able to stir his wife's enthusiasm to join them on a great journey.

Albert and Anita Hofmann left Zurich for the USA on September 26, 1962, aboard one of Swissair's first DC-8 jets and then flew on to Mexico City. There Gordon Wasson met them, having already prepared all they would need for the expedition. With him was Irmgard Weitlaner Johnson, daughter of Robert Weitlaner, and widow of Jean Basset Johnson, pioneering ethnographic researcher of Mexican mushrooms. The next day, they left for the south in a rented Land Rover. They traveled for two days past one natural marvel after another—the snow-covered volcano, Popocatépetl, which rises above the central Mexican plateau, then down into the Orizaba Valley, and on through fertile tropical vegetation. Continuing by ferry, they crossed the Papaloapan River (Nahuatl for "Butterfly River"), traveled through Tuxtepec, formerly an Aztec garrison, and finally came to the Mazatecan village of Jalapa de Diaz. It lay at a higher altitude in the federal state

> The most beautiful effects became apparent. Powerful, it was a true, complete Velada. There was singing, clapping, an ecstatic atmosphere. The young women sometimes nearly sobbed as they sang.
>
> *Albert Hofmann*

Albert Hofmann with his mushroom stone, 1984

of Oaxaca and was the starting point for their expedition.

Hardly had the foreigners reached the village center when the men—"there were no girls or women to be seen," Hofmann recalled—came out from their houses, shops, and bars and hesitantly approached the strangers, finally to crowd around the Land Rover. The four visitors were led to the village elder where Wasson presented his authorizations and recommendations from various officials which confirmed the scientific mission of the group of travelers. The village elder, a mestizo who likely could not read, was duly impressed by the official stamps and seals on the documents and, after greeting them, had a nearby barn put at their disposal for their stay. "I began to look around the village," Hofmann noted: "Ghost-like, the ruins of a large colonial era church that certainly had once been beautiful rose along the side of the village square that sloped up a hill. Now I began to see women with long braids of blue-black hair in long white red-trimmed dresses venture shyly forth from their huts to see the strangers."

Once the visitors had settled into their lodging, they were hungry from the long journey. An evening meal had been organized for them, and they were led to a typical mud hut with a straw roof where roast chicken, black beans, and tortillas were served along with beer and tequila, the beverages customary in Mexico.

> The gift of being able to communicate between the realm of spirits and supernatural powers and the ordinary world—a profound capacity found throughout the world and expressed in thousands of culture-bound manifestations of the human imagination—is pivotal to the art of shamanic healing.
>
> *Wade Davis*

The following day, they set off for the next leg of the trip through the Sierra Mazateca. There were no roads, only untraveled ways and small paths. The journey continued on mules. Wooden saddles take time to get accustomed to, but soon "this mode of travel proved to be the most pleasant I know," wrote Hofmann. The path led through swampy valleys, then along steeply sloping hillsides, and on through seemingly impenetrable rain forest, banana groves and coffee plantations. The travelers were impressed with the diversity and color of tropical vegetation and Hofmann in particular with countless species of wonderful butterflies. Shortly after sunset, they reached a small settlement where lodgings were even simpler than the day before. The warm climate enabled them to sleep on a covered veranda.

The next day's journey on the backs of mules took the expedition further south and to higher altitude. Along the way, Hofmann saw ololiuqui vines growing wild. Nightfall found them in the Mazatec village of Ayutla where they planned to spend several days. They found lodging in the house of Doña Donata Sosa de Garcia, the head of a large family and manager of the local coffee plantation. An annex was the temporary storage facility for freshly harvested coffee beans. Hofmann was delighted by the sight of the "young Indian women and girls in their bright, colorfully decorated garments as they returned towards evening, with sacks of coffee on their backs supported by headbands."

An opportunity for the researchers finally presented itself. They would benefit from their good relations with Doña

(. to r.) Gordon Wasson, Irmgard Johnson-Weitlaner, Albert Hofmann, 1962

Anita Hofmann pressing leaves
to extract juice

(l. to r.) Anita and Albert Hofmann, Irmgard Johnson-Weilaner

Donata. She took them to an old woman who gave them their first samples of the *Hojas de la Pastora*—unfortunately, only a few leaves; the blossoms and roots needed for a botanical identification were lacking, and the woman did not wish to tell them where the plants grew and could be freshly picked. Though mildly disappointed, Hofmann did not lose heart; it was a first clue.

They traveled higher into the mountains to overnight in San Miguel-Huautla, then descend to Rio Santiago. There, they met a teacher, Doña Herlinda Martinez Cid

107

whom Wasson had gotten to know on his earlier expeditions. One excursion took them through lush tropical vegetation to San José Tenango. After being unable to wash for days, they were overjoyed to find a hidden spring in the jungle which flowed into a basin. There Hofmann saw a hummingbird in the wild for the first time, "a shimmering, blue-green metallic jewel that flew among large liana flowers in the canopy of foliage."

Salvia divinorum

Meanwhile, Doña Herlinda used her connections and led the group of researchers to several curanderas. For this occasion, Natividad Rosa had dressed in a magnificent gown. She gave them a large sprig of the blooming *Hojas* plant that they had sought but was unwilling to conduct a ceremony. Apparently she did not wish to reveal the location of the sacred ritual to strangers and would not tell them where the plants grew. However, the next day she brought them a basket of fresh leaves from the plant. According to Hofmann, "it was a member of the genus *Salvia*, related to the well-known Meadow Clary or *Salvia pratensis L.* The plant has blue blossoms crowned with a white helmet and arranged along a twenty to thirty centimeter panicle, the stem of which tends to blue." Knowing that the active agent was in the extract drunk at ceremonies, Anita and Albert Hofmann crushed the fresh leaves with the help of an Indian girl using a stone press. They squeezed the juice through a cloth, mixed it with alcohol as a preservative, and bottled it in vials for later analysis at the Basel laboratory.

Ceremony with a Magical Plant

The day before they were to leave, Doña Herlinda finally succeeded in finding a curandera who would offer to carry out a ceremony for the group using *Hojas de la Pastora*. That evening they followed her along a narrow path that led up to the curandera's hut set apart on the mountain side. Obviously, no one in the village was supposed to know that the strangers were visiting a curandera. Once they arrived, they were greeted by Consuela Garcia, who locked the entry as soon as they all had gathered in the hut.

They seated themselves on bast mats placed on the clay floor and listened to the curandera's instructions, interpreted and explained by Doña Herlinda. A few candles lit the setting dimly as a spicy scent spread from a burning bowl filled with copal. With a practiced hand, Consuela Garcia prepared the magical drink from the salvia leaves they had brought. Hofmann refrained from participating in the ritual due to a badly upset stomach but his wife Anita took part along with Gordon Wasson. The curandera laid out six pairs of leaves for Wasson, the same number for herself, and three pairs for Anita. As with the mushroom ceremonies, the salvia leaves were distributed in pairs; the dosage adjusted for each individual.

The curandera crushed the leaves, thinned the pulp with water, poured it into a cup and consecrated it with smoke from copal incense. Before she would give Anita Hofmann and Wasson their cups, they had to confirm that they believed in the sacredness of the ceremony. Both nodded assent and were permitted to drink the bitter-tasting brew. Consuela Garcia murmured invocations, then extinguished the candles and left the group to await the effect. "After some twenty minutes, Anita whispered to me that she could see strange, brightly haloed images. Gordon too felt the effect of the drug," Hofmann noted.

After a while, the curandera relit the candle on her altar table and intoned prayers and incantations, half-spoken, half-sung. Finally, it was time for the ritual consultation. Wasson asked how his pregnant daughter was and was told both mother and daughter were doing well. Anita Hofmann asked about her children in Switzerland and was given the good news that they were safe and well. Both found their state of intoxication to be comparatively mild but clearly hallucinatory. After a closing prayer and thanks to the gods and goddesses of the plants and to all saints, the ceremony and an eventful night ended. In the same manner as they had left the village, the group was able to return before daylight, undetected. Now Hofmann and Wasson knew that the *Hojas de la Pastora* were used within the same ceremonial context as mushrooms. Moreover, they had enough material from the plant for Hofmann to make the planned botanical determination and chemical analysis.

The next morning, the band of explorers traveled on, but not without having adequately thanked Doña Herlinda. They left the fertile valley, climbed into the Sierra, and reached Huautla de Jiménez, the main town of the Mazatec realm, towards evening. At dinner in the town's sole inn,

Albert and Anita Hofmann, Irmgard Johnson-Weitlaner (behind), Doña Herlinda and assistant (front) in 1962

the travelers drank a toast to the success of their expedition.

The Spirit in the Pill

The next day, Gordon Wasson led the group to the curandera Maria Sabina who received them warmly. The shaman guided them to her new hut, since the house in which Wasson had attended a session had gone up in flames a few years later, apparently a case of arson in reprisal for revealing the secret of the *niños santos*—holy children—to foreigners. When Albert Hofmann told her that "it was possible to put the spirit of the mushrooms in pills, she was astonished and offered at once 'to be of service,' namely, to grant us a consultation."

They agreed to a session for the following night, and Hofmann spent the day looking around the small city. He then accompanied Wasson on a visit to the Instituto Nacional Indogenista, a state institution that attends to the concerns and problems of Indians. On the way back to the hotel, they met Father Aragon in front of the cathedral. Wasson knew him from his earlier travels, and they accepted his invitation for a glass of tequila in the sacristy. The priest's blessing and the spirit from the agave brandy put them in the mood for the ceremony that evening. At sunset they met in their hostess' house. Maria Sabina's pretty daughters Apolonia and Aurora had already arrived as well as a niece, numerous children, and Don Aurelio, an elder shaman. Then they all prepared by drinking cacao and eating pastry on the veranda.

It was the evening of October 11, 1962. Night had overtaken dusk as they entered the house and made themselves comfortable on the bast mats. Candles lit the setting. A few children and relatives soon fell asleep. The scent of copal made the stuffy air bearable. It was toward midnight that Maria Sabina deemed the moment had come for the ceremony. Solemnly, Albert Hofmann gave her a small bottle of pills and Herlinda told her through an interpreter that each pill with five milligrams of psilocybin contained the spirit of two pairs of mushrooms. The curandera examined the pills with a skeptical eye, briefly exposed them in incense smoke, and distributed them by twos to the adult participants. To Don Aurelio and her daughter Apolonia, who also was to serve as a curandera, she gave four pills each. She took the same number herself; Wasson and her daughter Aurora,

each received a pair, Anita Hofmann and Irmgard Johnson each one pill. Since Albert Hofmann was familiar with his synthetic psilocybin already, he wished to make up for the lost opportunity with the *Hojas de la Pastora*. A girl of perhaps ten years of age prepared the extract from five pairs of fresh leaves for him under the direction of Maria Sabina. It was said the juice was particularly potent when prepared by a virginal young maiden.

They swallowed the pills, drank the extract, and extinguished the candles. The participants lay on the mats to relax and wait for the effects to take hold. After a scant half hour, they heard Maria Sabina's voice as her daughters and Don Aurelio became restless. Herlinda interpreted and explained that Maria Sabina could not find a spirit in the pills. Hofmann knew that the pills took longer to act because absorption of psilocybin from the pills happened in the stomach. By contrast, when mushrooms are chewed, part of the active agent is already absorbed through the mouth's mucous membranes. He decided to give Maria Sabina, Apolonia, and Don Aurelio each a further pair of pills, giving them each a dose of thirty milligrams of psilocybin.

With the increased dose, the spirit from the pills soon appeared and inspired the shamans. Hofmann noted: "The prayers and chanting of Maria Sabina were fervently answered by her daughters and by Dona Aurelio's deep bass. Hearing the languid, ecstatic groans of Apolonia and Aurora gave the impression that the religious experience of the young women was mixed with sexual-sensual sensations in their state of intoxication."

Maria Sabina

Maria Sabina (right)
with her daughter

Hofmann's wife, Johnson, and Wasson all enjoyed a state of euphoria. Anita Hofmann had striking visions of exotic line patterns. While the strong effect of the psilocybin continued until dawn, Albert Hofmann's plant extract drink left him "in a state of heightened receptivity and intense sensitivity, but with no hallucinations." For the Basel chemist, much more important was the finding by the Mazatec curandera that his pills did indeed contain the spirit of teonanácatl, were equal in potency to the mushrooms, and in no way different. "That was confirmation from an expert that synthetic psilocybin was identical to the natural product. In parting, I presented her with a small bottle of psilocybin pills. She radiantly explained that now she could give consultations even when no mushrooms were growing."

Maria Sabina's stance that the psilocybin pills contained the spirit of the mushrooms was unusual. Most shamans were convinced that all plants possessed a "spirit" or a "soul," in effect the "group soul" of a species. Terence McKenna, a passionate advocate for magic mushrooms emphatically believed that the spirit in the pills was not identical with the one in nature. Hofmann disputed his claims in conversations more than once. As a scientist, he was firmly convinced that the isolated agent was identical to that found in nature. He allowed as well for the presence of "spirit" in the molecules, which discloses his magical worldview, when he repeatedly emphasized that LSD had found him, not conversely.[45]

A Chinese legend illustrates the situation: Several wise men noticed that people under the influence of alcohol changed and were convinced that the drink contained a spirit which took hold of them. They decided to capture this spirit. To this end, they placed the jar holding the alcoholic liquid on the fire to drive out the spirit. To prevent him from simply escaping into the air, they blocked the exit and allowed only a tiny opening through which vaporized material could escape and which they collected in a second jar. In their effort to find the "wine spirit," they invented distillation.

After heartfelt goodbyes, the visitors took leave of their hostesses and traveled by truck from Huatla de Jimenez to Teotitlan to retrieve their Land Rover. As they returned to Mexico City, they paused near Puebla to visit one of many ancient churches from the Spanish colonial era. To Anita Hofmann's great astonishment, she saw the same pattern in the richly decorated ornamentation above the altar that she had seen two days earlier while under the influence of the magic mushrooms. In

Mexico City, the group separated with some of them traveling on to the USA, and others to Switzerland—their heads full of unforgettable impressions and, in their baggage, plant samples.

Wasson and Johnson sent the *Hojas de la Pastora* to Carl Epling and Carlos D. Jativa at Harvard University's Botanical Institute for analysis. They turned out to be an as yet unknown species of salvia which the two explorers named *Salvia divinorum*. In 1964, Hofmann wrote the religious studies scholar, Karl Kerényi, "I would have suggested *Salvia divinatorum* because that would be a translation of 'Salvia of the Diviners.'" Chemical analyses of extract from the diviner's salvia in Basel's Sandoz labs were inconclusive. Since a self-experiment brought no effect, Hofmann conjectured that the agent was unstable. That proved to be his last effort with this plant. He refrained from any further investigation and wrote in 1979 that the chemical nature of the magical plant Ska Maria Pastora still remained open. It was not until three years later that the psychoactive agent of salvia, salvinorin A, first was discovered by Alfredo Ortega during systematic exploration of the occurrence of terpenes in several salvia species.[46] In 1984, Leander J. Valdés happened upon this substance a second time when researching the active ingredients of the Aztec salvia.[47] Independently of one another, they extracted juice from fresh leaves, isolated salvinorin A, and determined its structure. Salvinorin A belongs to the terpenoid salvinorins which differ markedly in structure from other hallucinogens. Next to the cannabinoids and a few other essential oils, they are the only psychoactive substances that are not alkaloids. In the 1990s, *Salvia divinorum* became a popular intoxicant and is still legally available in most countries.

The Consequences

Although Gordon Wasson's article in *LIFE* about hallucinogenic mushrooms may have caused many readers and some scientists to shake their heads, it did draw the attention of American youth who were straining against conservative middle-class mores of the 1950s. Animated by rebellious figures like James Dean, the Rock and Roll of Elvis Presley, and provocative tales from Beat authors, young people sought to break free from society's constraints. The lure of magic mushrooms seemed to promise novel and startling experiences and drew the first adventurers to hitchhike to southern Mexico in search of the intoxication and enlightenment Wasson had so enthusiastically described.

Only later did Albert Hofmann realize the far-reaching consequences that the coming together of indigenous culture and traditions with the thirst for knowledge in persons informed by Western cultures had set in motion. It was the magic mushrooms which gave Timothy Leary, the Harvard psychologist, his first high, sent hippies on pilgrimage to Mexico in the 1960s, and ultimately unleashed the modern psychedelic culture.

Maria Sabina, who revealed the secret of the teonanácatl to the Wassons, paid a high price for betraying the secret rituals. Soon after the ceremony with Gordon Wasson, her house was burned down because some believed her deed profaned

Psilocybe azurecens

their sacred traditions. Years later, she confessed that in the view of the official position of Cayetano, Wasson's informant, she felt she had no choice and felt pressure to fulfill the wish of the white people. In an interview in 1971, she said she "should have said no." She believed that "from the moment the strangers arrived, the *niños santos* lost their purity, their powers; they destroyed them—they will never again be at work."[48]

Scientific research was not the only source of profanation. The flood of tourism swept away the pristine culture of Huautla de Jiménez forever. Hofmann knew that the same mechanism held true for most ethnological research: "Wherever researchers and scientists discover and investigate the increasingly rare remains of ancient customs, their pristine nature is irretrievably lost. This loss is only partly offset if the results of the research bring lasting cultural benefits."

Fifty years after the decoding of the active principles of the mushrooms that contain psilocybin, over one hundred and eighty species across all continents—seventy-six in Mexico alone—are now known and new ones are being discovered constantly.[49] Mycologists such as Paul Stamets and Jochen Gartz have done invaluable work discovering and classifying the new varieties. Mushroom tourism to Mexico has largely come to a standstill because the mushrooms can now be found or grown in most countries. In scientific endeavors, because of its briefer duration of effect, synthetic psilocybin is frequently preferred over LSD.

Paul Stamets   Jochen Gartz

Friendships and Encounters

All real living is meeting. Martin Buber

Family Life

Albert Hofmann was a child of his time and social context. Driven by strong ambition, he was successful in his profession and moved upward socially. In the Swiss Army, he advanced to First Lieutenant. His views on work ethic, diligence, discipline, and the division of gender roles were traditional. In the 1960s, he maintained distance from the counter culture but was sympathetic towards the youth movement's closeness to nature and their ecological and pacifist attitudes. On the other hand, he had no understanding of their lack of discipline, or the unkempt appearance of many hippies, or the sometimes vulgar style of Beat literature.

Throughout his life, Albert Hofmann kept his family and professional lives separate. The topic of his work or professional problems was seldom brought to the family table. He often spent evenings working in his garden retreat, the converted shed which stood separate from the house. His son Andreas remembers: "He went there to work but afterwards came back into the family's world. That's why sometimes we didn't get to hang out with him much. Back then, no one spoke about party politics at home; politics were discussed only in the broadest sense of issues like development and the technologizing of the world, atomic war versus nuclear power. My father voted for the Free Democratic Party but did not always agree with their principles. The influx of foreigners bothered him as well as the loss of our country's autonomy and identity and the erosion of our traditions. He valued the notion of people being rooted in their natural surroundings. Papa was loving when he was around, but the parental care came from Mama. She was the guardian of the nest, concerned herself with our problems, and provided emotional security. My father was glad to be around us but didn't have much time for the family. Mostly, to protect his time, my mother shielded him from us.

I had a fine position in the family and benefited a lot from having a three-year

Still Life by Albert Hofmann, 1963   Ceramic Cat by Albert Hofmann, 1992

older brother, Dieter. The worst parental anxieties were already past and anything that he had put them through or was permitted to do was alright for me. As a child I had it very good. My parents generously kept me on a long leash. For many years, my father and I went running in the forest together on Sunday mornings, and we had some good conversations. That's when he opened my eyes to nature, to the seasons and their moods.

LSD was never discussed in our family, and we didn't know anything about his self-experiments. It wasn't until I was working in an architectural firm in New York from 1963 to 1966 that I incidentally happened to learn of the effect of LSD from a fellow employee, an architect and artist. He had tried it only once and said it had completely changed his life. His account made me realize the significance of LSD. I became interested, so I went to a lecture by Timothy Leary. Unfortunately, I didn't understand everything since my English was not good enough. I saw an article about LSD in an American magazine showing a photo of some man I didn't know, lying in a metal frame bed with a needle next to him. The caption said it was 'Albert Hofmann on an LSD high.'"[50]

Beatrix, the youngest daughter, has only good things to say about her parents: "I often had temper tantrums, but my mother was always understanding. She was very intuitive about people. There were no punishments in our parents' house. I was lucky in that my older sister Gaby had always wanted a sister and was very caring towards me. I idolized Gaby. As the youngest, I wasn't always being scrutinized and could develop freely. My father promoted anything creative: Drawing and painting or making music. He also planted a small garden with me. We children were often in Lucerne at my mother's parents during vacations. When my parents traveled, my grandparents came to Bottmingen and took over parental functions, like

> Friendship flows from many sources but is purest from respect.
> *Daniel Defoe*

116

Aurelio Cerletti and Albert Hofmann with wives in front of the Capitol in Rome on the occasion
of the first international meeting of the Collegium Internationale Neuro-Psychopharmacologicum
(CINP) on September 9, 1958

supervising homework. Our house was usually pretty lively. We often had visitors, and something was always going on."

Circles

Numerous friendships were cultivated by Albert Hofmann with fellow researchers, academics and artists. Despite his workload, he enjoyed being visited and often spontaneously invited people to his home. Hofmann was a good listener and approached others with empathy. His discoveries defied the neat categories of different disciplines. Hence, he came into contact not only with chemists, but with an array of ethnologists and ethnobotanists, biologists and mycologists, physicians and psychiatrists, theologians and religious studies experts, psychologists and therapists, philosophers and archaeologists, lawyers and politicians, writers and painters. In the course of his long life, Hofmann met nearly all of the important LSD researchers and therapists. With many, he enjoyed lasting and deep friendships so that professional questions and private matters often overlapped in his correspondence. He met many proponents of the counterculture as

> It is the lives we encounter that make life worth living.
> *Guy de Maupassant*

117

well as many who produced LSD underground. To be sure, he distanced himself from them more during his active professional career than in later years when his reservations diminished.

His friendship with writer Ernst Jünger and his relationship with Aldous Huxley meant much to him. At work, his favorite person to talk with was Aurelio Cerletti with whom he not only discussed professional matters but valued as a friend. Hofmann enjoyed his conversations with ethnobiologist and Harvard Professor Richard Schultes and mycologist Gordon Wasson. Both frequently spent days or weeks at a time as Hofmann's guest. He kept up a lively exchange with therapists and researchers like Hanscarl Leuner, Humphry Osmond, Walter Pahnke, and later with Stanislav Grof and Ralph Metzner. Many of them knew each other and this tight network of acquaintances extended across the boundaries of many disciplines and resembled the widely branching threads of a mushroom mycelium.

Interweavings

Among Anita and Albert Hofmann's private circle of friends in Basel were the Basel orientalist Rudolf Gelpke and his wife Li. Gelpke's book *Vom Rausch im Orient und Okzident* (*On Inebriation in the East and the West*), (Gelpke 1966) published by Klett Verlag, was well regarded. Other friends were poet, philosopher and bookseller Hans Werthmüller and his wife Heidi. Klett had also published his book, *Der Weltprozess und die Farben—Grundriss eines integralen Analogiesystems.* (*The World Process and Colors*)[51] Werth-

müller and Gelpke had corresponded about its contents and Gelpke gave it extensive praise in his own book. Since the 1950s, before Hofmann and Gelpke first met, both had been regular customers of Werthmüller's bookstore which appears in Hofmann's book, *LSD - My Problem Child,* as the setting for an LSD trip. They all knew the German writer and translator Philipp Wolff-Windegg, nephew of the Stuttgart publisher Ernst Klett, and his wife Mareile. Her father, Felix Georgi (1893–1965) was a professor of neurology at the Friedmatt, the psychiatric clinic of the University of Basel and had conducted experiments there with mescaline. Though Georgi knew Hofmann, the lifelong friendship between his daughter Mareile and the Hofmanns came about in a different way. She met Albert and Anita Hofmann together with her first husband, Swiss author Kuno Raeber. He was an admirer of German writer Ernst Jünger through whom he had met Albert Hofmann. After separating from Raeber, Mareile entered into a relationship with Philipp Wolff and they married in 1960. Wolff too met Hofmann through Jünger. It was a close-knit web of friends with enormous intellectual capacity linked by their interest in literature and philosophy. All five men, Hofmann, Gelpke, Jünger, Werthmüller and Wolff, published with Klett in Stuttgart.

In the 1960s, Albert Hofmann frequently hiked with Hans Werthmüller and Philipp Wolff. At regular gatherings of the three couples every one or two months with rotating hosts, Hofmann, Werthmüller and Wolff spoke little about politics; their interest in literature and art bonded them and, of course, private matters such as the joys and worries of parenthood were discussed.

Hofmann spoke most often of experiences during his many travels and of the remarkable people he met. But his qualities as a listener were so well developed that he became involved in the concerns of his friends. Mareile Wolff recalls that the wives remained somewhat in the background during these gatherings. LSD, of course, was always a topic of conversation. Hofmann repeatedly encouraged the two couples to try LSD and offered to accompany them. Heidi Werthmüller and Mareile Wolff were curious, but fear on the part of their husbands held them back. In the end, they all refrained in part due to the insistent warnings of Li Gelpke who described her upsetting and frightening experiences with psilocybin.

Hans Werthmüller

Another welcome guest was the poet Rainer Brambach who, together with Hans Werthmüller, received the Culture Prize of the City of Basel in 1982.

Hermit in the Crystalline World

Born on Christmas Eve in 1928, Rudolf Gelpke was the son of the engineer known as the initiator of Swiss shipping on the Rhine River. While still at the height of his creative powers, his father had withdrawn from public life to devote himself to philosophy and mysticism. The son was markedly influenced by his uncon-ventional father. At the age of twenty-three, Gelpke's first publication was a novel, *Holger und Mirjam*. His broad range of interests led him to study at universities in Basel, Berlin, Zurich and Tehran where he studied ethnology, philology, philosophy and the history of religion. His enthusiasm for T. E. Lawrence's book *Seven Pillars of Wisdom* convinced him to pursue Islamic studies which he finished in record time, obtaining his doctorate in 1957. He then traveled to North Africa and Iran for studies and served as correspondent in Tehran for the *Neue Zürcher Zeitung* and as a contributor to the linguistic and ethnographic *Atlas des Iran*. As early as his first study visits to Iran in 1958 and 1960, Gelpke examined the role of hashish and opium in Iranian intellectual history. In 1960 he qualified as a professor at the University of Bern; in 1962 his monograph on Iranian prose in the twentieth century was published. That same year he was appointed lecturer on Persian language and literature at the University of California in Los Angeles. The American lifestyle and academic routine were not to his liking, and he was unhappy. When family problems arose as well, he decided not to pursue the academic life any further despite his meteoric rise. From 1963 he lived for the most part in Tehran

> True friendship is a plant of slow growth.
>
> *George Washington*

but kept his residence in the USA. He converted to Islam in 1964, divorced his wife in Basel, and married an Iranian woman. During this period, he continued translating from Persian which brought his name to the attention of a large circle of literary connoisseurs.

Gelpke was consistently portrayed by contemporaries as having a fascinating appearance. He was tall, slender, and blond with alert blue eyes. Furthermore, he was a stimulating conversationalist, constantly generating ideas and an equally keen and curious listener. He expressed his opinions clearly and decisively and, according to Hofmann, was "very well informed, fanatically zealous in his work, impatient with mediocrity, yet charming, likeable, and engaging."[52]

Gelpke and Hofmann became friends in 1960 when Gelpke attended Hofmann's lecture in Basel on Mexican magic mushrooms. At the end of the talk, Gelpke introduced himself: He was a scholar of Islam and acquainted with Asian drugs from his own experience. After hearing about intoxicants used by the Indians, he was curious to experiment with them.

It was no problem at the time because Sandoz was generous in making LSD and psilocybin available to physicians and research facilities. One condition was that experiments be done under medical supervision. Since Gelpke's brother-in-law was a professor of anesthesiology at the University of Basel, this was no hindrance. In 1961,

Rudolf Gelpke

Hofmann provided him with one hundred dragées of LSD of 0.025 mg each and forty of psilocybin of 2 mg each. Between April and September, Gelpke had ten LSD trips and nine psilocybin experiments, only three of which were under medical supervision, the rest he did alone. Gelpke's personality reminds one of the Parsi drug researcher Antonio Peri, the main character in Ernst Jünger's novel *Heliopolis* whom Jünger described as a "hermit in the crystalline world." Gelpke published a thin volume of remarkable reports on his experiments in 1962 entitled *Fahrten in den Weltraum der Seele (Travels in the Universe of the Soul)* and dedicated it to Albert Hofmann. These reports also appeared in the periodical *Antaios* which Ernst Jünger and Mircea Eliade edited at Klett Verlag whose director was their common friend, Philipp Wolff. Hofmann and Gelpke met often. They saw each less frequently after Gelpke moved first to California and later immigrated to Iran as he seldom stayed in Switzerland. They did, however, remain in contact by mail. Gelpke described life in the USA and sent him newspaper clippings from there about LSD. For his part, Hofmann described his Mexican expedition in detail, and he touched briefly on the Cuban missile crisis which he and his wife missed while they spent a few days on the Island of Cozumel—"across the way from Castro"—and mentioned that the American psychiatrist and LSD researcher Sidney Cohen, whom Hofmann regarded highly, had paid him a visit in Basel.

Above all, however, Hofmann justified the position of his firm: "We, and especially the people from Sandoz in the USA, are presently experiencing very unpleasant things with these substances. The worst and most dangerous for the company was that a high Canadian official of the health ministry labeled LSD and Thalidomide[53] as the two most dangerous drugs which ought to be strictly banned in the country. That proves how poorly informed responsible persons often are, or how they sometimes let their actions be directed by an even worse informed press. If there ever were two drugs that did not resemble each other in the least, it is Thalidomide, which resulted in so many malformed babies, and LSD. The only thing they share in common is that both have often been mentioned in daily papers recently. To blunt groundless accusations that our company is trying to make money with a dangerous drug (as you know, we have distributed nearly all of the LSD and psilocybin gratis and only to qualified research organizations and to force the health authority to finally establish rules for distribution of these new kinds of substances, we have completely stopped distribution of LSD and psilocybin. … We proposed to the Food and Drug Administration that they should take over distributing LSD and psilocybin and we would make the substances available. So as you can see, lots of problems and no progress. It evidently will take longer for LSD and psilocybin to achieve the standing they deserve."

Gelpke perceived California culture to be shallow and on its way to the condition described by Aldous Huxley in his utopian novel *Brave New World*. This came from

an experience "with the substance which you once gave me. Its effect: degeneration; cynical and icy laughter from somewhere in the background; in the foreground World History as Big Business, Hollywood style— thousands of masquerades and cascades of color partly swallowed up by night and absolute cold. In the end, the only thing I had was the tiny flame of my own ability to love; for a few seconds, I 'tele-visioned' my wife in Switzerland with amazing clarity and objectively accurate, even to details like her blue jacket, etc."

Gelpke was pleased that Hofmann wanted to print a report from him in a contribution planned for the *Basler Stadtbuch* of 1964. During this time they changed to the more personal *Du* form. Anxious to have his friend's observations, Hofmann sent ololiuqui alkaloids to him in Tehran with precise details about its make up and instructions for its dosage. In turn, Gelpke described life in Iran and his experiences with the alkaloids he received. The effect of lysergic acid amine on him was "a soporific, slowing and dulling of the senses." The morning glory seeds had a similar effect on him. He undertook one of the experiments in the company of a Iranian woman he considered to be suitable. She "called out to a series of Islamic prophets and told of Khadija (the first wife of the Prophet) and recited endless but beautifully melodic verses of Persian poets." He described his intense preoccupation with different aspects of opium and was certain that "all of these drugs will disappear, together with heretics and rebels, into catacombs in the coming 'ash gray' mass civilization. I can't believe with Huxley in the potential and notion of the 'enlightenment and evolution of the

Woodcut by
Fred Weidmann

character and competency as an expert since they were assigning him as a diplomatic representative to Cairo. Hofmann's answer concerning Gelpke was effusive but he hedged the reason for their acquaintanceship as follows: "We became acquainted through an exchange of information about ethnographic questions, comparing particular aspects of Central American and Near Eastern ethnography. He closed his recommendation with: "In addition to his great intelligence, I am amazed at Dr. Gelpke's creative energy. In my opinion, as an expert in cultural and political questions regarding the Arab world, Dr. Gelpke is suitable in every respect." However, Gelpke decided against accepting the post and he remained in Tehran.

human race.'" He wrote an article on drugs for the periodical *Bild der Wissenschaft* and asked Hofmann for illustrations and to proofread the manuscript. Hofmann made few corrections—what concerned him most was that Gelpke tone down his praise of him: "You can't write what you've already said and absolutely must correct in the galleys, namely that my pioneering work in the area of psychotomimetics is 'ingenious.' 'Pioneering' is fine and that's already praise enough. To say anything more would be an exaggeration." Hofmann did worry about complications with the publisher: "I am curious whether this apology for intoxication, in particular so openly praising opium and hashish, will be accepted by the editors at *Bild der Wissenschaft*." To Hofmann's amazement, the article appeared without objection and was unchanged.

At the end of 1965, the Swiss Federal Political Department contacted Hofmann to inquire about Gelpke's

At the beginning of 1966, Gelpke greeted Hofmann on his sixtieth birthday: "From Capricorn to Capricorn, from continent to continent." Gelpke wrote that Klett Verlag definitely planned to publish his extensive manuscript on intoxication in the orient and occident and reiterated his views about LSD: "Now, I am more convinced than ever that among all sacred drugs, LSD is the quintessential key to reality and this reality has never before been so buried, so blocked off and inaccessible to the average person in our pseudo-real technological civilization." Hofmann replied to Tehran on the sixteenth of April, the anniversary of his first LSD high: "The LSD movement seems to be nearing its zenith," and he listed the periodicals that had devoted lengthy title stories to LSD; he mentioned that the Swiss tabloid *Blick* had recently discovered the topic and had published three articles about "LSD, the Drug from

> Jünger told me someone called him in the middle of the night to say he knew now what LSD stood for: Love Seeks You (Liebe Sucht Dich). Maybe that's so.
>
> *Albert Hofmann*

Hell," and he wondered: "I am curious what we'll get when this new wine that's coming along so fast has finished fermenting."[54]

In the fall of 1966, Gelpke's first comprehensive and systematic work in the area of drug research, *Vom Rausch im Orient und Okzident* (*On Inebriation in the East and the West*), appeared and was to be followed by two further volumes as part of a trilogy. His friend Werthmüller wrote: "The book is an apology for intoxication as well as a vehement attack on Western civilization, an attempt at a metaphysics of the phenomenon of intoxication, an attempt to bridge the gap between west and east, and not least a personal confession, a *document humain*."[55] Forty-five years later, Gelpke's picture of an openly sensual Islamic culture in Persia seems to stem from long forgotten times and contrasts sharply with current social realities in the Islamic Republic of Iran. When they met for the last time eight years after their first encounter, Gelpke's hair had grayed, he "had thinned considerably, and now was a truly fascinating figure." Gelpke returned to Switzerland in 1971 and died from a stroke shortly thereafter in Lucerne at the age of forty-three. In his obituary for his gifted friend, Hans Werthmüller said: "As a human being and a conversational partner, Rudolf Gelpke's fascination with the world was scintillating and, as with all radioactive elements, he was consumed by his own radiant power." Twenty years after his father's death, Gelpke's son Basil made a film for German television in 1993, *Albert Hofmann— LSD und sein Entdecker,* commemorating the fiftieth anniversary of LSD.

> In corruption of the famous words of Goethe, one might say 'If the eye weren't sunny, it couldn't see the sun; if matter weren't imbued with spirit, how could matter move the spirit.
>
> *Albert Hofmann in a letter to Ernst Jünger on December 16, 1961*

Mrs. Obrist, Ernst Jünger, Anita Hofmann, Albert Hofmann, Mrs. Mohler, and Alexander Jünger in 1949

Ernst Jünger and Albert Hofmann at the Rittimatte in 1978

Radiance and Convergence

Due to the nationalistic and elitist nature of his early work, the German writer, philosopher, military officer and entomologist Ernst Jünger was a controversial figure. He became known for his war diaries, essays, fantastic novels and stories. Born in 1895, Jünger distanced himself in the early 1930s from the National Socialist ideology, which he perceived as mindless totalitarianism. Jünger corresponds to the epitome of a German, at least in the cliché that Swiss often make of him: On the negative side were his exaggerated virtues of ambition, sense of honor, discipline, elitism and nationalism combined with martial rhetoric; on the positive side, he is regarded as one of the last significant, sensitive and thoughtful representatives of the nation of poets and philosophers in the tradition of Goethe.

Some of his writings testify to his drug experiments, the collection of surrealistic texts entitled *The Adventurous Heart, Visit to Godenholm,* the novel *Heliopolis* and his essay, *Annäherungen: Drogen und Rausch.* (Jünger 1970) Jünger experimented with ether, chloroform, hashish, cocaine, mescaline, psilocybin and LSD, among other substances. He used drugs for excursions into the metaphysical, for liminal experiences. In his younger years, he experienced total loss of control on hashish: In his hotel room he suddenly felt as if he were in a swingboat and stormed into the

> Drugs are the key—they don't open up more than what is in us but perhaps they lead to depths that otherwise remain unplumbed.
>
> *Ernst Jünger*

corridor, running through the crowded lobby in his pajamas. After that experience—a doctor had to be summoned—Jünger did not touch drugs again for years.

Hofmann portrays his friendship with Ernst Jünger in his book, *LSD - My Problem Child,* in more extensive detail than any other friendship, eloquent evidence of the significance the writer had for him: "Radiance is the perfect term to express the influence that Ernst Jünger's literary work and personality have had on me. In the light of his perspective, which stereoscopically comprises the surfaces and depths of things, the world I knew took on a new, translucent splendor. That happened a long time before the discovery of LSD and before I came into personal contact with this author in connection with hallucinogenic drugs."

Hofmann described what motivated him to contact Jünger: Early in 1947, he congratulated Jünger on his birthday as a "grateful reader." That letter marked the beginning of a friendship of over fifty years. The letters often had to do with Hofmann's work with hallucinogens about which Armin Mohler[56] had informed Jünger. Two years after establishing their first contact, they met in 1949. Soon, Jünger visited the Hofmanns quite frequently. Hofmann's son, Andreas remembers: "I didn't know anything then about how important Jünger was. To me he was the epitome of what we Swiss understand as a 'German' with his Prussian manner and his clipped speech. At home in Bottmingen, we had laid out a bocce court with a roller, inspired by my father's long tours of military service in Ticino where almost every grotto has one. When Ernst Jünger visited, we often played bocce and drank Chianti." On those occasions, Hofmann sometimes invited additional guests, the poet Rainer Brambach and Hans Werthmüller or Jünger's biographer Gerhard Nebel. Unlike the more formal invitations to the Hofmann house, the children were part of these relaxed summer meetings in the garden.

Two years after first meeting, they had their initial LSD trip together. Hofmann was particularly interested in how such a sensitive, artistically inclined person would react to LSD outside a medical setting. In case of the need for medical assistance, Hofmann asked his friend, the physician and pharmacologist Heribert Konzett, to participate in the experiment. As a precaution, he chose a dosage of fifty micrograms for Ernst Jünger. That proved to be too low as the effects were rather mild. Afterwards, Jünger said about LSD, "it's only a house cat after all, compared with the Bengal tiger that is mescaline or maybe a leopard"—words that surely bothered Hofmann. Jünger later revised his opinion. He acknowledged, "The dose was too weak; I waited for the stage performance, but it turned out to be only a serenade in the lobby."

Some ten years later, after the discovery of psilocybin, "we developed the idea in our correspondence of conducting a symposium to which we would also invite Rudolf Gelpke." (Jünger 1970) Their mushroom symposium was held in the spring of 1962 at Jünger's house. In the group were Konzett, Gelpke and Hofmann. To set the mood, Jünger's wife served hot chocolate, based on descriptions in ancient chronicles that the Aztecs drank *chocolatl*

before they ate of *teonanácatl*. An adequate dose was chosen this time and each person received twenty milligrams. Hofmann hoped he would be able to relive the delightful experiences of his youth in nature. But that was not to be. The high did not lead him and the others to bright realms. "With the increasing depth of inebriation, everything became yet stranger. I even felt strange to myself. ... Fear of death seized me, and illimitable longing to return to the living creation, to the reality of the human world. ... I slowly returned to the room. I saw and heard the great magician lecturing uninterruptedly with a clear, loud voice, about Schopenhauer, Kant, Hegel, and speaking about the old Gäia, my beloved little mother. Heribert Konzett and Rudolf Gelpke were already completely back on earth again, while I could only gain a foothold with great effort."

For Hofmann, entrance into the world of the mushroom was a confrontation with emptiness and a dead world. Returning to the world of the living creation was all the more delightful. "How wonderful to be among humans again," he remarked after coming down, as they sat together around a table to enjoy the midnight meal Jünger's wife had prepared and listen to Mozart. Hofmann was of the opinion that a psilocybin high was often gloomier and less enlightening than one with LSD. Jünger then spoke of it as an "earth mushroom." Hofmann recorded that, "For me, the experiments

> With these trials one has to take a certain degree of risk into account.
>
> *Ernst Jünger*

with LSD were more luminous than with the earth mushroom."

Their last joint experiment also took place in Jünger's home in Wilflingen, in February of 1970. There were just the two of them. This time Hofmann took 100 micrograms of LSD and gave Jünger 150 micrograms. Soon after he began to feel the effects, he recorded: "Our boat tosses violently" and the high quickly led them into wordless depths. "Words seemed to originate from an infinitely distant world that had become strange so that, smiling, I abandoned my efforts as hopeless. Jünger's experience seemed to be no different, but language was unnecessary; a wordless glance sufficed to communicate agreement." The LSD trip brought them an exhilarating convergence.

In view of the enormous and often unpredictable effects of LSD on consciousness, Jünger was of the opinion that it should only be accessible to an elite. At a Jünger symposium in 2000, Hofmann shared Jünger's opinion and agreed—in contrast to Aldous Huxley, who wanted to make the psychedelic experience possible for everyone.[57]

Well into old age, Jünger combined his annual trip to an insect exhibition in Basel with a visit to the Rittimatte, the later residence of Hofmann. There the two could be seen deep in conversation as they slowly walked across the meadow. During one of these walks, the passionate insect collector found a specimen of a species that was thought to be extinct. In contrast with Hofmann who

> Visionary experience is not always blissful. It is sometimes frightful. There is hell as well as heaven.
>
> *Aldous Huxley*

rather quickly offered friends the familiar *Du* form of address, Jünger maintained a reserved distance his entire life. Hofmann was one of the few friends with whom he used the familiar form. Their friendship was recorded in an extensive and substantial correspondence and lasted until Jünger's death.

Jünger's importance was underlined by the fact that in 1993 President François Mitterrand and German Federal Chancellor Helmut Kohl paid him a courtesy visit in his home in the Stauffenberg forest house in Wilflingen. Only after Jünger's death did it became known that he had converted in September 1996 to the Roman Catholic faith. He died in 1998 at the age of one-hundred and two. During the course of his life, he received countless medals, service crosses, honors, distinctions and literature prizes. Over two thousand people attended his funeral, among them Erwin Teufel, the Minister-President of Baden-Württemberg, a representative of the Federal government, five Bundeswehr generals, Spanish Prime Minister Felipe Gonzaléz and Anita and Albert Hofmann.

Almost a Friendship

As the son of British author Leonard Huxley, writing was a birthright for Aldous, born in 1894. His brother Julian was a biologist and a writer, his half-brother Andrew Fielding Huxley was awarded the Nobel Prize in biology. Aldous Huxley's mother died when he was fourteen. At twenty-one, he made writing his profession. His best known work is the disturbing futuristic novel *Brave New World*. In the summer of 1919, he married Maria Nys,

GRAN HOTEL BOLIVAR
LIMA · PERU

August 3ʳᵈ 1958

Dear Dr. Hoffmann,

Your letter of July 16ᵗʰ reached me just as I was setting out for South America, and I am writing now from Peru (the land of a most unsatisfactory and dangerous mind-changing drug – coca – still consumed in great quantities by the Indians – mainly, I am told, to suppress the pains of hunger, only too common in the high Andes).

What you say about

Cables: "BOLIVARCO"

1/

GRAN HOTEL BOLIVAR
LIMA · PERU

psilocybin interests me very much, and I hope that I may have an opportunity of learning more about this new door into the Other World of the mind while I am in Europe this autumn.

Do you intend to be present at the pharmacological Congress in Rome in September? It is possible that I may be there as an interested observer and learner – but I am not yet certain if I can manage it. My the address in Italy which will always find me (after

Cables: "BOLIVARCO"

Aldous Huxley, 1953

2/

GRAN HOTEL BOLIVAR
LIMA · PERU

August 25ᵗʰ or thereabouts is c/o Felice Archera 31 Corso Abruzzi Torino.

If we do not meet in Rome, I will try to visit you in Switzerland.

Yours very truly,

Aldous Huxley.

Cables: "BOLIVARCO"

a refugee from Belgium whom he met during the war. They immigrated to California in 1937, where he began a new phase in his work. The once sharp-tongued critic met Jiddu Krishnamurti, explored the world's great wisdom literature and discovered their common mystic origins. He turned his knowledge into *The Perennial Philosophy.* (Huxley 1949)

In 1953, Huxley contacted the British psychiatrist Humphry Osmond. He was interested in the latter's psychedelic experiments and offered himself as a subject. Osmond was not particularly enthused: "I didn't like the possibility, however remote, of being the man who drove Aldous Huxley to insanity." (Lee, Shlain 1985) Finally, he relented. In May 1953, under the supervision of a psychiatrist, Huxley took 400 milligrams of mescaline in his home in the Hollywood Hills. His essay *The Doors of Perception* (Huxley 1954) described this first psychedelic experience. In *Heaven and Hell* (Huxley 1957) he examined paths to mystical experience in general. He understood and described the effects of psychedelic drugs—based on the filter model of attention presented by British psychologist Donald Broadbent in 1958—as an opening of the gates of perception, an expansion of consciousness by the increased flow of unfiltered input to the brain.[58]

Aldous Huxley and his second wife Laura, who died at ninety-six in 2007, experimented with mescaline, psilocybin

> Blake said that "gratitude is heaven itself"—a phrase I was unable to understand before taking LSD but which now seems luminously comprehensible.
>
> *Aldous Huxley*

and LSD; Huxley appears to have taken psychedelic substances approximately ten times. As the two were traveling in Europe in 1961, Huxley contacted the discoverer of LSD at Sandoz. Hofmann described this meeting that was important to him in his diary: "Huxley phoned this morning from Zurich and invited me to meet him at the Hotel Sonnenberg. I immediately drove to Zurich with Anita. First meeting in the hotel lobby with A. Huxley and his wife, an Italian from Turin, a psychiatrist. A.H. was at the International Congress for Applied Psychology in Copenhagen (13–19 August), where he gave a lecture 'Visionary Experience.' Tomorrow the Huxleys are traveling on to the sea in Italy. Lunch on the covered terrace restaurant with a lovely view over the city and the lake with a bottle of Maienberger Beerli wine. Spoke about the magical drugs, in particular LSD and psilocybin, which the H.'s both have tried. A.H. believes that these drugs (which he would gladly rename, since 'drug' in the English-speaking world has disreputable overtones) have an important role to play in the current phase of the development of humankind. He believes that trials under laboratory conditions make no sense. Experiments could be important for artists, for religious purposes, for psychotherapy. The surroundings, the preparation for the trip, the physical and mental state are critical for the experience. The next book, which will appear in the spring, again takes up the problem of psychomimetics. A.H. left me an audio tape of his lecture on 'Visionary Experience' to copy. The H.'s want to experiment in Italy with LSD and psilocybin which are hard to procure in the USA and asked about them. This evening

I sent A.H. 100 tabs of psilocybin, 100 tabs of LSD, and 12 vials of LSD. A.H. wore a yellow freesia in his lapel. He recommended to Anita that she take LSD or psilocybin on a meadow of alpine flowers. She should look into the blue cup of a gentian blossom to experience the miracle of its beauty."[59] The next morning Hofmann received back the books he had sent Huxley to autograph with lovely dedications.

One year later, *Island* appeared, the novel Huxley had announced (Huxley 1973), in which he opposed his dystopian *Brave New World* with a positive utopia where natural science and technological civilization combine with Eastern wisdom to form a new culture. A magic medicine named "moksha" plays an important role in the life of the society living on an imaginary island. Huxley sent Hofmann a copy of his new book after it came out in March 1962 with the dedication: "To Dr. Albert Hofmann, the original discoverer of the moksha medicine, from Aldous Huxley." Although they met one more time at a conference, the nascent friendship had no chance to mature because of the advanced stage of Huxley's illness. He fell ill in 1960 with cancer of the larynx or, according to some sources, of the tongue. After responding well to radiation treatment, his cancer recurred in 1962. He remained active and with full mental powers until his death, but his physical suffering was great.

A few hours before he died, he scribbled (his voice had failed him) on a slip of paper: "LSD—try 100 micrograms intramuscularly." Against the advice of the doctor present, his wife Laura fulfilled his last wish. He died peacefully on November 22, 1963 at 5:20 pm, only hours after the assassination of U.S. President John F. Kennedy. In a letter to Hofmann on March 26, 1964, Huxley's friend of many years, Humphry Osmond, described that moment even if his description diverges in some points: "Sir Julian tells me he was writing up to the very last minute and, for your own ear… at the very end he took a quantity of LSD at his surgeon's advice and died very quietly and peacefully, moving out into the beyond. Since he had been in great pain and distress, this was a wonderful happening for everyone, and I know that Aldous himself would like the discoverer of LSD to know this, even though I do not think at the moment it is quite the time for publishing it widely."[60]

A certain ambivalence with regard to Huxley's ideas can be heard in Hofmann's words: "Huxley said in both of his books, *The Doors of Perception* and *Heaven and Hell*, in which he reported about his mescaline experiments, that the phantastica should take over the role of alcohol and nicotine in our society. Jünger did not agree. In our correspondence about drug issues he wrote: 'I can't agree with Huxley's idea that the masses could be given the opportunity for transcendence. If we take the matter seriously, we are not talking about comforting fictions but realities. And there, a few contacts are enough to open channels and pathways. How wrong Huxley was and how right Jünger was subsequently became clear."[61]

The Networker

During the 1960s and 1970s, Hofmann's correspondence with Humphry Fortescue

Osmond, whom he met frequently at conferences, was copious and friendly, if not always without undertones on Hofmann's part. Born in 1917 in southern England, Osmond studied medicine, completed his training in psychiatry during WWII and served as a military doctor with the Royal Navy. After the war, he worked at St. George's University in London where he began his studies of pharmaceutical treatment for mental illness and research with hallucinogens. It was in London that Osmond and his colleague John Smythies first conjectured that the symptoms of schizophrenia were similar to those caused by hallucinogenic drugs. In 1952 Osmond hypothesized that biochemical substances could be responsible for schizophrenia. He became known to a wider public as the man who gave Aldous Huxley mescaline, and, in a poetic exchange with the writer, coined the term "psychedelic."

Humphry Osmond

Their lengthy correspondence began in the early 1960s with a handwritten card from Osmond to Hofmann stating that Heacock and his colleagues "have confirmed your findings regarding Ololiuqui." Hofmann answered him in December 1961 and wanted to know where the results were published. In March of 1962 Osmond wrote that Hoffer had told him Harley Mason at Cambridge, England, had also found lysergic acid amine (LA) but wouldn't publish because Heacock had already beaten him

to it with his confirmation. He asked about LA for self-experiments and where in England he might get LSD. Hofmann thanked him and said that he could get LA 111 and LSD from Sandoz in London. In further letters, Osmond mentioned the analgesic effect of ololiuqui alkaloids and their use for pain relief by the Aztecs and the Spanish.

Osmond later described the experiments he and his colleagues ran with the alkaloids and came to the negative judgment already stated: "I can't see why anyone would ever want to take Morning Glories for either kicks or therapy—its effect on all three of us was just plain negative and I don't mean in a constructive way."[62]

Osmond liked to ask lots of complicated questions in handwritten letters, barely legible, but always warm and lengthy. His letters were rather careless and he often made inexact or ambiguous statements in regard to specialized questions. For example, one of his accounts of a self-experiment starts with "I took one pill" without further specifics. Hofmann's handwritten annotation on the letter, "What kind of pill?" shows his perplexity. In a longer report, Osmond described his experiments with monoethylamide of lysergic acid (LAE) for its analgesic and possible spermicidal action, of planned animal trials and his hope to find effective tranquillizers. He asked if any support might be available from Sandoz. Hofmann's marginal note, "Certainly not," leaves little room for interpretation. Internally, Hofmann and especially Cerletti discounted Osmond's animal trials. Cerletti in a note to Hofmann, "To tell the truth, the whole business is disappointing if not dubious. The way the enclosed report is put together, the flight of ideas from analgesics to antimitotics and spermicides to tranquillizers is more than suspect. What use would animal trials be to Dr. Osmond's pharmacological colleagues? I don't expect anything more than rubbish to come of this (and additional requests for a grant!!)," was Cerletti's clear judgment. Hofmann repeatedly tried to clarify matters by asking what exactly he had ingested and explained that the LAE mentioned had nothing to do with ololiuqui and that only LA (lysergic acid amide) occurred naturally in nature. Osmond then sent assorted data regarding his work, but it did little to answer Hofmann's questions.

Ironically, on April 19, 1966, the anniversary of Hofmann's first self-experiment, Osmond wrote an open letter to the *New York Times* in which he explained how the prohibition of LSD was counterproductive. He complained that the increasing repression made the work of researchers difficult. "Rather than prohibiting the use of LSD, it should be made available to researchers who can administer the drug with appropriate safeguards to carefully screened individuals." Hofmann concurred with Osmond, "I agree fully with your views." According to Hofmann, it was Sandoz' intention to pressure the state health authorities to give psychedelics new legal status.

At the beginning of 1967, Osmond sent four LSD samples, three capsules and one tablet from the American black market to Hofmann requesting that he analyze them. As was to be expected, the three capsules did not arrive intact, so Hofmann could only analyze a mixture of the three. The mix contained a total of 15 micrograms instead of the 250 to 350 micrograms per capsule indicated. The tablet contained 11 micrograms of LSD instead of the stated 500. Hofmann asked Osmond to treat this information confidentially and not to mention either himself or Sandoz. They agreed that this information shed new light on the extremely high dosages supposedly being ingested. Osmond thanked him, excused himself for the poor state of the samples, and threatened to send him further ones. Hofmann was not overjoyed and tended to discourage further inquiries in the future: "Meanwhile, the labs have been working in other areas than psychotropic substances. Nonetheless, we have found some new lysergic acid derivatives with strongly analgesic and apparently antidepressive action." Osmond reported that the Spring Grove Group of Kurland, Unger, Pahnke and Savage had confirmed the findings of the Saskatchewan group about LSD and alcoholism. The psychedelic experience was vital to therapeutic outcome, which Hofmann acknowledged.

After retiring in 1971, Hofmann wrote to Osmond that: "occupation with philosophy, poetry and

> Whoever uses psychedelics should treat them with greatest respect. When Aldous and I used them, we prepared the ambience and ourselves the day before. The day of the session was kept as a holy day, and there were beautiful fruits and flowers around. The result was that we had no negative experiences.
>
> *Laura Archera Huxley*

fine arts" had largely replaced chemistry in his life. There were two sides to their relationship. Hofmann seemed to like him a great deal as a person; their professional exchanges, however, caused Hofmann consternation. Osmond had an enormous network of relationships and was an excellent networker within the community of psychedelic researchers. Humphry Osmond remained active until his death in the USA at the age of 86 on February 6, 2004.

The Coronation

Since the 1950s, Hofmann had been friends with fellow researcher Finn Sandberg, a pharmacologist and professor at the Royal Pharmaceutical Institute in Stockholm. At Sandberg's recommendation, Hofmann joined the American Society of Pharmacognosy in hopes of seeing his friend more often. Hofmann wrote him about ongoing research in the Sandoz labs with a degree of openness that today would be unimaginable. They frequently described their projects and travel plans to each other and discussed pharmacological questions. Sandberg's letters were quite friendly, sometimes in German, often in English and, inexplicably, occasionally in French. Sandberg knew all three perfectly.

Finn Sandberg constantly traveled the world in search of interesting plant-based medicaments. Hofmann frequently asked his friend to provide intriguing and rare, difficult to obtain pharmaceutical plant samples from his travels to Russia, Pakistan, China or Cameroon. In return, Sandoz would send Sandberg alkaloids and seeds of rare plants. Their correspon-

Anita and Albert Hofmann in Stockholm

dence provides interesting insight into research of the time. Procuring plant materials could take months or even years. The samples received were not always those requested—the wrong plant component arrived or the samples were already spoiled on arrival. Hofmann wrote him, "Today I am coming to you with a request for a drug. It is *Lagochilus inebrians Bunge* (*Labiatae*), described by Bunge as an inebriating deciduous shrub. We would like to analyze it chemically. This dwarf shrub grows in the steppes between Bukhara and Samarkand. Hence, it is difficult to get plant material. I thought that, thanks to your connections behind the Iron Curtain, you might be able to get us this drug. Dried leaves would be best

Finn Sandberg at the private party
for Albert Hofmann's 100th birthday

for an analysis. Seeds would also be valuable in efforts to grow it here." One year later, Sandberg succeeded in procuring the desired samples in Samarkand; he wrote that they were on their way to Basel in a package. Hofmann replied: "Unfortunately there were no seeds, just buds and blossoms," and again requested seeds which did indeed reach Basel a few months later.

They frequently met at conferences, whether in the South Seas or in Berlin or in Stockholm. Sandberg wanted to see Hofmann honored in Sweden, his homeland, and proposed Hofmann for an honorary doctorate to Stockholm University. To document his proposal for university officials, he asked Hofmann to send a résumé, a list of his publications, and a summary of his scientific activities. These efforts proved successful. In March 1966 Hofmann wrote his friend: "I just received official notice from the Royal Pharmaceutical Institute awarding the honorary doctorate.... You

can well imagine how pleased I am with this great honor from the world-renowned and respected Royal Pharmaceutical Institute. It is you, my friend, whom I wish to thank for your initiative in presenting my publications to the collegium of professors. Knowledge of my work was prerequisite for their critical appraisal. My colleagues at Sandoz and senior management are delighted with this distinction. This honor contributes to the reputation of our pharmaceutical-chemical research laboratories." Hofmann made minute preparations, informed Sandberg of his exact travel plans, and asked several detailed questions about the procedure of events at the ceremony. "Is formal evening wear required for the ceremony? In this case is it a tuxedo or tails?" It is a tail coat! He also wished to know when it would be decided whether he would be giving a speech as he was not good at improvising. Since King Gustav VI Adolf of Sweden was among those honored, receiving an honorary doctorate in medicine, it was he who was the one selected to give the address at the banquet on May 31, 1966.

Just before his retirement, Hofmann inquired whether his friend could send him a sample of *Amanita muscaria* and mushroom material from Siberia since he thought fly agaric mushrooms from there contained alkaloids different from those found in Europe. Nothing points to the fact that Hofmann was already busy clearing out his desk. The Swedish-Swiss friendship and the shared passion for their work on pharmaceutical plants even survived Hofmann's retirement.

They did nothing less than inspire a generation of Americans to redefine the nature of reality. *Don Lattin, 2010*

Vision of a New Psychology

Timothy Francis Leary was born to Irish-French immigrants in Springfield, Massachusetts in 1920. His parents and Jesuit school gave him a strict Catholic education. At age 19, he attended the renowned military academy at West Point but left after eighteen months due to disciplinary problems. He began studying psychology at the University of Alabama in 1941 and was awarded a Bachelor of Arts degree two years later. He then worked as a psychologist in an army hospital in Pennsylvania until the end of WWII. After the war he resumed his studies at Washington State University earning his master's degree in 1946 and obtaining a doctorate in psychology from the University of California at Berkeley in 1950. That same year he set up a department of psychology at Kaiser Foundation Hospital in Oakland, California, where he encountered his college friend, Frank Barron. The two shared many interests, whether a drink together, playing tennis, or a preference for reading James Joyce over Sigmund Freud. (Lattin 2010) They carried out a psychotherapy study in 1955 which received wide notice and was much discussed. One third of the one-hundred and fifty patients treated improved, one third remained unchanged, and one third deteriorated. In the control group that received no treatment, the results were the same. The two established psychologists found the results to be sobering and prompted Leary to deeply question the relationship between physician and patient and to explore new psychotherapeutic treatment methods. He finally was promoted to clinic director and published nearly fifty articles which brought him respect in the field.

His book *Interpersonal Diagnosis of Personality* (Leary 1957), which was based on the analysis of hundreds of group treatment outcomes, presented his method for categorizing patients into different personality types with five levels of interpersonal interaction. Leary did not automatically consider patient behavior that deviated from the norm to be dysfunctional.

Timothy Leary, Richard Alpert, 1961

As long as symptoms of severe illness were not present, he thought such persons should be supported in managing their own lives. With that, Leary challenged the theory of behaviorism which held sway throughout America at the time and limited itself to one-sided observation, measurement, and alteration of behavior patterns. Leary's book became standard reading for American psychologists and gave him a solid reputation in academic circles. Younger colleagues especially found his approach to a modern psychotherapy to their liking. The personality test developed from his methodology has been used in psychological evaluations and tests for decades now.

Despite his success in psychotherapeutic work and research, Leary was frustrated and saw no prospects for his professional future. After nearly ten years at Kaiser Foundation Hospital, he resigned in 1958. He had reached an impasse in his private life as well. A few years earlier, his wife Marianne, whom he married in 1944 and who had suffered increasingly from depression, took her life, leaving Leary with their two children, Susan and Jack, eight and six years of age. He needed to take a break and gain distance from academic life.

In the winter of 1959, Leary traveled with the children to Florence, Italy. There he began work on a new manuscript, *The Existential Transaction,* which summarized his ideas for a new psychology. He met his old pal Frank Barron who was on sabbatical in Europe and told Leary about an extraordinary experience he had on a study trip in Mexico. A psychiatrist there had given him a small bag of so-called magic mushrooms which had given Barron "William Blake revelations, mystical insights, and transcendental perspectives." (Leary 1983) Leary was fascinated by Barron's extravagant report but also concerned about the professional reputation of his old friend. But Barron had even more to report: Professor David McClelland, Director of the Center for Personality Research at Harvard University was also in Florence at that time and, having read Leary's *The Interpersonal Diagnosis of Personality,* might be able to help him find a new job. The next day, Leary met McClelland and told him about his next book in which he promoted a new "existential" understanding of the psychotherapeutic process which took the patient, therapist, their environment and world views into account as an interactive system. Such a theory was new to McClelland, but he appeared to like Leary's plans and vision. After a while he said: "Okay, I am ready to offer you a job.... You're just what we need to shake things up at Harvard." (Leary 1983)

With his two children, Leary rented a spacious house in Newton Center, a suburb of Boston. He quickly acclimated to Harvard and went to work. He met Bill Wilson, the founder of Alcoholics Anonymous, and Charles Dederich, founder of Synanon, both representing extremely successful self-help groups for addictions. Leary always had the same question: "How do *you* change human behavior?" Whether encounter groups or client-

> A consequence of Leary's emergence as celebrity outlaw and counterculture symbol was that his earlier contributions to personality and clinical psychology have been largely overlooked.
>
> *Jeff Brookings,*
> *Psychology Professor*

centered therapies, all known methods appeared to take a long time to change habits established over the course of years. Soon, other colleagues became interested in researching new methods of behavior change. One young assistant professor in particular stood out: Richard Alpert. He was the son of a wealthy Boston family, had graduated from Stanford University, and had come to Harvard in 1958 as a lecturer in psychology. He was ten years younger than Leary. The two men were the only faculty members in their department who made themselves available to their students in the evening. Their offices were not far apart, and they soon became friends and decided to start a project together. Leary thought of Frank Barron, and McClelland agreed to bring him from Berkeley to Harvard and gave the green light for a one-year psychology research project. It was to start in the fall of 1960 which gave Leary, Barron and Alpert an entire summer to leisurely develop their plans.

Psychedelic Revelation

In high spirits and full of confidence, Barron and Leary drove to Mexico during the semester vacation and rented a magnificent villa with a swimming pool in Cuernavaca. Lying in the sun on beach chairs, they planned to lay out the content, goal, purpose and general framework of their project. Many friends and acquaintances who also came to Mexico for a warm weather break visited them, among them McClelland with his family and later Richard Alpert. One day, Gerhart Braun, an anthropologist at the University of

Mexico, stopped by and told them he had gotten a small bag of psilocybin mushrooms from a curandera which he would gladly share with those guests present. By then, Leary had read about magic mushrooms and, after some hesitation, he decided to try them. They did not taste good to him: "The smell was like crumbling logs or certain New England basements." (Leary 1983) But soon, he began to feel the hallucinogenic effects and everything began to quiver, to come alive. He watched his good friend Bruce, a logician and philosopher from Michigan, who had remained sober and was lost in a book: "The scientist! But he had no idea what he was observing. This professional revelation struck me as immensely comic.... Couldn't stop laughing." Timothy Leary's first psychedelic experience left unforgettable impressions with far reaching consequences. The forty-year old later said: "The journey lasted a little over four hours. Like almost everyone who has had the veil drawn, I came back a changed man.... In four hours by the swimming pool in Cuernavaca I learned more about the mind, the brain, and its structures than I did in the preceding fifteen-years as a diligent psychologist." (Leary 1983) It was the most "deeply religious experience" of his life. With expanded consciousness and his firm conviction that he had found the key to the upcoming research project, Leary returned to Cambridge.

> The use of hallucinogens as sacred or magical drugs which can be seen in different cultural contexts, can be explained by their capacity to provoke ecstatic experience under the right outer circumstances and corresponding inner preparation.
>
> *Albert Hofmann*

Academic Mushroom Circles

Barron was enthused by what Leary told him of his experiences. Both believed they had found a magic formula for bringing about thorough-going and very quick psychological change, and decided to design their project accordingly. Harvard seemed to be the ideal university for this even psychologist and philosopher William James,[63] previous lecturer at this elite university and founder of the profession of psychology in the United States, was acquainted with psychedelic experiences. In 1897 James described his experiments with laughing gas in his essay *The Will to Believe*.[64] His work *The Varieties of Religious Experience* made him world famous. In a short time, Alpert, Barron, and Leary met other students, doctoral candidates, and professors who were willing to assist and volunteer for their unusual project. In October 1960, they founded the Harvard Psychedelic Research Institute. Professor Mc-Clelland and a few of his colleagues had imagined the project somewhat differently but Harvard was a stronghold of academic freedom so Department Chairman Henry Murray gave the green light to the Harvard Psilocybin Project.

At the time, Aldous Huxley was a guest lecturer at Harvard. On November 8, 1960, Humphry Osmond brought Huxley and

> One may say truly, I think, that personal religious experience has its root and centre in mystical states of consciousness.
>
> *William James, 1902*

> It was astounding – I lay back, listening to music, and went into a sort of trance state. I saw a vision of that part of my consciousness that seemed to be permanently transcendent and identical with the origin of the universe.
>
> *Allen Ginsberg*

Leary together at a luncheon in Boston. Afterwards, Huxley commented to Osmond, "Seems like a solid chap. What do you think?" Osmond replied, "I don't know. Seems a bit stuffy, don't you think." Huxley answered, "Yes, perhaps." (Lattin 2010) However, Huxley offered to consult with them and suggested they also invite Huston Smith, professor of comparative religion at the Massachusetts Institute of Technology (MIT) in Boston to join the project.

The majority of the 38 subjects in the first experiment were post graduate students and colleagues at the university, along with good friends. Leary and Alpert procured the psilocybin in pill form from the Sandoz branch in Hanover, New Jersey. The dosages varied and were administered according to mutual agreement. Using a detailed questionnaire, a record was kept of the impressions and experiences of each subject. Three quarters of them described "very pleasant" experiences and nearly as many "a noticeable expansion of consciousness." For the first time, the notion of "set and setting" came up, according to which a psychedelic experience is informed by one's inner mental state and outer surroundings. Most of the experiments took place in Leary's tastefully decorated home rather than in sterile university rooms. Candles or a fireplace lit the room and the music of Bach, Mozart or Ravi Shankar played. Upon Huxley's recommendation, further experiments would include influential and creative persons and artists—among them writers William S. Burroughs, Allen Ginsberg, and Arthur Koestler. The percentage of positively-rated experiences among the nearly two hundred participants rose. Fully ninety-five percent found the psychedelic sessions "changed their life for the better." Summing up, Leary and Alpert considered psilocybin to enhance mental capabilities and creativity and recommended it as "instant psychoanalysis" for use in psychotherapy. To avoid the term "drug," they called psilocybin a "consciousness-expanding substance." (Weil 1963, 2)

The university administration noted the successful experiments and amazing results but was unable to dismiss concerns about the utility of the project. However, the enthusiastic reports awakened curiosity among the students and their friends. Some experienced a marvelous psychedelic experience at Leary's house or elsewhere in private quarters without being officially part of a study. Increasingly, a noticeable boundary formed between those who had had a psilocybin experience and those who did not belong to the inner circle of the initiated. Leary and Alpert made an effort to continue their experiments on the basis of the project as defined but already were thinking about a further study that could yield even more convincing results for the successful use of psilocybin in positive behavior change. The opportunity would soon present itself.

At Aldous Huxley's urging, Leary sent a detailed report about the Harvard Psilocybin Project to Albert Hofmann in the beginning of 1961. Hofmann answered him on February 22nd:

> I was just reading in a book by Aldous Huxley (The Perennial Philosophy) when your kind letter and your report on investigations with psilocybin was handed over to me. It was a friendly suggestion of Mr. Huxley to let me know the preliminary results of your studies, and I should like to thank you very much for having followed his suggestion.
>
> My own experiences with psilocybin and earlier with LSD convinced me, as I have written to Mr. Huxley two years ago, that the use of this kind of drug should not be restricted to pharmacology and psychiatry but that they should be studied also in respect to their faculty to open up new "doors of perception." It gave me therefore a great satisfaction to study your interesting approach using psilocybin as a consciousness-expanding drug.
>
> You have realized the importance of the environmental factor of surroundings for the quality of the effects of psilocybin. Many psychiatrists who use LSD or psilocybin as an aid in psychotherapy don't pay attention to this point. The results of your studies, with the aim of determining the conditions under which optimal positive reactions with psilocybin occur will also be important for the therapeutical use of this drug.
>
> The dosage you use (up to 30–36mg) seems to me extremely high. Was the psilocybin content of your tablets been checked?
>
> I take the liberty to enclose a copy of a paper which I read last autumn at the International Symposium on the Chemistry of Natural Products at Melbourne and a reprint of a preliminary publication on the same subject in EXPERIENTIA. You may be interested to hear that we have elucidated the secret of the third important magic drug of the Aztecs, of "Ololiuqui."

> Though LSD and some kindred alkaloids have had amazingly bad press, there seems to be no doubt of their immense and growing value.
>
> Bill Wilson, Founder
> of Alcoholics Anonymous

Surprisingly enough we have found there compounds to be closely related to LSD.

With one of the components (d-isolysergic acid amide) I experienced a mental state of complete voidness. Another Ololiuqui compound (d-lysergic acid amide) has narcotic properties. I would be pleased if the active principles of Ololiuqui could be enclosed later in your studies.

Please keep me informed on the symposium at the fall meetings of the American Psychological Association centered on psilocybin.

Looking forward to meet you in summer here in Europe.

I remain
Sincerely yours,
Dr. A. Hofmann

Please convey my best regards to Mr. A. Huxley.

Liberation Behind Bars

In the spring of 1961, two officials of the prison administration of the State of Massachusetts contacted Leary to ask about the possibility of providing them with graduate students to do research and therapy in their detention centers. They expected an immediate refusal because working with inmates was most unrewarding for psychologists; the prevailing wisdom was that criminals remain criminals. (Leary 1983) However, the officials had not reckoned with Leary's avant-garde ideas regarding behavior change. He agreed. Nonetheless, it did require several meetings and discussions until the prison authorities and the competent prison psychiatrist. Dr. Jefferson Monroe, were convinced of the therapeutic potential of psilocybin and the Concord

Prison Psilocybin Rehabilitation Project could begin. The effectiveness of the unusual and controversial therapy method would be demonstrated if the high rate of recidivism of released prisoners could be significantly reduced. Enough of the endless cops and robbers game—rather, as Leary put it, "turning convicts into Buddhas."[66]

The timing could not have been better for German-born Ralph Metzner, a doctoral student of psychology. When he heard of the prisoner project, he sought out Leary in his office, and told him of his strong interest in participating. At first glance, Leary thought Metzner, who was only a few years his junior looked "too academic, too dainty-British. Too ivory tower to be walking into a prison and taking drugs with hoodlums." Not until this meeting did Metzner learn that the psychologists would also take psilocybin which, however, only strengthened his interest in the project. Leary recognized the young psychologist's willingness to learn and invited him to visit him at home. After a joint psilocybin trip, Leary was convinced he had found a gifted psychologist and team member. For Metzner, it was "the most astonishing experience of my life."[67]

Soon thereafter, Leary, Metzner and colleague Gunther Weil strode through the iron gates of Concord Prison and met their first candidates—two murderers, two armed burglars, one embezzler, and a heroin dealer. The first therapeutic drug session was done with a dosage of twenty milligrams psilocybin each. The carefully prepared experiment intended "to free the personality temporarily," while under the influence of the hallucinogen, "from the neurophysiologic control patterns and genetic and cultural filters that imperceptibly rule our normal perceptions of the world." (Metzner 1992) It was a great success. The effect of psilocybin was to transform the doctor-patient relationship, freeing up both the psychologists and the prisoners from their fear of one another. Inmates and scientists experienced each other as persons of equal value and lost the sense of sitting behind walls. For Leary "This identification is not metaphorical. It is neurological. In scientific papers we called this process re-imprinting." (Leary 1983)

The therapy sessions continued and, as word of their success got around, additional prisoners asked to participate. By the fall of 1962, around thirty-five convicts had been treated by fifteen Harvard psychologists and colleagues in psilocybin-enhanced group psychotherapies. The goal was to effect positive changes in behavior and to reduce the rate of recidivism. The guidelines for the project were constantly reviewed and revised, and the authorities were regularly informed of the course of events. After every session, each of the inmates underwent extensive personality tests and the assessments were discussed together with the psychologists. Both sides were surprised and enthused by the results. Depression, hostility, asocial tendencies all declined, while ambition, a sense of responsibility, and cooperativeness increased. According to prison statistics of the day, on average 70 percent of inmates released on probation became recidivist. Of the participants in the Harvard Psilocybin Project during its first year only 25 percent reoffended, six due to violation of terms of probation and only two due to new crimes. During the second year, only 10 percent of the same group reoffended. (Leary 1983)

The Harvard psychologists could not exactly explain this success. They supposed that two factors accounted for the remarkable behavior changes. For one, psilocybin helped prisoners to recognize and identify alternatives through role-play—"free citizens versus prisoners." Second, once liberated from their former games, being part of a therapeutic group process that provided empathetic support, they could radically change their behavior and begin new lives.

The Man with the Mayonnaise Jar

English philosopher Michael Hollingshead was Executive Secretary for the Institute of Anglo-American Cultural Exchange in New York where he met the Anglo-Canadian physician and psychiatrist John Beresford, assistant professor for pediatrics at New York Medical College. In the summer of 1961, Beresford initiated Hollingshead into the secrets of psychoactive substances and mentioned that a number of prominent persons had already attained extraordinary experiences with them. That piqued Hollingshead's attention. Of the substances mentioned, mescaline interested him most, of the people mentioned, Aldous Huxley. The next day, Hollingshead phoned the writer in Los Angeles to learn the simplest way for him to get the drug. Huxley gladly told him but also mentioned a certain Dr. Albert Hofmann, a Swiss chemist, who discovered a substance which should be taken with great care, should he ever try it: "It is

> LSD seems to suspend the imprinted and conditioned brain circuits that normally control perception/emotion/thought, allowing a flood – an ocean – of new information to break through.
>
> *Robert Anton Wilson*

significantly more potent than mescaline," Huxley warned, but added that he had experienced incredible things with it. (Hollingshead 1973)

For Hollingshead, it was immediately clear that mescaline could wait. He had no difficulty getting the more potent substance. Beresford, too, wished to experiment with LSD and ordered a gram from Sandoz in Basel using the letterhead of the New York Medical College and the justification that he wished to test the effects of the drug on amoebas and use it as a control substance in a series of bone marrow experiments. By return mail he received a small, dark vial with packing slip H-00047 and a bill for $285. One gram of the substance in powder form was enough for around ten thousand doses each of 100 micrograms. Hollingshead received half the shipment. To be able to prepare reasonable doses, he dissolved the light brown power in distilled water, added exactly 5,000 teaspoons of powdered sugar, and mixed it into a paste which he put in an empty mayonnaise jar; that gave him around 5000 doses.[68] When he began to feel effects, he realized that despite his care during the procedure, some LSD had entered his system in an amount he later judged to be five times a normal dosage. He wasn't prepared for that but it ended well. After a first fright, he went out on his rooftop terrace and had a spectacular psychedelic experience. He called Huxley a second time, to tell him about his LSD trip and to thank him for the valuable tip. Huxley suggested he get in touch with Timothy Leary and told him of Leary's psilocybin projects in Harvard. The two keen minds met in the spring of 1962 for a lively conversation.

John Beresford
Michael Hollingshead, Harvard, early 1960s

Leary told him about his successful studies; Hollingshead raved about the potential of LSD. Despite his positive experiences with psilocybin, Leary was remarkably reserved. Everything he had heard up until now about lysergic acid seemed to him to be ominous; "Mushrooms and peyote grow in soil and have been used for thousands of years in the cultures of wise Indians. LSD, by contrast, is a laboratory product that quickly fell into the hands of physicians and psychiatrists. Besides, I was afraid." (Sirius 2008, 30) Hollingshead did not give up, and Leary invited him to live in his house for a while to be able to exchange ideas in the context of his friends and colleagues.

The mayonnaise jar made the rounds in Newton Center, too, and one evening in the comfortable circle of friends, Timothy Leary, though timid, dabbled with a sample from the magic pot and shortly thereafter began to experience a psychedelic revelation that outshone all of his psilocybin trips: "My previous psychedelic sessions had opened up sensory awareness, pushed consciousness out to the membranes. Psilocybin had sucked me down into nerve nets, into body organs, heart pulse, and air breath; had let me spiral down the DNA ladder of evolution up to the beginning of life on the

Timothy Leary (l.), Richard Alpert (r.), Copenhagen 1961

planet. But LSD was something different. Michael's heaping spoonful had flipped my consciousness into a dance of energy, where nothing existed except whirring vibrations, and each illusory form was simply a different frequency. It was the most shattering experience of my life." (Leary 1983, p.118) Leary recognized at once the enormous potential of this psychoactive substance for his ongoing projects but also suspected that LSD meant the end of their hopes of winning a Nobel Prize and becoming accredited Harvard professors. (Leary 1983, 120) His realization strengthened his commitment to psychedelic research; his hunch was to become reality.

However, before that Leary, Alpert and Metzner traveled to the International Congress for Applied Psychology in Copenhagen from August 13–19, 1961, accompanied by Aldous Huxley. Leary gave a lecture on "How to Change Behavior,"[69] Huxley talked about "Visionary Experience." Leary and Metzner returned to the USA, Huxley and Alpert traveled on to Switzerland where they met independently with Albert Hofmann—Huxley at lunch in Zurich, Alpert the next day in Basel where Hofmann learned for the first time of the Concord Prison Psilocybin Project. His diary notation: "Visit from a young American psychologist, Dr. Richard Alpert of Harvard University, Cambridge, USA, who also participated in the Congress in Copenhagen. He works in the group with Dr. T. Leary. He uses psilocybin with which he has a great deal of personal experience to prepare criminals for release. Prisoners receive psilocybin after extensive psychological preparation whereby Dr. A. himself usually also takes the drug. It often gives the patient insight into his relationship to others and his responsibilities. This is followed several days later by a discussion of the insights won to anchor them and, if necessary, another psilocybin trip. Dr. A. believes that the essential effect under psilocybin is for the true self to disconnect from the individual self that is bound to external circumstances and to become conscious of itself, which can lead to self-knowledge and healing. He also believes that people develop deep mutual understanding by taking psilocybin together and recognize the essential core common to all people and the meaninglessness or secondary significance of social position. A nice lunch on the Rhine terrace at Donati's."[70]

> The discovery of LSD could possibly be the most critical event in human history. Take it once and you know that all you've known about consciousness is wrong.
>
> *John Beresford, 1971*

143

The End of Peace, Joy and Magic Mushrooms

A variety of reasons contributed to the end of the Harvard psilocybin projects: For some time, students and young people had been consuming psilocybin and magic mushrooms outside of defined experiments; LSD was becoming ever more popular. Times had changed—instead of gray flannel suits, white nylon shirts, and narrow 1950s ties, men wore Indian shirts and longer hair; women went without bras, miniskirts replaced petticoats, and birth control pills were openly marketed. At Newton Center, illustrious guests came and went, among them Al Hubbard, Stanley Krippner, Charles Mingus, Robert Thurman and Alan Watts. Similarities of LSD experiences with the contents of Eastern spirituality were being discovered and discussed, and the erotic "side effects" of psychedelics were being enjoyed. Serious experiments alternated with hedonistic parties.

Soon rumors of drug-fueled orgies were making the rounds publically. Leary was surprised and confused by the emphasis on sexuality after having treated the psychedelic trips respectfully as purely psychological experiments and death-rebirth experiences. Huxley knew exactly what he was thinking: "Of course this is true," he told him, "but we've stirred up enough trouble suggesting that drugs can stimulate aesthetic and religious experiences. I strongly urge you not to let the sexual cat out of the bag." (Leary 1983, 114)

Reports critical of drug experiments at the venerable university appeared in the media. Official sources made it known that the CIA and FDA had kept a sharp eye on the projects and their directors from the start. A black market for hallucinogens had gradually developed among the students. Concerned parents contacted the authorities and the university. Still, spectacular therapy successes and personal experiences of new dimensions of consciousness made Leary, Alpert, and Metzner all the more determined, so that as Ralph Metzner said in retrospect (Ram Dass, Metzner 2010, 81), "The outer turmoil in society became less and less important, the more we became involved in the exploration of inner space." At Harvard, prejudice, envy, and ill will from conservative colleagues at the Center for Personality Research, whose students deserted to the progressive professors, stoked intrigues among the student body and resistance on the part of the university. Gordon Wasson, who from the beginning rejected the psilocybin projects, also exerted pressure on Harvard. He could not stand Leary. (ibid. 87) In the eyes of the department's chairman, McClelland, the operation of his department had been stirred up more than enough. However, an unfavorable article by a student was the final straw, putting an end to the Harvard Psilocybin Project.

Andrew Weil was no more than eighteen when he entered Harvard University in 1960. He had no experience with psychedelics, but he was quite interested in the psilocybin project which had only recently

> The visionary experience is the key to behavior change.
> *Timothy Leary*

> Our brains are designed to change.
> *Michael M. Merzenich, Neuroscientist*

begun. He and his friend Ronnie Winston, the son of a rich diamond merchant, contacted their advisor, Timothy Leary, who was not averse to giving them a role in his project, but when he learned their ages, he had to decline. Leary kept strictly to his agreement with the university administration of excluding any freshmen. With Alpert too they were biting on granite, but the students found another way to obtain magic mushrooms and carried out their own experiments privately. Frustration at not being permitted to participate in the prominent experiments with advanced students and lecturers festered in Weil. Jealousy entered the picture a year later when he saw that Alpert had cast an eye on his friend Ronnie and they apparently had taken psychedelic trips together in Newton Center. Andrew Weil knew of the precarious situation and the impending termination of the psilocybin project—he had caught wind of the university administration's intention to dismiss Leary and Alpert. In the end, the rejected candidate and spurned lover wrote an exposé for *The Harvard Crimson* in which he denounced Alpert and Leary's drug experiments outside the university and mentioned that psychedelics of all kinds were being given to freshmen at free-wheeling parties.

Weil's article did not miss its mark. On May 6, 1963, Nathan M. Pusey, the president of Harvard University determined that Timothy F. Leary, lecturer in clinical psychology, disregarded his employment agreement and was absent from Cambridge without permission, hence was being relieved of his teaching duties with immediate effect and his salary halted retroactive to April 30. Shortly thereafter Richard Alpert also was dismissed with the justi-

fication that he had given psilocybin to freshmen students. David McClelland, who brought Leary to Harvard in his day, commented succinctly: "The more drugs Leary and Alpert took, the less they were interested in research."[71] Weil gave it a second go with his article *The Strange Case of the Harvard Drug Scandal* in the November 5, 1963 issue of *Look Magazine*. Five years later, he regretted his behavior and apologized to Leary and Alpert. Leary accepted his apology with his customary smile while Alpert, now known as Ram Dass, remains undecided whether he can forgive him completely. (Lattin 2010)

After he left Harvard, Andrew Weil devoted himself to the study of altered states of consciousness. He studied with ethnobotanist Richard Evans Schultes, became a regular contributor to *High Times* magazine, and since the mid-1970s has spoken out against the U.S. War on Drugs. Later, he turned to health topics, researched alternative therapies, did pioneering work in the area of integrative medicine, and became a bestselling author. As one of the most influential and wealthy proponents of health in the USA, he is in demand as a lecturer and guest on television. His consulting organization on health questions, *Andrew Weil Lifestyle,* and a mail order company for health products are gold mines.

> The sexual impact is, of course, the open but private secret about LSD which none of us has talked about in the last few years. It's socially dangerous enough to say that LSD helps you find divinity and helps you discover yourself.
>
> *Timothy Leary*

> Tim was a chieftain. He stomped on the ground, and he left his elegant hoof prints on all our lives.
>
> *Hunter S. Thompson, 1996*

145

Not until 1977, was it disclosed that one of the opponents of Leary and Alpert's psilocybin projects, Herbert Kelman, a Harvard professor for social ethics, was on the payroll of the CIA which, as was well known, supported other kinds of projects with psychedelics. Kelman admitted having accepted money beginning in the 1960s from the Human Ecology Fund, an organization controlled by the CIA to finance the MK-Ultra projects, for purposes purportedly unrelated to drugs.[72]

Susan, Timothy and Jack Leary, 1963

Millbrook

> Which is better: to have fun with fungi or to have idiocy with ideology, to have wars because of words, to have tomorrow's misdeeds out of yesterday's "miscreeds?"
>
> *Aldous Huxley*

> It isn't merely the familiar image, a little more distorted or more colorful, it is a completely different program. And that is because LSD changes our senses, one sees better, one hears better, everything is more intense—to that extent Timothy Leary was right when he claimed it was also the most powerful aphrodisiac. The mechanism of LSD is quite simple: the gates of perception are opened and we suddenly see more—of the truth.
>
> *Albert Hofmann*

Long before the falling out and final verdict from Harvard University, the psilocybin project team had decided to take a break and refocus their efforts. There was no lack of ideas and motivation on their part, and they were receiving encouraging signals of support from a faithful following. As early as the summer of 1962, Leary, Alpert, Metzner and a few colleagues organized a six-week course in Mexico to train "trip guides" for the responsible use of LSD and other psychedelics. They and their partners traveled to Zihuatanejo with a group of thirty-five older students and

close friends. At the suggestion of Aldous Huxley and philosopher Gerald Heard, they adapted instructions from the *Tibetan Book of the Dead,* translated from "Anglo-Buddhist into Psychedelic American" during their LSD-sessions.[75] The text, detached from Tibetan symbolism and adapted to Western psychological concepts, described sequences that are comparable to LSD experiences. The first period is "that of complete transcendence—beyond words, beyond space-time, beyond self.... There are only pure awareness and ecstatic freedom from all game (and biological) involvements." (Leary, Metzner, Alpert 1971) In that condition, one could realize emptiness, the unbecome, the unformed, and the immortal. The second phase included various hallucinations but also unusually clear perception of external reality. The final phase comprised return to everyday reality and customary identity. The central message of the instructions read aloud was to neither fear nor desire phenomena that arise during the psychedelic sessions. The readings promoted accepting whatever appears with the greatest possible serenity and continuing meditation in the

Ralph Metzner and Timothy Leary, 1963

The Big House, Millbrook 1963

awareness that any distraction or unsettling thoughts came from within one's self.[74] "If the manual is read several times before a session is attempted, and if a trusted person is there to remind and refresh the memory of the voyager during the experience, the consciousness will be freed from the games which comprise 'personality' and from positive-negative hallucinations that often accompany states of expanded awareness." (Leary, Metzner, Alpert 1971)

It was not long before Mexican media learned of the illustrious group of tourists and their drug course and reported on beach parties in "LSD Paradise." The training program was stopped by the police and the directors and participants expelled from the country. Attempts to continue the course in the Caribbean, first on Antigua then on Dominica, likewise ran afoul of local authorities. Struck financially and emotionally, the group returned to the United States. The exiles could not go back to Harvard and didn't wish to return to the house in Newton Center, but they also did not wish to abandon their promising experiments and courses or the growing number of interested and

paying devotees. The fact that Leary, Alpert and Metzner always moved in the best of society and maintained good contacts in wealthy circles was now beneficial.

Peggy Hitchcock was a course participant and a granddaughter of William Larimer Hitchcock, founder of Gulf Oil Company. She received permission from her brothers, twins Billy and Tommy Hitchcock, the former a successful stockbroker, to house the homeless group in a building on the Hitchcock family's three thousand acre estate in Millbrook, a small town eighty-six miles from New York City. The "Big House" with its sixty-three rooms was the largest of the various buildings on the enormous grounds. Leary, Alpert, Metzner and their colleagues could not imagine a better place to continue their communal form of living and the psychedelic experiments undisturbed.

Bureaucratic Hurdles

With their projects freed from the constraints of the university, the spectrum of psychedelic experiments at Millbrook assumed new dimensions. However, the necessary supply of psilocybin and LSD could no longer be

147

ordered through the university. Nevertheless, on December 30, 1962, Leary ordered one hundred grams of LSD and twenty-five kilos of psilocybin from the English company L. Light & Co., an English co-contractor of Sandoz, on Harvard University letterhead. The company's director, Henry de Laszlo, thanked Leary but asked for more information about the purpose of the unusually large quantities—that much LSD would suffice for a million trips at one hundred micrograms. At the same time, he informed Albert Hofmann with whom he seems to have been acquainted, and both wondered why the order was not sent to Sandoz in Basel or to its American branch. Leary, too, seems to have been uncertain and on January 11, 1963, probably unaware that it was Hofmann's birthday, he sent an order to Basel, this time addressed to the pharmaceutical company Hoffmann-La Roche. They in turn forwarded it to Sandoz. Again, Leary ordered one hundred grams of LSD and twenty-five kilos of psilocybin and inquired about the availability and price of N,N-dimethyltriptamine (DMT), N,N-diethyltriptamine (DET), 6-hydroxy DMT, psilocin (4-hydroxy dimethytriptamine) and bufotenine (5-hydroxy dimethyltriptamine); once again the order was sent on the letterhead of his former employer, with Leary's note that he was the director of a research project studying the effects of psychedelic drugs; tissue and animal tests and further studies with voluntary subjects were planned.

For this purpose, Leary, Alpert, Metzner, Walter Houston Clark, Huston Smith and oth-

> The dangers of external change appear to frighten us less than the peril of internal change. LSD is more frightening than the Bomb!
>
> *Timothy Leary and Richard Alpert*

ers founded the International Federation for Internal Freedom (IFIF) on January 23, 1963 in Millbrook as a nonprofit psychedelic, educational and research organization. Independent study groups were planned plus a magazine, Psychedelic Review. However, the quantities of psilocybin and LSD they had ordered failed to arrive. Instead, they received Albert Hofmann's letter of January 24th in which he expressed his interest and how pleased he was with these projects. He told Leary that Sandoz would gladly provide the product but only directly, not through intermediaries. He mentioned the inquiry to Light & Co. and asked Leary to turn to him personally in the future. That same day, Sandoz quoted IFIF an offer with details of price, delivery, packaging, and methods of payment. The price was 75 Swiss francs per gram for psilocybin and 508 Swiss francs per gram for LSD. IFIF was requested to include the import license from the proper authority with their final order. Sandoz added that "the other substances mentioned in your enquiry can in principle also be supplied by us and we would be very thankful to you if you would let us know by next mail the quantities you intend to order for each product to enable us to prepare a special offer for your university. You may be assured that we shall not fail to do all in our power to satisfy you in every respect and thanking you in anticipation of your further news." Five days later, Yves Dunant, the general manager of Sandoz circulated an internal memo: "Mr. Mason warns against sending Dr. Leary the 25 kilos of psilocybin and 500 grams of LSD he ordered.[75] We will receive a letter from Dr. Henze next week with the necessary explanations." Two days later, a telegram arrived at Sandoz from L.G. Wiggins, vice president of Harvard University in which he stated that Harvard was not responsible for Alpert's and Leary's order of psilocybin and LSD.

On February 7th, the promised letter from Dr. Carlo Henze, manager of the U.S. branch of Sandoz, reached Yves Dunant in Basel. Among other things, he reported: "That there is ample evidence that LSD has been smuggled into this country from various outside sources, including Mexico, Israel, and perhaps Italy and that the federal authorities have looked upon this with increasing suspicion. … The reason for this interest, aside from the bad publicity, is inherent in the fact that certain groups outside the medical field have been playing around with hallucinogenic substances and that the drug has also found its way into the hands of drug addicts and other fringes of psychopathic personality groups.… I am writing to you today to recommend that no shipment of these compounds be made directly from Basel to any person in this country." He confirmed that Harvard University was not informed of the order; he concluded that while Dr. Timothy Leary was still a member of the university and was making use of Harvard University stationary, that he knew that Leary had been fired because of the irresponsible manner in which he and his associates had used hallucinogenic substances.[76] In a separate letter to Renz and Hofmann, Henze requested that they refrain at all costs from doing any further business. His information stemmed from, among others, FDA employee Harold O'Keefe who told Henze that there was abuse, the substances had gotten into the wrong channels and, regarding LSD: "Of all drugs that we know about, we know of none which deserve controlled handling to a greater extent than these."

On February 13th, Leary again turned to Hofmann, repeated his order, and mentioned that journalists were interested in their projects for an article in *LIFE*. A down payment in the form of a check for over ten thousand dollars was enclosed. Meanwhile, Leary's inconsistencies with regard to Harvard and the future direction of his projects had turned Hofmann's initial interest and delight into growing annoyance. His irritation shows in his handwritten note at the reference to media attention in the letter: "That apparently is the most important thing." Leary continued: "We feel that we are engaged in furthering the important and exciting work that you began. Life gets complicated at times when some of our colleagues fail to grasp its significance. Life must be equally complicated for you." Again Hofmann noted by hand: "Certainly after this letter!" The tone of Hofmann's response is businesslike but notably less friendly than in earlier letters: "Needless to say, our company will proceed in this matter strictly according to FDA regulations." And, "I note with some concern from your communication that you have given your research project a publicity (e.g. invitation to *LIFE* reporters) which can only be injurious to the scientific clarification of questions connected with the use of these substances." For its part, Sandoz sent Leary's check back to him and turned down the order for lack of an import license.

Leary and his fellow campaigners at IFIF still did not give up, as can be seen from Hofmann's internal communication of February 28th regarding a phone call from Richard Alpert: "Without prior notice I received a call from Dr. R. Alpert, a colleague of Dr. Leary, Harvard University, Cambridge, USA. He asked whether the order for one kilogram of psilocybin and one hundred grams of LSD had arrived and what our response was. I filled him in regarding the contents of our written response to Dr. Leary that should arrive shortly. Richard Alpert again explained the basis and goal of IFIF's approach. Since Sandoz USA apparently was not willing to take over distribution of LSD and psilocybin or responsibility for their use with respect to the FDA, IFIF had constituted itself as the central contact for a large number of research groups to relieve Sandoz of this task and enable the projects to continue their research with these substances. Based on past negotiations with the FDA, he believed that recognition of IFIF as a sponsor was forthcoming. As soon as they received the required approval from the health authority, IFIF would enter into a contract with other pharmaceutical companies for delivery if Sandoz chose not to supply the substances."

Leary made one more attempt; his letter of March 6th which spoke euphorically of IFIF landed on Hofmann's desk. A check accompanied the same order as received previously, this time for five thousand dollars, which Sandoz returned on March 19th. Hofmann became unsettled and made inquiries with several friends about Leary and their assessment of his character and the activities of IFIF. Among these contacts was a letter to Aldous Huxley on March 11th in which he summarized events up until then and asked him for information: "Some weeks ago our firm received an inquiry signed by Dr. Leary of the Harvard University for the delivery of 500 gr LSD and 25 kg Psilocybin to be used for the research project of the IFIF. Unfortu-

nately, the LSD, in connection with the Thalidomide-Affair and to some cases of misuse with Psilocybin and LSD, and to which greatest and widest publicity was given for the sole purpose of sensation, was classified as a very dangerous drug. These events caused our branch company in U.S.A. to stop delivery of those substances. It looked as if the IFIF could and would take the responsibility for the distribution and application of Psilocybin and LSD towards the FDA. In the above-mentioned inquiry Dr. Leary informed us that he would procure the necessary licenses from the FDA. With the reservation that the 'Clearance' by the FDA had to be settled, we sent in our quotation. After a short time, we received a greater order for LSD and Psilocybin and a cheque was enclosed for an advanced payment, but the 'Clearance' was missing. Furthermore, we got a very unfavorable impression by the fact that in the letter containing the order special attention was called to a visit by *LIFE* reporters and their great interest in the activities of the IFIF. In doing this the whole project seems to be treated with hasty publicity and undesirable sensation.

These were the reasons why our firm could not accept the order. Delivery is, of course, only possible, if the official licence [sic] from the FDA can be presented.... As you of course know, I am also personally convinced that the psychedelic substances offer, besides their usefulness in psychotherapy, as consciousness expanding drugs for educational purposes and for self-knowledge new and not yet fully explored possibilities. Unfortunately, the danger of an uncontrolled or unserious application with undue publicity and sensation is very great and

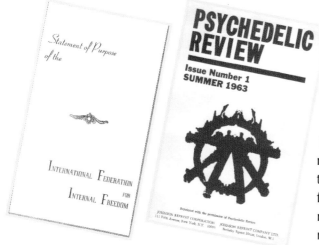

therefore the control of distribution and availability is of greatest importance.

In our Western civilization the Tabu [sic] is missing which regulates the use of psychedelic drugs by primitive people. It is difficult to replace Tabu by government regulations and therefore it is of paramount importance to know what kind of persons and organizations are dealing with the application and distribution of psychedelic drugs."

Huxley answered him on March 21st: "I have been annoyed and disturbed by the stupid and sensational publicity surrounding LSD and also by the cases of misuse which occasionally occur. Not wishing to add to the publicity, I have refused all invitations, in recent months to write articles about LSD or to speak over the radio. What is needed now is not talk, but solid work on the experimental-psychological and psychotherapeutic levels.

I have known Dr. Leary and his colleague Dr. Alpert for several years and have discussed their projects with them. … In general I am of [the] opinion that Leary and Alpert have done some very valuable pioneering work. They have had enthusiastic collaborators

of great ability such as Dr. Huston Cummings Smith, Professor of Comparative Religion at the Massachusetts Institute of Technology, and Dr. Alan Watts, the well known orientalist."

Huxley's favorable and supportive endorsement of Leary and Alpert succeeded in quieting Hofmann's mistrust, but changed nothing in his and Sandoz' position not to complete an order without approval from the FDA. Since the authorizations never arrived, Leary's repeated orders remained unfilled.

The refusal from Basel did not stop the psychedelic pioneers in Millbrook from carrying on with their studies and experiments. They were able to procure the necessary substances through other channels. The researchers gave lectures at universities and scientific conferences and published articles in professional journals. Interested and curious visitors came from around the world for discussions and psychedelic experiences, among them: Writer Robert Anton Wilson, later known as co-author of the *Illuminatus!* trilogy; London psychiatrist R.D. Laing, cofounder of the anti-psychiatric movement; Paul Krassner, journalist and publisher of the magazine *The Realist*, Willem A. Nyland, a longtime student of Gurdjieff, and many other friends and acquaintances from their Harvard days.

The Woman from Washington

She was attractive, blond, artistic, and the mistress of U.S. president John F. Kennedy, whom she had met in 1938 at the tender age of sixteen at a ball and on numerous occasions after that. By her mid-forties, Mary Pinchot Meyer was the ex-wife of CIA agent Cord Meyer and an avowed pacifist concerned about the course of history and the acute tensions between her country and the Soviet Union over the 1962 Cuban missile crisis. Timothy Leary's reputation as the talented leader of the psychedelic experiments at Harvard convinced Mary Meyer that he was the right person for her plans. In September 1963 she appeared at Millbrook and asked Leary to instruct her in guiding psychedelic sessions which she hoped to conduct with important people in Washington to convince those charged with U.S. foreign policy of the risks and futility of Cold War tactics. Only when she mentioned that President Kennedy would also be among those select did Leary stop encouraging her to bring them to Millbrook for sessions conducted by him. Subsequent meetings with her appear to have been fruitful as was an LSD trip taken together. There has never been any evidence that John F. Kennedy ever took LSD. Mary Pinchot Meyer's biographer wrote: "Mary's visits to Timothy Leary during the time she was also Kennedy's lover suggest that Kennedy knew more about hallucinogenic drugs than the CIA might have been telling him.... But the timing of her visits to Timothy Leary do coincide with her known private meetings with the president.[78]

There is controversy over whether or not the assassination of President Kennedy on November 22, 1963, was due to his foreign policy that emphasized peace and international understanding and disturbed the influential and powerful armaments industry and the military. Also

> The basic problems facing the world today are not susceptible to a military solution.
>
> *John F. Kennedy*

Mary Pinchot Meyer (r.), John F. Kennedy

disputed is the speculation of some chroniclers that LSD experiences could have induced a corresponding change in his consciousness and behavior. In any case, Leary received a phone call in early December he had been expecting from Meyer after Kennedy's death: "They couldn't control him anymore. He was changing too fast. They've covered everything up.... I gotta come see you. I'm afraid. Be careful." (Leary 1983, 194) Months passed and the two never met again. The murder of Mary Pinchot Meyer on October 12, 1964, remains unsolved. Similar to President Kennedy eleven months earlier, she died from two gun shots. According to her ex-husband Cord Meyer, it was "the same sons of bitches who murdered John F. Kennedy."[79]

Founding Years

In the spring of 1964, the Millbrook commune founded the Castalia Foundation along the lines of the spiritual community of the same name in Hermann Hesse's novel *The Glass Bead Game.* Hesse's Castalians maintained an ethically based educational system combining science and

PSYCHEDELIC SESSIONS

TIMOTHY LEARY & RALPH METZNER

FALL AND WINTER 1965/66
IN
NEW YORK, BOSTON, PHILADELPHIA, PITTSBURGH,
CLEVELAND, CINCINNATI, DETROIT, CHICAGO

THE CASTALIA FOUNDATION
announces
WEEKEND WORKSHOPS IN
CONSCIOUSNESS EXPANSION

Discussions and demonstrations of traditional and modern methods of expanding awareness. Eastern philosophic, Western scientific, religious, aesthetic and psychological interpretations of states of transcendent consciousness.

Permanent staff: Timothy Leary, Ph.D.; Richard Alpert, Ph.D; Ralph Metzner, Ph.D.

For information, write: CASTALIA FOUNDATION
BOX 175
MILLBROOK, N. Y. 12545

and body techniques. In the mid-1960s such courses drew many, especially young people seeking meaning.

Multimedia Spectacle

"Our purpose in being here is to expand our awareness. To assimilate and to see aspects of the psychedelic consciousness. To observe the phenomena of inner space. This is the Magic Theatre. ... So sit back and relax. Extend yourself to an aesthetic distance. You may have the opportunity of leaving your body. Leaving your mind. You are going on a voyage. The price of admission is your mind. For if you attempt to analyze and conceptualize, you will cheat yourself out of the opportunity to see things in a fresh manner." On April 5, 1965, Michael Hollingshead greeted visitors to the first performance of the Psychedelic Theatre with these words as they waited expectantly in New York's Village Vanguard jazz club in Greenwich Village for appearances by Richard Alpert, Ralph Metzner, Susan Leary, Alan Watts and jazz musicians Charles Mingus, Pete La Roca, Steve Swallow and Charles Lloyd. New kinds of lighting and

spirituality in socially beneficial symbiosis. The novel was written in the 1930s and first published in 1943 in Switzerland where Hesse lived after 1919. *The Glass Bead Game* was not published in Germany until after the Nazi era. Looking back, Hesse wrote: "It was for me to construct a spiritual space in which I could live and breathe. Despite all the poison released in the world, I had to make the realm of the mind and soul visible as existing and unconquerable. Hence my story was utopian, the image projected into the future, and the ugly present banished into a past that had been overcome."[80]

Leary's notions about a future society corresponded with Hesse's. He and his friends were seeking freedom for their experiments. To address their precarious financial situation, Leary and Metzner offered "Psychedelic Sessions" in Millbrook and other East Coast cities, weekend seminars on consciousness-expanding methods, such as meditation and yoga, without the use of psychedelics. Both of them had gathered experience in these disciplines during the past and on their visits to India in 1964 when they intensively studied Eastern mind

> Tim was just Tim. He didn't have the intellect that Ralph had and he didn't have the heart that I have, but he did have a sense of history and he was very much a scientist.
>
> *Ram Dass*

> Tim hated the word "guru." But, nevertheless, a regular cult built up around him. And you could not say he didn't enjoy it!"
>
> *Ralph Metzner*

sound effects reinforced the effect of the already innovatively choreographed show. The audience was enthralled.

Among the pioneers of the growing trend of multimedia shows in the 1960s were avant-garde artists Michael Callahan and Gerd Stern who founded USCO (The Company of U.S.) in 1962. They coined the term "intermedia," and the slogan "We are all one" hung above all their events. Together with lyricist/painter Steve Durkee, composer John Cage, artists Robert Rauschenberg, Richard Aldcroft and his Infinity Machine which projected kaleidoscopic images, they presented spectacular psychedelic art happenings combining technology and mysticism. Towers of slide projectors, stroboscopes, and audio systems sent a storm of abstract images, color compositions, and sound collages over an audience that had never before seen nor heard such a spectacle. Among the regular guests, co-producers, and contributors were the communications theorist and "Magician of the Media Age" Marshall McLuhan and the architect and philosopher R. Buckminster Fuller, coiner of the expression "Spaceship Earth." In the months following the successful premier, Leary and Metzner, together with USCO, pre-sented their "Psyche-delic Explorations," talks and discussions about psychedelic themes accompanied by electronic sound and Indian ragas, on Monday evenings in New York's New Theatre.

> Many of us would never have tried psychedelics if it weren't for Leary's popularizing them.
>
> *Rick Strassman*

"Contact is the only love," Gerd Stern, 1963

Peace Tabernacle, USCO, 1967

Changes of All Kinds

This period of creative activity came to an abrupt end in December of 1965 when the commune in the Big House was evicted. The owners believed the scene had gotten completely out of hand. Ralph Metzner recalls: "I think our reputation in New York was: Let's go up to Millbrook for the weekend and have sex and take drugs." (Ram Dass, Metzner 2010, 125) This gave Leary and his new wife Rosemary a reason to travel to Mexico on vacation with Leary's children Jack and Susan. However, the trip ended at the border in Laredo where customs officials found a small amount of marijuana on Leary's daughter and arrested both her and her father but released them on bail with probation. Disenchanted, the family returned to Millbrook where they were taken in again because of their difficult straits on condition that they conduct themselves in a more orderly fashion. That winter, with the help of dozens of friends, Timothy and Rosemary Leary set up the Leary Defense Fund. To add to his fund, Leary began an extensive publicity campaign in the media through articles and lectures about the historical and socio-cultural significance of marijuana and psychedelics.

In New York, Michael Hollingshead had joined the Agora Scientific Trust of John Beresford and Jean Houston. He moved back to London in 1965, where he opened the World Psychedelic Center. His legendary mayonnaise jar had been spooned empty by then, but he was able to replenish it from a source in Czechoslovakia. Interested novices had the opportunity of taking a first LSD trip in his apartment in Chelsea.

Meanwhile, Richard Alpert also traveled to London where he met with psychiatrist R. D. Laing and took several LSD trips with him. Together, they delved into and discussed the spiritual and therapeutic aspects of such sessions. Afterward, Alpert traveled via France to India where he dedicated himself to deeper study of meditation and yoga. He found his Guru, Neem Karoli Baba, also known as Maharaj, and converted to Hinduism; then he later returned to the USA as Ram Dass, "servant of God." In the 1970s, he founded the Hanuman Foundation which was concerned with the spiritual education of society; and together with Larry Brilliant and former Merry Pranksters activist Wavy Gravy, he set up the Seva Foundation which promotes health in Asia and Africa. As a spiritual teacher, Ram Dass was extremely active over the next decades imparting instruction in meditation and spirituality.

Turn on, Tune in, Drop out

In his autobiography, Timothy Leary recounted that the slogan "turn on, tune in, drop out" came to him under the shower. (Leary 1983) However, according to John Perry Barlow (Ram Dass, Metzner 2010) it stems from Marshall McLuhan, coiner of the phrase "the medium is the message" and the term "global village" concerning the meteoric developments in human communication and their effects on the media landscape. McLuhan also advised Leary about his appearances in public: "Associate LSD with all the good things that the brain can produce—beauty, fun, philosophic wonder, religious revelation, increased intelligence, mystical romance." Leary should always smile as soon as he sees that he is being photographed, and McLuhan emphasized that he should "Wave reassuringly. Radiate courage. Never complain or appear angry. ... A confident attitude is the best advertisement."[82] For Leary this advice came at an opportune moment. The youth movement of the 1960s was nearing its peak. The great majority of young people who identified with this subculture in the U.S. supported Leary's ideas about a new society built upon peace and mutual understanding. For their part, representatives of the social order of that time had problems with the former Harvard psychologist's concerns and expressed their vehement disagreement. The mood began to shift. Leary and LSD had long been the talk of the town and the entire country as leading media fed the hysteria about drugs with sensational material. Coverage was one-sided, seldom documented, and based mostly on statements from scientists who strictly rejected psychedelics or tendentious statements from agencies and government officials.

Local sheriff G. Gordon Liddy had long viewed Leary and the wild doings in Millbrook with suspicion, and for him, the right moment seemed to have arrived. Accompanied by thirty deputy sheriffs, he conducted a nighttime raid on the main building. The police found only a small amount of marijuana but that sufficed for Leary's arrest, even though it could not be proven to be his. This was not enough for a jail term, so he was again released on probation. A few years later, in 1972, Sheriff Liddy was sentenced to twenty years in prison as the leader of the burglars who broke into Democratic Party headquarters in Washington, D.C. to steal files meant to strengthen the reelection campaign of Republican President Richard Nixon. The incident, known as the Watergate Scandal, eventually led to Nixon's resignation; Liddy was released after serving four of his twenty years. Some years later, after Leary also had his prison time behind him, they began to appear in public together to debate the question "Duty or Freedom?" Their joint appearances, especially at colleges, delighted students who sided with Leary but gave Liddy due respect for having the courage to cross swords on stage with the champion of psychedelic and social freedom.

In allusion to the society of truth seekers in Hermann Hesse's novel *Journey to the East*, Leary founded the League for Spiritual Discovery on September 19, 1966, and registered it as a religious community. As the initials of the parent organization indicate, the holy sacraments were not bread and wine. Leary used an institutional vessel, this time a church, to spread his ideas and vision of a free culture based on individual responsibility. He, his wife Rosemary, Ralph Metzner, their friends and colleagues, called these psychedelic sessions "festivals;" multimedia events, lectures, music, light shows organized in Millbrook and New York. Leary's multimedia show *The Death of the Mind* was based on a scene in the Magic Theater

> What we have been, what we now are, we shall not be tomorrow.
>
> Ovid

in Hesse's novel *Steppenwolf*. With a group of New York filmmakers and artists, Ralph Metzner presented *The Illumination of the Buddha*. The shows were presented in other cities as well and even made it to stages on the West Coast. Bob Lowe and his students spliced together scenes cut from various shoots into the film *Turn On, Tune In, Drop Out*. On May 11, 1967, it appeared in movie theaters where it had a run of only one week. The main character, LSD, had meanwhile been outlawed, and the distributor pulled the film for fear of sanctions from the authorities.

The criminalization of LSD and other psychedelics made all further legal experiments with them impossible in Millbrook. The growing uproar surrounding Timothy Leary and the activities of the commune with its ever-changing residents and visitors led Ralph Metzner to leave the place he would always remember as an important milestone in his personal development with extremely mixed feelings. He moved to New York where he delved into the theories of Wilhelm Reich, and like Richard Alpert, occupied himself with yoga and meditation, but continued to visit Millbrook on weekends.

On the political stage, the U.S. government exhibited extreme con-cern with rampant illegal consumption of LSD among youth and the associated social and cultural up-heavals. Political and military figures were startled when otherwise peaceable hippies began anti-war demonstrations after the U.S. began bombing North Vietnam in March 1965 and invaded with ground troops shortly afterward. In the spring of 1966, the U.S. Senate began the first LSD hearings and discussed the entire spectrum of LSD use—as a therapeutic tool and as a weapon by the CIA—and subpoenaed pertinent representatives.

Senator Robert F. Kennedy questioned Timothy Leary, among others, who presented his typical mix of fact, fiction, and fun with customary rhetorical brilliance which hit home with very few senators. Attitudes hardened, and the chasm between the establishment and innovators grew. Up until the time LSD and all other psychedelics were declared illegal, Leary had spoken out for their controlled and responsible consumption. He expressed this in his testimony to the U.S. Senate and had no objections were the government to take over the control of LSD instead of a radical ban which he thought would only encourage underground production and the black market.

Timothy Leary, Human Be-In, Golden Gate Park, January 14, 1967

Fuel of the Sixties

It is not surprising that LSD first came into circulation as an inebriating drug in the United States, the country in which industrialization, urbanization, and mechanization, even of agriculture, are most broadly advanced. These are the same factors that have led to the origin and growth of the hippie movement that developed simultaneously with the LSD wave. The two cannot be disassociated. *Albert Hofmann, 1980*

A Molecule Changed the World

No other psychoactive substance has changed the world more fundamentally than that molecule whose unsuspected effect Albert Hofmann experienced in Basel on April 19, 1943. That same year, physicists at Los Alamos opened the Pandora's Box of the twentieth century and developed the atomic bomb. Two years later it was dropped on Hiroshima and Nagasaki with an effect more deadly than anything previously known. Researchers of consciousness, philosophers, and psychologists spoke of the effects of LSD as the "spiritual atom bomb," an apt comparison in many respects as history would show. After attending a concert by the Grateful Dead, the hippie and acid rock group of the 1960s *par excellence*, eighty-year old mythologist Joseph Campbell commented: "The Dead-

There is the highly significant timing of the discovery of LSD – in 1943, at the height of WWII, within months of Enrico Fermi's fist controlled nuclear chain reaction, which led directly to the building of the atomic bomb; as if it was to be a kind of psycho-spiritual antidote to this death weapon.

Ralph Metzner, 2008

heads are doing the dance of life and this, I would say, is the answer to the atomic bomb."[84] In his address talk at the International Symposium, "LSD - Problem Child and Wonder Drug," held in 2006 in Basel, American publicist Michael Horowitz described LSD as *The Antidote to Everything*. He mentioned that Aldous Huxley speculated as he wrote his novel *Brave New World* that the antidote to the modern world would be the discovery of a blessed drug that could bring genuine ecstasy. The person who found such a substance would be among the greatest benefactors of a suffering humanity.[85] Oil and LSD, Horowitz said, are both fuels, both have their high peaks, but only one will someday be exhausted. He cited Timothy Leary who wrote in 1963: "The nervous system can be changed, integrated, expanded in its function. These possibilities naturally threaten every branch of the Establishment. The dangers of external change appear to frighten us less than the peril of internal change. LSD is more frightening than the Bomb!" (Leary 1970)

158

DROP ACID
NOT
BOMBS !!

Horowitz concluded that 1943 was important as the year of the birth of an all-purpose antidote, another kind of bomb, an epiphany bomb. Useful antidotes are hard to find, ecstatic adventures should not be missed.[86]

The Bohemians of Manhattan

For most Americans, WWII was far away across the Atlantic. They knew it only from radio, newspapers, and the few living newsreel images in movie theaters. After the Allied invasion of the coast of Normandy in June 1944, they expected the war to end soon. The clique of students at Columbia University in New York and their friends, among them poet Allen Ginsberg, writer Jack Kerouac, his buddy Neal Cassady, and other young literati and artists, all yearned for peace and freedom. In 1948, writer William S. Burroughs joined them. In the 1950s, they were the most prominent representatives of the beatniks, a generation in ferment. They took leave of the university context and sought a more exciting life, different from that of their parents. With the books they wrote, they made literary history.

The term "Beat Generation" was coined by Jack Kerouac;[87] their works[88] became the seedbed of a primarily literary subculture and contained all the elements to be found a few years later among the hippies: Rejection of a one-dimensional materialistic world view, pursuit of a lifestyle of hedonistic excess, interest in Eastern philosophy, drug experiments, and alternative forms of communal life and sexuality. A group of young writers, which included Kenneth Rexroth, Michael McClure, Gary Snyder,

Philip Lamantia and others, formed what became known as the "San Francisco Renaissance," the 1940's beatnik scene on the West Coast. Poet and City Lights bookseller Lawrence Ferlinghetti published their books as well as those of the New York beats drawn to San Francisco where the connoisseurs of the art of living met for stimulating drinks and discussions in the now historic Vesuvio bar in the trendy North Beach district.

The poets were young, the print runs of their books small, their influence on society modest. While many young people and intellectuals took notice, conservative circles disapproved of their provocations and obscenities. Memories of the horrors of WWII were still raw and the excesses of the growing Cold War were already casting crippling shadows over society, culture and politics. But the seeds had been sown and, with the birth of the counterculture of the 1960s, they began to sprout.

From the Laboratory into the Cuckoo's Nest

Whether under the care of responsible physicians or in the experiments of the intelligence services, LSD got into the heads of people whose brains were ready and open to learning its potential for expanding consciousness and heightening creativity, and were willing to implement it.

Aspiring writer Ken Kesey enrolled at Stanford University in 1959 to take graduate courses in "Creative Writing" while he worked on his first manuscript. To afford the tuition and supplement his pocket money, he took a job as a night aide in the psychiatric ward of the Veterans

"Flashback" cartoon by Ron Cobb

(l. to r.) Jack Kerouac, Allen Ginsberg, William S. Burroughs, 1944

Hospital in Menlo Park, California. Shortly after starting, he took part, unsuspecting like all the other voluntary subjects, in a MK-Ultra study financed by the CIA to investigate the effects of psychedelics. Kesey's LSD experiments turned out positively; he enjoyed them completely, underwent a creative boost, and processed the experiences together with his adventures in the psychiatric ward, into his novel *One Flew Over the Cuckoo's Nest.* (Kesey 1972) With Jack Nicholson in the leading role, the tragicomedy was filmed by Milos Forman in 1975 and won five Oscars. In an interview shortly before his death in 2001, Kesey repeatedly claimed that LSD substantially enhanced his creativity: "There's something about seeing reality with a new light shining on it that goes right from your eyes to your fingertips. I would not have been able to write so well without LSD. I'll take acid every time, it's a short cut to enlightenment given us at the end of the century for

those of us who wanted to go on to better realities and understand it with respect: the door's been opened and this is the key that opened it.'"

Can You Pass the Acid Test?

Ken Kesey's doors of perception had opened wide and the key stayed in his hands. A friend provided him with a different key, one to the hospital medicine cabinet, and Kesey succeeded in smuggling out a considerable supply of LSD pills. That made it possible for him to realize his plan to share what were for him the undeniable benefits of LSD with as many people as possible.

With a group of artist and writer friends, among them

> I got high on psychedelics before I was ever drunk. I never smoked. Then LSD came by. And to me it was the most wonderful thing that had ever happened. ... And, of course, the best drugs ever were manufactured by the government.
>
> *Ken Kesey, 1999*

Neal Cassady, Carolyn "Mountain Girl" Adams, activist Wavy Gravy, journalist Paul Krassner, and writer Stewart Brand, the technology geek among the early acid heads, Kesey founded the Merry Pranksters in the spring of 1964. They bought an old school bus, painted it from front to rear in the most dazzling colors and christened it "Further." In mid-June, they left San Francisco on their great psychedelic tour of America. The Warlocks, a rock group built around guitarist Jerry Garcia, accompanied them. When they learned that this name was already being used by another group, they changed it to The Grateful Dead. The cheerful troupe intended to liberate youth from their conformity and lethargy. The vast quantity of LSD tablets originally intended for secret CIA research projects now became fuel for equally momentous experiments—the legendary Acid Tests.

The Merry Pranksters created a furor wherever they went; their Acid Test Parties surprised expectant youth, frightened their parents, and overwhelmed politicians. The Grateful Dead played, there was dancing and laughter and LSD in generous supply. Posters lettered large with the question "Can You Pass the Acid Test?" announced their events on short notice. This question about passing the psychedelic initiation was a serious one. "Kesey and the Pranksters dropped a tab of LSD into the belly of America. They wanted to turn the country on,

> As an innocent girl from a middle class New York family in the Bay Area, I came to these crazies! And then LSD yet! I thought: Yes! That's it! I was convinced that within one or two years no one would wear a tie—worldwide! And that everybody would love each other!
>
> *Carolyn Garcia*

to do for the nation what LSD had done for them as individuals and as a community. They wanted to show Cold War America an alternative and apparently a much more adventurous, harmonious, and fun way to live." And "Further" became a symbol: "The bus was both the vehicle by which to make this new lifestyle visible and a prototype of that lifestyle itself. Are you 'on the bus'? asked the Pranksters, 'or not'"? (Turner 2006, 63)

Ken Kesey and the Pranksters worried little about the consequences of their Acid Tests. Although most of the thousands of new LSD consumers managed this carefree form of introduction into the extraordinary realms of their consciousness fairly well, the charge of a certain degree of irresponsibility in their handling of the powerful substance is valid in retrospect. At least the settings promoted positive trips; the intention of the organizers to challenge the banality of a superficial society met a need. In any case, they earned the monument Tom Wolfe erected for them with his novel *The Electric Kool-Aid Acid Test*. (Wolfe 1968)

Timothy Leary and his team valued and praised LSD just as highly, but they warned against improper use. However, this was not the reason the Pranksters did not find Leary when they visited Millbrook in the summer of 1964. He was on an experimental three-day trip, and the people in Millbrook were reluctant to give Kesey and his companions some of their LSD since their own supply was running low. (Wolfe 1968) But later on, the members of the best known psychedelic communes of the East and West Coasts became close friends and appeared together on many different occasions.

Carolyn Adams, later, the
wife of Jerry Garcia, with
daughter Sunshine

Ken Kesey

Ken Kesey aboard the bus Further, during the Summer
Solstice Great Bus Race, Aspen Meadows, Tesuque,
New Mexico, 1969

The Hog Farm

Hugh Romney was reputedly given his stage name of Wavy Gravy by Blues singer and guitar player B.B. King. Romney was active in the avant garde scene in Greenwich Village in the Early 1960s and then went to California where he and his wife, with various friends, including some Merry Pranksters eventually moved to a hog farm in Sunland, Tujunga, California. At that time the Merry Pranksters were traveling on the West Coast in their bus "Further" putting on the Acid Tests with their house band, the Warlocks, who later became the Grateful Dead.

The hog farm still exists as a communal family in Laytonville and Berkeley, California. Larry Brilliant and his wife, Girija, Wavy Gravy, Ram Dass and an eclectic group of friends established the Seva Foundation, a public health organization working primarily in sight restoration and eye health internationally.

Chemistry in the Underground

In the early 1960s, the use of LSD, then still legal in the USA, spread rapidly among young people. Anonymous production grew apace in backrooms, garages, basements or professional laboratories equipped for that purpose. Then in 1962, the U.S. Congress passed new drug safety guidelines, and the FDA restricted the use of LSD to research, prompting the first arrests for alleged misuse. That same year, the first underground lab was dismantled,

> If it can be saved at all, the world will be saved by rebels.
>
> *André Gide*

and sixty-two thousand doses of mediocre quality LSD were confiscated.[89]

LSD, in substantially greater quantities and considerably better quality, originated with Augustus Owsley Stanley III. Born January 19, 1935, he arrived at the University of California at Berkeley in 1963. As a young student there, he had his first experiences with drugs and decided, with the help of his girlfriend who was a doctoral candidate in chemistry, to manufacture LSD in his bathroom. Before long, the police raided his home laboratory but found only precursor chemicals. Stanley then moved to the Los Angeles area, began professional production of LSD and, within the shortest possible time, distributed an estimated one to ten million doses before he headed back north. In July 1966, he met Tim Scully; within a year they had produced around three hundred thousand doses of high quality LSD in Richmond, California, at a potency of 250 to 300 micrograms, which became known as "White Lightning" and sold at two dollars a dose. Other legendary products they brought to market included "Monterey Purple" and "Owsley." Thereafter known as Owsley "Bear" Stanley, he became the major provider for the Merry Pranksters and their Acid Tests.

Owsley Stanley (l.) and Jerry Garcia, 1969

The Trips Festival

After countless Acid Test Parties, Ken Kesey, Stewart Brand, and the rest of the Pranksters organized the Trips Festival in the Longshoreman's Hall in San Francisco in January 1966 with the support of impresario Bill Gra-

> Myth is the secret opening through which the inexhaustible energies of the cosmos pour into the human cultural manifestation.
>
> *Joseph Campbell*

ham. Owsley Stanley financed the event, bought the Grateful Dead their first functional amplifier system so that in the future they could appear before a larger audience, and became their sound engineer. Gerd Stern of the Company of Us came from New York and installed his projectors and stroboscopes. The Trips Festival was the biggest psychedelic event, the largest LSD party on the American West Coast. In the meantime, California had already declared LSD illegal and posters promised a psychedelic experience without LSD. Nonetheless, as expected, more than enough was available. A shopping bag full of freshly made LSD from Stanley's trusty lab was passed around. It was a unique

The Grateful Dead in the Greek Theater, Berkeley, June 1985

Concert Poster, 1966

meeting of beatniks of the 1950s with hippies of the 1960s, the psychedelic scene of the West Coast and the turned-on technophile multimedia scene of the East Coast. As Jerry Garcia remembered it: "Thousands of people, man, all helplessly stoned, all finding themselves in a roomful of other thousands of people… It was magic—far out beautiful magic." In 1967, Owsley Stanley was arrested and sentenced to three years in prison. After his release, he continued to work for the Grateful Dead. In 1996, he moved to Australia with his wife Sheilah; he died on March 12, 2011, in a traffic accident. The entire output of his LSD production is estimated at around 460 grams which is about four million trips.

Dionysian Festivals

The lyricist and song writer Robert Hunter is known for the poetic and playful texts he wrote for the Grateful Dead. When talking about the creative stimulus of LSD, he enthused: "Sit back picture yourself swooping up a shell of purple with foam crests of crystal drops soft nigh they fall unto the sea of morning creep-very-softly mist…and then

sort of cascade tinkley-bell like (must I take you by the hand, ever so slowly type) and then conglomerate suddenly into a peal of silver vibrant, uncomprehending, blood singingly, joyously resounding bells.[90] … By my faith, if this be insanity, then for the love of God permit me to remain insane." (McNally, 2002, 42-43) Like Kesey, Hunter was one of the volunteer subjects in the CIA's LSD experiments at Stanford University. The intelligence service didn't know what to do with his boost in creativity. He used it himself to write *Dark Star*, one of the most popular songs of the Dead.

The Grateful Dead gave their concerts the same progression as an LSD trip, providing their audience an optimal set and setting. That was especially true of the legendary, long improvisations of guitarist Jerry Garcia, dubbed "Captain Trips" by Deadheads. The band's relationship to its fans, the "Deadhead" family," was special and involved mutual appreciation. The Dead didn't perform for an "audience," they made music for their community. From the group's first concerts, psychedelics were a part of Deadhead culture: "Feelings

165

of openness with others was [sic] often facilitated by the use of hallucinogenic drugs," as Deadhead Amy Cross explained, and "these experiences would often strip away defense mechanisms built up over a lifetime, and allow people to see others more directly, and thus increase the feelings of family relationship." (Carroll 2007)

Joseph Campbell

We have world-renowned mythologist Joseph Campbell to thank for deep insights into the social and cultural function of legends, fairy tales and traditions of human development. He advised his friend George Lucas during the making of the first trilogy of the Star Wars films regarding the life of heroic Luke Skywalker. At the invitation of guitarist Bob Weir and percussionist Mickey Hart, Campbell attended a Grateful Dead concert in February 1985. Although he had traveled much during his life, and seen and experienced many things, he was excited and overwhelmed by the performance as he described it in a lecture shortly thereafter: "I had a marvelous experience two nights ago. I was invited to a rock concert. I'd never seen one. This was a big hall in Berkeley and the rock group were the Grateful Dead, whose name, by the way, is from the Egyptian Book of the Dead. And these are very sophisticated boys. This was news to me.... Rock music had never seemed that interesting to me. ... But when you see a room with eight thousand young people for five hours going through it to the beat of these boys.... The genius of these musicians—these three guitars and two wild drummers.... Listen, this is powerful stuff! And what is it? The first thing I thought of was the Dionysian festivals, of course. This

energy and these terrific instruments with electric things that zoom in.... This is more than music. It turns something on in here (the heart). And what it turns on is life energy.

This is Dionysus talking through these kids. Now I've seen similar manifestations, but nothing as innocent as what I saw with this bunch. This was sheer innocence. And when the great beam of light would go over the crowd you'd see these marvelous young faces in sheer rapture—for five hours! Packed together like sardines!! Eight thousand of them! This is a wonderful, fervent loss of self in the larger self of a homogeneous community. This is what it's all about!" [91]

Hippies? Hippies!

Who were these hippies, few of whom would have called themselves such but most of whom would have considered themselves to be "hip." People in the smoke-filled jazz clubs of the 1940s and 1950s were called "hip" or "hipsters." The term was used by African-Americans who wanted to indicate that they were up on the latest trends. Linguists derive "hip" from the West-African "hipi," which meant "to open one's eyes." [92] Many young people in the 1960s had their minds opened after they saw through the senseless affluence and conspicuous consumption of middle-class culture and the inflated scenarios of Cold War intimidation. In his 1961 essay "What's Wrong with the Clubs," Kenneth Rexroth used the expressions "hipster" and "hippies" to refer to young people infatuated with beatnik nightlife; Michael Fallon was first to use the term "hippie" to describe counterculture in San Francisco in his article in the fall of 1965.[93] As successors to the beatniks, hippies expanded and practiced the beatnik alternative world view—their life style made cultural history.

A Peaceful Cultural Revolution

The youth movement of the 1960s, which largely originated with hippies in the USA and England, was a psychedelically inspired cultural revolution without bloodshed. It was fueled by LSD, rightly called a "politically active pharmaceutical."[94] "Nevertheless, the socially and culturally motivated upheavals of the earlier 1960s should not be considered identical to those that occurred in 1968, when students around the world vehemently campaigned for primarily political changes. Philosopher and political scientist Herbert Marcuse (1898–1979), whose theories significantly influenced the student movement of the 1960's in Germany, succeeded in bringing down the protests and revolt to a common denominator. He claimed that "Critical Reason" is characterized by precisely the kind of imaginative experimentation being practiced by the counterculture: "Such commitment and creativity is able to break free from the predominant fixation on middle-class instrumental reason and discover new ways to live and new forms of consciousness."[95] His commentary convincingly augmented the ideas and theses of Aldous Huxley, Ken Kesey, and Timothy Leary regarding psychedelic liberation: "The *trip* comprises the experience that artificially and briefly replaces the self formed by established culture. At the same time, artificial and private liberation anticipates in distorted form a requirement of social liberation; the

revolution has to be a revolution of perception that accompanies the material and spiritual modification of society and produces a new context. Awareness of the necessity of a revolution in the manner of perceiving, of a new sensorium, is perhaps the true kernel of the psychedelic pursuit."[96]

For the youth of the 1960s, creating a counterculture was, to some extent, a moral duty in the face of such blatant social evils: Wars, racism, sexual discrimination, hostility towards sensuality, environmental degradation. LSD helped to sensitize and enhance awareness of these issues. It was a change of spirit that caused so much commotion in the establishment that President Richard Nixon declared Timothy Leary to be "public enemy number one" shortly before he himself had to step down because of criminal scheming in connection with the Watergate scandal.

When Albert Hofmann was asked, in connection with the celebration of his 100th birthday, whether he would subscribe to the old hippie dictum, "if all generals would take a successful LSD trip, world peace would follow more or less automatically," he carefully replied, "I cannot answer that.... But I think it would be worth a try. That reminds me of a story: once a young woman came to my laboratory. I asked her, how she got into the factory and she said in English: 'I can pass everywhere, I am an angel.' And then she said: 'You have to help me see that the American president gets LSD.' Her name was Joan, like Saint Joan

> I think it needs be established, firmly, flatly, and finally, that what we call the '60s would never have happened had it not been for the psychedelic sacraments.
>
> *Tom Robbins*

Nick Sand in his laboratory, late 1960s

Nick Sand on his houseboat in Sausalito, north of San Francisco, late 1960s

Nick Sand with Amanda Feilding, director of The Beckley Foundation, Basel 2006

of the French. I still ask myself how she ever got into the Sandoz building. Of course I couldn't give her anything." (Bröckers, Liggenstorfer 2006)

Chemists for a Better World

Whereas the father of Nicholas Sand worked, among other jobs, as a chemist on the Manhattan Project for the American atom bomb program during WWII, his son, born in 1941, turned to the same profession but applied it to peaceful applications and questions. At age fifteen, he began to practice yoga, took an interest in spirituality and Eastern philosophy, and in 1961 took his first mescaline trip, triggering a lifelong interest in psychedelics. While still in college, he regularly visited the commune in Millbrook and acquired his first experiences with LSD. After finishing a degree in anthropology, he decided to devote his life to the production of psychedelic drugs. Knowing that his behavior was criminal under prevailing law, he saw his disobedience as action in the service of a higher good. In 1967, he moved to San Francisco, set up a laboratory, and began producing DOM and MDA.[97]

A year later, he met Tim Scully whose fellow lab assistant, Owsley Stanley, was in prison; Scully now taught Sand how to make LSD. In their hidden lab in Windsor, California, north of San Francisco, they successfully produced LSD of the highest quality on their first try. Their "Orange Sunshine" became one of the most popular and well-known underground brands. Estimates of the quantity manufactured range from a few hundred thousand to several million doses. When they learned that penalties for drug crimes were determined according to the *weight* of the quantity confiscated rather

> When I took over production, I knew full well that I would land in jail eventually. The only question was when! But we had to do our thing! And took prison into account—like a sort of alternative service.
> For humanity!
>
> *Nick Sand, 2010*

than the number of doses, they came up with blotter paper as the vehicle for the substance instead of sugar cubes. As many as 900 trips could be dropped onto a sheet of blotter paper with a syringe, making it much easier to distribute.

However, the lab was discovered and both were arrested. Sand was sentenced to fifteen years but was paroled after nine. He used the opportunity to flee to Canada, set up a new lab, and in 1996, he was arrested again. His laboratory was so well equipped that the Royal Canadian Mounted Police used it as the set for their training videos. Sand remained in jail in Canada until the end of 2000 when he was extradited to the U.S. to complete his prison sentence. Shortly after his release, Nick Sand visited the LSD Symposium in Basel in January 2006 to pay his respects to the discoverer of LSD who had just turned one hundred. During an interview for the TV documentary *Inside LSD*, an extremely charming and good-humored gentleman spoke of the years he spent underground producing large quantities of LSD. Nick Sand had a clear conscience and did not regret his activities in the least. This attitude may help account for the fact that the interview was cut from the October 2009 broadcast of the film on the National Geographic Channel.[98] What was important to him, was a different and better future; as he said a year later: "We wanted to turn on the world. A world with colors and flowers, and temples with swans, you know, that was my vision!"[99]

Human Be-in poster,
Bowen & Mouse 1967

Flowers in Their Hair, Love in Their Hearts, LSD in Their Heads

In 1967, Scott McKenzie sang: "If you're going to San Francisco, Be sure to wear some flowers in your hair. … For those who come to San Francisco, Summertime will be a love-in there." The song traveled around the world. It became the anthem of California hippies and a symbol of the "Summer of Love." That "summer" began in mid-winter with a "Human Be-In" which drew over twenty thousand mostly young people to San Francisco's Golden Gate Park for a happening of a special kind. "Human" heralded a new humanity, the renewal of human values in the face of a Philistine society and bellicose politics, and "be-in" an apolitical coming together in contrast to the sit-ins used for strikes at American universities. Timothy Leary came from snowy Millbrook to mild California to recommend that participants "Turn On, Tune In, Drop Out." New York Beat poet Allen Ginsberg chanted Indian mantras, "cosmic breath modulations"[100], which he accompanied on his harmonium. The flower children sang "All You Need is Love," celebrating love with flower power and countered the horrors of the Vietnam War with "Make Love, Not

Parents who suspect their offspring are turned on via LSD should be suspicious if the youngsters suddenly espouse a oneness with God and the universe, if they are suddenly super-knowledgeable about life and love, if they hear and see things no one else does, and if their pupils are dilated.

Ann Honig, Journalist, 1967

War." The historic event was accompanied by the rock bands Big Brother and the Holding Company, Country Joe and the Fish, Jefferson Airplane, Quicksilver Messenger Service, and the Grateful Dead, all of which were founded in San Francisco in the mid-1960s. Not only the musicians, but most of the other performers and thousands of visitors were well acquainted with cannabis and LSD.

One neighborhood near Golden Gate Park, Haight-Ashbury, became famous in 1967 as the center of the Summer of Love and the American hippie movement. Almost daily, national media reported details on flipped-out kids, their colorful, offbeat clothing, the new psychedelic music style, and their drug culture attempting to interpret an entire generation's attitude towards life. *TIME* Magazine for July 17, 1967 headlined: "The Hippies: Philosophy of a Subculture." In August *CBS* aired its documentary: "The Hippie Temptation." Tens of thousands could not resist the temptation and streamed into the area around the intersection of Haight and Ashbury Streets dubbed "Hashbury" by writer Hunter S. Thompson. He wrote: "San Francisco in the middle sixties was a very special time and place to be ... but no explanation, no mix of words or music or memories can touch that sense of knowing that you were there and alive in that corner of time and the world. Whatever it meant...There was madness in any direction, at any hour... You could strike sparks anywhere. There was

> Rock music and drugs belong together like man and woman. One without the other is unthinkable. The song "Sex and Drugs and Rock and Roll" by Ian Dury gives you the program of the entire history of rock music.
>
> *Christian Rätsch*

a fantastic universal sense that whatever we were doing was right, that we were winning... And that, I think, was the handle—that sense of inevitable victory over the forces of Old and Evil. Not in any mean or military sense; we didn't need that. Our energy would simply prevail. We had all the momentum; we were riding the crest of a high and beautiful wave."[101]

The spirit of the hippies and the Summer of Love are still in the air of the neighborhood which has become a favorite destination for tourists from around the world. The head shops, which used to offer all imaginable paraphernalia for the sophisticated consumption of consciousness expanding drugs—and often those substances themselves in backrooms—have become souvenir shops. No summer lasts forever, no culture, nor counterculture or subculture. The Summer of Love in San Francisco and the Monterey International Pop Festival that was held in June of 1967 are widely regarded to have been the highpoints of the hippie movement. More than two hundred thousand people flocked to the County Fairgrounds in Monterey, that picturesque California coastal town, to hear the already famous rock groups.

The Diggers

They adopted the name of the original Diggers who, in the middle of the seventeenth century, proclaimed their vision of a society without private property and purchasable belongings. The American Diggers arose in San Francisco in the mid-1960s as a mix of young people from the beatnik underground and the artists' scene, the New Left, the human rights and peace movements. As the San Francisco Mime Troupe, they staged political street theater and happenings; as representatives of an alternative, libertarian tribal culture, they opened the first Free Clinic in Haight-Ashbury where they offered free treatment to drug addicts and aided the poor and homeless.

The Diggers' happening, "Death of a Hippie," symbolically carried the Summer of Love to its grave on October 6, 1967; that also signaled the end of the hippie movement for its "founding fathers." However, the initial and defining criteria of this historic and unique youth movement—expanded consciousness, altered perception of reality, social, cultural, and political change marked by a universal vision of a better world—are more relevant today than ever.

Sex and Drugs and Rock and Roll

The eroticizing properties of all kinds of psychoactive substances have been documented for thousands of years. Timothy Leary described LSD as "the most powerful aphrodisiac ever discovered by man." (Leary 1970) With inspiring songs, melodies and rhythms of pop and rock bands, with stimulating psychedelics, their unbounded zest for life and their light-hearted love lives, the hippies freed sexuality from the prudish fug of the 1950s. Throughout human history, religious or political watchdogs of public morality have repeatedly succeeded at tabooing all forms of sensuality, and time after time, social impetuses and upheavals are needed in order to reverse the inhibition of sexuality, exuberance and celebration. Renowned American journalist and Beat author Lawrence Lipton (1898–1975) is said to have "recommended that ethnologist Margaret Mead not seek 'the sunniest and simplest attitude towards sexuality' in Samoa" but among the hippies," and wrote: "As far as hippies are concerned, the sexual revolution is over and won." (Lipton 1965)

Michael Bowen evoked the distant past when he organized the first Human Be-In in San Francisco in 1967 and announced it on the cover of the *San Francisco Oracle* as the "Gathering of the Tribes." Ever since prehistoric times, the shaman beat the drum in monotone, hypnotic rhythms to induce trance states in the tribesmen. In many such sacred rituals, plant-based drugs enhanced perception in participants. When singing and dancing, they experienced extraordinary states of intoxication, felt literally beside themselves, received answers to pressing questions, and gained visions and insights into their futures. With the rise of monotheistic religions, the archaic customs of shamanic tribal rites were systematically suppressed but have experienced a revival since the 1960s.

For Hindus, Krishna ranks far up in the community of goddesses and gods; many believe he actually once lived. Krishna is also known as the incarnation of Vishnu as sensuous Govinda, the flute playing "cowboy." He is said to have once stolen the clothes of the Gopis, young shepherd girls, as they bathed in a river. He invited them to dance naked for him to his melodies. In return he promised: "Oh, chaste and pure girls, I know your hearts' desires and thoughts. I will fulfill your wishes; you shall count on my presence in the coming weeks and months."

The cult of Dionysus, named after the Greek god of wine,

> The road of excess leads to the palace of wisdom.
>
> *William Blake*

intoxication and ecstasy, was known for its orgiastic rites. There is dancing, flirting, drinking and feasting to the music of flutes and the rhythms of tambourines, and what today is known as "free love" was widely practiced between genders. As the son of Zeus and Demeter, goddess of fertility, Dionysus, in his aspect as Iacchus, also took part in the Eleusinian Mysteries at Eleusis: "The central idea of the elite was to drink wisely and suitably during the symposium. 'Suitably' meant to become drunk. Once achieved, one was held to be aristocratic, reputable, and an accessible human being by one's peers. Poets of antiquity spoke of this often."[102]

Martin Luther (1483–1546), the Reformation theologian and reformer, saw no reason not to praise zest for life along with the fear of God: "Whoever loves not wine, women, and song remains a fool his whole life long." And: "Young people should not be sad rather cheerful and happy. A cheerful nature befits youth." The Middle High German word *Minne* means "love." The Minnesingers, also known during the twelfth century as troubadours, lived during a time of societal and cultural transformation and, like hippies hundreds of years later, sang praises to love. A comparison of musical styles shows that: "Like Rock, Minnesang was made up of familiar subgenres such as those about love unfulfilled (elevated songs) and those about love consummated (dawn songs)," with the Minnesinger serving as singer/songwriter and the minstrels as the singers' back up bands.[103]

> The only people for me are the mad ones, the ones who are mad to live, mad to talk, mad to be saved, desirous of everything at the same time.
>
> *Jack Kerouac*

Sounds of the Sixties

Dynamically evolving during the 1960s, rock music reflected the attitudes of the younger generation and the viewpoints of the counterculture better than did any other art form. Within a very few years, it fanned out in a myriad of different stylistic directions strongly influenced by drugs, especially LSD. The earliest use of the term "psychedelic" in music was a version of "Hesitation Blues" by The Holy Modal Rounders, a folk duo familiar only to connoisseurs, on their debut album in 1964.[104]

In the mid-sixties, the genre later known as "psychedelic rock" or "acid rock" appeared in California. Its development was closely associated with hippie culture and was affected by the electrification of the folk scene. Pioneers of the genre were the Grateful Dead, Jefferson Airplane, the Electric Prunes, the Doors, and the Byrds. The word "psychedelic" first appeared in two album titles in 1966: *The Psychedelic Sounds of the 13th Floor Elevators* (by the 13th Floor Elevators, of course) and *Psychedelic Moods* by The Deep.

Singer-poet Jim Morrison and keyboardist Ray Manzarek founded The Doors in 1965. Morrison suggested the Los Angeles group's name after using mescaline, reflecting a link to psychedelics. He was inspired by lines from the poet William Blake: "If the doors of perception were cleansed everything would appear to man as it is, infinite."[105] With their debut album, they were among the first rock groups to break the usual convention of limiting songs to three-minutes with "The End."

That same year, the Jefferson Airplane from San Francisco played their first shows;

they are considered to be one of the most important representatives of psychedelic rock. Their first album *Jefferson Airplane Takes Off* appeared in 1966. Shortly thereafter, singer Grace Slick joined the band. Their second album *Surrealistic Pillow* followed in 1967 and contains her two best known songs which she wrote while with her previous band, The Great Society. They are "Somebody to Love" and especially "White Rabbit," which referred to the fictional world of Lewis Carroll's children's novel *Alice in Wonderland*, giving it a psychedelic slant but encoded to avoid censure and allowing it to be played on the radio.

Jimi Hendrix, genius of the guitar, also drew much of his musical inspiration from LSD trips—he named his band the Jimi Hendrix Experience. Their debut album in 1967 carried the title *Are You Experienced,* in keeping with Kesey's question "Can You Pass the Acid Test?"

The undisputed pioneers of psychedelic music in Europe included the Beatles and Pink Floyd who are considered to embody a prototypical psychedelic rock sound. The dividing line between psychedelic rock and other genres is fluid. Some music experts and historians include bands like Yes, King Crimson, Soft Machine, East of Eden, Hawkwind, Emerson Lake and Palmer in this genre. Music is by far the art form most frequently characterized by the word "psychedelic." However, the designation "psychedelic music" is vague and sometimes misleading because it was applied to completely different pieces and bands from folk to jazz. The

Album Cover for "Seven Up," by Walter Wegmüller

Grateful Dead, as the psychedelic band par excellence, in contrast to their extravagant concert appearances, sound like a normal country rock band on many studio recordings while the early works of Frank Zappa which contain many psychedelic sound elements are not included in this category due to his unequivocal rejection of drugs. In the mid-1960s, many jazz musicians like John Coltrane and Miles Davis were inspired by LSD, yet did not label their compositions and work as psychedelic. In Coltrane's *A Love Supreme* these influences can be clearly heard. The gifted saxophonist confirmed: "I perceived the interrelationship of all life forms." It's a matter of record that Charles Mingus, Rahsaan Roland Kirk, and Dizzy Gillespie turned on with LSD given to them by Timothy Leary and Allen Ginsberg.[106]

Typical attributes considered to be psychedelic in music were the application of feedback, wah-wah and echo e music using the sitar, and electronic instruments. The Mellotron or synthesizer, invented during this time, made novel "spacey" music possible with atmospheric floating sound carpets. Whether with the help of psychoactive substances or innovative recording techniques, the musicians' urge to experiment was unbounded. Elements of classical music also found their way into popular pieces, such as the trumpets and cellos on the Beatles' album, *Sgt. Pepper's Lonely Hearts Club Band*, or Procol Harum's "A Whiter Shade of Pale," influenced by Johann Sebastian Bach and considered by some to be psychedelic.

Lyrics of the period were influenced by Eastern religions or showed touches of surreal or esoteric color. Further influences flowed in from the writings of beatniks, science fiction and fantasy literature.

Hermann Hesse's legendary novel *Steppenwolf*, which appeared in 1927, is better known than the rock band of the same name which achieved great popularity on the West Coast in the late 1960s. Their hit, "Born to be Wild", quickly brought them worldwide acclaim as the title song to the cult film *Easy Rider*. In "The Pusher" they indicted profit-oriented traders of hard drugs; in "Don't Step on the Grass, Sam" they objected to Uncle Sam and authorities getting involved with regulating marijuana. Their "Magic Carpet Ride" takes listeners on a psychedelic trip with a "flying carpet."

The trend towards multimedia presentation, to a kind of psychedelic synthesis of the arts, had already begun with surreal band names such as Vanilla Fudge, Iron Butterfly or Quicksilver Messenger Service and could be seen in the graphically extravagant, brightly colored concert posters, fantastic record jacket designs, playful texts, and light shows which imitated the colorful intoxication of an LSD trip. Acoustic impressions of a trip were rendered in a piece by Pink Floyd, "Interstellar Overdrive" and in the album *Cottonwoodhill* by the group Brainticket, formed around the Belgian multi-instrumentalist Joël Vandroogenbroeck. Iron Butterfly induced a trip-like trance with their song "In-A-Gadda-Da-Vida."

Some bands were dubbed "psychedelic" because their members spoke euphorically about their drug experiences, others because their music lent itself so well to listening during a trip, even if the musicians had never taken LSD. The fact that most rock musicians of the time were inspired by Albert Hofmann's discovery and references to psychedelic experience were pervasive makes it difficult to differentiate styles. The media and censors seized upon the subject of intoxication among musicians and accused many groups of glorifying drugs, sometimes erroneously. That is how the single by The Byrds, "Eight Miles High," ended up on the banned playlist in the U.S. and was boycotted by radio stations, although its lyrics were merely describing guitarist Gene Clark's first plane trip to London.

In Germany, a new musical scene emerged in the late 1960s called "Krautrock" that freed itself from the American and English models. It was characterized by a unique mix of haunting, ethereal sounds from electronic instruments and elements of music of contemporary composers like Karlheinz Stockhausen and experimental psychedelic rock. The greatest psychedelic influence came from bands like Amon Düül II, Can, Guru Guru and Tangerine Dream. The Berlin Krautrocker Ash Ra Tempel met Timothy Leary in 1972 in Bern and used the occasion to hold a jam session. It led to the release

> In the beginning we were creating our music, ourselves, every night... starting with a few outlines, maybe a few words for a song. Sometimes we worked out in Venice looking at the surf. We were together a lot and it was good times for all of us. Acid, sun, friends, the ocean, and poetry and music.
>
> *Jim Morrison*

> We must always remember to thank the CIA and the Army for LSD ... Everything is the opposite of what it is, isn't it? They invented LSD to control people and what they did was give us freedom.
>
> *John Lennon*

the following year of the legendary album *7-Up* with a cover illustration by Swiss painter Walter Wegmüller. During the recording session a bottle of 7-Up dosed with LSD circulated and gave the album its name. "The guy at the mixer console inserted clever noise intermezzi at regular intervals; Leary himself played the rock star, moaning and howling with a throaty voice while accompanied by a ten-man Big Band pounding out earthy rock that gradually sounded ever more psychedelic. After a while, the music left behind any connection to the earth's gravitational field and drifted weightlessly in space, passing strange planet-feedback melodies as it searched for the center of the universe."[107]

Acid House, Psytrance, Goa Trance

Several different psychedelic music styles developed in the late 1980s between Europe and Goa in India, the ultimate destination of many sixties-era hippie trails, where DJs played their music at beach parties. Young people, paying homage to the life style and drug use of the Flower Power era, joined them. LSD consumption had faded in the 1970s, but was revived during the rave and techno parties of the 1990s, along with the use of magic mushrooms and MDMA. "The psychedelic revolution never ended. It only needed to travel halfway around the world to a solitary beach at the end of a dusty road where it could freely change and develop into a new paradigm without pressure from the state or media: Goa consciousness," according to Goa Gil, a representative of this music and life style. (Rom, Querner 2012)

Burning Man, 2006

The Desert Lives

With the words "Eros, fire, and acid," a participant in a blog got to the heart of the Burning Man Festival of 2009 held in Nevada's Black Rock Desert. Held annually since 1986, Burning Man has gradually developed into the wildest gathering of the American art and psychedelic scene, attracting visitors from around the world. Attendance has grown from the initial twenty "Burners" to the over fifty thousand in 2010 who enjoyed a week of eccentric and radical self-expression, constructed bold and crazy sculptures, consumed impressive quantities of hallucinogens, and swore to be entirely responsible for themselves. Experts such as Ann and Alexander "Sasha" Shulgin and relevant organizations like MAPS and Erowid were available on-site for psychedelic counseling. This unique anarchic, hedonistic spectacle ends with the ritual burning of the gigantic wooden Burning Man statue. It is a matter of honor that all participants help clean up afterwards and leave no trace upon the festival grounds.

175

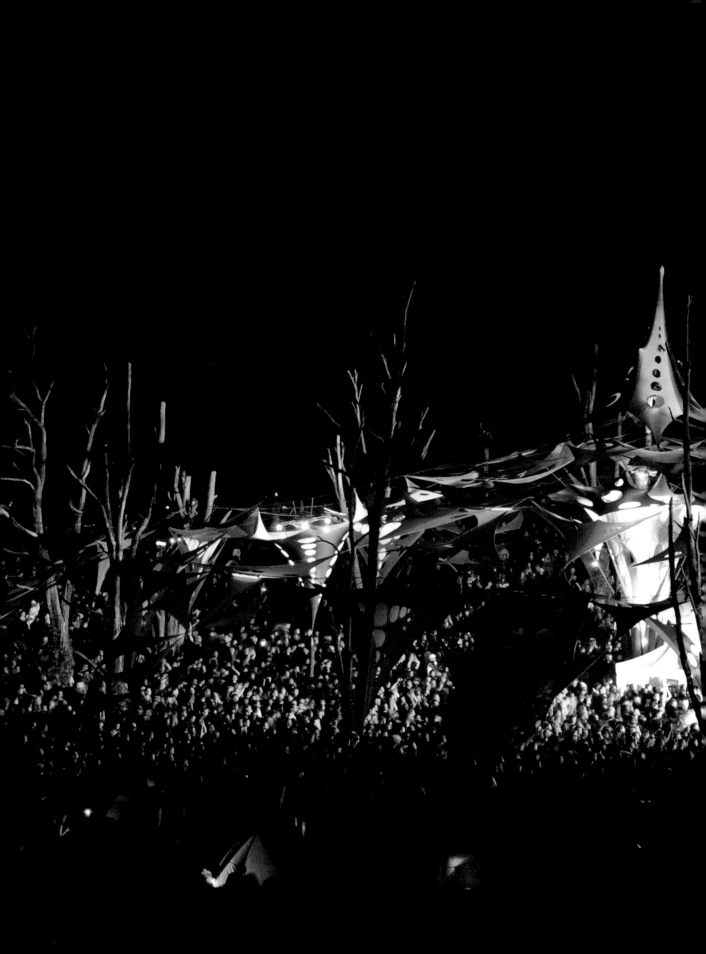

O.Z.O.R.A. Festival, Hungary 2009

Lucy in the Sky with Diamonds

On August 28, 1964 Bob Dylan visited the Beatles in their suite in the Delmonico Hotel in New York. He offered them a joint and the Beatles inhaled their first marijuana. Ringo reached for the joint first and soon began to laugh; before long they all were laughing. Paul McCartney was delighted and said it was the first time in his life that he truly could think.[108] From that point on, marijuana and hashish became the Beatles' constant companions from breakfast to their "Hard Day's Night." One day, their London dentist invited them for dinner, and with LSD for dessert, he put them in a state which we have to thank for masterpieces of pop music. In August 1966, their album *Revolver* appeared with the song "Tomorrow Never Knows." John Lennon's lyrics were inspired by *The Psychedelic Experience, A Manual Based on the Tibetan Book of the Dead* (Leary, Metzner, Alpert 1964) which contained instructions for safely conducting and sensibly processing psychedelic experiences. According to his biographer Albert Goldman, Lennon interpreted sections of text for his song, and tape-recorded them shortly before his third LSD trip in January 1966. When the LSD started to take effect, he listened to

Sgt. Pepper's Lonely Hearts Club Band album cover, 1967

> It (LSD) opened my eyes. We only use one-tenth of our brain. Just think what we could accomplish if we could only tap that hidden part! It would mean a whole new world if the politicians would take LSD. There wouldn't be any more war or poverty or famine.
>
> *Paul McCartney*

the passage again and was so pleased with the results that he decided to build the LSD experience into a song.

In August 1966, the Beatles gave their last regular concert in front of 25,000 people in San Francisco's Candlestick Park. They absorbed the spirit of optimism tangible throughout California and, inspired by that atmosphere and their LSD experiences, went to work in their studio. Five months later, in June 1967 their most important album, *Sgt. Pepper's Lonely Hearts Club Band*, appeared and became a milestone in rock history. It showed new musical possibilities and fully exploited the technical capabilities of studios of that time. An orchestra and the Mellotron were used to create music that could never be adequately performed live. For the first time, the Beatles printed the texts to their subtly profound, sometimes surrealistic songs on the cover. The record jacket, a photographic collage showing the Beatles in costume in front of a wall of pictures of famous personalities, such as Stan Laurel, Mae West, Bob Dylan, Shirley Temple, Aleister Crowley, and Marlon Brando, was honored with a Grammy and chosen as the Best Album Art of All Time by *Wired* in June 2010.

John Lennon and George Harrison were largely responsible for the psychedelic influences. "Within You Without You," featuring George Harrison playing sitar, reveals the influence of Indian philosophy and expresses his search for meaning. According to the Beatles, the initial letters of their legendary song "Lucy in the Sky with Diamonds" had nothing to do with LSD, a recurrently stubborn rumor which the band always denied.

The playful nature of the album perfectly matched the mood of the Summer of Love and became a kind of musical "Bible" of the counterculture, while the Beatles became its cultural spokesmen. Once it appeared, the band sent a copy autographed by them all to Albert Hofmann. To make their message of love accessible to everyone, they performed the programmatic song "All You Need is Love," which had only appeared as a single, in June 1967 on the BBC satellite broadcast "Our World." The Grammy awards of 1968 selected *Sgt. Pepper's Lonely Hearts Club Band* as the best album, and in 2003 *Rolling Stone* put it first in their listing of the "500 Greatest Albums of All Time."

Woodstock

Almost overnight, Richie Havens became famous after opening the Woodstock Music and Art Festival on that late Friday afternoon of August 15, 1969 with the song "Freedom," all alone onstage with his acoustic guitar. The band that was due to open the show was stuck in traffic and the stage had not yet been completed. Instead of the sixty thousand visitors expected, over four hundred and fifty thousand people eventually made the pilgrimage to this farmland in upstate New York, and the festival became a legend. Also unforgettable was Joe Cocker with his interpretation of the Beatles classic "With a Little Help from My Friends." The British rock and blues singer and his band were one of more than thirty rock groups from the USA and England. to stand on the stage during the following three days and nights.

Carlos Santana's appearance was the start of his great career. Inspired by a good dose of LSD, he ignited a guitar inferno. This was an ambiguous experience for him. His band was sent onstage sooner than planned, and he was still totally high. He had wanted to come down first but the producers did not care. He was told that they could either play right then or not at all! "The guitar neck, it felt like a electric snake that wouldn't stand still....The neck is going like that ... and inwardly, I'm just, I remember saying, over and over, "God, I'll never do this again, ever! If you can just keep me in time and in tune, that, that's all I ask. That was my first mantra... and then the sound of hearing the music coming from within me, through my body, through my fingers, through the amplifier, through the speakers, up into the audience as far as you can go, and then come back to you. You know, uh, it was a scary thing... I don't recommend it for anybody, you know, to go on stage high on LSD, trying to perform... but, by God's grace, the performance that they got...was very electric." The enthusiastic audience didn't notice, and Santana on LSD whipped them into frenzy, especially with the ten-minute

> Whenever I hear the Beatles, I hear the enchanting melody of "Lucy in the Sky with Diamonds" in my head. I don't really know if this title is a reference to LSD. But something of an LSD trip resonates in this song. So, my "problem child" had somehow a hand in it.
>
> *Albert Hofmann*

> Sometimes I have the feeling that the 1960s were a lot wilder than we ever appreciated.
>
> *Daniel Cohn-Bendit*

Wavy Gravy and crew arrive at the airport en route to Woodstock

Aerial of Woodstock Festival, 1969

instrumental piece "Soul Sacrifice," which was captured in the documentary film *Woodstock—Three Days of Peace and Music*. When Santana saw himself in the film, he was somewhat satisfied: "Not as good as it could have been, but not bad."[109] Despite the chaos in front, behind, and on the stage, many other musicians, groups and visitors took similar impressions and memories home with them. Even today, it remains uncertain how many groups appeared and in which order. For this reason, what is true of the Woodstock myth holds true in many respects for the entire psychedelic epoch: "Anyone who can remember the sixties, probably wasn't there."[110]

Members of the Hog Farm Commune had already proven themselves at different festivals and were responsible for security at Woodstock as well. They helped see to it that Woodstock became a symbol of a peaceful community. They settled quarrels and looked after the countless victims of unprepared drug trips due to the uncontrolled availability of LSD.

His debut album *Are You Experienced* had already been out for two years; his experiences with LSD, which were definitely conducive to his musical creativity, stemmed from several years earlier. The festival had officially ended and programming of acts had gotten completely off track when, on Monday morning, Jimi Hendrix played his alienated version of the *Star Spangled Banner* for around forty thousand listeners; it was too extreme for many ears. "Machine gun salvos, aerial attacks and the explosion of mortars"[111] could be heard between distorted guitar-riffs. Nonetheless, this legendary guitar solo became the high point of Hendrix's career and his appearance in the Woodstock film is one of the most analyzed scenes in music or concert film. Singer-songwriter Melanie Safka, known only by her first name under which she still performs, once spoke of her impression that she was the only person there who was *not* on drugs.

The chaos, improvisation and solidarity of the Woodstock Festival reflected the spirit of the hippie and youth movements in America of the 1960s as was also true for most young people in many other parts of the globe. They resonated with a sense of oneness with the world, with the importance of friendship, freedom,

180

and love. Or, as Jerry Garcia put it: "The thing about Woodstock was that you could feel the presence of time travelers from the future who had come back to see it. You could sense the significance of the event as it was happening. There was a kind of swollen historicity—a truly pregnant moment. You definitely knew that this was a milestone; it was in the air."[112]

Hair

The pop and rock musical *Hair* was first performed in New York City on October 17, 1967, and became one of the most popular musicals ever. In a loosely connected set of scenes, it described the life of a hippie commune during the Vietnam War waiting for the blissful Age of Aquarius to dawn. The story represented most of the attributes of the alternative culture of the 1960s that was hated and opposed by the majority of society and politicians: Starting with long hair –"they should go to the barber!"– the clothing from second hand shops or Indian boutiques—"they should first of all wash themselves!"– and on to anti-war demonstrations– "shirkers! Communist pigs! Enemies of the State!" A key scene in the song "Hashish, "which lists all the known legal and illegal drugs, has the main character Claude taking an LSD trip. A musical portraying the values of the Flower Power generation left the conservative public duly indignant while Hair became a cult show to countless young people around the world whose dreams and aspirations it mirrored. It was translated into many languages and remains popular in many countries; in 1977 Milos Forman directed a film version.

Swinging London

Carnaby Street and King's Road were originally insider spots for hippies and backpackers, but soon were overrun by voyeuristic tourists. In November 1966 John Dunbar, Peter Asher, and Barry Miles, with the support of Paul McCartney, opened the Indica Gallery in Mason Yard. This bookstore and art gallery became a trendy place where later, John Lennon and Yoko Ono would first meet. The following month John "Hoppy" Hopkins and Joe Boyd opened the UFO Club on Tottenham Court Road in which groups like Pink Floyd, The Incredible String Band, and Procol Harum began their careers "with quantities galore of LSD and psychedelic silk-screen posters."[113]

London became the center of European rock music in the 1960s. Free concerts were given in Hyde Park with tens of thousands in attendance. Indian gurus enhanced the colorfully clad scene. One of the places to meet was "Middle Earth," a trendy pub named after the land of the Hobbits from J.R.R. Tolkien's bestseller *Lord of the Rings,* later filmed by Australian director Peter Jackson; the hippie magazine *Gandalf's Garden,* named after the magician in Tolkien's trilogy, was popular reading. Brightly colored, shimmering clothing was to be found in a hip boutique on Kings Road called "Granny Takes a Trip." Its slightly sloping floor meant that, even when sober,

> My experiences with hallucinogenic drugs have not shaken my political convictions for a second. They have sharpened my perception, and sensitized my awareness, opened my senses to things my analytic mind had long been aware of: There is more than one reality and consequently also more than one truth.
>
> *Günter Amendt*

Pink Floyd's first public concert in London's
All Saints Church hall in Talbot Street, Notting Hill, 1966

Gandalf's Garden store in Chelsea, London, late 1960s

customers needed to take care to keep their balance when rummaging through the extravagant clothes. Barry Miles and John Hopkins published the *International Times*. To inaugurate this first underground magazine, they gave a party at the legendary Roundhouse in Chalk Farm on October 15, 1966, a vacant locomotive hall, where Miles personally handed out well-dosed sugar cubes to the nearly two thousand visitors.

The fourteen hour *Technicolor Dream* at Alexandra "Ally Pally" Palace on April 29, 1967 was the largest underground psychedelic event in London with nearly ten thousand attending and comparable to the Acid Test parties in the USA. All the bands that started their careers in the UFO Club played. Even Pink Floyd, who had played a gig in Holland the previous evening, caught a ferry back to England and with their introduction to "Interstellar Overdrive," brought the crowd out of their pleasant LSD-induced trance around three-thirty in the morning. "Then came the rebirth of energy, another day, and with the sun a burst of dancing and enthusiasm." (Miles 1997, 181)

Trips Around the World

The psychedelically inspired youth movement of the 1960s, which began in the USA and England, quickly spread to the European continent and soon thereafter around the world. In Holland, Amsterdam became a meeting place for international hippies with its newly created cultural centers: The Melkweg in a former milk processing factory, and the Paradiso in a former church, and as the home of the Netherlands' "oldest hippie," Beat poet Simon Vinkenoog.

In West Germany, these years were marked by the economic miracle of the 1950s, and increasing prosperity provided distraction from coming to terms with the Nazi past. Consequentially, the growing counterculture was increasingly politically motivated. The antiauthoritarian opposition coalesced in universities and found expression in a powerful student movement. More light-hearted but no less influential impulses came from the music scene. The Beatles began their career in Hamburg's "Star Club." In all the larger cities, young people flocked to rock concerts in newly opened cellar clubs. The psychedelic music scene was extremely diverse. Student and hippie communes caused a stir as did artists with their Happenings.

Several thousand Danish hippies founded the Freetown Christiania, an alternative residential and working settlement in Copenhagen in 1971. Based on self-regulation and democracy, it operates independently of state authority. The motto of the nine hundred persons belonging to the community today is: "Freedom, Love, Harmony." An essential principle in Christiania is that drug consumption be done freely and self-responsibly.

In Switzerland, the stories of folklorist Sergius Golowin concerning magical realism and "forbidden fairy tales" inspired a group of young, fanciful hippies. They called themselves "Härdlütli" as the "good folks" or nature spirits are called who, according

Gandalf's Garden magazine cover, September 1968

to one legend, live deep beneath the rock cliffs upon which stands the city of Bern. Together with the musician Polo Hofer, they ran for a seat on the Bern city council in 1971 and in 1979. At Golowin's suggestion, they reintroduced Fasnacht (Carnival) to Bern in 1979 after a gap of one hundred and fifty years, because, as they remarked, "the authorities in a city are only as good as their carnival is."[114] Although such achievements may seem inconsequential, it should not be overlooked that the tiny Alpine country was no less psychedelic in the 1960s than other Western countries. In any case, at the end of 1971, Swiss authorities refused to cooperate with a U.S. request to extradite Timothy Leary who had fled after a minor marijuana offense and spent nearly two years in Switzerland. This did not go unnoticed by Albert Hofmann who expressed his satisfaction to Leary a few days later in a greeting card.

Swiss airlines began offering a direct flight in 2010 from Zurich to San Francisco. The California city still is associated with freedom, love and flower children. To advertise the service, Swiss decorated an Airbus A-340 in the style of a VW bus of the hippie generation and used the song "If you're going to San Francisco" in radio ads. The "Flower-Power Jet" flew for a year and a half and was also available as a model airplane.

The principal reason for the draconian prohibitive measures, however, was the goal of attacking the youth movement, hippies and the like, who opposed the Establishment and the Vietnam War, and whose 'cult-drug' was, above all, LSD.
Albert Hofmann

Brotherhood of Eternal Love

John Griggs began his professional career as an ordinary marijuana dealer in Laguna Beach, south of Los Angeles. His life changed radically when he and his motorcycle gang stole a Hollywood producer's sizable supply of LSD at gunpoint. After a series of amazing trips, Griggs had no doubt that he had found the elixir of enlightenment. This experience led him to the commune in Millbrook where Timothy Leary recommended that Griggs found his own church, as he himself had recently done and described in a pamphlet.[115] Leary's pamphlet declared LSD, which had a short while earlier been declared illegal, to be a sacrament. On October 16, 1966, Griggs and thirty of his friends founded the religious community of the Brotherhood of Eternal Love.

Most of the members of the new congregation were vegetarians and practiced their own syncretic form of piety drawn from Christianity and various Eastern religions. Like their leader, they were primarily drug dealers and moved with him to a remote ranch in rural southern California. They initially dealt in quantities of a few kilograms but expanded their activity by importing several tons of high quality Red Lebanese and Black Afghan hashish, rare and choice morsels for American consumers. In the late sixties and early seventies, the Brotherhood became the largest sales organization of narcotics in the United States and exercised significant influence on international trade in hashish from the Middle East, primarily from Afghanistan and Pakistan. After the arrest of Owsley Stanley, they began doing business in LSD with Nick Sand and Tim Scully. In the summer of 1969 alone, the Brotherhood dealt an estimated one hundred thousand of the legendary "Orange Sunshine" tabs out of an entire production estimated to be somewhere over ten million. (Schou 2010) Their

> The uncontrolled change in consciousness, which legal and freely accessible drugs including psychedelic plants would affect, is extremely threatening to a culture based on domination and ego.
>
> *Terence McKenna*

Haight-Ashbury, San Francisco 1966

businesses were largely undisturbed until the Brotherhood's fortunes turned. After the first arrests for marijuana offenses, the church's founder Griggs died in August of 1969, allegedly from an overdose of psilocybin (Schou 2010, 190), although according to some sources, from an overdose of PCP. (Lee, Shlain 1985, 248)

As early as February 1968, Timothy Leary had decided to withdraw from public life and settled comfortably in one of the cottages on the Brotherhood's Idyllwild Ranch with his wife Rosemary. While on a trip to Laguna Beach, police stopped Leary's car, discovered two marijuana roaches and arrested him. Due to differences in the interpretation of the marijuana laws, Leary was not sentenced until January 1970 when he received ten years in prison plus a further ten years for the same offense during an attempted border crossing into Mexico in 1965. In September of 1970, the Brotherhood financed the Weathermen, a leftist underground organization in the U.S., to break Leary out of a San Luis Obispo prison and to arrange his flight to Algeria where he joined fugitive Black Panthers.

During that turbulent summer of 1969, the sinister Ronald Hadley Stark entered the scene. Only one photo of him exists but countless rumors circulated, mostly wild stories, about the traveling businessman also known as Terrence W. Abbott. Manifestly criminal, he was known for his contacts with the Palestinian Liberation Front, his ties to the Japanese Mafia, as an informant for the CIA, and as a drug smuggler. In New

> Any man who has once proclaimed violence as his method is inevitably forced to take the lie as his principle.
>
> *Alexander I. Solzhenitsyn*

York, he told Millbrook's owner, William Mellon Hitchcock, of a French LSD transaction. Since Hitchcock wished to have nothing more to do with drugs, he referred Stark to the Brotherhood of Eternal Love. When he appeared at the Ranch and was

Man's magazine, 1961

met with mistrust, he allegedly offered them a kilo of pure LSD. No one had ever seen that much LSD at one time. Stark explained that he knew a simple method for making excellent LSD and described his plans for production with the support of his diverse high-level international contacts. Stark spoke ten languages and appeared to have access to Czech sources for the necessary materials as well as a production facility in Paris at his disposal. He became a gray eminence in the psychedelic movement and the largest manufacturer of LSD by the end of the 1960s. Speculation over the amount of LSD produced in his hidden labs ran up to twenty kilos, enough for one hundred million doses. (Lee, Shlain 1985, 248)

During this period, criminal elements took over the Brotherhood and pushed out the peace-loving founders. Their large drug smuggling deals of all kinds ended miserably.

A concerted police action destroyed the church organization in August 1972 with the arrest of fifty-seven people and confiscation of half a ton of hashish, over one hundred liters of hashish oil, and one and a half million "Orange Sunshine" tabs. The last member of the "Hippie Mafia," as *Rolling Stone* described them,[116] was arrested thirty-seven years later on September 26, 2009, as he re-entered the USA from Afghanistan with his real passport.

Demonization

Shunting LSD off into illegality proceeded in installments and began in the USA in the mid-1960s. Increasing consumption by young people of LSD took on frightening dimensions in the eyes of society and perspective of politicians. LSD had left the clinics of psychiatrists and intelligence services and gotten out of control. Once the CIA and the Army determined that psychedelics were of no use for their purposes, these governmental authorities became as actively involved in anti-LSD propaganda as they had shortly before been in their covert human experiments. They fanned fears and spread false reports, such as that LSD damages human genetic material. They supported scientists who represented the view that LSD caused psychoses and suppressed research exploring and documenting its promising therapeutic applications. The FDA and various

other U.S. health agencies consistently exerted influence on American politicians to prohibit LSD research and consumption.

Mass media campaigns tending towards a hysteria parallel to earlier political furors about a Communist menace, reiterated threats of LSD's dangers to mental and physical health. *TIME* warned that, like an epidemic, "The disease is striking in beachside Beatnik pads, and in the dormitories of expensive prep schools; it has grown into an alarming problem at UCLA and on the UC campus at Berkeley. And everywhere the diagnosis is the same: psychotic illness resulting from the unauthorized, nonmedical use of the drug LSD-25."[117] *LIFE* went one better with their sensational lead article "LSD: The Exploding Threat of the Mind Drug that Got Out of Control."[118] The evidence that LSD caused brain damage supposedly lay in the fact that so many young people with LSD experience showed little desire to adopt the middle-class life style of their parents and instead were protesting ever more insistently against the Vietnam War and fundamentally questioning political authority. The establishment became alarmed and saw public and political order endangered. In 1971 American President Richard Nixon declared the War on Drugs and one year later pronounced the former Harvard psychologist Timothy Leary to be the "most dangerous

LIFE, March 25 1966

Flash, July 1966

187

man in America." This was shortly before Nixon became the first U.S. president to step down from office due to criminal machinations in the Watergate Scandal.

Verdict and Prohibition

In the spring of 1965, the FDA withdrew approval to use psychedelics in psychotherapy. At the beginning of August, under pressure from Washington, the management of Sandoz considered stopping production and distribution of LSD, amounting to nothing short of a recall of all remaining stock from their subsidiaries. Excluded were the USA, Canada, Australia and England where Sandoz was in contact with "official instances" and sought adequate transitional solutions. First, an inventory was taken in Basel: In addition to pure substances in "processed galenic form," there were 18,500 ampoules of one hundred micrograms of LSD and some two hundred pills of 25 micrograms each. The total quantity came to nearly 3,000 grams or six million single doses, an "enormous stock." Added to that, were 473 grams of psilocybin and 108 grams of psilocin. The company planned to store the pure substances and ampoules in their narcotics locker, destroy the pills, and then resume supplying the "legitimate researchers in direct contact with Sandoz" specified allotments from the supply of ampoules.

> It is well known that prejudice, ignorance, and special interests are involved in the current classification of drugs as legal and illegal and intoxicants.
>
> Albert Hofmann

> Alcohol, nicotine, and prescription sedatives do more damage to Americans every day than LSD has done since it was discovered in 1943.
>
> John Perry Barlow

Official institutes, such as the Chemical Defense Establishment in London, would also be supplied in the future with pure substance on a case-by-case basis.[119]

Eight months later, in mid-April 1966, Sandoz decided to end any further distribution of LSD and psilocybin. That applied not only to the United States which received the news from the Pharmaceutical Division in Hanover, but to all other countries as well. Sandoz' press agency in Basel announced: "Although we never have marketed LSD-25, which was first discovered in our laboratories in 1943, or psilocybin, which was first isolated from a Mexican mushroom in Sandoz laboratories in 1958, the special circumstances which led to our decision warrant further explanation." A description of the compounds and their effects followed along with the information that Sandoz had made both substances "available to qualified researchers in laboratories and clinics throughout the world at no cost. Thanks to strict, self-imposed safety measures, it was possible to avoid misuse of these substances by unqualified persons. Unfortunately, however in recent times the increasing misuse of hallucinogenic drugs by young people abroad has come to our attention." The statement continued with this reference to hysteria in the media: "This situation has worsened in part due to the uncontrollable flood of articles in the tabloid press that awakened unhealthy interest in LSD and other hallucinogens through distorted representations to the lay public." Underground production and the black market also played a role because, "in recent times, certain starting materials for production of LSD became generally available on the chemicals market, making possible production by irresponsible circles primarily interested in smuggling and black market trade." Although LSD is still associated with the name Sandoz, for the pharmaceutical company in Basel, a historic chapter was closed with this action. "Moreover, the last Sandoz patent for LSD expired in 1963."[120]

On October 6, 1966, LSD was declared illegal in California and subsequently across the whole USA. The Comprehensive Drug Abuse Prevention and Control Act passed on October 27, 1970. Article II, the Controlled Substances Act (CSA), lists nearly all known hallucinogens (LSD, psilocybin, psilocin, mescaline, peyote, cannabis, MDA) together with heroin as regulated substances with high potential for misuse and no demonstrable medical benefit.

In the Federal Republic of Germany, the fourth Narcotics Equality Act took effect on February 25, 1967, subjected LSD to the provisions of the opium law, the forerunner of today's Controlled Substances Act. LSD is also banned under applicable UN conventions, the Single Convention on Narcotic Drugs (1961) and the Convention on Psychotropic Substances. (1971) The complete ban of LSD in West Germany was issued in

---

Translation of Sandoz Press Release, April 18, 1966
Sandoz AG Press Service

Several days ago the North American Pharmaceutical Division of the SANDOZ Inc issued a press release with immediate effect. All further distribution of the drug known as lysergic acid diethylamide, also known as LSD-25, and psilocybin, a compound used for purposes of research will cease. This decision pertains not only to the USA, but to all other countries, including Switzerland. Although we have never marketed LSD-25, which was discovered in our laboratories in 1943, nor Psilocybin, which was first isolated in SANDOZ Laboratories from a Mexican mushroom in 1958, the particular circumstances that have led to our decision warrant further explanation.

LSD and psilocybin are hallucinogens, i.e. compounds that influence sensory perception. LSD was particularly important for modern psychiatric and psychopharmacological research because even a scant quantity affects the psyche. SANDOZ made this compound and the less powerful psilocybin available to qualified researchers in laboratories and clinics throughout the world at no cost. Thanks to strict, self-imposed safety measures, it was possible to avoid misuse of these substances by unqualified persons. However, in recent times the increasing misuse of hallucinogenic drugs—particularly by youth abroad—has come to our attention. This situation has worsened due in part to the uncontrollable flood of articles in the yellow press awakening unhealthy interest in LSD and other hallucinogens through distorted representations to the lay public.

Underground production and the black market have also become decisive factors; in recent times certain starting materials became generally available on the chemicals market which made LSD production possible for irresponsible circles primarily interested in smuggling and black market trade. Moreover, the last SANDOZ patent for LSD expired in 1963. Although it is clear that the tight restrictions in force at SANDOZ allowed almost none of our production of LSD and psilocybin to enter black market channels, the new situation has convinced us we can no longer be responsible for distribution and delivery of these substances. The proper authorities will have to put in place adequate measures for controlling production and distribution of hallucinogenic materials while providing for legitimate research interests and preventing fraudulent use.

Translation of An Important Communication Regarding Lysergic Acid Diethylamide (LSD-25)

We have learned of individual instances of the administration of lysergic acid diethylamide (LSD-25) which has led us to emphasize that it is not possible to predict its effects, and undesirable reactions can occur. Thus, a subject who appears to be entirely normal may in fact harbor latent schizophrenia or some other latent psychiatric condition that manifests itself after (administration of) LSD-25, or the degree of euphoric release or intensity of the hallucinations can lead to behavior that could be embarrassing or even dangerous for the particular patient or their surroundings if supervision is prematurely ended or totally lacking.

For these reasons, we must ask the treating physician to assume complete responsibility for the effects of LSD-25, the use of which requires particular caution relative to the statement of indications and care, and ask you to sign and return the accompanying *declaration*

shown below) which indicates the quantity of LSD-25 requested and sent.

A number of sensational and in part distorted accounts about the effect of LSD-25 have appeared in popular magazines and in the daily press. Therefore, we ask that you exercise caution and publish your findings only in professional journals.

Declaration

The undersigned confirms that he wishes to utilize lysergic acid diethylamide (LSD-25), is informed of its effects and properties, and is aware of the possibility of unforeseen reactions. He declares he will assume entire responsibility for the utilization of the compound.

Date: _____

Address: _____

Signature: _____

1971. In the following years, the USA pressured all countries of the world to generally prohibit the use of hallucinogenic substances; Switzerland complied in 1973. LSD and all other psychedelics were referred to as "narcotics," and their possession and consumption became punishable. The first arrests were made and the first sentences of life imprisonment were handed down in the USA.

These rigorous measures brought promising research to a virtual standstill and meant the end of many successful therapies. State institutions were forced to accept the ban, and the few scientific studies of psychedelics operating under strict requirements were carried out at hospitals and universities. It is estimated that during the mid-sixties, nearly 40,000 psychiatric patients were treated with LSD psychotherapy, and thousands of volunteers participated in the LSD studies reported in over 3,000 scientific papers. (Hintzen, Passie 2010)

A considerable number of therapists, however, did not wish to stop using this drug which was so helpful in treating their patients. They chose instead to ignore the law and continue their treatments illegally.

Underground Therapy

From 1961 on, psychotherapist Leo Zeff had used LSD with countless patients. He was among the pioneers in psychedelic psy-

> For many doctors it was a panacea, especially for patients who were no longer open to psychotherapy or psychoanalysis. At the time, I received touching letters from people whom LSD had freed from years of suffering.
>
> *Albert Hofmann*

chotherapy and known for his carefully prepared sessions. As a former army officer, he respected the government, but when it banned hallucinogenic substances, he decided to continue his successful therapies underground. Zeff was only one of many who chose not to concede to the draconian measures mandated by the authorities and politicians and continued to operate despite the threat of legal penalties. As a safety precaution, he took the pseudonym "Jacob" and only after his death, was his real name disclosed. (Stolaroff 1997, 2004)

Leo Zeff

In the late 1970s, when "Adam" was mentioned, many knew it referred to MDMA or Ecstasy. Hardly anyone knew that Leo Zeff originated the name for this soft drug which, in his opinion, could restore one's original state of innocence. Alexander Shulgin, the chemist who an article in *The New York Times Magazine* called "Dr. Ecstasy," introduced Zeff, a Jungian psychologist, to the drug in 1977 when it was still legal. Shulgin had rediscovered MDMA in his private lab in California in the 1960s. It was first synthesized by the pharmaceutical firm Merck in 1912 and registered on Christmas Eve of that year with the German Patent Office as an appetite suppressant. This amphetamine derivative quickly established itself as an empathogen in the party scene and as an effective adjunct in psychotherapy, especially for posttraumatic stress disorders.

In his preface to the book *Secret Chief*, the story of Leo Zeff, by Myron Stolaroff, Albert Hofmann wrote: "In the illegality of his time it was unthinkable to publish the excellent results of his therapy. ... It is therefore praiseworthy that today, nine years after his death, a friend has undertaken the task of publishing the details of the therapeutic methodology of this intrepid PhD psychologist." (Stolaroff 2004, 23)

The Empire Strikes Back

Since the mid-1960s and certainly since the worldwide ban on LSD and all other hallucinogens, consumption of the "Fuel of the Sixties" has continued to climb. Underground production has long since reached professional scale, equally matched by upgraded competency among law enforcement and political authorities. With the support of the majority of society, the War on Drugs was proclaimed. Whether marijuana, LSD, or heroin, whether individual consumers, street dealers, or chemists in hidden labs, narcotics agents made no distinctions. Consequently, the courts and prisons rapidly filled with a new category of "criminals."

"Operation Julie" was one of the largest police actions of all time. After lengthy surveillance and investigation by nearly eight hundred detectives and undercover agents, a host of British policemen stormed a professionally equipped LSD lab near the tranquil town of Tregaron in rural Wales. Around six million top quality LSD tablets valued at several million British pounds sterling were confiscated. During simultaneous actions and raids in Britain and

> Anything that alters consciousness is a threat to the existing order. That is one point of agreement across the entire political spectrum.
>
> *Timothy Leary*

France, one hundred and twenty people were arrested and £800,000 pounds sterling in Swiss bank accounts seized. During the resulting trials, seventeen accused were sentenced to a total of 130 years in prison. Among the operators of the laboratory were chemist Richard Kemp, anthropologist Lewis Daly, a professor of cryptozoology at the University of Wales, the American writer David Salomon, and other chemists and physicians.

Crime Scene Missile Silo

Exactly when and where William Leonard Pickard, scion of a wealthy intellectual family, began manufacturing LSD is not known. His first arrest was in December 1988 in a warehouse in Mountain View, California, after a neighbor reported strange odors to authorities. Police found 200,000 doses of LSD and Pickard was sentenced to five years in prison. After his release, he enrolled at Harvard University and devoted himself to studying drug abuse in the former Soviet Union, where, since its dissolution in 1991, many chemists who had lost their jobs operated freely in the ever expanding black market. Subsequently, Pickard became the deputy director of the Drug Policy Research Program at the University of California in Los Angeles.

Leonard Pickard met Albert Hofmann in February of 1996 at the scientific symposium, Worlds of Consciousness, held by the European College for the Study of Conscious-

William Leonard Pickard,
Cambridge 1997

The Inquisition ended in 1819, but in many areas of psychotherapy and medicine, the U.S. government has taken up where the Vatican left off.

Robert Anton Wilson

ness in Heidelberg; they spoke at length about underground LSD production and Pickard's studies at Harvard. Soon thereafter, Hofmann sent him a copy of his book, *LSD - My Problem Child*, with the dedication: "With warm memories of our meeting in Heidelberg. "In the end, Pickard's undiminished passion for producing the substance in considerable quantities led him once more to calamity.

After a month-long trial based on circumstantial evidence, a federal judge sentenced William Leonard Pickard on November 25, 2003, to two consecutive life sentences and his partner Clyde Apperson to thirty years in prison. The charges read "conspiracy to produce more than ten grams of LSD" and "possession with intent to sell more than ten grams of LSD." The book Hofmann had signed was seized upon Pickard's arrest, together with an edition of Alexander and Ann Shulgin's book *PiHKAL: A Chemical Love Story* containing a thoughtful dedication. Both books were presented as evidence by the State's Attorney to the panel of jurors. The Department of Justice celebrated the announcement of the verdict with a ponderous press release describing their arrest as the "seizure of the largest LSD laboratory in the history of the Drug Enforcement Agency (DEA)." Around "91 pounds" or over forty kilos of LSD were seized according to the report. All the media, including the Associated Press and respected papers such as the *San Francisco Chronicle* and the *Los Angeles Times*, accepted the quantities stated without question. Four months later, DEA Administrator Karen

Tandy confirmed the amount seized before a committee on appropriations: "In Operation White Rabbit the DEA broke up the world's leading LSD producing organization led by William Leonard Pickard. It was the largest seizure of a single operational LSD laboratory in the history of the DEA. On November 6, 2000, DEA agents seized approximately 91 pounds of LSD, 215 pounds of lysergic acid (a chemical LSD precursor), 52 pounds of iso-LSD (a by-product of LSD production), and 41 pounds of Ergocristine (an LSD precursor with which an additional 27 pounds of LSD could be produced) from a decommissioned missile silo near Wamego, Kansas."[121] At a dose of 200 micrograms, that would mean Pickard and Appleton had produced 200 million LSD trips from their nearly 40 kilograms of LSD and had been capable of producing another 50 million with the 27 pounds mentioned. However, it later turned out that the 91 pounds did not refer to LSD, but to the entire weight of all seized substances and equipment.

This trial, the longest in the State of Kansas in twenty six years, lasted eleven weeks. Pickard denied all charges and entered an appeal, knowing that either way arduous years were imminent. His daughter was born three weeks after his arrest; his wife finished medical school and has since worked as a physician.

Dedication to Freedom

British-Canadian psychiatrist John Spencer Beresford was an assistant professor of pediatrics at New York Medical College. In 1961 he became interested in researching LSD and resigned his post. Together with psychology student Jean Houston and her friend Michael

Corner, a medical student, he founded the Agora Scientific Trust in Manhattan. It was the first private organization in the world dedicated to researching the effects of LSD on human consciousness. Several years later, Jean Houston and Robert Masters summarized their impressive studies and their personal LSD experiments in their groundbreaking work on the great variety of psychedelic experiences. (Masters, Houston 1966)

Beresford originally was committed to reserving the use of LSD as an adjunctive tool to scientifically trained specialists only and was troubled by Timothy Leary's call to "tune in, turn on, drop out." Later, however, he became increasingly convinced of its potential for heightening experience in the realms of hedonism, creativity, and consciousness with appropriate application. He revised his opinion and generally opposed the medicalization of psychedelics which restricted their use to medicine and psychotherapy.

Between 1964 and 1974, Beresford practiced in New York City and was also an assistant professor of psychiatry at York University in Toronto. As a consequence of the increasingly harsh War on Drugs, he left the academic milieu and founded the Committee on Unjust Sentencing. Their advocacy focused on the unfortunate situation of people who having run afoul of the law because of psychedelics, subsequently landed

> As a rule, the reporting about LSD resembles coverage by an extraterrestrial ethnologist who researches the phenomenon of human auto traffic only at emergency rooms.
> Mathias Bröckers

> The crazy thing is that it was the CIA that turned us all on; and banning it also was just the thing—that really got the counter culture going!
> Ken Kesey

in prison, in many cases with life sentences. On several occasions Beresford joined rounds of discussions by the U.S. Sentencing Commission[122] pleading fervently for freedom for all those who had been condemned for psychedelic drug infractions and explaining the difference between those substances and hard drugs.

Together with German activist and publisher Werner Pieper, Beresford organized the first International Conference on Prisoners of the War on Drugs in conjunction with the 1996 Worlds of Consciousness Congress held in Heidelberg. He organized a similar conference in 1999, the first International Drug War Prisoners Conference at York University in Toronto, Canada.

Outrage

In the summer of 1993, writer Peter Stafford first informed Albert Hofmann of the existence of "LSD prisoners," as they were termed by John Beresford in April during a lecture at the University of California in Santa Cruz. (Stafford 1992) Hofmann was appalled and wrote to Beresford: "I became deeply moved and terrified when I learned that people were sentenced to decades of imprisonment for possession of LSD.... I did not even know that LSD prisoners were in jail in the USA. The stories of victims you report seem incredible to happen in a civilized society, very shocking. What kind of administration is that which commits such criminal acts." And: "I express my highest admiration for what you did and do to bring to people's attention and to the Sentencing

> Freedom is being allowed to think your own thoughts and live your own life.
>
> *John F. Kennedy*

John Beresford, 2007   John Beresford in Heidelberg, 1996

Committee what is happening to the victims of such an unbelievable jurisdiction. I do hope that you will be successful in your endeavors to set free those poor people." And in conclusion: "Your report about the LSD prisoners and what you undertook for them is the most important event that came to my knowledge at the occasion of the 50th anniversary of LSD. My heartfelt thanks!"[123] Beresford's answer described the prisoners' plight in detail and spoke of his efforts to personally assist them with legal help to shorten their sentences.[124] Hofmann replied:" I do not understand the hard sentences if I compare them with the sentence Owsley had to serve, the man who produced and sold hundreds of grams of LSD. He told me that when he was arrested the police found him with 180 grams of pure substance; and he only had to serve 3 years! This happened in the sixties."[125]

Three years later upon his ninetieth birthday, Albert Hofmann received a stack of heart-wrenching letters from LSD prisoners directly or indirectly via John Beresford and answered them all personally. As the extracts from his letters to various women and men, mothers and fathers in prison in England, Ireland, and the USA show, Hofmann's outrage over their arrest for possession or use

John Beresford and Albert Hofmann in Heidelberg, 1996

of LSD is quite clear as is his deeply felt sympathy. To a mother in Dublin, he wrote: "My knowledge of the English language does not suffice to express my feelings and my admiration when I read the excellent enthusiastic description of the effects which your LSD experiences had on your life. I share your letter as one of the most beautiful documents testifying the mind opening power of LSD…. I can only wish that you remain capable to retain your eyes and heart open for the reality of the wonder and beauty of life."

To a chemist in California: "I would not believe it if I would not read it in your letter, a 30 years sentence for preparing a psychopharmacon! …This happens in the USA, the protagonist for justice and freedom in the world!!! There are no words to characterize such a hypocrisy. The prohibition of LSD, which was prepared as a medicament, which is a medicament of the higher order, that works on the very core of the human being, on the consciousness, started in the USA. It is a shame that the rest of the world follows this bad example." To a young woman in Dublin: "24 years sentence for possessing and using a pharmacological agent. You did not hurt anybody, you did not disturb society. The American society is already disturbed, punishing people who make use of their right, guaranteed by the Charter of Constitution, "the pursuit of happiness." To a man in California: "Your letter…impressed me deeply. It is a wonderful letter containing clear thoughts, deep insights and a philosophy of life I share with you. If only the people who are responsible for the insane laws regarding the use of psychedelic drugs would try themselves these kind of psychopharmaca, they would become conscious of the harm they produced by the draconian prohibition of psychedelics."[126]

During the closing ceremony of the LSD Symposium on January 15, 2006, on the occasion of Albert Hofmann's 100th birthday, John Beresford presented him with a carefully composed album of letters and photos from women and men incarcerated in the USA. They congratulated the discoverer of LSD and told of their tragic circumstances. None of the cases involved weapons or violence, and financial interest seldom played a role. Beresford was accompanied by Natasha Pickard whose husband Leonard was sentenced to two life sentences for conspiring to produce and sell LSD, and also by Karen Hoffmann, who, as a young Dead-head, was sentenced to life in prison for distributing LSD but after ten years in jail, gained early release in 2002. Hoffmann was arrested during the DEA's Operation Looking Glass,[127] known among Dead-heads as Operation Dead End, which focused on the LSD-consuming public at Grateful Dead concerts.

> John Beresford was a significant player in the psychedelic movement in the West.
>
> *Ram Dass*

> I have always had a high regard for John. I experienced him as a true humanitarian and healer; he gave selflessly of his energy and caring for those in great need. I'd like to think of him as a friend and ally in the work towards a more just and enlightened society.
>
> Ralph Metzner

195

Humane Therapies, Transpersonal Visions

Genuinely new territory in science can only be gained if, at a decisive point, one is willing to abandon the foundation upon which the existing science rests and, so to speak, jump into the void. *Werner Heisenberg*

Divine Lightning

As a brain researcher in Prague in 1956, George Roubiček was one of the first in the Communist Eastern bloc to carry out systematic studies with LSD. He was particularly interested in the effect of LSD on the brain's electrical activity. His approach was to administer a large dose of LSD to each test subject in a dark room and record their physiological parameters throughout the entire experiment. Some three hours after ingesting LSD, subjects were exposed to oscillating flashes of light in varying frequencies from a stroboscope, permitting measurement of how a subject's brain waves were affected. When Roubiček was looking for subjects among his students at Charles University, Stanislav Grof, a medical student, raised his hand. Patience was required, however, because Grof first had to graduate before he could qualify as a subject for these experiments. Nonetheless, since there was a shortage of assistants, he was able to help with several sessions. Soon after he graduated in the fall of 1956 with a degree in medicine and in the philosophy of med-

icine, he was ready. Grof, born in 1931, now a young medical intern, contacted his professor again. His first LSD experience, accompanied by his brother Paul who had also studied medicine, was the turning point in the life of this man who was to become a world-renowned researcher of consciousness. "I felt that a divine thunderbolt had catapulted my conscious self out of my body. I lost my awareness of the research assistant, the laboratory, the psychiatric clinic, Prague and the planet. My consciousness expanded at an inconceivable speed and reached cosmic dimensions. There were no more boundaries or difference between me and the universe." (Grof 2006) This "divine lightning" inspired Grof's career. His first LSD session was enough to convince him that the conventional psychodynamic model he had

> Stanislav Grof is one of the world's greatest living psychologists. He is truly a pioneer in every sense of the word and one of the most comprehensive psychological thinkers of our era.
>
> *Ken Wilber*

This portrait of Albert Hofmann by German artist Bernd Brummbär, was painted in homage "to the great biochemist, inventor of LSD and courageous pioneer of altered states of consciousness," 2007 studied at university could not satisfactorily explain this experience. "This day marked the beginning of my radical departure from the monistic materialism of Western science.... I felt strongly that the study of non-ordinary states of consciousness, in general, and those induced by psychedelics, in particular, was by far the most interesting area of psychiatry I could imagine. I realized that, under the proper circumstances, psychedelic experiences—to a much greater degree than dreams, which play such a crucial role in psychoanalysis are truly, using Freud's words, a 'royal road into the unconscious.' And right there and then, I decided to dedicate my life to the study of non-ordinary states of consciousness." (Grof 2008)

> In forty years, I have never met anyone who has deeply experienced transcendent realms and in spite of that still held on to the Western materialistic scientific world view.
>
> *Stanislav Grof*

> I know of no work that so well incorporates the findings of Freud, Jung and Rank, adding fresh insights which the methods of those psychotherapists never could have achieved.
>
> *Joseph Campbell*

After graduating, he completed training as a psychoanalyst and was hired by the Psychiatric Research Institute in Prague. He investigated the effects of LSD until the mid-1960s and used it quite successfully as a psychotherapy adjunct in over three thousand psychedelic sessions, carefully documenting each case. This invaluable collection of material was the basis for the theories and models he later described in several books. According to his observations, treatment of alcoholics, drug addicts and depressive patients brought the greatest and quickest success. For patients exhibiting psychoneuroses, psychosomatic disturbances, and character neuroses, lasting improvements were usually not sustainable without a systematic working through the various problem areas during a series of multiple LSD sessions. Grof used LSD in accompanied trials as a means of self-exploration and insisted that all persons involved in treatment, from nurses to physicians or psychiatrists, be familiar with the effects of LSD from personal experience, a requirement that was adopted by many researchers.

Thirty Years of Research

In 1965, Stanislav Grof was invited to the USA for an international conference on Psychotherapy with LSD; after which he embarked on a lecture tour. Upon returning to Czechoslovakia, he received an invitation from Joel Elkes, professor at Johns Hopkins University in Baltimore, Maryland, offering him a research fellowship. Grof was engaged in work in Prague and did not wish to thoughtlessly abandon professional and private contacts at home. Nonetheless, after hesitating a short while, he accepted the enticing offer. When the fellowship ended, he decided to remain in the USA. From 1967 to 1973, he was Clinical and Research fellow, Assistant Professor of Psychiatry and later, Chief of Psychiatric Research at Johns Hopkins University.

The program at Johns Hopkins was one of the world's most enduring and influential project to ever study the therapeutic benefits of psychedelics. The program's first studies of LSD had begun in the early 1950s and ended nearly thirty years later. They were

(l. to r.) Stanislav Grof, Hanscarl Leuner and coworkers, ca. 1970

Albert Hofmann at the Maryland Psychiatric Research Center with Walter Pahnke and Helen Bonny

initially carried out in the research department of Spring Grove State Hospital and, after 1969, at the Maryland Psychiatric Research Center in Catonsville. The program was directed by Albert A. Kurland, a physician and Director of the Institute, who was the group's driving force.

Early experience with LSD was gathered from trials with chronic schizophrenic patients. As with other drugs, LSD was ad-

ministered daily. Researchers soon discovered that tolerance to LSD developed after a few days of regular use, after which it had little effect. Albert Hofmann had also established that "LSD does not act as a true medicament; rather it plays the role of a medicinal aid in the context of psychoanalytic and psychotherapeutic treatment." After these first rudimentary trials, research was largely halted for several years. In the early 1960s, a young psychologist, Sanford Unger, brought new initiatives to the Institute. Unger considered visionary experience to be a decisive therapeutic factor and formulated principles of psychedelic therapy and methodology for clinical evaluation.[128] Stanislav Grof, Walter Pahnke, Charles Savage, and Richard Yensen, along with Kurland and Unger, were among the best known members of the dynamic team. Grof recalled: "The period between 1967 and 1973 that I spent at the Maryland Psychiatric Research Center in Catonsville, Maryland, was a time of exciting team cooperation with a group of passionate and congenial researchers," during which he could contribute important experience and his theories which were as yet little known. Under his guidance, the group developed a blend of the European psycholytic and American psychedelic approaches and called it "psychodelytic." Grof had earlier suggested combining the deep psychological insights of psycholytic therapy with the strong motivation to change behavior which psychedelic

> Hippies—they've gathered a great deal of experience in this area—have said: of every five trips, one is a horror trip and four are good; this has to be taken into account. Psychiatrists say: it can be extremely valuable to confront the negative side of your consciousness.
>
> *Albert Hofmann*

therapy induced.[129] As a result, the group began to focus more on the analysis and processing of psychedelic experience. In particular, they no longer considered negatively experienced events as failures but gave them the attention Grof felt they warranted due to their potential for transformation. In further studies, the team systematically investigated psychedelic therapy's prospects for successful treatment of various psychopathologies, for training psychiatric personnel, for use in the care of terminally ill cancer patients, and for treatment during withdrawal of heroin and alcohol addicts.

Encouraged by earlier promising results with treating addictions, the research group at the Maryland Psychiatric Research Center randomly divided one hundred and thirty-five alcoholics into two groups. One received a high, one-time dose of 450 micrograms of LSD with the intent of freeing them from their deadlocked addictive patterns through an overwhelming experience; the other group received moderate, one-time doses of 50 micrograms. Six months later, an evaluation team independently ranked 53 percent of the higher dosage group as "essentially rehabilitated" as compared with 33 percent of the lower dosage group. Eighteen months later, the differences between the two groups had nearly vanished. The results from this study were all the more remarkable since all the patients had only undergone a single LSD session combined with a few hours of psychotherapy before and after the trial. Most surprising for the therapists were the dramatic improvements in many patients in the control group who had only received 50 micrograms of LSD, as the low dosage was considered to be an "active placebo" without noticeable therapeutic effect.[130]

Encounter With Death

A further indication for LSD-assisted psychotherapy came from the treatment of seriously ill and dying persons. Independently of each other, author Aldous Huxley and pediatrician Valentina Wasson, wife of mushroom researcher Gordon Wasson, were the first to suggest administering psychedelics in conjunction with therapeutic accompaniment to terminally ill patients. A pioneer in LSD treatment for terminal cancer patients, Eric Kast investigated the use of LSD as an analgesic, in studies which he carried out in the early 1960s at the Chicago Medical School.

At Maryland Psychiatric Research Center, Walter Pahnke systematically explored the effects of psychedelic therapy on cancer patients. Following Pahnke's early death in 1971, Grof took charge of medical treatment. The study investigated the changes in mental states and in the physical pain of patients but also how the patient's attitude towards dying was affected. Over a number of years, more than one hundred cancer patients were given LSD or DPT—dipropyltryptamine—a similar but significantly shorter-acting substance.

Many patients reported a distinct reduction in negative emotions, such as anxiety, despondency, tenseness, and insomnia, as well as diminished avoidance of social situations. Furthermore, LSD therapy had a marked though unreliable influence on acute physical pain. Many patients who did not respond to conventional analgesics reported that a single LSD session reduced their pain for weeks, some for even months, and others were completely relieved. The most spectacular changes came in attitude

Joan Halifax

towards death and belief about a life after death. Nearly all patients with spiritual sensibility found they feared death less and tended to a stronger belief that the soul or consciousness survives biological death. Successful therapy also had a positive influence on relatives of these patients, allowing them to bear more readily their mourning and ineluctable loss. For some thirty percent of cancer patients, an LSD session brought dramatic improvement on the parameters measured and moderately positive change for another forty percent. The remaining thirty percent showed no significant change after treatment.

Grof considered the treatment of the terminally ill to be the most interesting and least controversial indication for LSD psychotherapy. He believed that the possibility of quickly reducing psychic and physical suffering for dying persons met with less resistance than other areas of application. Although this treatment was tried almost exclusively with cancer patients, his opinion is that it is appropriate to use it for people with other life-threatening illnesses. His observations showed that for some patients, LSD psychotherapy could

not only aid in preparing for death but might prolong life or even bring recovery.

With his first wife, anthropologist Joan Halifax, who assisted in these studies, Grof presented their results in *The Human Encounter with Death*. (Grof, Halifax 1977) Along with an extensive description of their analyses, they elucidated the phenomena of dying and death from comparative cultural, philosophical and spiritual perspectives. They came to the conclusion that "Death and life, usually considered to be irreconcilable opposites, appear to actually be dialectically interrelated. Living fully and with maximum awareness every moment of one's life leads to an accepting and reconciled attitude toward death. Conversely, such an approach to human existence requires that we come to terms with our mortality and the impermanence of existence. This seems to be the innermost significance of ancient mysteries, various spiritual practices, and

> Which states of consciousness do we want to show present to our children, those shown on RTL television or the one found with meditation? The one found with alcohol or the one found with LSD?
>
> *Thomas Metzinger*

201

rites of passage." A rabbi, who, on his own initiative, had participated in an LSD training program at the Research Center, sought words that did justice to his harrowing encounter with death and subsequent spiritual rebirth. What came to his mind were words spoken by Leonardo da Vinci as he was dying: "While I thought that I was learning how to live, I have been learning how to die," and he turned them around and said: "I thought I was dying, but I was only preparing to live."

The Cartographer

In our everyday consciousness, we experience our identity as firmly delimited. In altered states of consciousness, such as dreams, ecstasy, trance or intoxication, boundaries between the self and the external world shift in many ways. At the start of the twentieth century, American psychologist William James pointed out that "Our normal waking consciousness, rational consciousness as we call it, is but one special type of consciousness, whilst all about it, parted from it by the flimsiest of screens, there lie potential forms of consciousness entirely different. We may go through life without suspecting their existence; but apply the requisite stimulus, and at a touch they are there in all their completeness." LSD apparently provided that stimulus. In his first book, *Realms of the Human Unconscious: Observations from LSD Research*, (1975) Grof provided a systematic survey of states and contents of consciousness that appeared in his patients during LSD therapy

> Lose your mind and come to your senses.
>
> *Fritz Perls*

sessions and illustrated them with striking protocols from his therapeutic practice.

The initial sessions usually resulted in the recall of long-buried experiences from early childhood. These were not merely remembered but literally re-lived. Birth and death are undoubtedly the two most important constants in human life. The experiences of death and rebirth are thus central to psychedelic sessions. Grof concluded that psychedelic therapy is a new version of that which "since time immemorial, powerful procedures have existed... that appear to facilitate such experiences in individuals as well as groups... either on special occasions, such as rites of passage and initiation rites, or as a matter of everyday practice in ecstatic cults." In the course of the many therapeutic LSD sessions he guided, Grof observed how frequently memories of the period surrounding birth came up, always corresponding to a particular phenomenology and fixed pattern. He discerned four phases in the psychological experience of time before and after birth, that corresponded with psychopathological syndromes and correlated with specific memories from postnatal life. During the first phase of a normal pregnancy, the fetus experiences *oneness* with the mother. After onset of labor and first contractions, this experience changes to *hell*. During contractions which lead to expulsion, the experience is one of *struggle*. And, finally, the fetus emerges newly born into the light. In Grof's experience, these phases shape one's psyche for the rest of one's life depending on which of these phases was decisive and how they were experienced. Grof called them "perinatal matrices" or behavior and thought patterns from the period surrounding birth. Grof considered a series of LSD sessions with high doses to be necessary for bringing the biological, emotional, philosophical and spiritual contents of the perinatal level up to consciousness. "In this process the individual has to face the deepest roots of existential despair, metaphysical anxiety and loneliness, murderous aggression, abysmal guilt and inferiority feelings, as well as excruciating physical discomfort and the agony of total annihilation. These experiences open up access to the opposite end of the spectrum—orgiastic feelings of cosmic proportions, spiritual liberation and enlightenment, a sense of ecstatic connection with all of creation, and mystical union with the creative principle in the universe."

The greatest challenges to Western psychology are the "transpersonal experiences" of Grof and many of his patients that comprise the entire gamut of states and phenomena known from spiritual traditions and parapsychological research. To this day, most psychologists do not consider them authentic and interpret them symbolically or pathologically. Grof divides them into two categories, the first one comprising expansion of awareness within the framework of "objective reality." He further divides this into several subgroups: Experiences that involve temporal expansion of awareness such as embryonic and fetal memories; collective and race-specific experiences; experiences of an earlier incarnation; precognition; clairvoyance; clairaudience; and time travel. Among the experiences belonging to spatial expansion of awareness are self-transcendence in interpersonal relationships; identification with other persons, groups, animals, plants, and inorganic material; out-of-body travel;

and planetary or cosmic awareness. Examples of spatial narrowing of awareness include organ, tissue, and cell-awareness. The second category comprises experiences that go beyond the framework of "objective reality;" here Grof includes mediumistic and spiritist experiences, encounters with superhuman spiritual beings, unknown life forms and deities, as well as archetypal and mythological experiences.

Expanding of the Image of Humanity

In the mid-1960s, a third force joined pathology-based psychoanalysis and behavioral therapy, namely, humanistic psychology which was given its theoretical underpinnings by its founder Abraham Maslow.[131] He is known particularly for his "hierarchy of needs," a developmental model of behavior which is often represented as a pyramid. He proposed a psychology of spiritual health and human self-realization in place of the pathology-based models. The core tenets of humanistic psychology purport that individuals have the potential for unsuspected possibilities to understand themselves and alter their self-images, basic outlooks, and behaviors. This potential can be developed if a clearly defined climate of favorable attitudes is achieved. According to humanistic psychologists, psychic disturbances arise when external influences block the self from evolving. Carl

> Human beings are part of the whole we call "the universe," a part that is delimited in space and time. We experience ourselves, our thoughts and feelings, as something separate from the rest, a kind of optical illusion of our consciousness.
>
> *Albert Einstein*

Rogers based his client-centered psychotherapy on Maslow's concept, developing it further for practical application in therapy. Both Maslow and Rogers understood the humanistic idea as a counterforce to dehumanization in our culture.[132]

However, the humanistic model of psychology had no place for the myriad forms of mystical and paranormal experience that Grof's patients underwent during LSD sessions, for which the term "transpersonal" was coined. The limitations of the psychodynamic model became clear to Grof during his very first experience. From then on, he believed that, even with all the means at their disposal, the natural sciences cannot explain life and all of its phenomena. These concepts made Grof the real father of transpersonal psychology. Along with the initiators of Esalen Institute, Michael Murphy and Dick Price, he founded the International Transpersonal Association (ITA) in 1978 and remained its chairman until 1982 and coeditor of the journal, *Transpersonal Psychology and Psychotherapy*, for several years.

In the last years of his life, Maslow supplemented his five-level hierarchy of needs with a sixth—striving for transcendence—thus acknowledging the concerns of transpersonal psychology.[133] His addition recognized not only the basic humanistic aspects but religious and spiritual experiences of the psyche, "peak experiences," which go beyond everyday awareness.

> Our great human adventure is the evolution of consciousness. We are in this life to enlarge the soul, liberate the spirit, and light up the brain.
>
> *Tom Robbins*

The foremost representatives of transpersonal psychology, in particular Stanislav Grof, Abraham Maslow, and Ken Wilber, contributed significantly to classifying and reassessing altered states of consciousness. Their interpretation departs strongly on several points from Western scientific tradition: "Normal" waking consciousness and "altered" states of consciousness are by no means distinctly separate but flow one into the other to build a spectrum of consciousness. Altered states of consciousness are no longer to be regarded as pathological deviations from a "normal" mental state; rather they must be understood as forms of expanded experience and taken seriously. Their contents often display paranormal aspects that cannot be attributed to fantasies, hallucinations, or recalled images. The reality that becomes accessible to us in altered states of consciousness may be more comprehensive than the one we experience in our familiar understanding of space-time. Transpersonal psychology considers altered states of consciousness to be harbingers of spiritual evolution that can prompt and spur personal growth.

The Spectrum of Consciousness

Much conceptual confusion and many contradictions amongst different schools of psychology and spiritual teachings stem from ill-defined and unclear boundaries regarding which levels of consciousness are concerned. American philosopher and consciousness researcher Ken Wilber designed a model that integrates all states of consciousness into one spectrum. (Wilber 1977) His clarification of terms and concepts partly reconciles apparently contradictory ideas and competing disciplines. Wilber's model is a multidimensional description of human identity ranging from unity with cosmic consciousness through different stages, which Wilber terms "bands," to the constricted sense of identity that is peculiar to the consciousness of self.

In agreement with many spiritual teachings, Wilber starts from the assumption that the innermost consciousness of human beings is identical with the absolute reality of the universe, which is named according to its lineage tradition, Brahman, Tao or God. He calls this dimension "Spirit;" it is in no particular place, therefore unending, and timeless, therefore eternal.

At the *level of spirit*, humans identify with the universe, are at one with it. In the *philosophia perennis* or eternal philosophy, as Aldous Huxley described this essence of all spiritual wisdom traditions, this level is the only "real" state. Hence, the innermost consciousness of humans, called Atman or Christ, is identical with the highest reality of existence.

The "transpersonal bands" represent a zone of the spectrum that goes beyond individual personhood in which one transcends the boundaries of his individual organism but is not aware of his identity with the universe. This part of the spectrum contains the phenomena described by Grof, from the archetypes of C.G. Jung to extra sensory perceptions.

Only at the *existential level* does a strict separation of the ego and the external world occur. Human beings identify with their three-dimensional organisms existing in space and time. This level includes the personal will as well as the "biosocial bands,"

Ken Wilber

as Wilber refers to the cultural patterns of family relationships and social conventions, and to the areas that color experience, such as language, logic and ethics.

At the *level of ego*, a person no longer feels like a total organism of body and soul but identifies himself by means of a mental image with reasoning and an ego. No longer does the person consider himself as just a body but as possessing a body and often, when experiencing parts of his own psyche as alien and separate, splits them off. This shrinks identity further down to parts of an ego. Psychic features that are too painful or incompatible with the person's world view are excluded, forming a foreign object. Wilber calls this the *shadow level*.

This highly condensed summary cannot do justice to the complex relationships between the individual levels and sub-levels. Wilber's core statement is that our sense of identity continuously narrows the further we move away from the level of spirit. The assertions of a particular psychological school or philosophical model can be associated with the levels of consciousness to which those systems and therapy approaches correlate. It is indisputable that the greater part of our dreams can be interpreted through the psychodynamic model. For proponents of the transpersonal approach, it is just as clear that there are dreams which are lucid, predictive, or archetypal and which cannot be reasonably explained within that narrow framework. Hence, it makes no

> Experience is not what happens to us; it is what we do with what happens to us.
> *Aldous Huxley*

sense to interpret a lucid dream at the Freudian level of the ego.

Lama Anagarika Govinda, a prominent representative of Tibetan Buddhism, put it this way: "These cases are not to be understood as separate, successive levels, but as mutually interpenetrating principles—from the subtlest all-radiant consciousness that penetrates everything to the material consciousness which appears as body."

Wilber's method clarifies many apparent contradictions and distinctions between various models: Two opposing theories can both be true if they are being applied to *different* levels of the spectrum of consciousness. Wilber offers a model for synthesizing contrary theoretical approaches in which diverse psychological schools and the great wisdom traditions have equal standing. Ken Wilber became the most important theoretician of transpersonal, or as he later called it, integral psychology.

Human Potential

California psychologists Michael Murphy and Dick Price met during their student days at Stanford University in the early 1950s. Studies in comparative religion and Indian philosophy had led Price to Harvard University where he met Alan Watts and lived with him for a time. Murphy traveled to India and the Ashram of Sri Aurobindo, near which the futuristic city Auroville came into being. After several years, inspired by Eastern philosophy and psychedelic experiments at Harvard, they both returned to San Francisco. Together, they wanted to realize a project that would make new forms of thought and study, beyond established

university and scientific enterprises, accessible to the growing ranks of young people searching for new insights and experiences in the realm of human development. Dick Price was an attentive member of the audience at the lecture given by Aldous Huxley in San Francisco in 1960 entitled "Human Potentialities." Huxley had long delved intensively into Eastern traditions and wisdom. In his book *The Perennial Philosophy* (Huxley 1949) he wrote: "It is only by making physical experiments that we can discover the intimate nature of matter and its potentialities. And it is by making psychological and moral experiments that we can discover the intimate nature of mind and its potentialities. In the ordinary circumstances of average sensual life these potentialities of the mind remain latent and unmanifested."

Price and Murphy quickly decided to give realization of human potential an appreciable boost. Murphy's grandmother had put a magnificent property near Big Sur on the Pacific coast at his disposal free of charge. It was dusk as the two young entrepreneurs viewed their future location for the first time. As they entered the main house, a young man held a pistol in their faces and asked: "Who are you and what do you want here?" It was Hunter S. Thompson, the watchman employed by Murphy's grandmother. Ten years later, that watchman would publish his novel *Fear and Loathing in Las Vegas,* which became an international best seller after the release of the film version featuring Johnny Depp. Dick Price's father provided generous financial support for their project. With the encouragement of Aldous and Laura Huxley, Alan Watts,

View from Esalen Institute, California

Gerald Heard and Gregory Bateson, Esalen Institute was launched in 1962. It became one of the most influential centers worldwide for new kinds of research and training. Michael Murphy described the basic objective of the workshop of the future as follows: "Esalen Institute exists to promote the harmonious development of the whole person. It is a learning center devoted to ongoing research of human potential which transcends religious, scientific and other dogma. It is devoted to the theory, practice, research, and founding of organizations to facilitate social advancement and offers seminars to this end for the general public; it organizes conferences, research programs, periods of residence for artists, scholars, scientists, and religious teachers, offers work-study programs and sponsors semi-autonomous projects."

Among the first teachers and course instructors were such luminaries as the founder of Gestalt therapy, Fritz Perls; historian of economics, Arnold Toynbee; theologian Paul Tillich, two-time Nobel prize winner Linus Pauling, psychotherapist Carl Rogers, behavioral researcher B.F. Skinner, family therapist Virginia Satir, nature photographer Ansel Adams, anthropologist Michael Harner, parapsychologist J.B. Rhine, dolphin and consciousness researcher John C. Lilly, Tao teacher Chungliang Al Huang, as well as Stanislav Grof, Timothy Leary and Richard Alpert. The Institute also offered various courses on "drug-induced mysticism;" in some therapies, psychedelics were utilized.

An Alternative

Stanislav Grof did research and taught at Esalen Institute from 1973 to 1987. Since LSD therapy was no longer lawful, together with his wife Christina, he sought other, non-pharmacological methods at Esalen for bringing about altered states of consciousness. They discovered that

> I like to imagine a future in which humanity will overcome all racial, gender, national, cultural, political, and economic divisions and create a global community.
>
> *Stanislav Grof*

certain breathing patterns led to states of consciousness similar to those achieved with LSD and then integrated these techniques into a new therapy approach they called "Holotropic Breathwork."[134] The most important aspect is strongly accelerated deep breathing, a kind of intentional hyperventilation. Special instrumental music, selected according to the particular phase of the experience, and simple therapeutic bodywork reinforce the effect of forced breathing. The entire process takes between one and a half and three hours; it involves several progressively more intense phases, achieves a peak, and then subsides. Holotropic breathing is done most often in group settings. Participants form teams of two in which one member, under the direction of the therapist, accompanies the other member who lies on a mat with eyes closed. During the course of a session, strong emotional outbursts might occur resulting in a catharsis which the partner facilitated through physical contact. Afterward, participants processed their experiences creatively, often by painting mandalas and talking about their experiences in the group. The technique shows some similarity to rebirthing[135] and has the power to open up a person. Hence, Holotropic Breathwork is also used to complement other therapies for overcoming blockages and enhancing entry into the spiritual realm. Nonetheless, Grof considered it to be an unsatisfactory substitute for LSD therapy. He is a firm opponent of the present drug prohibition and has repeatedly spoken out for legalization of psychedelic substances.

Esalen became Grof's place of residence and work for many years. "Since my first visit in 1965, it has offered me many opportunities to conduct seminars and workshops

(l. to r.) Dagmar and Václav Havel, Stanislav Grof

and share my material with open-minded and sympathetic audiences. In the last five years it has become my home base and a unique emotional and intellectual resource. In this extraordinary natural laboratory of the human potential movement I met many creative people pioneering in experiential psychotherapies, and had the opportunity to relate their work to my own. This made it possible for me to integrate the observations from LSD research into a broader theoretical context. Of particular value have been the experiences from a series of experimental educational programs for professionals, which my wife Christina and I have been conducting at Esalen. These events, which organically combine didactic input, intrapsychic exploration and group work, and have a guest faculty ranging from Mexican and North-American shamans to theoretical physicists, have become an invaluable source of inspiration."

In the late 1980s Grof left Esalen and moved north of San Francisco to Mill Valley. There he trained therapists in Holotropic Breathwork, wrote books, and gave lectures. In Prague, where his remarkable career had begun, in recognition of his life's work, he

(l. to r.) Václav Havel, Stanislav and his brother Paul Grof

received the Vision 97 Prize from the Dagmar and Václav Havel Foundation bestowed on October 5, 2007 by Václav Havel, former president of the Czech Republic.

Interaction at Esalen

Albert Hofmann was a guest at Esalen Institute in February of 1984 for an informal gathering concerning psychedelics and spirituality. Stanislav Grof had personally invited him and conducted an interview with him to introduce the Swiss chemist to the other participants. Hofmann felt at home in California: "Thank you for inviting me to Esalen. I really enjoy this very beautiful landscape. It is so wonderful to be here and to experience the atmosphere at this institute with old friends and colleagues. It has been a great

experience for me." During his stay, Hofmann met for the first time Christian Rätsch, an ethnologist from Hamburg as well as Ralph Metzner who recalled: "Stanislav Grof organized an informal meeting of some twenty psychedelic researchers to debate the potential for these substances in therapy and consciousness research and to compare them with each other. Albert Hofmann was there, Andrew Weil, Christian Rätsch, and others. At the time, MDMA was known but was not yet illegal. Of course we tried out this substance together. I baptized it an 'empathogen' in its effect because it quite easily put one into a state of empathy, which is extremely valuable in therapy and in all interpersonal relationships. In one conversation during this session, Albert said to me and others in English: 'with this substance, matter and mind are one.' A while later I said to him, as I was thinking of his discovery of LSD, 'for those who love Her, Nature reveals her deepest and most beautiful secrets.' Albert squeezed my hand in silent agreement. In January of 1984 I got a small card from him with a photo of the Rittimatte, in which he referred to the meeting at Esalen. He wrote in English: 'I am happy to collaborate with you and our California friends in order to help people to open their eyes and minds for the message of the Creation, its beauty and wonder.'"[136]

The use of entheogenic drugs in all cultures has always been incorporated within a religious-ceremonial setting. Thus, the experience becomes that for which man has ever yearned most deeply, *unio mystica* and its resulting bliss.
Albert Hofmann

Mushrooms Instead of Fish

While Leary and Alpert's Concord Prison Project was dedicated to "sinners," the Good Friday experiment, dubbed the "Miracle of March Chapel" in the annals of psychedelic studies, dealt with the "blessed." With the approval of Timothy Leary, his doctoral advisor, Walter Norman Pahnke (who already had a medical degree), wanted to explore whether administering psilocybin to subjects in a religious setting triggered or favored mystical experiences; the experiment related to his dissertation for Harvard Divinity School. For practical reasons, he chose psilocybin rather than LSD because its effects lasted half as long. He set out to "gather empirical data about the state of consciousness experienced [on drugs]" to compare with his "typology of mysticism." Although Leary had recommended that he gather his own psychedelic experiences prior to the experiment, Pahnke preferred to wait until his thesis had been approved so no one

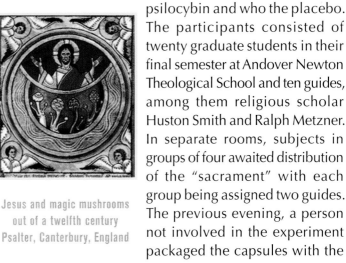

Jesus and magic mushrooms out of a twelfth century Psalter, Canterbury, England

could accuse him of bias. The experiment was conducted on Good Friday, April 20, 1962, during a worship service in the Protestant Chapel of Boston University. Subjects could move freely between a main space and three secondary spaces while being discreetly observed.

The experiment was designed as a classic double blind scientific study: Neither the participating students nor the investigating researchers knew who had received the psilocybin and who the placebo. The participants consisted of twenty graduate students in their final semester at Andover Newton Theological School and ten guides, among them religious scholar Huston Smith and Ralph Metzner. In separate rooms, subjects in groups of four awaited distribution of the "sacrament" with each group being assigned two guides. The previous evening, a person not involved in the experiment packaged the capsules with the

Robert Venosa, *Enlightenment*, oil on canvas, 90 x 120 cm, 1977 drug and placebos for each group. At ten-thirty a.m., all thirty participants got identical-appearing capsules: Half of the subjects and one of the leaders in each group received capsules containing 30 milligrams of psilocybin, while capsules containing nicotinic acid, a short-acting stimulant, were given to the remaining ten subjects and the other five leaders. Eighty minutes after the subjects had ingested the capsules, Howard Thurman, an African-American pastor, began conducting a service that lasted over two hours ending at two-thirty in the afternoon. It quickly became evident who had received the placebo and who the active ingredient. Ten of the twenty subjects sat attentively in the pew. Among the other ten, some wandered through the chapel, some lay on the floor or stretched out on a pew, and one sat at the organ and played strange chords. Five of the attendants also behaved oddly. Over Pahnke's objection, Leary had seen to it that the attending guides also be included.

At half past four, the students were systematically questioned and subsequently allowed to go home. During the days following the experiment and once again after six months, the participants completed the same nine-part questionnaire. Pahnke wanted to use these evaluations to determine the quality of the subjects' encounters and quantify the degree of their mystical experience.

This important effort to compare altered states of consciousness in mystics with those induced by psychedelics was docu-

That was probably the first time that an empirical scientific experiment examined something like "religious feeling." And the mystical experiences of the young theologians was "mind-blowing"!

Ralph Metzner

mented in Pahnke's publication, *Drugs and Mysticism.* (Pahnke) In the first part, he described and defined the characteristics of mystical experience based on numerous examples and quotations from mystics. Pahnke determined that particularly characteristic of their experience was primarily a sense of unity, in terms of absorption of the individual within the whole, of the merging of relative with absolute, subject with object, personhood with divinity. All further characteristics of the mystical state he interpreted as consequences of this central experience of unity: Among these, transcendence of time and space, the perceived poverty of language to adequately express the experience, and feelings of overwhelming joy, love, and holiness.

The second part presented the results of the experiment. His findings were unmistakable: Nine of ten students from the psilocybin group reported deeply moving mystical and religious experiences and sensations. No one in the placebo group had comparable experiences and that group fell far short on all the parameters measured. The second questionnaire completed after six months showed that for eight of the ten who had received psilocybin, positive effects were still present. These subjects emphasized their heightened sensibility and perception and described deep insights into the transcendence of their existence. The experiment also had a positive effect on their daily lives: They lived more consciously, reflected more upon their lifestyles, and displayed greater social engagement. Pahnke believed the positive consequences were due to the fact that the church service had provided a safe and familiar framework for the drug experience. It was clear to him that

Walter and Eva Pahnke with daughter Jennifer

Albert Hofmann and Rick Doblin at the conference of the International Transpersonal Association, August 1983, Davos, Switzerland

psychoactive substances in a church were a controversial subject. "To some theologians, the awareness that it appears possible to experience mystical consciousness... with the help of a drug on a free Saturday afternoon at first appears ironic and even profane" Pahnke remarked. In addition, the experiment raised the question as to whether mystical experiences are based solely on neurological processes and questioned the basic tenet that a mystical experience has to be earned through asceticism or years of meditative practice.

About twenty years later, a young Boston psychologist, Rick Doblin, investigated the long-term effects of the Good Friday experiment for his doctoral thesis. (Doblin 1991) It took him four years to find nineteen of the original twenty participants. Sixteen agreed to complete the same questionnaire as before. The results were astonishing: All answers were practically identical to those from a quarter century earlier. Nine of the ten participants who had taken psilocybin confirmed that their one-time psychedelic experience had enabled them to lead a more aware and spiritual life, and they had gained a more nuanced understanding of

questions regarding life and death. They reiterated that the experiment had been a positive influence. However, several subjects also related difficult moments during the experiment when they had feared they might go insane or die. Pahnke had suppressed the fact that he needed to inject one student with an antidote; that student had immediately wanted to follow the pastoral calling to spread the good news of Christ, had left the chapel, and gone out into the street from where he had to be retrieved. Of those in the control group, only one participant reported that the experiment had given him much. However, it was not the church service that

> There is almost a rule of thumb for those worlds of experience: the deeper the drug experience, the more impossible addiction becomes. What precludes these drugs from having addictive potential from the beginning is the ritual setting of the ecstasy and the sacramental interpretation of the realities that emerge. For my part, I use the term "sacrament" in an emphatically magical, sacerdotal sense in comparison with which the symbolism of Catholic sacramentalism pales. Of course our sanctified host was tinged with a drop of Albert Hofmann's famous problem child, lysergic acid diethylamide—so it would deserve to be mentioned in the same breath as soma and peyote.
>
> *Peter Sloterdijk*

213

had positive consequences for him but the decision he made to try psychedelic drugs himself at the next opportunity. In his follow up report, Rick Doblin judged the results of the Good Friday experiment to be largely positive; this led him to found the Multidisciplinary Association for Psychedelic Studies (MAPS) in 1986, a worldwide organization dedicated to the study and promotion of psychedelically-aided psychotherapies. Reverend Mike Young, today in his seventies, was one of the subjects who had received psilocybin. He is a family friend of President Barack Obama and conducted the memorial service for the President's grandmother in December 2008. Young described his personal insights on Good Friday of 1962 as the most profound spiritual experience of his life and to this day, is not tired of inviting Christian churches and leaders responsible for theological training to enter into, as he calls it, "entheological dialogue."

Like Pahnke some forty-five years earlier, psychiatrist Roland Griffiths at Johns Hopkins University in Baltimore wished to explore whether, and to what extent, psilocybin could trigger mystical experiences, but not in the context of a worship service. His study (Griffiths 2008) provided impressive confirmation of the results of the innovative Good Friday experiments. Two thirds of the thirty-six subjects indicated having had a mystical experience under the influence of psilocybin. Even fourteen months after the one-time trial, they reported feeling better than before the experiment: More satisfied, creative, self-assured, flexible, and optimistic. As Dede Osborn, a sixty-eight year old business consultant put it: "I feel more centered.... I don't seem to have those self-doubts like I used to have." As with the other participants, she had not previously taken psychedelics but had regularly participated in religious or spiritual activities.

The Missing Taboo

In November 1964, Walter Pahnke sent Albert Hofmann his dissertation, published in book form as *Drugs and Mysticism*. Hofmann's comments about the experiment were encouraging; he inquired as to whether the examining committee was "still under the influence of the Leary-Alpert affair" and how Pahnke's work had been received by Harvard University, since he did not believe that Pahnke's "Good Friday experiment could have been carried out in good old Europe." Hofmann used this letter of thanks to expand on the subject in the title and regretted that his English was not adequate for expressing himself as clearly as he would have liked: "I hoped to give you my final answer and my final personal view on the question of drugs and mysticism. The true mystical state of consciousness being the very aim, the deepest sense of human life, the innermost core of religion, one cannot be careful and

> We picked our subjects for diversity of culture: devout Christians, Muslims, agnostics. We found that all had comparable experiences! I think we are dealing with a region of the human soul that is something like the actual foundation in which our human yearning for religious orientation might be anchored.
>
> *Roland Griffiths*

> At least part of the meaning of LSD today is this: that chemical technology has made available to millions the experience of transcendence of the individual ego which a century ago was available only to the disciplined mystic.
>
> *Frank Barron*

delicate enough in treating this problem. From this, i.e., from the faculty of seeing more and more of the true reality, depends essentially the future of mankind.... I must confess that in this context many basic questions still remain open for me, e.g., who should be allowed and when should one be allowed to use these drugs to induce a state of mysticism. (Allowed, of course not in the sense of governmental restriction or release but in respect to personal ethical responsibility.)... Your work is a further convincing example of the importance of set and setting for the development of different effects of psychedelics. You show, e.g., that the psychotic reactions which led to the designation 'Modell Psychose' for the action of this kind of substances follow from the special view of the psychiatrist and his setting. A very important question, in fact a crucial one, is whether there is a lasting beneficial impact of the psychedelic induced mystical experience on the everyday life (love, wholeness, harmony of emotion and intellect). This would be even more important than the question whether the drug induced mystical experience is in every respect identical with the spontaneous mystical state. The spontaneous mystical experience occurs probably because an individual's mind has grown consciously or unconsciously to such a state that the enlightening must occur spontaneously and that therefore he is able to realize his insights in his everyday life. If on the other side mystical consciousness is induced by a psychedelic to somebody who is actually not prepared to it, then it will probably not have a lasting beneficial effect on this personality;

on the contrary, it may be harmful. This raises again the problem mentioned above: who is worthy to take a psychedelic? In the light of these thoughts, one would say: Everybody to whom a mystical experience could happen also spontaneously. But who knows this?"[137]

In conversations and lectures, Albert Hofmann repeatedly emphasized that in shamanic tribal cultures, the plants of the gods were considered sacred and magical medicine that could only be used under certain conditions and consumed before they could develop their beneficial healing and therapeutic effects. The gods threaten to punish their desecration or abuse with sickness, insanity or death. "In our Western civilization the taboo is missing which regulates the use of psychedelics by primitive people. It is difficult to replace taboo by government regulations and therefore it is of paramount importance to know what kind of persons and organizations are dealing with the application and distribution of psychedelic drugs."[138]

Vast Emptiness, Nothing Holy

Very few people who visit a traditional Christian worship service expect or even hope to have a mystical

> What should a rationalistic, materialistic, and rather unbelieving society do with drugs that bring visions? Should they be completely banned? Who should have access to them? Scientists for research projects? Psychotherapists? Philosophers, who seek to understand thought processes? Artists hoping for heightened creative powers? Mystics? Hedonists?
>
> *Sidney Cohen*

> We have simply looked away. If you choose not to integrate such drugs into our culture, that causes great damage as well.
>
> *Thomas Metzinger*

experience in that environment. Consequently, it is questionable whether the sermon in Pahnke's experiment was a decisive catalyst for the religious experience. His choice of a church service as setting is a demonstrative reminder that originally longing for and ultimately experiencing God was the goal of religiously motivated assemblies.

The growing interest in LSD and Eastern meditation techniques in the 1960s was an indication of the increasing importance of finding one's self and meaning in life. Being sought were direct experiences and personal discoveries, not the rigid rituals, admonitions, doctrines, and codes of behavior offered by religious institutions. Many people described their psychedelic peak experiences as mystical, spiritual, or religious and their descriptions closely resemble those of persons who have had a spontaneous religious revelation. For some, such states of expanded consciousness represented a first and often dramatic encounter with hitherto unknown dimensions of their minds. A few left it at that; for others, the relatively short excursion into the realm of expanded awareness was as if a door to paradise had opened briefly and then closed again. That finite moment, that glimpse into spiritual spheres, sufficed to trigger the desire to explore and plumb the depths of these other worlds.

In many people, LSD experiences awakened an interest in living spirituality but seldom in institutionalized religions. Very few joined an established Christian religious group based on their experiences; a few were drawn to charismatic sects. In contrast, a steadily growing number of people were attracted to millennia-old practices of shamanism. Life in a tribal group, in harmony with the laws and rhythms of nature and archaic rituals, was a major attraction for people seeking new forms of community and a new relationship with nature.

Journeys to the East

Exerting the greatest pull upon Westerners search for meaning, India has often been idealized as the cradle of spirituality. Yearning for the mysterious wonderland in the East dates from late antiquity, when young Greeks traveled to India to listen to the wisdom of the Brahmins. In many lands over the centuries, people have sought to find a path to the legendary land of the Orient. In the modern era, ever since Hermann Hesse's novel *Journey to the East*, became a household name, many more have sought to gain access to India's natural treasures and wisdom. Another of his narratives, called *Sehnsucht nach Indien* (Longing for India), expresses a yearning awakened in Hesse in early childhood. His ancestors had been missionaries in India and his mother was born there. In the course of a three-month trip to Asia in 1911, he became acquainted with the Muslim, Hindu, and Buddhist worlds and later often wrote of them. His best known story is *Siddhartha*, a novella that describes the life of a young Brahmin who is admired by all and dedicates his life to the search

> As for psychedelics, it has been pointed out that they only accomplish their objective if you work with them. That is true as well for religions.
>
> Brother David
> Steindl-Rast

> Those wise ones who see that the consciousness within themselves is the same consciousness within all conscious beings attain eternal peace.
>
> Katha Upanishad

for the All One, the Atman. Hesse became the most popular writer of the 1960s and an icon of the hippie movement.

A trip to the Orient in a VW bus or as a hitchhiker became an unforgettable and formative rite of passage for countless young dropouts. Their image of India was of ascetic Hindu sadhus with long hair, who kept apart from society and all convention and smoked hashish in chillums, or of exuberantly colorful psychedelic temples and their idols. The archaic and anarchic aspects of Indian culture became a symbol of freedom, forming a counterpoint to what was perceived as the elaborate and boring lifestyle of the West.

The Beatles traveled to India and learned Transcendental Meditation from Maharishi Mahesh Yogi; Allen Ginsberg became a Buddhist, the Harvard trio composed a psychedelic handbook modeled after instructions found in the *Tibetan Book of the Dead* (Leary, Metzner, Alpert 1971), Timothy Leary adapted texts from the *Tao Te Ching* for his *Psychedelic Prayers*, Stanislav Grof became a student of the Siddha Yoga master, Swami Muktananda, and at rock festivals, the sounds of Ravi Shankar's sitar were to be heard.

In the Here and Now

During their time at Harvard, Timothy Leary, Richard Alpert and Ralph Metzner cultivated an intensive exchange of ideas with Aldous Huxley and Alan Watts, both widely recognized experts on the spiritual traditions of the East. Their study of the teachings and practices of Buddhism soon showed them that Eastern traditions were replete with knowledge about transcendent states of consciousness and meditative practice. Richard Alpert wanted to learn more about these topics first hand and decided in 1967 to travel to India, which he considered to be the source of this knowledge. He hoped to meet yogis, monks, or gurus who could help him better understand his psychedelic experiences and teach him to achieve mystical states without pharmacological support.

For several months, he traveled with a young man who knew the country well. They crisscrossed the subcontinent, visited temple sites and ashrams. Despite countless new impressions and marvelous scenery, Alpert was disappointed. He concluded that the spiritual tradition was no longer vital in India and there were no wise men and saints for him to meet. Having had enough traveling as a tourist, he planned to return home. When his companion announced that he was going into the mountains to meet with his guru, Alpert at first resolved not to go along. Besides, Buddhism interested him more because he thought it was extremely clear, clean, and an intellectually ideal subject matter. For him, Hinduism seemed too emotional, garish, and colorful like the images of its gods. Only after some hesitation, did Alpert decide to accompany his companion into the Himalayas. The evening before their arrival, he left the house at night and looked up at the starry

> The moment someone begins to do that which he has always wanted, a new life begins.
> *R. Buckminster Fuller*

> It required two World Wars, Hitler and Stalin, the threat of nuclear war and environmental destruction and, in many cases, a hefty dose of LSD to render Europeans sufficiently humble to seek their lost spiritual center elsewhere.
> *Stephen Batchelor*

217

sky, remembering his mother who had died the previous year of a spleen condition.

Alpert's first impression of Neem Karoli Baba, his companion's Guru and known to his followers as Maharaj, was mixed. He was not sure what to make of a man whose first question was how much he earned in the USA and whether he would give him his car. That same evening, Maharaj called Alpert to him and said: "You looked up at the stars the other night," and "you were thinking about your mother." Since no one else had known about this, Alpert was astounded—how could this be? The guru continued: "Your mother died last year" and "before she died, her stomach got very big." Alpert remembered that it had been her spleen. The guru closed his eyes briefly, then looked him directly in the eyes and said in English: "Spleen." This released an uncontrolled burst of emotion in the psychologist. He felt confused and was unable to account for the experience; he was unsure of what had happened to him. That evening as he rummaged in his shoulder bag, he found a small container of LSD tablets that he had brought to India—less for his own use and more because he hoped to find holy men who could tell him what they thought it was all about and how they would evaluate its utility. During his travels, he had given the substance to a few sadhus and monks and had gotten various answers. One Buddhist monk thought it gave him a headache, another respondent said it helped him to meditate, and a third

> We were convinced that we had found a new path and could reach the destination with the aid of psychedelic drugs faster than Hindus or Buddhists had done.
>
> *Ram Dass*

asked where he could get more—all information for which he would not have had to come all the way to India. The brief episode with Maharaj, however, impressed him. He assumed that the guru would have something substantive to say about LSD and decided to ask him when the opportunity arose.

The next morning, he was called to Maharaj and, as he entered, heard him say, "Where is the medicine"? Alpert was at first mystified, because he was not used to hearing LSD called "medicine" but then understood and went for his supply. Maharaj wanted to know whether the medicine bestowed siddhis, supernatural powers. This question also bewildered Alpert at first. The pills were highly dosed, each containing 300 micrograms of LSD. Alpert put one in the hand of the guru who examined it carefully and asked for more. So, Alpert gave him a second and finally a third, all of which Maharaj swallowed at once. Alpert remained with him the entire morning and noticed they seemed to have no effect, which impressed him but he could not explain. Back in America, he recounted the episode to friends and mentioned it in lectures. Gradually, doubts began to creep in. Had the guru perhaps not swallowed the LSD but thrown it over his shoulder? On his next trip to India, the second chapter unfolded. The guru summoned him again and asked: "Did you give me medicine when you were in India last time?" which Alpert affirmed. "Did I take it?" With some hesitation, Alpert also affirmed this. "What happened?" When Alpert answered 'nothing,' he dismissed him. The next day Maharaj took up the matter again.

"Have you got any more of that medicine?" Alpert brought the remainder of his pills and poured a powerful dose of 1200 micrograms into the Guru's hand. As if in answer to Alpert's unspoken doubt, Maharaj pointedly put each pill into his mouth and swallowed it. He asked whether he should drink water and how long it would take before he felt something. But most of all, he wanted to know: "Will it make me crazy?"

"Probably," was Alpert's honest answer. Maharaj crept under his blanket. When he resurfaced, he looked completely insane. Alpert began to regret having given the old man such a powerful dose and imagined the consequences of his irresponsible behavior. The guru let him squirm but not for very long. After an hour, he laughed at Alpert and, looking completely normal, asked him: "Have you got anything stronger?" He explained that such substances had been known in the Kulu Valley long ago but that this ancient wisdom had since been lost. His assessment of the medicine was that it was useful, but not a true samadhi. "To take them with no effect, your mind must be firmly fixed on God. Others would be afraid to take. Many saints would not take this … If you are in a place that is cool and peaceful, and you are alone and your mind is turned toward God, then you may take the yogi medicine." He said it allowed one to achieve greater awareness, to welcome the saints and visitors from higher spheres. The disadvantage was that one could not remain in that state; that it was much better to become a saint than to just receive a visit from one, but that "LSD won't do that for you … Love is a much stronger drug than LSD medicine." (Ram Dass 1976)

Alpert became his disciple, converted to Hinduism and changed his name to "Ram Dass"—"Servant of God." Several more times, the American was amazed by Maharaj with his siddhis and the precise knowledge of what was going on in his chela's head. Alpert recognized that the East possessed excellent "maps of human consciousness" which would make it possible to better understand and classify many of his own extraordinary LSD experiences. In the course of his sadhana, his practice of different yoga and meditation techniques, he found he could access many of these states of consciousness without pharmacological support. Nonetheless, Ram Dass considered LSD to be a suitable tool and appreciated it as an unsurpassed resource for self-assessment.

After several years and many further lessons from his master, Ram Dass himself became a spiritual guide and teacher. His book *Be Here Now* (Ram Dass 1971) became a bestseller in the scene and "to be in the here and now," a popular motto for life. Back in the USA, Ram Dass established several nonprofit foundations based on his teacher's life principles "to love and nurture everyone" and "to serve and love everyone." In February of 1997, he suffered a life-threatening stroke from which he has slowly recovered but that has forced him to spend his subsequent life in a wheelchair. He moved to the Hawaiian island of Maui from whence he shares his wisdom with a large group of international followers via the Internet and his books. His two latest titles are *Be Love Now* (Ram Dass 2010) and that same year, *Birth of a Psychedelic Culture*, with Ralph Metzner and Gary Bravo.

Buddhists and Psychedelics

In the summer of 1996, the American Buddhist magazine *Tricycle* focused on the topic: "Psychedelics—Help or Hindrance?" In response to their survey regarding consumption of psychedelics, nearly 1,500 readers responded, of whom eighty-nine percent described themselves as practicing Buddhists. Of these, eighty-three percent reported having consumed psychedelics; more than forty percent said that LSD or mescaline had sparked their interest in Buddhism; and twenty-four percent still consumed psychedelics. Most of those surveyed reported they no longer took drugs, while seventy-one percent believed that the use of psychedelics could "provide a glimpse of the reality to which Buddhist practice points." Fifty-nine percent saw no essential conflict between Buddhism and psychedelics, while the remainder were of the opinion that drug use and Buddhism were incompatible.[139] Another survey done a few years later found that sixty-two percent of Western Buddhists have taken psychedelic drugs; of these, eighty percent practiced Tibetan Buddhism.[140] Apparently many Buddhists in the West found that psychedelic experiences opened the door to spirituality. Further, there is an extant American Buddhist subculture which continues to consume psychedelics.

> We are all prisoners of our minds. This realization is the first step on the journey to freedom.
>
> *Ram Dass*

(l. to r.) Ram Dass, Jack Kornfield, and Stanislav Grof at Esalen

Ecologist and Buddhist

For anthropologist and ecologist Joan Halifax, psychedelic experiences, engagement in the antiwar movement, the study of tribal cultures, and the pursuit of Buddhism went hand in hand. Together with Stanislav Grof, her husband at the time, she treated terminal cancer patients at the Maryland Psychiatric Research Center and co-authored *The Human Encounter with Death*. (Grof, Halifax 1980) From then on, dying and death remained a supremely important issue for her. After years studying the Dogon tribe in Mali and the Huicholes in Mexico, Joan Halifax turned to Buddhism. In 1979, she founded the Ojai Foundation in California, a site for spiritual encounter, and in 1990, the Upaya Zen Center in Santa Fe, New Mexico, a center for Buddhism, Zen training, and courses for accompanying the dying. Her psychedelic experiences in younger years were decisive in developing her empathy for terminally ill people whom she helps focus on living the time remaining to them composed and, often pain free. "Spending seventeen straight hours with a patient on the day when the patient took LSD, giving them a tremendous amount of support before and after the LSD session. This sounded

Roshi Joan Halifax   Vanja Palmers

like an unbelievable endeavor. But truly, this was a contemporary rite of passage, which probably would not been needed at all had our society and culture been responsive to the question of death."[141]

Zen Priest and Animal Welfare Advocate

Vanja Palmers, the son of an Austrian entrepreneurial family grew up in Lucerne. His family took over a textile factory in Switzerland and built it into a worldwide brand. When they sold the company, Palmers came into an inheritance of millions. At that point, the wild years of his youth and a goodly amount of psychedelic experience lay behind him. "Over forty years ago, I used LSD often. These experiences were a turning point in my life;" and "LSD shattered my worldview." As a child he had dreamed of becoming the richest man on earth. However, his experiences with LSD revealed to him that satisfaction in life was not related to money.[142] One consequence of this recognition was his entrance into the San Francisco Zen Center and later into Tassajara Zen Monastery in nearby Green

Gulch, where he spent ten years meditating and was ordained as a Zen priest. Upon returning to Europe, he established the ecumenical Haus der Stille (House of Silence) in Puregg, Austria, with Benedictine monk David Steindl-Rast; he also founded Felsentor, a center for animal rights and spiritual seminars on the steep slope of Mount Rigi in Switzerland where Joan Halifax also teaches regularly. "Since there are very few *Zendos* (meditation halls) in Switzerland in remote areas where one can also stay overnight and hold multi-day *sesshins* (meditation retreats), the idea arose of finding and creating such a place."[143] Vanja Palmers provides "worn-out" livestock a peaceful place to retire in the animal sanctuary located there. While the community is guided by Buddhist teachings, the center considers itself interreligious. The Center is jointly managed by a Franciscan sister; in the Zendo, built in Japanese temple style, there is a black Madonna in addition to a statue of Buddha. Palmers is convinced of the value of his LSD experiences and sees no contradiction between spiritual practice and the use of substances which open the mind. He was very happy to have met Albert Hofmann, whose discovery had so influenced his life, several years before Hofmann's death.

Instant Nirvana

The Buddhist philosopher Lama Anagarika Govinda (1898-1985), with his contrarian point of view, was an important bridge builder between religious thinking in Tibet and European culture.

> If God dropped acid, would He see people?
>
> *Steven Wright*

German-born, with the given name Ernst-Lothar Hoffmann, he lived in Asia from his thirtieth year on but spent his last years in the USA. His book *Buddhist Reflections* contains a short essay entitled "Back Doors to Enlightenment: Thoughts on the Expansions of Consciousness through Drugs."[144] Govinda makes it clear in the opening sentences what he thinks: "Notoriously, there are no limits to human folly." He is referring particularly to "LSD, which is put forward by certain gurus as a means of meditation. Invoking Jean Gebser, he emphasizes that the path to enlightenment does not depend on expanding but rather on intensifying consciousness. He notes that accumulating ever more unrelated fragments from within is comparable to the stockpiling of isolated facts in Western science. The "atomism" of rational knowledge which takes physics as its model is reflected in the "images of psychedelic art, which are put together as if from a thousand splinters and fragments."

The main difference between states of consciousness induced by LSD and by meditation is "that LSD deprives us of all control," whereas meditation "is a creative activity which lets a meaningful cosmos arise out of the untamed conflict of inner powers." Meditation gradually creates an inner center which leads us to its core in the depths of our consciousness. The effect of LSD, however, is to take us away from this center. An LSD experience is "an ever more fragmented multiplicity of unrelated and constantly shifting projections of unconscious contents." According to Govinda, using LSD flushes to the surface the heritage of our past and ultimately the entire universe, the totality of all forms of being, of all conditions of life, "from the blind outpourings of bestial demonic drives and brutal passions to the emanations of divine enlightened beings." In his thinking, these LSD visions, however, should not be confused with the true Buddha nature of humankind. And even if LSD triggers experiences resembling those achieved through meditation, they still are worthless to the person involved because the knowledge for interpreting this symbolic psychic language is lacking. That is what comes of skipping over the path from the periphery of normal waking consciousness directly to the inner core at the depths of consciousness. The spiritual path consists of pressing forward gradually while making use of all thought, feeling, and intuition. For Govinda, LSD is not a suitable tool for traveling the spiritual path. Whoever uses this substance to descend to the depths of universal consciousness "is swallowed up by it or else drifts like a rudderless ship lost on the limitless wastes of the ocean."

A more optimistic position regarding spiritually motivated use of drugs is represented by Buddhist teacher Jack Kornfield: "Many people who took LSD, mushrooms, or whatever it was, along with a little spiritual reading of *The Tibetan Book of the Dead* or some Zen texts, had the gates of wisdom opened to a certain extent. They began to see that their limited consciousness was only one plane and one level and that there were a thousand new things to discover about the mind.... They began to see the dance in much greater perspective." Kornfield spoke from his own experience: "I took LSD and other psychedelics at Dartmouth

> Anyone who has already been there without drugs, no longer needs them.
>
> *Walter Houston Clark*

Stanislav Grof with
Lama Anagarika
Govinda at Esalen

Myron Stolaroff with
Albert Hofmann at the
Rittimatte, 2002

though I was studying Eastern thought before then, but they came hand in hand as they did for many people. It is true for the majority of American Buddhist teachers that they had experience with psychedelics either right after they started their spiritual practice or prior to it. I even know of cases where people were genuinely transformed by their experience in the way that one would be from an enlightenment experience. They are rare."[145]

Myron Stolaroff represents a position diametrically opposed to that of Govinda. After his first LSD experience in 1956, he declared LSD to be humankind's most important discovery. He gave up his job as an electrical engineer to systematically study the effects of LSD, founding the International Foundation for Advanced Study in 1961. He was particularly interested in whether LSD could reinforce meditation. He describes the general framework in his article "Are Psychedelics Useful in the Practice of Buddhism?" In his opinion, to successfully integrate psychedelic experiences, it is necessary to

possess an ethical foundation, to be well informed about the effects expected, and to understand the significance of set and setting. Stolaroff makes the case for a high dose during an initial experience to reach transpersonal levels and enable an expanded perspective. In addition, he recommends the use of breathing techniques to maintain mental stability during the drug experience. If these conditions are met, spiritual practice can benefit from psychedelics. He believes that a further drug experience is only useful after the contents of the previous one has been fully processed through meditation

Cosmologist of Joy

Alan Watts, the British philosopher of religion, like his friend Aldous Huxley, had thoroughly studied Eastern wisdom teachings before either of them ever came in contact with psychedelics. This contrasts with Ram Dass and many others who found their way to Eastern wisdom through psychedelics. Alan Watts, born in 1915, introduced the West to Eastern spirituality, in particular Taoism and Buddhism. His special area of interest is the Buddhist path of Zen which posits that all sentient beings and the entire universe possess Buddha nature and it suffices to recognize this to be liberated. Zen is described as "the pathless path" and means to live every moment to the fullest. However, direct access to this insight is blocked by endless inner dialogue, stubborn ideas, and judgmental notions. Zen always strives for experience and behavior to be in the present moment. Its practice consists of *zazen*, sitting in absorption. An equally important practice, perhaps better termed "lifestyle," is attentiveness in day-to-day life, complete engagement in one's tasks without distracting preoccupations. Zen means to eat when hungry and to sleep when tired. Alan Watts saw Zen as the most direct path to spiritual liberation. In 1936, just twenty-one years of age, he published his first book, *The Spirit of Zen*.

Two years later, Watts emigrated to the USA where he continued studying Buddhism in New York; his book *The Way of Zen* appeared. Watts moved on to California where Oscar Janiger introduced him to mescaline. After that, he participated in various studies at the University of California at Los Angeles in which a team led by Keith Ditman, Sterling Bunnell, and Michael Agron investigated the effect of LSD. Psychedelics fascinated Watts. He corresponded at great length about the commonalities of psychedelics and Zen with Aldous Huxley and Timothy Leary, as well as with Anagarika Govinda, with whom he had become friends during Watts' last years. Nevertheless, they remained of differing opinions. Watts attests to the potential of psychedelics to afford people access to higher spiritual levels, expanded states of consciousness, and religious experience. His concluding commen-

> Psychedelic substances are simply instruments like microscopes, telescopes or telephones. A biologist doesn't always keep his eye glued to a microscope, he steps back and works with what he has seen.
>
> *Alan Watts*

> Since the Enlightenment, the analytic mind focused on technical mastery has been most highly valued. A person busily occupied in the world in this sense is usually not open to other states of mind. These then are most probably denigrated or considered to be pathological.
>
> *Christian Scharfetter*

Alan Watts

tary is found in his book, *The Joyous Cosmology* (Watts 1972) which deals with his psychedelic experiences. Watts advised: "When you get the message, hang up the phone."

Psychosis and Enlightenment

From a phenomenological point of view, an acute schizophrenic psychosis can scarcely be differentiated from a mystical state in a healthy person. The difference lies in the fact that, afterwards, mystics can integrate their experiences into a religious tradition whereas psychotics with the same experiences remain alone, misunderstood, stigmatized socially, and shunned and ultimately flee into their own delusions. Conventional Western psychology does not have a model at its disposal to recognize extraordinary states of consciousness and considers ecstatic states and mystical experiences to be pathological. Psychology in the Freudian tradition only deals with what, metaphorically stated, happens in our cellar and on the ground floor. It equates mystical with psychotic experience and does not take account of the fact that our minds can access countless levels of consciousness.

The most important criterion for distinguishing between a psychotic and a mystical experience remains to what extent alien experiences can be integrated into normal consciousness and everyday experience. The degree to which exceptional experiences can be integrated into the personality structure determines the dividing line between psychosis and mysticism. Psychotic states are bizarre experiences of reality which remain unintegrated. Aldous Huxley was convinced that these experiences do in fact tell us something about the nature of the universe and that they are of value, but only if we are able to integrate them into our conception of the world and apply them to daily life.

According to the psychotomimetic approach, LSD induces a state of mind imitating psychosis. But are states of consciousness induced by LSD truly psychotic, i.e., manifestations of temporary mental illness? Psychotic experiences are typically "split," whereas LSD-induced experiences are usually integrated into waking consciousness and everyday life. The American consciousness researcher Terence McKenna commented ironically: "LSD causes psychotic behavior in those who have never taken it!"

Tool of the Mind

Even under difficult conditions not conducive to positive experiences found in early experiments with LSD, many subjects experienced states closely resembling those described by mystics and saints. The possibility to induce such experiences with pharmacological means triggered a fierce debate about the value and authenticity of this chemically induced "instant mysticism." Critics claimed that LSD and related substances represent an illegal and illegitimate shortcut that stimulates experience for which users are unprepared. A comparison with travels in the outer world readily suggested itself. We use modern means of transport to reach foreign continents within a matter of hours without faulting the means as unauthorized shortcuts. Grof compares the significance of LSD in psychiatry with the microscope in biology or the telescope in astronomy. The technical means do not bring to life the micro and macrocosms, but simply give us the opportunity to observe and explore them in a previously unknown way. In the same fashion, LSD does not create extraordinary mental and psychic phenomena but merely brings to light processes that are already present in the psyche to which we would otherwise scarcely have access. Timothy Leary summed it up: "Rejecting drugs as a tool would be like rejecting the microscope because it makes seeing too easy. I think people deserve every revelation they can get."

> Visionary experience is not the same as mystical experience. Mystical experience is beyond the realm of contradictions. Visionary experience is still within that realm. Heaven entails hell, and 'going to heaven' is no more liberating than is the descent into horror.
>
> *Aldous Huxley*

> LSD: It is not a matter of its being similar to mystical experience; it is mystical experience.
>
> *Walter Stace*

> The important thing about psychedelic experience is that it is completely democratic. You do not have to scrub the floor of an ashram for years before you reach your goal; you simply go straight to the end goal.
>
> *Terence McKenna*

Creativity and Art

And indeed, the first non-medicinal self-experiments with LSD were carried out by writers, painters, musicians, and other intellectuals. LSD sessions had reportedly provoked extraordinary aesthetic experiences and granted new insights into the essence of the creative process. *Albert Hofmann*

Intoxicated Literati

Since the very earliest literature, writers' guilds have been accompanied by intoxicating drugs of all kinds. A passage in the *Epic of Gilgamesh* celebrates gripping the flask: "He drank the beer—seven jugs! And became expansive and sang with joy. He was elated and his face glowed." One issue of the Swiss periodical *Du* was devoted to alcohol as the fuel of the poets. (*Treibstoff Alkohol—Die Dichter und die Flasche*)[146] In his article "Das letzte Glas" (The Last Glass), Wilfried Schoeller concluded that "alcohol should be paid royalties as the most powerful progenitor of literature imaginable." He thus calls to mind such notable literary friends of drink as Jean Paul, Edgar Allan Poe, Upton Sinclair, Jack London, Malcolm Lowry, Ernest Hemingway, F. Scott Fitzgerald, William Faulkner, E.T.A. Hoffmann and many others. Joseph Roth drank wine and liquor at breakfast, and his last book was *The Legend of the Holy Drinker*.

Hashish proved to be equally inspiring. François Rabelais scattered hidden allusions to cannabis throughout his books. The mysterious herb "pantagruelion" in his novel *The Life of Gargantua and Pantagruel* (1532–1564) is nothing other than marijuana, which he dared not mention openly out of fear of being persecuted by the church. *Much Ado About Nothing* is not a prophesied commentary about today's drug policies but a comedy by William Shakespeare, of whom it is documented that he used "weed" or cannabis.

In mid-nineteenth century Paris, members of the Club des Hachichins" used hashish both to stimulate their creativity and to study the drug's effect upon them and their beaux-arts. This artistic and intellectual elite included Théophile Gautier, Charles Baudelaire, Gérard de Nerval, Alexandre Dumas and the painter, Eugène Delacroix. Psychiatrist Jacques-Joseph Moreau, who published *Du hachisch et de l'aliénation mentale* (*Hashish and mental illness*) in 1845, was also a club member. His study was the first methodical treatise on the influence of drugs upon the central nervous system.

Albert and the LSD Revelation Revolution by Alex Grey, oil on wood, 2006

Through self-experiments, American student Fitz Hugh Ludlow explored the psychological states and physiological effects of hashish use. His compelling accounts tell of walking a tightrope between heaven and hell in various states of intoxication using remarkably high doses: "It was during a stroll, that one of the strangest phenomena of sight which I have ever noticed appeared to me. Every sunbeam was refracted into its primitive rays; wherever upon the landscape a pencil of light fell, between rocks or trees, it seemed a prismatic pathway between heaven and earth. The atmosphere was one network of variegated solar threads, tremulous with radiance and distilling rapture from its fibres into all my veins." Ludlow's documentary novel *The Hasheesh Eater*, published in 1857, immediately became a true sensation and is regarded as a classic today.

The solanum mandrake is also known as *Mandragora*, or *Alruna—the Omniscient*. It was added as a stimulant to beer in ancient Egypt and was made into mandragora wine by the Romans. Today, it can be enjoyed in the Basque region as mandrake schnapps, high in alcohol content but not hallucinogenic. Depending on how it is prepared, the magical herb is used as a relaxing drink to relieve pain or sleeplessness, but also, when very carefully dosed, as an aphrodisiac. "It's intoxicating effect inspired the imagination of early historians, on up to novelists, cartoonists, and modern film makers."[147]

Bee God and Sacred Mirrors

Archeological discoveries on all continents suggest the versatile use of psychoactive substances. Since prehistoric times, artistic transformation of inner images and visions as well as representations of external events related to hallucinogens have been found in nearly all shamanic cultures. Among the most significant examples are the famous cave drawings of Tassili n'Ajjer in Algeria, made between 7,000 and 10,000 years ago. They show a being, apparently wearing a protective mask, known as the "Bee God of Tassili" holding mushrooms in its hands while its body is rimmed with them. The dashed lines leading to its head may indicate the effect of the drug on its mind. For many anthropologists, this image is the earliest reference to use of psychoactive mushrooms. At the time these cave paintings originated, the Sahara was a fruitful savannah that supported farming, beekeeping and livestock. And, where cattle graze, mushrooms containing psilocybin grow on their dung almost everywhere in the world.

The Huichol Indians live in the Sierra Madre Mountains of West Central Mexico. They are closely bound to the world of their gods, consider all natural phenomena to be animated by numinous powers and identify no separation between religion and everyday life. Their shamanic world view is rich in myth and shaped by potent visions brought on by their ritual use of the peyote cactus *Lolophora williamsii*. The Huichols portray their visionary images in flamboyantly lush colors with fascinating ornamentation in paintings worked in thread, yarn or wool, nearly all of which include stylized peyote buttons. Equally fanciful and colorful are their peyote-inspired sacred animal figures and masks, embellished with appliqued glass beads.

Mushroom runner
of Tassili

Bee God of Tassili

Huichol thread
picture

Some ethnologists believe that the masks, which traditionally showed rather grim expressions and were quite grotesque, are now being made as attractive, colorful "psychedelic art" to appeal to growing numbers of tourists.

At the age of ten, Peruvian curandero and artist Pablo Amaringo was served his first drink of ayahuasca, a jungle brew made from a liana, *Banisteriopsis caapi*, found in tropical rainforests and the leaves of the chacruna shrub, *Psychotria vieridis*. The slightly bitter drink is also known as Yage and contains dimethyltryptamine (DMT), a consciousness expanding hallucinogen. It is considered to bring mental clarity, to purify the spirit and, with a strong enough dose, to induce striking visions. Common side effects are diarrhea and vomiting which serve to cleanse the body.

Amaringo came to the attention of the West through ethnologist Luis Eduardo Luna and ethnopharmacologist Dennis McKenna, who first met him during the course of an ethno-botanical project in Pucallpa, eastern Peru, in 1985. He had stopped practicing as a shamanic healer in 1977 and had since been eking out a living from his paintings. When Luna and McKenna suggested that Amaringo paint pictures of his visions, his exceptional genius became apparent. Even many years after

Enkidu ate the food until he was sated; he drank the beer- seven jugs! And became expansive and sang with joy! He was elated and his face glowed. He splashed his shaggy body with water, and rubbed himself with oil, and turned into a human.

The Epic of Gilgamesh

Peyote leads the self back to its true sources.
Antonin Artaud

his last ayahuasca visions, Pablo Amaringo could paint them from memory down to the smallest detail. Thus began his most intense period of artistic creativity. Luna and Amaringo documented a cross-section of his psychedelic paintings with text and pictures in a splendidly illustrated book, *Ayahuasca Visions: The Religious Iconography of a Peruvian Shaman.* (Luna, Amaringo 1991)

The humid climate throughout broad parts of the Northern hemisphere during the Middle Ages favored the infestation of grain, particularly rye, with ergot, the fungus that serves as the starting material for LSD. The consumption of contaminated flour frequently caused mass poisoning or ergotism. Its effects ranged from acute intoxication to severe hallucinations with associated physical symptoms. Artists such as Pieter Brueghel the Elder and Matthias Grünewald depicted the sufferings of those so afflicted in their paintings. Many of the apocalyptic paintings of Hieronymus Bosch (circa 1450–1516), populated by demons and mythical creatures, gnomes and monsters, are thought to have been painted after experiencing hallucinogenic effects from mild doses of ergot.

With the appearance of LSD in the 1960s, the relationship between psychoactive substances and art suddenly changed. Whether it was painting, fashion, music,

Alex Grey with Albert Hofmann, Basel 2006

> The cultures of ancient peoples have all been shaped by the use of particular drugs.
>
> *Ernst Fuchs*

> In the mail. The Hashish Eater, a book by Fitz Hugh Ludlow, recently published in German by Sphinx Verlag in Basel. Albert Hofmann sent it to me. He keeps me up to date about these kinds of things.
>
> *Diary entry from Ernst Jünger, April 3, 1982*

design or architecture, the impact of LSD was apparent in all areas of artistic and creative endeavor. Ten years after the emergence of the term "psychedelic," the creative work of a generation of artists who had experienced new dimensions of perception resulted in the innovative and visionary forms described as "psychedelic art" or "psychedelia."

Among the best known psychedelic artists is Alex Grey, born in 1953, the son of a graphic designer. Grey studied first at the Columbus College of Art and Design in Ohio from 1971 to 1973 and later at the Boston Museum School, where he met his wife, artist Allyson Rymland. Together, they experienced their first psychedelics. For five years, Grey worked in the Anatomy Department of Harvard Medical School, assisting in the preparation of cadavers, and gained detailed knowledge of the human body. He went on to teach anatomical drawing and sculpture for ten years as a lecturer at New York University. Today, he is a freelance artist teaching courses in spiritual painting.

Alex Grey, *Theologue—The connection of man with the divine consciousness weaves the structure of space and time, in which the self and its surroundings are embedded,* acrylic on canvas, 457.2 x 152.4 cm, 1984

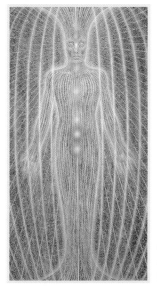

Alex Grey, *Spiritual Energy,* oil on canvas, 60 x 210 cm, 1986

Alex Grey's 1986 series of twenty-one life-sized, anatomically exact paintings of the human body were his first important artworks. The individual paintings represent different levels of the body. They show the skeleton and outer shape of the body, the bloodstream, the vascular system and neural pathways, the chakras and the meridians, up to the "spiritual" person and his aura. He called this series *Sacred Mirrors.* Grey considers himself a kind of shaman, his pictures as healing art for a society alienated from nature and hyper-immersed in technology. Many of his works clearly show the influence of altered states that he experienced in his younger years. One LSD trip was unforgettable: "The vision I had in 1976 changed my work and the focus of my life. My wife and I were intrepid psychonauts doing psychedelic exploration, questioning all reality. Our discoveries during this period of experimental mysticism became the basis by which we live our lives. Together, we had an experience of what we refer to as the *Universal Mind Lattice.* Wearing blindfolds and lying in bed we took heroic doses of LSD…. Our bodies transformed into toroidal fountains of light… The energy that was flowing through all these different toruses, these cells, was love energy. It was intense and ecstatic. We were participating in a network of love energy uniting all beings and all things. That was the true reality, that we are all interconnected on some very fundamental primordial level, and that this interconnectedness is the subtle body of the cosmos—and we are each an important node in that infinite network. It amazed me that Allyson had experienced the same transpersonal space at the same time. This changed our work. There was nothing more important."[148] In 2005, Alex Grey expressed his great appreciation of Albert Hofmann and his discovery of LSD in a portrait entitled *St. Albert and the LSD Revelation Revolution.*

Having already studied literature, history and psychology, Isaac Abrams (born 1939) was drawn to art. He tried his hand at painting but did not consider himself an artist, that is, not until 1965 when he participated in his first LSD experience in an experiment at the Dream Laboratory in Brooklyn. There, psychologist Stanley Krippner was studying the effect of hallucinogens on the creative process. In Abrams that process took a complex form, as Jean Houston and Robert Masters noted: "During the LSD session, he discovered that there was also a rich inward life spiritual, pre- or extra-logical, irrational or going beyond reason. At the same time, he first became aware of the world as possessing a balance, a harmony, above all a unity not evident to him before."

> A visionary is a person who sees through things; nothing obstructs his gaze; he discovers dizzying crystalline regions, chronicles unknown worlds. He knows the magical incantations to tame the most guileful hell; he creates an equilibrium between the supernatural and nature.
>
> *Marcel Brion*

(Masters, Houston 1968) For Abrams, that was the beginning of his career as a distinguished artist. In that same year he opened New York's first gallery for the new art form. To train further, he traveled to Vienna in 1972 to study under Ernst Fuchs, a prominent representative of fantastic art, and found someone with whom he could talk about LSD. Abrams' oil painting *All Things are One* appeared on the cover of Masters and Houston's *Psychedelic Art.* (ibid)

A New Dimension of Art

Stimulated by the LSD experiments of Göttingen physician and psychotherapist Hanscarl Leuner, Richard P. Hartmann, also a doctor as well as a gallery owner, initiated a two year series of experiments at the Max Planck Institute in Munich. Thirty well-known German and Austrian artists, including Alfred Hrdlicka, Arnulf Rainer, and Friedensreich Hundertwasser, took LSD for the purpose of discovering "valuable insights into the the process of painting."(Hartmann 1974) Hartmann meticulously logged his observations and the artists' impressions during sessions. His evaluations should be assessed in view of his assumption that LSD induces model psychoses. Thus the artists participating suspected that the paintings they created during the experiment would be compared to those of the mentally ill. Another reservation was their fear of exposure and perhaps even damage to their reputations since the canvases were to be exhibited publically at the conclusion of the study. In the end, the artists gave in to their curiosity and the allure of participating in the experiment.

In his summary, Hartmann stated that: "LSD principally elevates to a new level of awareness, so therefore generalizations about the experimental results are difficult to make. However, some trajectories related to the depth of intoxication could be seen. At different phases of these experiences, some common features emerged. However, since the condition and constitution of each

Isaac Abrams, *Walking Through Oneness*, oil on canvas, 160 x 122 cm, 2007

participant and the subject's mental state and circumstances differed, there was no such thing as a standard dose. On the contrary, LSD neutralizes those standards which an artist often follows without being aware of them and the resulting images under LSD do not always fit into the viewers' standards." (Hartmann 1974) Aside from the artists' individual reports about the state and depth of their intoxication, their sensory impressions, altered perceptual abilities, and their feelings of wellbeing or uneasiness, Hartmann was unable to draw any general conclusions about the degree or quality of artistic activity while they were under the influence of LSD.

The Creativity Pill

Ever since his first LSD experience as a volunteer subject under Sidney Cohen at the Veterans Hospital in Brentwood in Los

Angeles in the spring of 1954, psychiatrist and cell biologist Oscar "Oz" Janiger (1918–2001) recognized the creative potential of the hallucinogen. Between 1954 and 1962, first at the University of California's Irvine campus and later in his private practice in Los Angeles, he studied the effects of LSD on nearly a thousand people—lawyers, housewives, students, physicians, office workers, engineers, actors, artists—keeping accounts of their experiences during guided sessions. He was among the first to focus on the creativity-enhancing effects of LSD on artists. In contrast with most of the LSD experiments at the time, which were being carried out in hospitals or psychiatric clinics, Janiger's experiments took place in an environment he had chosen to make as comfortable and conducive as possible to a psychedelic experience. His medical offices contained an especially comfortable furnished room with a welcoming atmosphere and a

233

view onto the garden. Later, numerous celebrities such as Anaïs Nin, Aldous Huxley, Cary Grant, Jack Nicholson and Stanley Kubrick were among his clients who enjoyed the pleasure of the "creativity pill," as Janiger termed LSD.

Janiger became famous for an experiment he carried out in 1968 in which he had seventy artists paint a Kachina doll, a favorite of the Native American Hopi tribe.[149] The subjects each painted a picture of the doll at least once before and then once again an hour after taking LSD. Art historian Carl Hertel examined and compared the more than 250 paintings. Though he did not specify qualitative differences, he found those painted while under the influence of LSD were brighter in color, more abstract, and the painted Kachina dolls often filled the entire canvas. With one exception, all of the participating artists deemed LSD to be an effective tool for boosting and expressing creativity.

Albert Hofmann reported on his very first experience with LSD to the effect that it had enriched his inner visual world: "Now, little by little I could begin to enjoy the unprecedented colors and plays of shapes that persisted behind my closed eyes. Kaleidoscopic, fantastic images surged in on me, alternating, variegated, opening and then closing themselves in

Sidney Cohen

Oscar Janiger

circles and spirals, exploding in colored fountains, rearranging and hybridizing themselves in constant flux." This experience is typical of psychedelics—mescaline or psilocybin can also trigger synesthesia. Fantastic visions are frequently generated by acoustic perceptions. It makes no difference whether one feels like Albert Hofmann, who was enchanted by the compositions of Mozart, or one prefers the spheric sounds of Pink Floyd.

In assessing to what extent LSD can enhance the creativity of people, Oscar Janiger distinguishes between "creativity" as an asset, i.e., the capacity to be creative, and "art" as the possible result of inspiration and creativity. It is certain that LSD cannot turn someone into an artist overnight. However, if creative potential lies dormant in someone, it can be awakened by a psychedelic experience. Janiger's studies show that, analogous to the diversity of psychedelic experience, the power of creative expression resulting from LSD use also varies. In virtually all cases, however, in the eyes of the experimental subject, the "creative process" gained from LSD positively influences the implementation of an artistic idea. Participants in all groups mentioned the following features, among others, as enhancing their creative process:

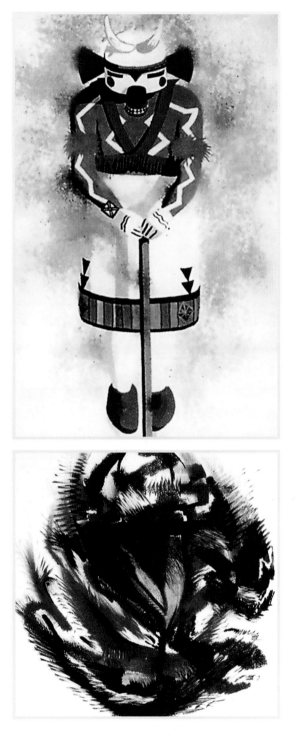

Two representations of a Kachina doll, one painted prior to and one while under the influence of LSD

- They provide a rapidity of thought that accelerates creative thought processes.

- They provide a basic emotional excitement and sense of significance.

- They widen consciousness to include both broad cosmic ideas and yet sharpen perception to see significance in the tiniest details.

- They cause things to appear to compose themselves into natural harmony.

- They intensify colors so that everything appears brilliantly illuminated from within.

- They free the individual from preconceptions. They fuse the individual with the object perceived—a phenomenon that Picasso says is the most important feature of looking at things creatively. When you paint an apple, you should be an apple. (Dobkin de Rios 2003, 110)

Psychedelia

Renowned Basel art dealer and gallery owner Ernst Beyeler—his *Fondation Beyeler* in Riehen, Switzerland, enjoys a worldwide reputation as a top-notch collection of art—wrote to the authors of this book on the occasion of Albert Hofmann's one-hundredth birthday to say:

"In my homage, I wished only to add my voice in praise of Dr. Albert Hofmann rather than to criticize the effect of LSD in art. Dr. Albert Hofmann deserves nothing less for his exemplary influence and life… He and I touched upon this in a conversation and discussed some of the relevant literature. It

235

appears that LSD has not brought any artistically significant results beyond a certain liberation of caprice. Further serious research would be required to come up with truly convincing results in art; I have not heard anything about such results. The example of Francesco Clemente, one of our best known modern artists is familiar to me. I know that he takes drugs and has visited Dr. Albert Hofmann. What I have observed is a certain loss of inhibition which has resulted in art that is openly erotic but not more so than his earlier works. On the contrary; a certain shallowness and profanation seem to have resulted. Heightened artistic effects seem to be found more in music. (Beatles, etc.)"[150]

The psychedelic art created in the 1960s and largely influenced by LSD has chiefly been ignored to this day. Creative work of the period is an expression of a particularly imaginative, varied and often ecstatic aesthetic to be found in the fine arts, in fashion, film, design and even in architecture. Reservations about psychedelics still appear to play a role in the fact that few curators and art historians have developed an objective

Claudia Müller-Ebeling

LIFE, September 9, 1966

> A psychedelic artist is one whose works clearly are influenced by a psychedelic experience and who recognizes and acknowledges this influence on his art.
>
> *Robert E. Masters and Jean Houston*

perspective on the broad range of psychedelic art.

However, in the sense suggested by Ernst Beyeler's words, further serious research has been done by among others, Oscar Janiger, Jean Houston and Robert Masters, art historian Claudia Müller-Ebeling, and Christoph Grunenberg, curator and director of the Tate Liverpool who put it this way: "The lingering disdain for psychedelic art and culture shown by serious historians and researchers is more than selective amnesia. The reasons are complex and lead directly to the essence of the psychedelic experience. We are dealing with an aesthetic that is normally relegated to the realm of applied arts, that is poor taste and artistic aberration, and that fights a losing battle against the point of view sanctioned by art historians and institutions that focuses instead on the aesthetic and theoretical purism of Pop Art, Minimal, and Concept Art. There appears to be a deep-seated mistrust of the frenzy of forms found in psychedelic art and its suspicious closeness to pop culture; apparently, the principles of high modern and formalism still prevail." (Grunenberg 2005)

Grunenberg was responsible for organizing the exhibit *Summer of Love*, the very first representative show of psychedelic art. In the press release it says: "Precisely

Mati Klarwein, *Annunciation*, oil and tempera on canvas, 128 x 88 cm, 1961.

Born in Hamburg in 1932, resident of Mallorca, where he died in 2002, psychedelic artist Mati Klarwein was world famous for his album covers for Santana's Abraxas and Miles Davis' Bitches Brew. He also did covers for Gregg Allman, Jerry Garcia, and Earth, Wind and Fire. Andy Warhol called him "my favorite painter;" he was a friend of Timothy Leary and Jimi Hendrix and he painted portraits of Brigitte Bardot, Michael Douglas, and Jackie Kennedy.

because we generously borrow today from the abundant reservoir of stylistic and design elements of the art and music of the 1960s and 1970s, it is important to go beyond mere nostalgia and sharpen our perception of the fundamental creative and visionary potential of that period. The exhibit holds many surprises. Not only does it place the revolutionary character and significance of art and politics in those years in a new light, it also gives us an idea of the upheavals during a period that continue to affect our thinking and behavior."

The exhibition opened at the end of May 2005 at the Tate Liverpool and included over 350 paintings, photos, films, lightshows, environments, posters, record album covers, and documentary material from Europe, the USA, South America and Japan. After appearing at the Schirn Kunsthalle in Frankfurt and the Kunsthalle Vienna, it closed in the summer of 2007 in New York after a well-received run at the Whitney Museum of American Art. Works by Isaac Abrams, Richard Avedon, Lynda Benglis, Harold Cohen, Richard Hamilton, Robert

Indiana, Yayoi Kusama, Richard Lindner and John McCracken showed for the first time the variety and richness of psychedelic art. The breadth and importance of this as yet largely under-appreciated genre of contemporary art was evident. Among the important environments in the exhibition was Mati Klarwein's *New Aleph Sanctuary*, created between 1963 and 1971. It combined many of the motifs he had used in sketches for various Santana album covers into a spectacular installation. Verner Panton's walkthrough amorphous furniture landscapes articulated utopian settings for unencumbered relaxation. Visionary architecture and city planning were represented by works from Archigram, Hans Hollein, Haus-Rucker-Co and others. (Grunenberg 2005)

The exhibit *Psychedelic—Optical and Visionary Art Since the 1960s* in the San Antonio Museum of Art in Texas from March to August 2010 augmented art history's understanding of psychedelic painting with work from established artists such as Frank Stella, Bridget Riley and Victor Vasarely.

A New Perspective

The expansion of consciousness through psychedelics such as LSD was reflected in the expansion of forms of artistic expression. The choice of available media multiplied with developments in electronics and innovative multimedia techniques. Computers, slide projectors, light shows, and modern audio systems made multi-sensory spectacles possible, a psychedelic aesthetic feast for the senses at all levels. Multimedia presentations by Andy Warhol and his factory artists were a component of the *Exploding Plastic Inevitable* performance and stage

H.R. Giger, Untitled, pencil on paper, 29 x 21 cm, 2005. Giger's gift for Hofmann's 100th birthday

shows by the avant-garde rock group Velvet Underground. Color TV, new illustrated magazines, and four-color printing became popular in the 1960s and brought more visual variety into people's

The entry door to Jacabaer Kastor's Psychedelic Solution, the fabulous shop for psychedelic art in Greenwich Village, New York

homes. Op and Pop Art's flashy effects with their glowing colors and abstract geometrical patterns were reminiscent of the recurring forms seen by Klüver during mescaline highs.[151] In discotheques, light shows featuring gyrating, kaleidoscopic projections sent guests on drug-free trips, while at home, the burble of lava lamps suggested hallucinatory psychedelic experiences. Posters in neon colors, sensual and effervescent, decorated the walls of student pads all over the world and, where budgets allowed, they hung amidst streamlined plastic furniture by Colombo or Verner Panton. Fashionably dressed women wore geometrically patterned

Kerim Seiler, Alice, textile object, 7.45 x 14 m, 2008. The Swiss artist's installation consists of an inflatable textile model of the LSD molecule. From outside, the sculpture molecule penetrates the roof of the Kunsthaus Zurich and becomes part of the group exhibit *Shifting Identities* in the interior.

mini-skirts or pants while trendy men wore shirts or ties in floral and paisley patterns. As Diana Vreeland, chief editor of *Vogue* magazine said, "It was a marvelous time. In the '60s you were knocked in the eyeballs. Everybody, everything was new." Hippies combined the intoxicating color of clothing with the psychedelic rush of the wearers.

In November 1940 with only twelve copies, Walt Disney's arduously produced movie *Fantasia* became the first cartoon with multi-channel sound. It was a giant flop and nearly bankrupted the fledgling company. Some thirty years later, the ingenious film was an insider's tip among hip youth, and its distributors reworked it to match the taste of the 1960s. Psychedelic posters advertised the masterpiece, which became a huge success as a "trip film." Young moviegoers could not get enough of the dancing flowers, mushrooms, and elves, of Bacchus intoxicated by rainbows and the abstract round dance of swirling, colorful patterns—all synchronized to classical music

by Bach, Beethoven, Stravinsky, Mussorgsky and Tchaikovsky, whose dynamics and charm were discovered and enjoyed as a side effect by Rock fans. At the time of production, the effect of LSD was as yet unknown, and it was only rumored that Walt Disney consumed mushrooms, but he did produce the first psychedelic film with this milestone in animation.

Encounters with Artists

Many psychedelic artists made contact with Albert Hofmann. The Italian painter Francesco Clemente, originally from Naples, mentioned by Ernst Beyeler earlier, experimented with LSD and counted his favorite writers, Allen Ginsberg and Gregory Corso among his friends. Clemente delved deeply into Hindu spirituality during a long stay in Chennai, India. In the mid-1980s he returned to New York where he met Andy Warhol and Jean-Michel Basquiat, with whom he teamed up on various projects. One summer day in 2001, Clemente and his family arrived unannounced at the Rittimatte, simply to thank Albert Hofmann. He gave Hofmann a catalog of his work that was being exhibited at the Fondation Beyeler, took a few photos, and politely said good bye.[152]

After a particularly hellish LSD trip that had eventually resolved itself in heavenly visions, Jürg Kreienbühl (1931–2007), the Basel painter known for his magical realism, turned to his friend Albert Hofmann. He wanted to learn how to interpret such experiences, as he was unclear whether they were mere illusions or pointed towards some deeper personal transformation. Hofmann explained that: "LSD, as a biochemical agent, only triggered his visions, but had not created them and that these visions rather originated from his own soul." Kreienbühl had taken an LSD trip with his childhood sweetheart Eva, with whom he could not break despite the fact that he already had a family. It had turned from an anticipated night of idyllic love into a night of terror and mutual estrangement but had ultimately brought healing insight.

Robert Indiana's *Love* paintings are legendary. His most famous appeared on an eight cent U.S. postage stamp in 1973.

The artist became aware of his selfishness, egotism, finally also his lovelessness: "Amid flowing tears, I was enlightened with the knowledge that true love means surrender of selfishness and that it is not desire but rather selfless love that forms the bridge, to the heart of our fellow human beings. Waves of ineffable happiness flowed through my body. I had experienced the grace of God."

Swiss artist H.R. Giger became internationally famous in the 1960s for his surrealistic and visionary airbrushed posters. The moment that film director Ridley Scott saw a copy of *Necronomicon*, a large-format overview of Giger's most creative period of work, he recognized him to be the person he needed as artistic designer for his film Alien and the creation of the extraterrestrial monster. *Alien* is a highlight of science fiction movies. Giger won the 1980 Academy Award for special effects. From his many years of friendship with Albert Hofmann, Stanislav Grof, and Timothy Leary, Giger was accustomed to being asked about his drug consumption. Charming and gracious as he is, he could not resist answering a journalist's question with a mischievous smile: "Oh, you know, I really can't say anything for

the record. LSD is still banned, so it isn't good to talk about these things."[153] He described his first LSD experience of February 1970, which he put into his art, as "one of my strongest and most unpleasant dreams." (Giger 1977) Years later, Giger did add

Martina Hoffmann, *Lysergic Summer Dream*, oil on canvas, 2006

Matteo Guarnaccia, *War is Over*, mixed media collage, 90 x 120 cm, 2007

that he subsequently had a number of very pleasant experiences with LSD but even better ones with psilocybin mushrooms.[154]

Magical light effects and long exposure times are the ingredients characterizing the work of American art photographer Dean Chamberlain. Using his special techniques which have been described as "painting with light through space and time," he creates stunning photographic paintings. Along with portraits of musicians like David Bowie, Madonna, and Paul McCartney, his series of *Psychedelic Pioneers*— Laura Huxley, Timothy Leary, Ram Dass, Alexander Shulgin, Oscar Janiger, Stanislav

Grof and John Lilly—occupy a prominent place in several collections. His portrait of Albert Hofmann shows the chemist, photographed from outside, behind a window of his work room, sitting at the table and looking out on the Rittimatte. It was a successful idea that perfectly corresponded to the photographer's aesthetic taste but it did not please Hofmann at all. The picture showed a lot of the

> Warhol refused to eat anything other than chocolate bars when he was traveling with all the LSD disciples because he was convinced that they would put something in his orange juice or water or in the scrambled eggs.
>
> Georg Diez

241

house's front which he perceived at once and protested: "But you can't represent me that way, so much concrete and so little green, when, after all, I am such a man of nature."[155] Somewhat crestfallen and slightly disappointed, Chamberlain went back to work and reduced the proportion of the facade.

Comic Strips

Even the earliest cave drawings were "organized in spatial sequences, provided images or other symbols that convey information and/or produced an aesthetic effect on the viewer."[156] This description can be applied equally to the comics. In the 1960s, comic strips underwent a psychedelically inspired boom as underground art.

One of the best known and most outstanding representatives of this "sequential art"[157] is Robert Crumb: "Well, the hippie revolution happened," he recalled. "In 1964 I first got laid, I met my first wife Dana, and all these protohippies in Cleveland... They started taking LSD and urged me to try it, so Dana got some LSD from a psychiatrist; it was still legal in '65. We took it and that was totally a road-to-Damascus experience.[158] It knocked you off your horse.... And then

Matteo Guarnaccia, *The Trickster*, 33 x 48 cm, ink on paper, 1995. Albert Hofmann first met the artist in Milan in 1982 on the occasion of the release of the Italian edition of *LSD-My Problem Child*, issued by the same press as Guarnaccia's books. The publisher asked the artist to look after the couple from Basel, and Hofmann's first question was: "Are you experienced?" Guarnaccia, born in 1954, answered, "Yes, I am." After returning home, Hofmann wrote the artist that his art was "amusing and philosophical," and that he had achieved "the maximum in expressing psychedelic fantasies." They visited each other, and Hofmann accepted Guarnaccia's invitation to give the opening talk at the psychedelic culture festival Starship in Milan in 1996.

it changed the whole direction of my artwork. Other people who had taken LSD understood right away what was going on, but the people who hadn't, my co-workers, they didn't get it."[159] Crumb began his career as a comic strip artist in 1967 in San Francisco with his characters Fritz the Cat and Mr. Natural, and drew the cover illustration for Janis Joplin's album *Cheap Thrills*.

The comic strip scene is still enriched by the Fabulous Furry Freak Brothers and Fat Freddy's Cat, the creations of Gilbert Shelton. He first studied sociology in Texas, and then switched from graduate school to art school where he met Janis Joplin. Shelton was drafted, but to his great relief, was exempted from military service after admitting he had taken LSD.

Artist Art Spiegelman's youth was spent in the marijuana smoke-impregnated and LSD-inspired hippie scenes of New York and San Francisco. He cast his father's memories of the Holocaust in the form of the cartoon novel *Maus* which earned him the treasured Pulitzer Prize.

Underground comic artist George DiCaprio, father of movie actor Leonardo DiCaprio, illustrated the brain circuit theories

242

Robert Crumb, album cover of Janis Joplin's *Cheap Thrills*

Gilbert Shelton, Grateful Dead, *Shakedown Street*, album cover, 1978

of his friend Timothy Leary in his comic strip *Neurocomic Timothy Leary*. Father and son operate the Hollywood film production company called Appian Way. For several years, they have been planning a film on the life of the former Harvard psychologist with Leonardo DiCaprio in the lead role, with Leary's goddaughter Winona Ryder as Rosemary Leary, and Leary archivist Michael Horowitz as creative consultant.

In Germany, Gerhard Seyfried from Berlin, and in France, Jean Giraud, known under his pseudonym "Möbius," like dozens of other graphic artists and painters contribute, with psychoactive assistance, most creatively to that increasingly popular blend of graphic art and literature, the comic strip.

Art Instead of LSD

Pre-perforated blotter paper sheets proved to be the ideal medium for liquid LSD which is drizzled onto the absorbent paper. From the mid-1970s on, so-called "blotters" became the customary medium for distributing LSD, the sheets ever more imaginatively decorated with colorful motifs and symbols. The single hits had images of Robert Crumb's Mr. Natural, the yin-yang symbol, or the eye on the pyramid pictured on the dollar bill. Some sheets are adorned all over with works of famous psychedelic artists and cartoonists, ranging from Alex Grey's phantasmagoria to Gilbert Shelton's Fat Freddy's Cat, and too with portraits of psychedelic icons such as Albert Hofmann, Alexander Shulgin and Timothy Leary.

The increasingly diverse decorated blotters became so popular that some bright minds turned them into a new art form. Soon, poster shops were offering a wide array of attractive sheets as "Blotter Art," while copies signed by the artists or the luminaries depicted, were being offered for sale in the

243

CHEMICAL SALVATION?

J.C.T.

The Chemical Salvation Comic by Brother Mel A. Tonin (text) and Sister Sara Tonin (image) from the Church of Trick, for Albert Hofmann's 100th birthday—first distributed to visitors at the LSD Symposium in Basel in 2006—is a parody of the evangelical missionary tract widely distributed in the USA by publisher Jack Chick

art trade. To be more suitable for printing, these blotters were no longer absorbent and rather than provide food for the brain, they provided wall decoration for the eyes. Since the 1980s, blotter art has been a profitable niche in the psychedelic art market with signed sheets reaching prices in the several thousands of dollars.

High in Hollywood

Cary Grant first learned of LSD in 1958 from his third wife, Betsy Drake, an actress who underwent successful LSD treatment at The Psychiatric Institute of Beverly Hills. Drake was one among hundreds of prominent patients who sought the treatment involving

Robert Crumb, *Mystic No. 1*, 1968

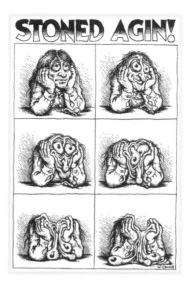

Robert Crumb, *Stoned Agin*, 1971

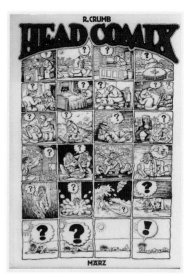

Robert Crumb, *Headcomix*, Frankfurt 1970

Timothy Leary blotter

innovative therapy at the widely known clinic run by psychiatrists Arthur L. Chandler and Mortimer A. Hartmann. Others treated there included Daniel Ellsberg, the whistle blower whose later release of the *Pentagon Papers* concerning the Vietnam War precipitated a political scandal. Grant's relationship with Betsy Drake was not his only troubled and unsatisfying relationship with women. Unresolved problems with his mother negatively influenced all his female friendships and had destroyed several of his marriages. As 1958 ended, Grant decided to begin LSD therapy with Hartmann himself and arrived at his goal of healing after seventy sessions: "I have been born again. I have just been through a psychiatric experience that has completely changed me … I had to face things about myself which I never admitted, which I didn't know were there. Now I know that I hurt every woman I loved." LSD therapy gave him the ability to love and helped him to become a happier person and a more successful actor. He called Dr. Hartman "My Wise Mahatma."[160] Grant was the first celebrity to make the therapeutic use of LSD known to a broader public. His description of his successful therapy appeared in the 1959 September issue of *Look* magazine, garnering wide attention.

That same year, movie star James Coburn was treated by Oscar Janiger with a 200 microgram dose of LSD which he remembered many years later: "It was phenomenal. I loved it. LSD really woke me up to seeing the world with a depth of objectivity. Even though it was a subjective experience, it opened your mind to seeing things in new ways, in a new depth." LSD also helped the actor professionally: "One of the great things about LSD is that it does stimulate your imagination. And it frees you from fears of certain kinds." (Brewer 2002)

Between them, Oscar Janiger, Sidney Cohen and Betty Eisner, Chandler and Hartman got half the prominent people in Hollywood high, made them healthier, and helped some script writers, actors and directors soar to new cinematic heights.

No cinematic glory was achieved by the B-movie *The Trip* in 1967, with a script

Artist Stevee Postman created this blotter art to mark the 60th birthday of the discovery of the psychedelic effect of LSD. The blotter is the standard American format of 7.5 x 7.5 inches and perforated into 900 "hits." Printed with soy-based dye on a chlorine-free, non-acidic and of course LSD-free hemp-based paper mixture.

Announcement of Mark McCloud's contribution at the LSD Symposium in Basel in 2006

by Jack Nicholson and the acting talents of Susan Strasberg, Peter Fonda and Dennis Hopper. They should have known how difficult it is to represent an LSD experience in a motion picture, whether the trip is a good or a bad one. "Looking back, however, it is a remarkable film for its time because it attempts to treat a socially relevant theme of the day cinematically (right up to the psychedelic colors). Also interesting is how it fails to do so: The film has and conveys no feeling for the point at which the story's tragedy ends and the absurd begins."[161] A year later, Nicholson and Strasburg failed again with their film *Psych-Out*, which, like *The Trip*, looked at the highs and lows of outsiders, of hippies, and their LSD experiences ranging from euphoria to paranoia.

As an actor, Jack Nicholson finally achieved his breakthrough with the film *Easy Rider*, the road movie *par excellence*. Featuring Nicholson, Peter Fonda and Dennis Hopper in the lead roles, it expressed, like no other movie, the yearnings of America's youth of the 1960s for freedom and it became a cult classic. A central scene is an LSD trip in a cemetery in New Orleans; this portrayal also falls short of depicting an actual psychedelic experience but is at least cinematically

convincing. The tragic ending shows the other face of America of the time: That of reactionary rednecks and Southerners who talk of freedom, but aggressively react to those who take it for themselves.

Actor Larry Hagman (1931–2012) found that "LSD was such a profound experience in my life that it changed my pattern of life and way of thinking. ... You lose your ego, which led me into to having no fear of death, because you've been there, experienced it and it ain't so bad, as a matter of fact it's wonderful."[162] Like Cary Grant, his colleague Hagman also recommended that: "It ought to be mandatory that all our politicians should do it, at least once."[163] His LSD experiences were so important to him that he planned to attend the LSD Symposium in Basel in January of 2006. Most of all, he wanted to congratulate Albert Hofmann on his one-hundredth birthday and thank him for his discovery. At the last minute, however, another deadline interfered and the meeting between the "Villain of Dallas" and the discoverer of LSD never took place.

Patient Cary Grant

I had decided to put LSD on the tongues of the other three. The scene shows the Lord's Supper, which was already clear to me as we filmed. At the same time, it gave a hint about how sadly the film ends.

Peter Fonda, 2010

I don't really like drugs, but LSD was good for me. I think all politicians should take LSD.

Cary Grant

Source of Inspiration

> I regard consciousness change to be of the very highest importance. For, the whole evolution of mankind consists in modification and expansion of consciousness.
> *Albert Hofmann*

From Uranium to LSD

To some a demigod, to others a lunatic, Alfred M. Hubbard remained virtually unknown in his lifetime. The quirky inventor and pseudo-scientist was one of the strangest people to popularize LSD in the USA. Looking at his appearance, his stocky body, short haircut, winning smile, and twinkling eyes, one would never suppose that before Jerry Garcia of the Grateful Dead, Hubbard was the first "Captain Trips" in the history of LSD and was known as "the Johnny Appleseed of LSD."

Alfred M. Hubbard

Hubbard's life story is full of holes and rumors such as claims that he provided black market uranium for the Manhattan Project constructing the U.S. atom bomb, and participated in the CIA's MK-Ultra operations as a psychotherapist. Born in Kentucky in 1901, Alfred "Al" Hubbard, at age eighteen built the "Hubbard Energy Transformer," an apparatus that supposedly transformed radioactive rays directly into electrical energy. The *Seattle Post Intelligencer* reported that with this device, he powered a boat for three days non-stop, going back and forth on Portico Bay off Seattle; and in 1919, he sold a fifty-percent share of his patent to a company from Pittsburgh for seventy-five thousand dollars.

During prohibition Hubbard managed to make a living as a taxi driver in Seattle. His next invention was much more profitable. Using a sophisticated communications device kept in the trunk of his cab, he was able to direct rum smugglers safely to shore undetected by the Coast Guard. However, he was caught by the FBI and sentenced to eighteen months in prison.

His activities during the 1930s remain a mystery and he resurfaced only during WWII. Thanks to his knowledge of electronic communications he got a job as an agent at the Office of Strategic Services (OSS), the predecessor of the CIA. During his service, he appears to have become involved

Albert Hofmann enjoyed a long friendship with German painter Wolfgang Maria Ohlhäuser. This portrait of the chemist was made in 2003.

in a plot to secretly ship heavy armaments from San Diego to England via Canada. When the apparently illegal deal was uncovered, he avoided prosecution by emigrating to Vancouver where he became a Canadian citizen. Soon after he arrived, he founded a boat rental company, became the director of a uranium mine, and later the owner of several companies that traded in uranium. By the age of fifty, he had fulfilled his dream of becoming a millionaire and owned airplanes, a huge yacht, and his own island. Despite all this, he remained unhappy and desperately sought some higher meaning in life. The miracle happened while he was hiking: He claimed an angel appeared to him and prophesied that something extremely important for the future of humanity would soon appear in which he would play a significant role. Hubbard had no idea whatsoever what he should be looking for. That changed in an instant when he stumbled upon an article in a science magazine mentioning the behavior of rats that had been fed LSD. Hubbard found out who was directing the experiments and obtained LSD from him. After his first trip, he knew what the angel had meant.[164]

Al Hubbard left his uranium empire behind and became a psychedelic missionary. He secured a PhD in biopsychology from a diploma mill and participated in LSD experiments on alcoholics conducted by psychiatrists Humphry Osmond and Abram Hoffer. These experiments were being directed by physician Ross McLean in Hollywood Hospital in New Westminster, British Columbia. After a quarrel with McLean, Hubbard left the clinic. Thereafter he divided his time between Canada and Menlo Park, California, where he was

(l. to r.) Myron Stolaroff, Rita Hubbard, Al Hubbard, Willis Harman, around 1960

hired by Willis Harman of Stanford Research Institute to manage the Alternative Futures Project, which focused on developing future-oriented strategies for companies and the government. LSD sessions were occasionally used to promote creative potential and support further studies. Soon, Harman and Hubbard agreed on the goal of "making an LSD experience available to political and intellectual leaders of the entire world."[165] Among the intellectuals was the writer Aldous Huxley, who lived in Hollywood, and had Al Hubbard to thank for his first LSD experience in 1955. In the process, Hubbard met psychiatrist Oscar Janiger, whom he kept well supplied with LSD from then on; Janiger treated countless celebrities in the capital of rich and beautiful people, setting their artistic talents pulsing.

Myron Stolaroff, a Stanford graduate and technical planning director with Ampex, a leading company for tape recorders, first learned of LSD in a lecture by Gerald Heard, a historian and philosopher in 1956. Stolaroff was a devout Jew and dedicated researcher and could not believe that a man as gifted as Heard could speak so favorably of a drug, mentioning Huxley's positive experiences as an example. Although Stolaroff remained skeptical, his curiosity was piqued because he too was looking for deeper meaning in life. Upon Heard's advice, he wrote Hubbard and mentioned his spiritual quest, asking for more information about the promising substance. Hubbard called Stolaroff shortly thereafter and a few weeks later, gave him exactly 66 micrograms of LSD in Hubbard's apartment in Vancouver. He experienced his first trip as life-altering religious moments that granted him deeper insight into his mind. (Stolaroff 1994) Impressed and highly motivated, he returned to California and now knew where his future calling lay: "In one day I learned more about reality and who we are as human beings than I had ever imagined before. I considered it the most important discovery I would ever make and that there was nothing more important for me to do than to realize the entire potential LSD offered."[166]

Myron Stolaroff quit his job and founded the International Foundation for Advanced Study (IFAS) in March 1961 where, with Al Hubbard, he dedicated himself to investigating the creativity-enhancing properties of LSD. During the next five years, until LSD was made illegal in California, nearly 350 people participated in their experiments. The results of an initial study with 153 subjects excited them. A remarkable 83% of subjects found the psychedelic experience to positively influence their personal development. Improved capacity to love and be loved was noted by 78% and 69% experienced more profound communication

with others. The same percentage felt better able to understand themselves and others, while 71% experienced greater self-confidence, and 83% developed a broader view of the world. (Markoff 2005, 60) Stolaroff remained as director and president of IFAS until 1970; during that time he and his colleagues conducted a total of six studies with LSD. His letter to Albert Hofmann of February 26, 1963, reports: "Al Hubbard has told me of his very interesting visit with you and your firm last fall in Switzerland. The other night, having dinner with Gordon Wasson in New York, I also had the opportunity to hear of some of your adventures in Mexico." He then introduced his IFAS foundation and requested help in filling out a new FDA form authorizing his LSD orders with the American branch of Sandoz.

Open Minds, Open Systems

The first computers appeared in the late 1950s. Some considered them to be merely equipment for large companies to automate the management of cash flow and other administrative tasks. Others soon recognized the possibility that digital machines could simulate the human brain. Among those who were interested in artificial intelligence and were attempting to imitate the human mind with mainframe computers were the "mechanists," in contrast to "humanists" who strove to extend the range of human intelligence with smaller personal computers. They developed

> Any sufficiently advanced technology is indistinguishable from magic.
> Arthur C. Clarke

the Arpanet, precursor to the Internet, which was, at the time, primarily used by the military. Many engineers and technicians, brilliant and shrewd inventors, had heard of LSD and were interested in the possibility of using it to increase their cognitive abilities.

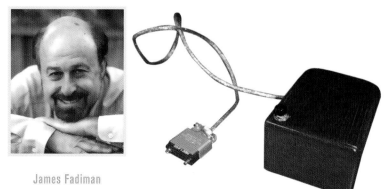

James Fadiman

Engineer Doug Engelbart's
first computer mouse

Charles Savage, a physician who had been carrying out LSD studies since the early 1950s, joined the Hubbard and Stolaroff IFAS team. James Fadiman, the youngest employee, who joined in 1962, soon became an important member of the Advanced Study Group. He had studied psychology at Harvard where Richard Alpert was his advisor. The two met in 1961 in Paris as Alpert was en route to a conference in Copenhagen with Leary and Huxley. On that occasion, Alpert confided to Fadiman that "the biggest thing in the world has happened, and I would like to share that with you," whereupon he pulled out a small vial and sent Fadiman on his first LSD trip. (Markoff 2005)

One of the first IFAS subjects looked after by James Fadiman was Douglas Engelbart, the inventor of the computer mouse, who was born in 1925. He is one of many engineers who enhanced their creativity using guided LSD sessions. Engelbart described his "copy and paste" process as a major step forward of "collective intelli-

In the 1960s the idea was to transform civilization according to our ideas and to transform IBM mainframes into personal computers.... We had the money and the time to do it, and we took LSD, which gave us the crazy idea of trying it all out.

Stewart Brand

gence;" his group was instrumental in the development of electronic word processing. It is an irony of history that the psychedelically inspired humanists were mainly financed by the Pentagon and NASA, two branches of a federal government that in a short few years later would make every effort to try to destroy a movement that, in its eyes, had gotten out of control.

The IFAS experiments helped Kevin Herbert, a programmer and software developer, assume more responsibility and make important decisions. His job at Cisco Systems, a company that specialized in developing computer networks, was demanding and stretched his abilities. Time and again, LSD helped him solve intricate technical problems: "I think that LSD can help you out of these problems you've been wrapping your mind around for weeks. It can give you a fresh perspective on a problem that's so complex that it's not good enough to try to explain it to a coworker."[167] In January 2006, Herbert arrived in Basel from the USA to participate in the LSD Symposium. He wanted to personally congratulate Albert Hofmann on his birthday and on his discovery of LSD which had so changed the Californian's life and work and led to smarter programs and software for our computers. He told a journalist: "LSD must be changing something in the internal communication of my brain. Whatever my inner process is that lets me solve problems, it works differently, or maybe different parts of my brain are used," and LSD "takes me to another world and into another brain state where I stop thinking and start knowing."[168]

Michael Gosney, the initiator of the Digital Be-In and head of a multimedia company, was clear about the relationship between the Internet and drugs: "The vanguard of the computer industry consists of creative people, who, like any creative community, are more inclined to experiment culturally. It's been unspoken for many years that the crown jewel of the U.S. economy has been so influenced by 'soft' drugs like marijuana and LSD."[169] Bill Gates unabashedly responded to an interviewer's question whether he had ever taken LSD: "My errant youth ended a long time ago." When the journalist persisted and asked what that meant, Gates answered: "It means that there were things I did under the age of twenty-five that I ended up not doing subsequently."[170] One of the first employees at Microsoft was Bob Wallace. He wrote the program for QuickSoft and introduced the concept and reality of Shareware, the sharing of software by many users. He was known as an "online drug guru" and, shortly before his death in the summer of 2002, he bequeathed a large share of his assets for psychedelic research.

Steve Jobs (1955–2011), broke off his study of art after only one semester. He became interested in Eastern philosophy, had his first experiences with LSD, let his hair grow and traveled to India during the early 1970s. Back in California, he met a young engineer, Steve Wozniak, who worked for Hewlett-Packard and also was acquainted with LSD. On April 1, 1976, the two hippies founded a company they called Apple in Los Altos and produced one of the first personal computers in Jobs' garage. It was empty because Jobs had sold his old VW bus to raise start-up capital; together with the sale of Wozniak's pocket calculator, they had one thousand seven hundred and fifty dollars. Vegetarian and Buddhist Steve Jobs enthused about his youthful experiences and counted his LSD trips and the journey to India as the "two or three most important things I ever did in my life."

When he was conceiving of the iTunes Player, which displayed dancing patterns in color on the monitor in time with the beat of the music, he recollected and grinned: "That takes me back to my youth." (Markoff 2005) In 2010 he praised the iPad as the "most advanced technology in one magical and revolutionary device." Jobs, the unconventional thinker, became an agile business man and a billionaire. Apple's slogan, "Think different" from the year 1997 could just as well have come thirty years earlier from the counterculture of the 1960s.

"Computers are coming to the people," said Stewart Brand in

> There were things about [Jobs] that people who had not tried psychedelics – even people who knew him well, including his wife – could never understand.
>
> *Steve Jobs obituary*, NY Times

> The personal computer is the LSD of the 1990s.
>
> *Timothy Leary*

an article about the developing computer scene around San Francisco in 1972 and "That's good news, maybe the best since psychedelics."[171] For Brand as for Leary, the computer is the new LSD, a new technology for opening the mind, changing society, and creating open systems. The information age had begun.

All is One

As a new IFAS staffer in December 1962, twenty-four year old James Fadiman was responsible for guiding Stewart Brand during his first LSD experience. Brand was one of 153 subjects in the first study and received two doses of LSD within an hour. He was then asked to meditate on a large yin-yang symbol painted on a wall while he listened to classical music through head phones. Although Brand was slightly annoyed by the arranged procedure, he not only liked the experience of altered perception, it decided the course of his life. He met Ken Kesey and joined the Merry Pranksters where he encountered Richard Alpert, Allen Ginsberg, Jerry Garcia and other artists and writers who had gathered around the "tripping" troupe.

One day, Stewart Brand began to produce imprinted buttons which could be pinned onto collars and the front of jeans jackets, showing which causes the wearer supported or opposed by means of the symbols depicted. He described the motive for this: "One afternoon, probably in March in 1966, dropping a little bit of LSD, I went up onto the roof and sat shivering in a blanket sort of looking and thinking.... And so I'm watching the buildings, looking out at San Francisco, thinking about Buckminster Fuller's notion that people think of the earth's resources as unlimited because they think of the earth as flat. I'm looking at San Francisco from 300 feet and 200 micrograms up and thinking that I can see from here that the earth is curved. I had the idea that the higher you go the more you can see earth as round. There were no public photographs of the whole earth at that time, despite the fact that we were in the space program for about ten years. I started scheming within the trip. How can I make this photograph happen? Because I had now persuaded myself that it will change everything if we have this photograph looking at the earth from space."[172]

One week later Brand stood in the middle of campus at the University of California at Berkeley with a box of buttons which said: "Why Haven't We Seen a Photograph of the Whole Earth yet?" The very next day after the *San Francisco Chronicle* reported Brand's action, NASA released a satellite image showing the earth as it rose behind the moon. In the fall of 1968, Brand published the first edition of his

Stewart Brand

> The discovery that one's own deepest being is one with the All frees a person from the burden of time, from fears, and cares. It liberates from the chains of alienation and isolated existence.
>
> *Ken Wilber*

John Perry Barlow

WHOLE EARTH CATALOG

access to tools

Fall 1968
$5

Whole Earth Catalog of 64 pages, which sold for five dollars and offered "Access to Tools," clothing, books, implements, seed, machines, all products for self sufficient hippies and their communes. The products had to satisfy certain criteria: Tools and equipment had to be useful, easy to employ, of high quality or economical, not widely known, and easy to order by mail. The catalog was conceived as a practical source for holistic thinking and acting people. From 1974 to 1985 Brand published the periodical *CoEvolution Quarterly*. In 1984 the *Whole Earth Software Catalog 1.0* appeared and in 1989 the *Electronic Whole Earth Catalog* as a CD-ROM; *Whole Earth* has been on the Internet since the spring of 2010. In a speech at Stanford University in 2005, Apple founder and CEO Steve Jobs compared the *Whole Earth Catalog* with the Internet: "It was a sort of like Google in paperback form, 35 years before Google came along."

Legal, Illegal, Digital

The first two generations of computer hackers to gain ill repute in the 1960s and early 1970s came out of the newly created university departments for computer science. They transformed centrally-controlled mainframes into virtual small computers and introduced multi-user systems which allowed greater access to the computers. The third generation emerged in the late 1970s, non-academic hackers and long-haired hippies who ultimately created the personal computer. In his article in *TIME* of March 1, 1995, "We

> Hence, everything is bound up together. Heaven and earth, air and water. All these are only one thing: not four, not two, and not three, but one. Where any are lacking, there is incompleteness.
>
> *Paracelsus*

> LSD induces a profound state. The ego vanishes and one feels part of a whole, is at home both in heaven and on earth; one feels oneself to be secure in the universe and to merge into a general consciousness.
>
> *Albert Hofmann*

255

Owe It All to the Hippies," Stewart Brand wrote: "The counterculture's scorn for centralized authority provided the philosophical foundations of not only the leaderless Internet but also the entire personal-computer revolution." For Sweden's Linus Torvalds, who as a student in the 1990s, developed the open source operating system Linux, boundless openness is the driving force behind his free software, the pleasure in interchange, the challenge of visionary thinking and of fair behavior.

The Well—Whole Earth 'Lectronic Link—operates like the *Whole Earth Catalog*; it is a loosely connected community committed to using the new form of communication. They created the first relationship network, a harbinger of cyberspace before the Internet and Facebook. Among those who, in 1985, founded the club as an online community of intelligent and informed world citizens, were Stewart Brand and Larry Brilliant. Brand's best known words stem from the Hacker's Conference in 1984: "Information wants to be free," which touched upon the sobering fact that it was ever harder to control information. The visionary club attracted the best minds of a new generation, one of whom was John Perry Barlow, born in 1947 on a Wyoming cattle ranch.

Barlow had heard of Pahnke's Good Friday experiment during his studies and when a friend asked him in 1966 whether he was interested in psychedelics, he just nodded. His first LSD trip, at an Ali Akbar Khan concert, changed his consciousness and his life within a matter of hours. Barlow became one of the early song writers for the Grateful Dead and later made no secret of having taken LSD "at least a thousand times." (Hayes 2000) He joined The Well in 1986 along with Mitch Kapor, the developer of Lotus 1-2-3 and a teacher of Transcendental Meditation, and John Gilmore, a top-notch employee of the computer company Sun Systems. In July 1990, Barlow, Kapor, and Gilmore founded the *Electronic Frontier Foundation* (EFF), the goals of which were to protect the free expression of opinions and self-determination in the Internet, i.e., open systems for open minds.

The term "Cyberspace"—cybernetic space—was first seen in 1984 in the novel *Neuromancer* by the science fiction writer William Gibson. The word was used in a literary context as the explanation for a "consensual hallucination of computer-generated graphic space."[173] John Perry Barlow remarked on how it combined aspects of humanistic hippie ideals of the 1960s with those of the nascent world of electronic networks in his speech entitled "A Declaration of the Independence of Cyberspace" at the World Economic Forum in Davos in 1996. The call for a "civilization of the mind" described a somewhat peculiar sounding but coherent blend of psychedelically driven hippie subculture with the entrepreneurial flair of high tech yuppies in Silicon Valley. Both aimed for a more humane, fair, and independent society and decisively shaped public perception of the new network, the Internet. "At the end of the twentieth century, the

> The Greeks of antiquity called the creation "cosmos," meaning "jewel." Humans had not yet polluted the world. Today, we experience the earth as a jewel only when viewed from the cosmos, the image that space travel has given us of the planet, blue and radiant in sunlight, floating in infinite space along the path preordained since time immemorial.
>
> *Albert Hofmann*

long predicted convergence of the media, computing and telecommunications into hypermedia is finally happening... At such moments of profound social change, anyone who can offer a simple explanation of what is happening will be listened to with great interest. At this crucial juncture, a loose alliance of writers, hackers, capitalists and artists from the West Coast of the USA has succeeded in defining a heterogeneous orthodoxy for the coming information age: The Californian Ideology."[174]

Gaia

On December 24, 1968, Commander Frank Borman pointed the Apollo space ship in orbit to the horizon of the Earth's moon. When he looked out, his breath caught and he whispered into the microphone: "Oh, my God, look at that picture over there! Here's the earth coming up!" Astronaut Bill Anders then shot one of the best known photos of all time, "Earth-rise," the earth ascending, a symbol of our planet. For the first time, people could *see* that we are all circling around the sun on Spaceship Earth.[175] For the first time, humankind could behold our habitat, its blue oceans, green forests, brown desert sands and glittering ice at the polar caps, all surrounded by a gossamer-thin layer, the atmosphere that allows earth's inhabitants to breathe and live. The thought and realization that we are part of a greater whole had found graphic expression.

At the same time, the British chemist, biophysicist and physician James Lovelock along with the microbiologist Lynn Margulis devised the Gaia Hypothesis which described the earth with its atmosphere as a living organism. They called this biosphere "Gaia" after the Greek

> Immersion in the psychedelic experience provided the ritual context in which human consciousness merged into the light of self-awareness, self-reflection, and self-articulation – into the light of Gaia, the Earth herself.
>
> Terence McKenna

They flew to the moon and discovered the earth

earth goddess, a self-organizing dynamic system in the infinity of the universe.

Throughout his life, Albert Hofmann confirmed the fact that LSD had helped him recapture the mystical experiences of nature of his youth: The feeling of oneness with the universe and the recognition of the necessity to care for the delicate ecological equilibrium of life on earth. It is nature herself, the spirit of nature in the form of plants that provides for the psychedelic experiences which sharpen the senses of humans for an enhanced awareness of the world and promotes a symbiosis between humans and all that surrounds them. "That is something unique," Hofmann pointed out, "and it is contained in these plants that have been used as sacred drugs for 3,000 years and in which I discovered these LSD-like compounds." (Bröckers, Liggenstorfer 2006, 18) What was unique pertained not only to all flora and fauna, but to all sentient beings, as it is said in Buddhism. Hofmann recalled a young man who thanked him and told him: "I grew up in the city but, ever since I took LSD, I walk in the forest again." (Ibid, 17) Hofmann emphasized that "He recognized that what was truly important was not the houses, factories, offices, which we need and use, but that on which we live, the

Albert Hofmann with John Allen, pioneer in biosphere science and inventor of Biosphere 2, during his visit to the project in Tucson, Arizona, 1988

> The most valuable knowledge consists in realizing once more where humans belong; to be part of living nature.
>
> *Albert Hofmann*

> Progress in the natural sciences makes the wholeness of the world and our oneness with it clearer in our minds. When our realization of the complete unity is not only intellectual, but opens up our whole being to the light of total consciousness, then this realization becomes radiant joy, all encompassing love.
>
> *Rabindranath Tagore*

sun and the moon and the earth, the meadows and flowers, all those things that grow, that are alive, that is what we need."(Ibid, 17)

These insights and developments during the 1960s and 1970s marked the beginning of the modern global ecological movement. Norwegian philosopher Arne Naess (1912–2009) who coined the term "Deep Ecology," was the founder of Norway's Green Party. In the 1960s, he was a guest lecturer at the University of California in Berkeley, and he relates that his LSD experiences during that time significantly influenced his later thinking.[176] He called his ecological philosophy "Ecosophy" according to which humankind's role, being part of the organism Earth, is as keepers and protectors of the basis of life on Gaia. The concept of sustainability has been known since the beginning of the 18th century, but it first entered into public consciousness in 1972 in the report from the Club of Rome, *The Limits to Growth*,[177] in the sense of a "condition of global equilibrium."

John McConnell proposed the first Earth Day in 1968. Every year since 1970, institutions, organizations, universities

Paul Stamets

Paul Stamets and Albert Hofmann, Psychoactivity Conference, Amsterdam, October 1998

and millions of people around the world use April 22nd to contemplate protection of the planet and its climate. At the suggestion of the government of Bolivia, the UN General Assembly declared April 22nd as International Mother Earth Day.

On September 15, 1971 a small group of young peace activists left Vancouver on an old fishing boat to prevent a U.S. atomic test off the coast of Alaska. They gave the action a name that elucidated the expedition's program: Green + Peace = Greenpeace. Grown from this band of committed hippies into one of the most influential and powerful environmental movements, Greenpeace has never shied away from directly confronting polluters through spectacular campaigns and protest actions. At sea, on land, and in the air, they point to abuses of the environment and thereby create pressure on industries and politicians throughout the world.

Symbiosis

Mushroom expert Paul Stamets traces his keen ecological conscience back to his experiences with psychedelic mushrooms. He found that such mushrooms are more likely to grow in areas that are ecologically threatened or damaged, as if they wanted to offer a solution to the people there. "Before the impact of human civilization, psilocybin species were largely restricted to narrowly defined ecosystems. Many thrive after ecological catastrophes. Landslides, floods, hurricanes, and volcanoes all create supportive habitats for many psilocybe mushrooms. This peculiar affection for disturbed habitats enables them to travel, following streams of debris... psilocybe mushrooms and civilization continue to coevolve. Today, many psilocybes are concentrated wherever people congregate—around parks, housing developments,

> Just as plants form sex organs to mate with bees, so too they marry humans—and this contact gives humans access to worlds that would remain inaccessible without plants.
>
> *Ernst Jünger*

> The first person to perceive his surroundings as a whole and recognize the power inherent in it was a shaman, a primordial shaman.
>
> *Galsan Tschinag*

schools, churches, golf courses, industrial complexes, nurseries, gardens, city parks, freeway rest areas, and government buildings—including county and state courthouses and jails! This successful adaptation is a comparatively recent phenomenon…. The way these mushrooms have evolved in close association with humans suggests an innate intelligence on the part of the mushrooms." (Stamets 1996, 16)

Ethnobotanist Kathleen Harrison can look back on over thirty years of field studies of psychoactive plants and mushrooms in Latin America and on Hawaii. Her collaboration with healers and shamans influenced her direct and feminine relationship with nature. She is aware that she does not find understanding everywhere in academic circles when she represents the opinion that: "Nature loves it when we take psychedelics and wander around, appreciating her, in a state of respectful awe and gratitude… I'll personify her—this grand, sentient, multi-formed presence. Some call her Gaia, an ever-transforming yet metastable entity who is far more than the sum of her amazing parts, but we'll just call her nature here. She is embodied in all the living things, the elements,

Kathleen Harrison

the planet and, some say, the heavens."[178] In a state of expanded consciousness, Harrison recognizes how, in all details, everything around her makes for a whole that thrives in miraculous fashion—a paradise which could not be more beautiful and perfect.

Albert Hofmann once remarked that he had trouble understanding how people admire and marvel at the design of a Ferrari but cannot seem to perceive the unimaginable fantasy, the endless variety and immeasurable beauty of nature.[179] Harrison is convinced that the feeling of deep love for nature rewards us with insight and joy. This love also triggers the impulse to tend and protect her. This principle of the interplay between spirituality and ecology has been deeply rooted in all native populations since time immemorial. We are in the process of remembering and re-learning it and psychedelics can help with that.

The view that nature is sending messages to us humans is not only held by Kat Harrison and Paul Stamets. As the caretakers of nature, shamans in all cultures mediate between humans and the "other-than-human-persons," as animism researcher Graham Harvey has articulated it. He found that animism best expressed the idea of a relationship between humankind and mushrooms: "Maybe sometimes the mushrooms just want to help us join in the big conversation that's going on all around us."[180]

One always assumes that science demystifies. However, if one probes deeper, even more marvelous things are revealed. When I see and know how everything is constructed, how our perception functions, how our consciousness comes about, then that is all so wonderfully constructed according to plan and so sophisticated that one can only marvel. Those aren't just words, they are facts!

Albert Hofmann

For psychologist Ralph Metzner the psychedelic, ecological, and other movements that developed in the 1960s all go hand in hand. "The decade of the 1960s was a time of several interconnected movements of socio-cultural transformation that profoundly changed Western society, and more indirectly other countries in the world as well: The environmental movement, the women's liberation movement, the anti-war movement, the civil rights movement, the revolution in sexual and family relations, and an explosion of new forms of expression in music and the visual arts."[181] In his books about sacred mushrooms and ayahuasca, he references reports from researchers and scientists who, on the basis of their impressive psychedelic experiences in the early 1960s and during the rest of their lives, became environmental activists as Metzner did himself.[182]

Nobel Prizes

The discovery of the structure of deoxyribonucleic acid, DNA, the genetic information of humans, in 1953 created a scientific sensation. Francis Crick and James Watson received the Nobel Prize for Medicine in 1962 for their "discoveries concerning the molecular structure of nucleic acids and its significance for information transfer in living material." At least Crick was under the influence of LSD while deciphering the form of DNA as a double helix. He confided to a scientist friend later that he occasionally took low doses of LSD to boost his capacity for thought and that other academics at Cambridge took small doses of LSD to free themselves of preconceived notions and allow their genius free course. Crick later publically began to promote the legalization of marijuana.[183]

With his contributions to understanding quantum field theory, Richard Feynman revolutionized twentieth century theoretical physics. He was involved in the development of the atom bomb at Los Alamos during WWII. His famous speech on December 29, 1959 at the California Institute of Technology in Pasadena, "There's Plenty of Room at the Bottom," is regarded by specialists as the founding document of nanotechnology. Feynman received the 1965 Nobel Prize for physics for his work in quantum electrodynamics describing elementary quantum field theory interactions. His keen interest in expanding human consciousness led the brilliant scientist to friendships with John Lilly and Richard Alpert. From Lilly he learned how to experiment with LSD in an isolation tank, and from Alpert how to have out-of-body experiences while in the tank.

American chemist Kary Mullis, was awarded the Nobel Prize in 1993 for discovering the polymerase chain reaction (PCR) that is based on the cyclically repeated copying of DNA with the help of a DNA polymerase and nucleotides. The method is indispensable today for detecting viral infections, hereditary disorders,

> What would opening the doors of perception bring? Nothing less than global peace.
> *Ralph Abraham*

> Another aspect of the psychedelic vision for me that has been profound is the sense that everything is alive or at the least, there is no distinction between what we call living and non-living.
> *Andrew Weil*

producing genetic fingerprints, and for the cloning of genes. In his autobiography, he describes his experiments with LSD in the 1960s. He doubts that he would have made his discovery without psychedelic drugs and personally conveyed this to Albert Hofmann.[184] He is of the opinion that "There are a lot of people for whom psychedelics have been really beneficial. But I wouldn't recommend it to everyone. Some are just not ready but society would benefit from letting people who are ready for psychedelics to have legal access them." (Mullis 1989)

As an expert on dynamical systems theory or chaos mathematics, emeritus professor of mathematics Ralph Abraham has written more than a dozen books. He discussed chaos and order with his friends Terence McKenna and Rupert Sheldrake in their *Trialogues at the Edge of the West.*[185] Interviewed in 1991, he explained how psychedelic insights had influenced mathematical theories: "In the sixties, a lot of people on the frontiers of math experimented with psychedelic substances. There was a brief and extremely creative kiss between the community of hippies and top mathematicians. I know this, because I was a purveyor of psychedelics to the mathematical community.... To be creative in mathematics, you have to start from a point of total oblivion. Basically, math is revealed in a totally unconscious process in which one is completely ignorant of the social climate. And mathematical advance has always been the motor behind the advancement of consciousness."[186]

The 1970s were a time of stagnation for American physicists. Jobs were scarce. The trend was back to conformity. It was reason enough for a few eccentric and eager young physicists to found the Fundamental Fysiks Group in Berkeley in 1975 and consider daring new theories. They held seminars at Esalen in which Western scientific theories such as quantum entanglement and Bells' Theorem were discussed and compared with the millennia-old traditions of Eastern philosophy leading to innovative discoveries. Bathing in the hot springs and LSD both provided the necessary stimuli. The group led modern physics in a new direction, revived quantum theory (Kaiser 2011), and was deemed worthy of a cover story by *TIME* magazine. A string of publications resulted, among them Fritjof Capra's bestseller *The Tao of Physics.*

Few researchers, engineers, scientists, designers, and artists have publicly spoken of their stimulating experiences with LSD and other psychedelics. In most cases, it is the people who are successful who can afford to admit having consumed psychoactive drugs and break the social taboo that existed even before psychedelics were illegal. Colleagues are not as likely to look askance at a Nobel Prize winner, and it is unlikely to cost such a person his job.

Thanks to the mind-opening stimulus of LSD many movements and developments came into being and a number of discoveries and inventions ensued. Under ideal conditions, psychedelics are, as they have been throughout human history, a source of inspiration.

Peak Experiences

Stanley Kubrick's film *Dr. Strangelove: or How I Learned to Stop Worrying and Love the Bomb* appeared in theaters in 1964 with acting genius Peter Sellers in the main role as the immigrant German scientist who, in the course of the Cold War, was a special advisor to the President of the United States. It is believed that Kubrick's model for Dr. Strangelove was Herman Kahn, the American futurologist and head of the RAND Corporation, contracted to advise the U.S. Armed Forces. Instead of looking at the sense-lessness of an atomic war that could destroy all humanity, Kahn developed omnipotent fantasies of grandiose scenarios planning for what would come afterward, more than "strange" and completely unrealistic notions about how a part of the population could survive. He

Dock Ellis

told a reporter early in the 1970s: "We (scenario writers) take God's view. The president's view. Big. Aerial. Global. Galactic. Ethereal. Spatial. Overall. Megalomania is the standard occupational hazard." A few years later and apparently a few trips smarter and wiser, he went into raptures over the counterculture that had since emerged: "I like the hippies," he explained to a journalist in 1968, "I've been to Esalen. I've had LSD a couple of times. In some ways, I'd like to join them."[187]

All his life, radical philosopher and soci-ologist Michel Foucault was in search of a new identity, hunting novel experiences. Following Nietzsche, Foucault felt that new identity could only be created by the large, extreme experience in which the subject tore away from itself. Foucault described this experience as a particular point in his

life which bordered on the unbearable. An LSD trip that he took in 1975 at Zabriskie Point in Death Valley, California, brought Foucault to this point which "requires the utmost in intensity and sheer impossibility" and which he later termed the best experience of his life.[188]

Competitive sports are not normally a playing field for acid heads—with one exception. On June 12, 1970, pitcher Dock Ellis became a baseball legend as he won for the Pittsburgh Pirates against the San Diego Padres with a no-hitter while he was under the influence of LSD. It was an incredible achieve-ment while in such a state, since a no-hitter signifies the special and extremely rare achievement of a pitcher not allowing a single base hit during an entire game. Ellis had swallowed a trip thinking he had that day free and the game would be played the following day. In an interview in 2008, he said "I can only remember bits and pieces from the game…. "I was psyched. I had a feeling of euphoria…. The ball was small sometimes, the ball was large some-times, sometimes I saw the catcher, some-times I didn't. Sometimes, I tried to stare the hitter down and throw while I was looking at him. I chewed my gum until it turned to powder. I started having a crazy idea in the fourth inning that Richard Nixon was the home plate umpire, and once I thought I was pitching a baseball to Jimi Hendrix, who to me was holding a guitar and swinging it over the plate."[189]

Ways of Life

Those whose eyes have been opened in a blessed moment and have merged their outer and inner sight are able to be aware of the miracle of creation in their everyday lives.
Albert Hofmann

Another Discovery

In the early 1960s, after more than twenty fulfilling years of residence in their house in Bottmingen which was a rural suburb of Basel when they first arrived, the Hofmanns wished to trade their increasingly urban setting for a quieter one with better air quality. Tax advantages in the canton of Basel-Land outside city limits and the desire of many city dwellers for country living meant that suburban villages grew up all around Basel. Within a few decades, an agglomeration of single family dwellings and housing developments littered the environs of the town. It was enough to prompt nature lovers to consider changing locations. While Anita Hofmann yearned for the mountains of her childhood in Graubünden, she did not wish to leave her circle of friends in Bottmingen and Basel city proper. She would have preferred to remain in Bottmingen where she was active in local education, but she understood and respected her husband's great dream.

While visiting the Diems, a couple who lived in the small village of Burg in the Leimental, a valley near Basel, the Hofmanns found the area very appealing. Their friends put them in touch with a farmer who wished to sell a large parcel of land above the village called Rittimatte. The property is sheltered by forest and a broad expanse of mountain ridges; from it, one's eye is led downward on the left to the gentle hills in nearby Alsace, on the right to the foothills of the Upper Rhine Valley; beyond, lie the summits of the Vosges mountain range and the Black Forest peaks with valleys extending down to the tri-border region. The Hofmanns knew at once: This was the place! One Sunday in the summer of 1963, the family traveled to picnic on the blossoming Jura meadow and to visualize plans for their new house.

After later acquisitions, the property came to nearly twenty-thousand square meters (almost five acres), a large portion of which was farmland on which nothing was allowed to be built; moreover, part of it lay on French territory. Hofmann liked to tell about his negotiations with

The first summer   Family Christmas around 1971

the landowner: "The farmer wanted three francs per square meter. I told him, 'I won't pay that!' and then added, 'I'll pay you four!'" and enjoyed the surprised look on the farmer's face.[190] Rudolf Gelpke wrote to Hofmann in February 1964: "I truly hope that everything is going well for you, dear Albert, and that the dream of your 'Burg [castle] in Burg' (that appearance late last summer was unforgettable and serves as a bright and often consoling memory to me) is becoming reality." And so it did. The Hofmanns' modern new home was built in the mid-1960s according to plans designed by architect Wendelin Gelpke, Rudolf's brother.[191] However, from the beginning, collaboration with the planner did not go well because Gelpke did not sufficiently satisfy Hofmann's wishes. Ultimately, Hofmann and his friend's brother had a falling out, but fortunately, Hofmann's son Andreas was also an architect and had just come back after several years in the USA. He took the matter in hand and, in particular, reworked the interior in close consultation with his parents. In October 1968, Anita and Albert

Hofmann with their youngest daughter Beatrix were able to move into their new home. They both were happy with their "paradise" as they called it. Albert Hofmann repeatedly referred to the Rittimatte as "my second biggest discovery."

The Hofmanns had the access road from the village enlarged from a narrow forest path to a small paved street. The wall of the house's entryway has a large ammonite embedded into it which, along with two other fine specimens, was found by Hofmann during the excavation work. The entry leads into a spacious living room separated by two stair steps from a work area and the library. The living area is for dining, drinking tea, reading and receiving guests. A grand piano was sometimes used for house concerts. In the living room suite, Anita and Albert Hofmann each had their favorite seats facing large front windows looking out on the surrounding meadows, hills, and valleys. A swimming pool was also built into the ground floor which the Hofmanns, both passionate swimmers, used nearly daily for over two decades. In the rear of

266

Room with a view

The Hofmann's home on the Rittimatte

Living room looking into the study area

The third bench commemorating Hofmann's 100th birthday

the house were Anita's personal room and Albert's small "snug," as he called his study. As in Bottmingen, Anita planted a garden with a large variety of flowers. Over the next twenty-five years they planted 25 cherry trees, for Hofmann a "plant of the gods," plus several mirabelle and green plum trees. Visitors appreciated the Rittimatte brandies, homemade from the fruit. With his grandson Simon, Albert Hofmann made his first wooden bench, which stands on French soil. There is a second one, a "secret" bench down at the edge of the forest, planed from a tree trunk where Hofmann sometimes withdrew for a nap or to be alone with his thoughts in peace. A third bench was a gift from the commune for his one-hundredth birthday; it stands in Swiss territory, closer to the house and along the path, and was thus easier for him to reach.

Paradise Found Again

The commune of Burg was part of the canton of Bern until 1994, when it became

267

part of the canton Basel-Land. The village is situated in the shadow of a cliff upon which stands the castle (German: Burg) that gave the village its name. Burg had 251 inhabitants at the end of the eighteenth century of whom 64 were entitled to vote. The village reached its peak population near the end of the nineteenth century. By 2010, as two hundred years earlier, it was again down to just 250 inhabitants or "Burgtaler" as they called themselves. The newly arrived married couple quickly became active in the community. On Ascension Day, the Hofmanns celebrated the "Banntag," a traditional Swiss custom, in the "Schützehüsli" (clubhouse) and often attended classical music concerts up in the castle. Hofmann also frequently enjoyed watching the village's amateur soccer tournaments and talking shop with the fans. He became involved with the community administration, serving as auditor for two years; however, local politics interested him less than the life of the villagers and their welfare. If he did not like something, he made it clearly known. A story is still told around the regulars' table about a Penance Day sermon in the Reformed Church parish hall: The pastor was holding forth with bloodthirsty accounts from the Old Testament until Hofmann indignantly interrupted and asked him to please stop going endlessly on with these dreadful stories.

Hofmann's commute during his last working years was now somewhat longer. It took him down through the village below the castle and by way of Metzerlen on past the pilgrimage town of Mariastein with its Benedictine monastery and Black Maria in stone, venerated by quite a variety

Drawing of Burg

of faith communities. Proceeding further down into the valley to Flüh, from where, via Biel-Benken, through his former place of residence, Bottmingen on to Basel, Hofmann would finally arrive at the Sandoz factory site along the Rhine. It took him about forty-five minutes by car, so a self-experiment followed by a bicycle ride was not advisable. However, thoughts of those days could evoke a chuckle from the still vigorous chemist. In his account of his life which he wrote to be read at his funeral, Hofmann emphasized the importance of their new home: "From the mutual plans of the family, that house on the Rittimatte arose, in which we spent many years, enriched by visits from our children and grandchildren and friends. While Anita found an exhilarating fulfillment in tending her beloved flowers in the garden and in the house, as she had back in Bottmingen—my time was spent in the quiet of my work space with literary activity, publications and lectures—some still in connection with my professional role, but also with recording my thoughts and personal insights into natural philosophy. On the Rittimatte, my life has come full circle, also in the sense that I again found my childhood paradise, the same countryside as on Martinsberg, where I was so blessed as a boy, the Jura meadow with the same flowers, and the same view into the distance."

The Company

From May 1929 until his retirement in the summer of 1971, Albert Hofmann worked a total of 42 years for Sandoz. Six years after joining the firm, he was able to obtain his own laboratory with an assistant. In 1946, he was promoted to be an authorized representative, in 1952 to director of research for the Depart-

ment of Natural Products. In 1954 the company congratulated him:

This coming Sunday, May 16, twenty-five years will have passed since you started as a young chemist armed with knowledge from Karrer's school. You immediately began your work as a research chemist with great zest and success in the area of heart glycosides and made significant contributions to clarifying the constitution of scillaridin. Then you moved to ergot alkaloids, our oldest and most important area, where you achieved significant success in degradation reactions and partial synthesis and in hydrogenation of ergot alkaloids and clarification of their constitution. You let the whole world know about lysergic acid diethylamide and the observation of its effect on you. You have become an authority in the area of ergot alkaloids and not only manage your department, but also do fruitful experimental work in it.

We do not wish to list all of your successes here but rather to express our special satisfaction that your work has

Colleagues congratulate the newly appointed vice-director, December 1951

In his new office as deputy director, 1959

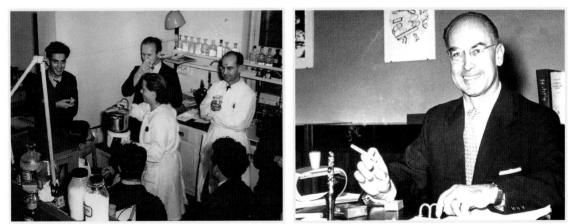

Final meeting with Arthur Stoll of the Sandoz research department, April 1956

resulted in a series of compounds that already contribute significantly to the commercial success of our pharmaceutical division.

On the occasion of the twenty-fifth anniversary of your employment we wish to offer our heartfelt congratulations and sincere thanks for your loyal, successful, and dedicated work during a quarter of a century.

As a token of our appreciation, we are presenting you with a monetary gift with the wish that you may use it for something which brings you much enjoyment and will be a pleasant reminder of this special day.

Hofmann bought himself "a gold wrist watch and an appealing, ancient slate table," as he mentioned in his letter of thanks.

After thirty years with Sandoz in 1959 he was named Deputy Managing Director.

Although more occupied with management concerns, he still worked in the lab as often as possible.

When Hofmann neared the end of his professional career in 1967, he had an unpleasant disagreement with the General Director, Carl Maurice Jacottet, over the renewal of his contract. Jacottet did not wish to meet Hofmann's demands and bluntly turned him down in no uncertain terms. In view of his impending retirement, Hofmann swallowed his annoyance and accepted the offer.

By contrast, his relations with colleagues over the years were always excellent. On the occasion of his fortieth anniversary of service in 1969, they wished him happiness and gave him many presents. Hofmann thanked them correspondingly warmly:

My wish to have a good telescope became a reality faster than I had expected. This

The Sandoz factory site and the Rhine River, early 1970s

Marc Moret

wish arose from living in our new home above the haze and light pollution of the city and viewing the twinkling, starry heavens. The microcosm of atoms and molecules in which the chemist works is matched by the macrocosm of the stars in which planets circle suns like electrons around atomic nuclei. Viewing the magnificence of the heavenly bodies in the infinity of space reasonably complements the world view of chemistry—the invisible, miniscule world of atoms and molecules.

Our human life has its locus neither in the microcosm of atoms nor in the macrocosm of space, but in that wonderful intermediate realm in the biosphere of our good earth. From this vital realm you have given me delightful flowers, among them lilies which I especially love, and good wine, a psychopharmacon proven over thousands of years which makes the spirit glad in the proper dosage—of great importance for all psychopharmaca.

On the occasion of the anniversary of my employment that you so wonderfully arranged for me, I would like to thank you all for the pleasant collaboration and the many signs of personal attachment that I have enjoyed over the past four decades. I wish you all the best of luck, health, happiness, and success in your professional activity in the service of our company, the prosperity of which is our common concern.

Hofmann published around 150 articles in professional journals, many of them in *Helvetica Chimica Acta*. Hofmann's chief scientific work is the monograph that appeared in 1964, *The Ergot Alkaloids*. A lecture he gave in a workshop to the German Society for Pharmaceutical Plant Research in the fall of 1958 in Tübingen entitled "The Chemistry of the Ergot Alkaloids" forms the core of his book. The first two short sections concern the botany of the ergot fungus and the history of ergot and its active ingredients. The far greater part

271

relates to the chemistry of ergot alkaloids and their derivatives. He concludes with their pharmacology and therapeutic use. The significance of his work for science and for the reputation of Sandoz can be seen in a letter which then-General Director Arthur Stoll sent in August 1964 to thank Hofmann for sending him the book:

The copy of your book on ergot alkaloids which you sent to me with the thoughtful dedication brings me great pleasure. I would like to sincerely thank you for this renewed sign of your longstanding devotion and congratulate you on your success in presenting the contents and form of such an important area of pharmaceutical chemistry in which we worked together for so long. With this, you have released me from an imprudent promise I made to Enke Verlag to write a small monograph on ergot, which I could not keep due to overload at work. I assume that Enke Verlag will now be completely satisfied.

As nearly as I could tell with the requirement currently imposed upon me to spare my eyesight, you have presented the material from A to Z which you master like no one else, clearly and fully, thereby demonstrating the importance of ergot alkaloids both in pharmaceutical chemical research and in pharmacology and medicine. That is highly praiseworthy and I am convinced that recognition from the field will not be lacking.

Your book shows that thorough scientific work is carried out at Sandoz that can readily stand alongside any being done at universities.

I too would like to express my grateful acknowledgement and remain with best wishes for your health and work and with my heartiest greetings.

Yours, A. Stoll

Arthur Stoll

In today's world where research in large enterprises is extremely focused and coordinated, the freedom that Hofmann enjoyed in those days is hard to imagine. He largely chose his areas of investigation himself, corresponded openly and extensively with colleagues about ongoing projects, investigated plants sent to him by friends, and on his own initiative pursued potentially interesting substances. In his self-experiments, he was also able to involve interested coworkers unhindered. Free exchange of ideas was possible at international congresses. Thus, he participated in a meeting of the German Society for Pharmaceutical Plant Research in Berlin, traveled to Stockholm for a professional chemistry conference, traveled from the USA via Tahiti to New Caledonia where he participated in an historic international symposium on medicinal plants from lands around the Pacific Ocean, then went on to Australia and Japan, a tour around the world.

He owed this freedom to his superior, Arthur Stoll, who had repeatedly praised him for his work, as he did when congratulating Hofmann when his paper on ergotamine was published in *Helvetica Chimica Acta*. However, there are also background noises. The Sandoz archives of Novartis indicate Arthur Stoll as the inventor first named on every patent up until 1952. Concerning Stoll's contribution to these inventions, Hofmann mentions that Stoll was hardly to be seen in the laboratory "because he was exclusively occupied by management duties even then." Stoll did take the patent documents of his coworkers' home on weekends to review. His "improvements" made things worse and mostly had to be canceled, which was a rather delicate matter. In any case, that is how Stoll's name came to be listed on the patent documents. Hofmann was not the only one affected by this problem during this period at Sandoz. When one of them asked why Stoll's name was listed on the patent, the chief answered: "Herr Doctor, surely you know why the publication appears under my name—so that it will be read."

Farewell to Sandoz

On July 1, 1971, Albert Hofmann retired at age 65. He did not plan to become inactive and looked forward to the next stage of his life. In September he wrote a detailed letter to Humphry Osmond and closed with his plans for the future: "Chemistry is replaced at a good proportion by occupation with philosophy, poetry and fine arts." Hofmann was in top mental and physical form. Up until his retirement he suffered every spring from asthma attacks triggered by a serious pollen allergy. For this reason, he fled as often as possible to the mountains of Graubünden, mostly to Pontresina in the Engadin. Near the end of his career, his allergy diminished

and nearly disappeared. While he was still working, he usually wore glasses until his shortsightedness was offset by farsightedness as he aged. From that point on, he never required either glasses or a hearing aid.

Sandoz' increasingly problematic relationship with his discovery and sometimes with Hofmann himself made it easier for him to leave. The corporate culture at Sandoz changed during the 1960s. Important positions in pharmacology and medical biology research turned over; ambitious careerists were eager to turn pharmaceutical research inside out. Ideas from chemists and pharmacologists regarding development of medicaments were now largely outweighed by sales projections from the marketing department. Jacottet's insensitive rebuff of Hofmann still gnawed at him after the end of his last four years and left him feeling unfairly treated. Nonetheless, he made an appointment with the general management to take leave on his last day but he was not received. This parting left Hofmann with mixed feelings. His energy never flagged during his working days and he remained dedicated to his employer until the end. Now, however, he had much more time to enjoy his days with Anita on the Rittimatte. Hofmann's retirement also required adjustments on her part. He had been absent during the daytime and she now had to become accustomed to having her husband around the house all the time. He could not cook and pre-emptively pretended to be inept. If he had to manage alone, however, he mastered the daily chores without a problem.

It was not until eighteen years later that Hofmann described, in a letter to the new general director of Sandoz, Marc Moret, the course of events under his predecessor and attached copies of his correspondence with Jacottet. The new management was unable to intervene in disputes that lay so far in the past. However, as a conciliatory gesture and in recognition of Hofmann's contributions, they augmented his pension fund by a sizable amount. On his eightieth birthday the corporate management congratulated him with a flower arrangement and a mollifying letter: "On your great day, we recall with pleasure your successful activity as director of the natural materials department of our chemical research in pharmaceuticals and thankfully acknowledge all you have contributed during your forty-two years of service to our company. The numerous articles you have published also bear witness to an extremely prolific professional life marked by many distinctions. We sincerely wish that you may long remain healthy and able to pursue your varied interests in the areas of philosophy, literature and the arts. Our wishes for a happy birthday and for a satisfying year in 1986 include your dear wife and the members of your family."

Father and Apostle

Two months after Hofmann retired, he and Timothy Leary first met in person on September 3, 1971, at the restaurant of the Lausanne train station. Leary and his wife Rosemary were living in the vacation village of Villars-sur-Ollon in the Valais. With the help of the Weathermen in September of 1970, Timothy Leary had escaped from jail to Algeria where he and his wife

found refuge with the exiled Black Panthers. In Algiers, ideological conflicts soon arose with Eldridge Cleaver, one of their leaders. Cleaver spied on them, had their apartment searched, and intercepted their mail. The couple decided to flee again. Under the pretext of attending a conference, they wanted to leave for Denmark which they had determined to be a country willing to receive them. After a nerve-wracking, nail-biting event with customs officials, they boarded a flight for the north. On an intermediate stop in Geneva they learned from French psychiatrist Pierre Bensoussan, who had supported them earlier, that CIA agents were waiting in Denmark to arrest Leary. They decided to remain in Switzerland and go underground. Bensoussan led Leary and his wife to the wealthy arms dealer Michel Hauchard, a dazzling personality who provided them with a chalet in Villars-sur-Ollon in the canton of Vaud. Hauchard proved to be a gallant host with extensive contacts, among them the prominent Swiss attorney, Horace Mastronardi, who anticipated a request for extradition from the U.S. government and applied for asylum for Leary in Switzerland.

It was in this climate of uncertainty that the father of LSD met its apostle. "Our greeting under the sign of our fateful connection through LSD was heartfelt. Of medium build, slender, resilient, sprightly, his face surrounded by brown, grey-streaked and slightly curly hair, he looked boyish, with bright, laughing eyes; Leary seemed more like a tennis champion than a former Harvard lecturer," was the impression described by Hofmann in his diary. He continued: "T.L. took me in a car on the road along the lake to Buchillon where he had a lunch reservation at the restaurant 'Au grand Forêt.' Good conversation in a gazebo over perch filets with a bottle of white wine. His dismissal from Harvard University supposedly was due to the behavior of his colleague Alpert who involved students in his homosexual behavior with the help of drugs. My objection to Leary's drug cult: Involvement of young people and publicity in the early stages of experiments. Leary's response: In the USA, young people age quickly as a result of the surfeit of information and the permissive, affluent society. He admitted that the publicity was a mistake he would no longer make. However, he believed that someone had to make that error.

After lunch, a Mr. Hauchard appeared who led us to his table where some young people from Paris sat: A translator of L's last book, a novel, he had written in Algiers with collaborators. The trip back to Ouchy to the large apartment of Mr. Hauchard, where waited Rosemary Leary and a hippie couple from the USA. Rosemary has wide dark eyes, would like to have children. She was operated on for that reason in Lausanne.

Evening walk with T.L. and the hippie along the lake. Dinner in a waterfront restaurant, at the end of which Dr. Horace Mastronardi, L.'s attorney also appeared. He called my attention to the three points of the probation conditions: No statements about the U.S. government, Vietnam, drugs. Our meeting should remain secret. He's 95% certain that he will secure asylum for his client or at least permission for departure to a country that would accept him. Dr. Mastronardi inquired, as had Mr. Hubbard, whether Sandoz might

be interested in L's library and drug documentation, which I denied."

The encounter left Hofmann with "the impression of a likable person who is convinced of his mission and states his views with a sense of humor but is uncompromising; he is imbued with a faith in the miraculous effects of psychedelics and extreme optimism leads him to underestimate or even overlook undesirable facts and dangers." However, Hofmann was of the opinion that it was a disservice to dub Leary an apostle of drugs since he had always differentiated between addictive narcotics and warned against their use.

Two months after their meeting, Leary was arrested by the Swiss police and put into solitary confinement. The American extradition request was processed before the appeal for asylum. Leary's mentor, Hauchard, was able to arrange for less harsh treatment and indulge him with choice food, providing him with reading material, a typewriter and stationary. On December 29, 1971, one month after his incarceration, Switzerland rejected the U.S. request for extradition but did not offer political asylum. Instead, he received a limited residency permit and was freed. Hofmann learned of the matter on the last day of December and on New Year's Day 1972 he expressed his delight that the "most

> Leary's indiscriminate publicity for the consumption of LSD contributed to its prohibition which ended scientific research. On the other hand, Leary's propaganda and Oscar Janiger's enthusiasm put LSD in the hands of the spiritual elite, such as Aldous Huxley, or of famous patients like Cary Grant.
> *Albert Hofmann*

dangerous man in the USA" was being permitted to remain in Switzerland:

Dear Timothy,

Returning from a trip to Stockholm, I heard about the decision of our authorities that you will not be extradited to the USA. What a relief! I am confident that Mr. Mastronardi will be successful in getting permission for you to stay in Switzerland. Are you now free to travel in our country wherever you like so that you can visit to the Rittimatte? All my best wishes for you and Rosemary in the New Year and, kindest regards,

Cordially, Albert

One month later during the legendary Fasnacht (carnival) in Basel, the two met again. Also present was the writer and bookseller Michael Horowitz, Leary's archivist and director for over thirty years of the Fitz Hugh Ludlow Memorial Library in San Francisco. Leary was a close friend of Horowitz and godparent to his daughter, actress Winona Ryder. Horowitz recalled: "A bright cold afternoon in February 1972. I am sitting in the back seat of a new Toyota, juggling a super-8 movie camera with one hand and a small microphone attached to a portable tape deck with the other. The two gentlemen in the front seat are having a spirited conversation which I am trying to record despite the noise of the car engine, and to film de-

A legendary snapshot of the second meeting on February 24, 1972 on the Rittimatte

spite the bumpiness of the ride. They are speaking of the previous night, when they joined in the celebration of the Fasnacht, an annual Swiss-style all-night party.

We are driving south through the center of Basel. Some 29 years earlier, the driver of the car had traveled this same road on a bicycle as the first person to experience the effects of LSD, a 250-microgram detonator to his nervous system. The man in the passenger seat, who publicly proclaimed he has taken 311 LSD trips, is listening attentively. He is wearing a bomber jacket and white sneakers, in contrast to the well-tailored dark suit of the driver.

Like a pair of psychedelic tourists visiting a sacred shrine, the passenger and I pepper our tour guide with questions about that fateful April day in 1943. He responds with precise details, a little surprised by the reverence we are giving him. This is just the beginning, we could have told him. Wait until you come to California!

As we drive along the historic route, they begin arguing about who should be permitted to take LSD. Albert says it is

> What I learned from Tim didn't have anything to do with drugs but it had everything to do with getting high. His die-hard fascination with the human brain was not all about altering it, but about using it to its fullest.
>
> *Winona Ryder, godchild of Timothy Leary*

safe and productive only for mature individuals, while Timothy says there was a good reason that it was embraced by the young, who were exposed to more information and a wider range of experience than their parents. It is too late for them; only the young can create a better world. An awkward silence leads to a new topic: the beauty of the Swiss countryside.

We are climbing a steep road from the village of Burg to Albert's impressive home on the crest of a hill. He takes us on a tour of the spacious house and grounds. I tag along behind them, shooting footage and grappling with the microphone. After walking along a well-traveled path through the woods to the French-Swiss border, we return to coffee and cakes graciously served by Frau Hofmann.

On the drive back to the train station Albert pulls over to the curb and turns off the engine. "That house is where we lived at the time. I never thought I would get there that day. My assistant who had ridden with me at my request asked permission to leave. I told her fine, but in fact I was in a panic. My wife and children were away. It was just me, and I barely managed to crawl to my bed.'

'It was the first bad trip, too,' comments Tim. 'There was no precedent. You must have felt that you poisoned yourself.'

'Yes, but in the end it was good. In the morning it was fantastic.'

'For me, the world changed forever,' says Tim. 'I would have remained a boring professional psychologist the rest of my life, making money and accomplishing nothing.'

'Instead of the most dangerous man in the world,' I remark. No less than the

LSD was also a topic at Fasnacht in Basel in 1972

president of the United States had said that, and we later learned Tim's movements were being tracked by the CIA and Interpol.

We all get out of the car. Leary asks me to give Hofmann the movie camera to shoot us in front of the house where Albert had died and been resurrected. That bit of footage turns out to be the only part of the movie in focus.

A little later we turn off the road—the Acid Highway—and continue to the train station where Albert drops us off, leaving with handshakes and a promise to see each other again." It did happen, but not until nearly twenty years later in Hamburg

277

Rittimatte, 1971

Postcard from January 1, 1972 to
Timothy Leary with a sketch of Rittimatte by Philomene Duttwyler, the
mother-in-law of Albert Hofmann's
daughter Gaby Duttwyler-Hofmann

H149 Burg i.L., 1.1.72
Rittimatte

Dear Timothy,
Returning from a trip to Stockholm I
learnt about the decision of our authorities
that you will not be extradited to the USA
What a relief! I am confident that Dr.
Mastronardi will be successful in getting a
permission for you to stay in Switzerland.
Are you now free to travel in our country,
wherever you like? So that we can plan
a visit to the Rittimatte.
All my best wishes for you and
Rosemary in the new year and kindest
regards
Cordially
Albert

278

on the occasion of the fiftieth birthday of LSD in 1993.

Hofmann himself recorded the following about this second meeting at the Rittimatte: "We drove together to my house in the countryside where we continued our conversation from last September. Leary seemed changed. He gave the impression of being agitated and distracted so that this time a productive conversation was not possible." Hofmann's judgment did not take into account that Leary had been out celebrating Fasnacht with a group of Basel friends the night before and was simply exhausted.

Meanwhile, Leary had finished his *Confessions of a Hope Fiend*, the story of his escape and, with the help of Hauchard and Roman Polanski, was able to sell the publication rights. With his share of the advance money, he bought a gold-colored Porsche in which he traveled through Switzerland from then on. He spent time in Carona, Ticino, with Christoph Wenger, a great-nephew of Hermann Hesse; Alpert was also staying there on his way back from India. Leary made contact with the Swiss myth researcher, Sergius Golowin, and met Rudolf Gelpke in the apartment of poet Urban Gwerder, the publisher of the underground magazine *Hotcha*. Leary had not lost his legendary smile and appeared to be satisfied. Within, however,

he felt dependent, uprooted, and missed his friends. Since the U.S. government undertook further action to nullify Leary's residence permit, he began to look for another host country. The situation was even worse than two years earlier since new verdicts against him had been handed down for alleged drug dealing in connection with the Brotherhood of Eternal Love. The only safe country appeared to be Austria under Bruno Kreisky's government. Rosemary was suffering badly from the uncertainty and constant stress, so with a heavy heart, the pair decided to separate and she returned to the USA. Through Hauchard, Leary met the attractive Joanna Harcourt-Smith, a wealthy thirty-year old woman. They fell in love and traveled together to Vienna where Joanna had good friends. Leary remained there only briefly because he felt unsafe and he accepted the invitation of a nephew of the Afghan king whom he had met in Switzerland. Leary's stay in Kabul was even briefer than that in Vienna. Upon landing in 1973, he was taken into custody by Afghan authorities based on a warning from the American consulate. Several days later, pressure from the U.S. government resulted in Leary being flown back to the USA in the company of two CIA agents without formal extradition orders; and there he remained incarcerated until 1976.

Legacies

Dr. Hofmann's legacy includes not only a remarkable chemical but the discoveries resulting from his investigations in ethnomycology, anthropology, and history. *Stanley Krippner*

The Problem Child

Since his youth, Albert Hofmann's artistic talents had been apparent to him but he was unaware of his ability to write. Perhaps he needed some distance after his retirement before settling down to write the story of his discovery. Work on the manuscript stretched over several years. In the summer of 1978, he received a proposal from Klett-Cotta Verlag to publish his book and in the fall of 1979, *LSD - My Problem Child,* first appeared in German. The book was officially launched on September 18th in the guild hall of Restaurant Safran in Basel with every seat occupied.

The author himself presented his new release, followed by a discussion in which a group of his friends participated, including his former colleague Aurelio Cerletti, physician and author Walter Vogt, poet Ernst Jaeckle, and Basel publisher Dieter Hagenbach, who represented the younger generation. Hofmann's diary entry: "Over 100 invited guests. Ernst and Liselotte Jünger and Dr. W. Jaeckle came to tea at Rittimatte. Dinner at 6:30 at the Restaurant Safran with representatives of Klett-Cotta: Dr. Thomas Klett, Friedrich Kar, Dr. Stehelin, Mrs. Dericke and others, also Dr. Walter Vogt and Dieter Hagenbach with their wives. At 8 p.m. introduction by Dr. Klett, then my talk 'What moved me to write this book.'" In his remarks, Hofmann explained what he meant by "problem child:" "Children with normal talents are usually not problem children; rather it is the particularly talented, those with exceptional abilities. They most often go their own way; sometimes their successes delight us, but their unusual and often dangerous antics worry us. In keeping with the metaphor of the title, the book describes how the father of LSD experienced the birth of this, his problem child, its development and career, and the hopes he held for its future. This book was written from a different point of view than previous ones from medical specialists or drug enthusiasts, because its 'father' is a chemist who has recorded all the characteristics of his offspring, virtues and vices, with

280

the critical eye of the scientist. And I don't think that the father's loving gaze, which could not be entirely excluded, has distorted the objective picture." Hofmann pointed out several times that he believed that a problem child was not one who caused its parents worry, but one for whom the parents must remain especially concerned. With his book, Hofmann wished to correct some of the legends surrounding the circumstances of its discovery which had even found their way into medical text books. "You will find descriptions of how the crazy Dr. Hofmann entertained the people of Basel during that first LSD trial with his acrobatic skills on a bicycle, or how he rode his bicycle into the office of his superior during that first LSD experiment. So, a first-person report on how LSD really came to be was not superfluous." The real "reason I wrote this book is the question that presented itself as a result of the LSD experiments, namely the nature of the relationship between mind and matter, which in turn relates to another fundamental problem of philosophy, the question: What is reality?"[192] His remarks about this subject occupied the greater part of his talk, but not of the book. Several years later, he clearly formulated his thoughts on these basic philosophical questions in *Einsichten Ausblicke.* (*Insight Outlook*)

Regarding the panel discussion, he noted that the remarks of

> I see the true importance of LSD as a way of providing material aid to meditation aimed at the mystical experience of a deeper, more comprehensive reality. Such a use accords entirely with the essence and working character of LSD as a sacred drug.
>
> *Albert Hofmann*

Aurelio Cerletti, whose participation he was able to secure at the last minute, carried the most weight. "At the end of the one-hour discussion, I asked Professor Werner Stoll to sum up, which he kindly did. Then reception with refreshments. All our children [were there] with their spouses. By and large, a successful occasion." Two days after the presentation, he was pleased by "good reviews" of the book and its presentation in the local press.[193]

LSD - My Problem Child provides the first comprehensive and direct insight into the fascinating story of LSD from its discoverer. The foreword describes the mystical experiences of his childhood. It concludes by putting his designation of LSD as a problem child into context: "I believe that if people would learn to use LSD's vision-inducing capability more wisely under suitable conditions, in medical practice in conjunction with meditation, then in the future this problem child could become a wonder child." The book describes in layman's language how Hofmann came to study chemistry, his discovery, its far-reaching consequences, and resulting encounters with notable people. The most space is devoted to the period between the discovery of the effects of LSD in 1943 and the Mexico expedition in 1962. A chapter follows about his friendship and joint experiments with Ernst Jünger and another about his encounters with Aldous Huxley. The excerpt from his correspondence with the writer Walter Vogt near the end of the book is certainly worth reading but seems somewhat arbitrary. In the concluding chapter, *LSD-Experience and Reality*, he summarizes the knowledge he gained from his LSD experiences and sketches his hopes for the problem child. The quality of the

Interview with André Ratti on the Swiss TV program "People, Technology, Science" on October 14, 1979 on the occasion of the publication of *LSD - Mein Sorgenkind*

illustrations, which like the text of the original German edition are printed on yellow paper, is unsatisfactory and does not do them justice. The book has few references to literature and sources, an index is lacking, and the final page contains a few obsolete formulae of chemical compounds. Despite these minor shortcomings, Hofmann's legacy has become a standard work on psychedelics. It met enormous interest in the German-speaking world and is still reprinted repeatedly.

On September 25, 1978, Albert Hofmann left on a three-week trip to the United States. In New York he had dinner with Alfred van der Marck, chief executive of the well-known publishing house McGraw Hill, and Joan Halifax, who was responsible for reviewing the English translation. At the suggestion of Jonathan Ott, who had already translated Hofmann's manuscript, the book would appear in a special edition in 1980 alongside Gordon Wasson's new book, *The Wondrous Mushroom*, and the joint project between Richard E. Schultes and Albert Hofmann, *Plants of the Gods*. All three titles had already been printed and the marketing and sales departments were ready to present the books to retailers and the media, when the board of directors learned of these new releases listed in the publisher's catalog under "Science." In their eyes, all three books belonged under "Drugs" instead and in no way fit the image of McGraw-Hill. Despite the reputation of the authors and the enormous expenses already incurred, the top management exerted their

> I see the true importance of LSD as a way of providing material aid to meditation aimed at the mystical experience of a deeper, more comprehensive reality. Such a use accords entirely with the essence and working character of LSD as a sacred drug.
>
> *Albert Hofmann*

authority to summarily forbid any sales support for all three titles, fired van der Marck and his coworkers, and eliminated his edition. Hence, the first edition of *LSD - My Problem Child* was barely noticed by the U.S. book trade and media with correspondingly low sales. Shortly thereafter, the stock was remaindered at a steeply reduced price. For the Swiss author, the categorical rejection from New York was difficult to understand and bitterly disappointing.

When Los Angeles publisher Jeremy P. Tarcher, who already had a catalog that attracted attention, learned of his New York colleagues' reversal of course, he found it incomprehensible. Consequently, he took on the problem child, secured the publishing rights, and brought it out under his imprint. On precisely the "fortieth anniversary of the first LSD trip," on April 16, 1983, "a copy of the new edition of *LSD - My Problem Child* in a luxurious binding" arrived in the mail.[194] With only a slight delay, the English language edition of the history of LSD achieved remarkable success, seeing several more printings and smoothing the way for more translations.

The Translator

At the invitation of Jonathan Ott, Hofmann came to America in the fall of 1977. He gave a lecture in Seattle at the University of Washington and then traveled on to Port Townsend to participate in a conference on hallucinogenic mushrooms[195] organized by Ott and the real reason for this tour of the USA. There, Hofmann, antiquities researcher Carl A.P. Ruck, and Gordon Wasson first presented their theory that a substance similar to LSD played an important role in the ancient Greek mysteries of Eleusis.

At their first meeting, Hofmann told his host of his book project. Since Ott spoke only a modest amount of German, they conversed in English. He had learned the language in high school and pursued it for another year in college which gave him good comprehension but limited facility to express himself. To Ott's great surprise, Hofmann spontaneously asked him to translate his book when it appeared. Hofmann countered Ott's misgivings by encouraging him with the explanation that he preferred a chemist with LSD experience as translator over an expert in the German language without knowledge of the subject. Furthermore, Hofmann would help him by reviewing his translation. Even before the German edition appeared, Hofmann sent him segments of the material for translation. After the English manuscript was completed, Hofmann came as promised to Vashon Island in the State of Washington to visit Jonathan and Patty Ott. Within ten days they went through the translation together from start to finish until both were satisfied with the result. In his diary Hofmann wrote: "Oct. 2nd flew with Patty and Jonathan to Seattle and to their house on Vashon Island. Worked on the translation. Fell in love with Patty who is good at everything, sings as she accompanies herself on the lute, improvises an inversion table, rolls marijuana cigarettes, prepares a blow of cocaine, cooks exquisitely, etc."

By the mid-1980's, Ott had emigrated from the USA and the Hofmanns visited him in Mexico for the housewarming of their newly built home, Rancho Ololiuqui. Ott had underestimated the effort required

Albert Hofmann with Jonathan Ott

Anita and Albert Hofmann, Jonathan Ott, 1977

to complete it and worked day and night with his second wife, Kjahel, a Mexican, to complete the basics before the aging married couple arrived from Switzerland. The high point of their several-day visit was a ceremonial LSD trip taken by the two couples.

The Media

Hofmann's relationship with the media was ambivalent. During his career, he published exclusively in professional journals and sought no publicity in the mass media. It irritated him that Timothy Leary sought contact with journalists for scientific projects at Harvard to generate publicity, and Hofmann told him of his disapproval both in letters and in person. After a bad experience with the *Sunday Mirror*, which shortened an article he had approved and then published it under a sensational title, Hofmann sent an internal note to the communications department at Sandoz requesting that: "In the future I would like to keep my distance from any journalists' requests for interviews." However, he did not remain by his refusal for long, but reaffirmed it almost reflexively if he was dissatisfied with an article. In most cases, the journalists succeeded in persuading him to change his mind. At his 100th birthday celebration, the authors of this book overheard a telephone conversation in which he firmly declined to be interviewed by a Russian journalist. But when the journalist showed up unannounced at his door with a camera man and sound engineer for an interview and photos, after a brief exchange, Hofmann invited them into the house. He spent several hours with them, entertained them, and posed a half hour for photos. Afterwards,

> I firmly believe that contemporary spiritual use of entheogenic drugs is one of humankind's brightest hopes for overcoming the ecological crisis from which we threaten the biosphere and jeopardize our own survival, for Homo sapiens is close to the head of the list of endangered species.
>
> *Jonathan Ott*

285

he said that it had been one of his best interviews.

Articles in the press seldom left him cold. He found them either wonderful or was enraged about shortened quotes or gimmicky titles. The article which piqued him the most was one published in *Stern* on the occasion of the publication of his book. The reporter for the German magazine made an appointment to discuss LSD and he began their conversation with the words "LSD saved my life." The visit took place in the afternoon and the journalist appeared to be listening closely so that Hofmann spontaneously invited him to dinner and even to stay overnight. Hofmann was appalled when the article dealt not only with LSD but drugs in general and with heroin in particular. It was the time of the *Wir Kinder vom Bahnhof Zoo* (a sensationalist book and drug movie released in 1981) and the article consequently contained photos with captions such as "Drug death in Berlin." Hofmann noticed the omission of his clear statements and felt betrayed. The journalist had apparently shown interest in order to lure him out of his reserve and then had twisted his statements. In a long letter to the managing editor, Henri Nannen, Hofmann complained: "I received Mr. Axmann on the recommendation of Klett-Cotta Verlag for a conversation about my recently published book *LSD - My Prob-*

Stern, No. 39, Fall 1979

lem Child. The publisher dispelled my concerns that the article might exploit the topic of LSD subjectively for sensational effect by telling me Mr. Axmann had received galley proofs of my book and thus was well acquainted with my critical attitude towards these sensitive problems and that *STERN* guaranteed serious coverage." Hofmann spent two pages laying out his objections and emphasized that he had written the book to provide a wider public with an objective picture of LSD: "An LSD experience involves a confrontation with one's self and surroundings when the boundary between I and thou, I and one's surroundings, eases or completely dissolves and other layers of reality enter consciousness.

My book illustrates and documents in detail what is described in brief above and also was the topic of my conversation with Mr. Axmann. I gave him the interview without asking for an honorarium and devoted two full days to this with the same goal that underpins my book to objectively enlighten regarding LSD.

Now I discover that the article in *STERN* by this Mr. Axmann presents me as an uncritical spokesperson for unbounded use of LSD, who ascribes powers to this substance that border on the fantastic, and attributes the monstrous attitude to me that 'thousands of narcotics victims did not bother him.'

With shameless evasiveness Mr. Axmann denied me the review of his manuscript that he had promised and instead merely read those passages to me over the phone that I could agree to. The piece is not only pointless, it is dishonest; my critical statements about the LSD problem are reversed. Mr. Axmann told me when we first met that LSD had saved his life and during our discussions he pretended to have an exaggerated enthusiasm for LSD that I did not share. In his version of the interview, however, he takes the opposite position and presents me as an LSD dreamer without scruples.

How superficially informed Mr. Axmann was can be seen in the caption of the first illustration which says: 'Ergot was known as a narcotic in the Middle Ages.' Ergot from rye is still not known as a narcotic and in the Middle Ages it was only used by midwives to initiate labor. I do not know to what extent an editor is accountable for such an erroneous article that is damaging to someone's scientific reputation and moral standing."

Henri Nannen did not regard it necessary to personally respond but had his secretary write a few brief lines of justification. After that, Hofmann visited Hagenbach at the publisher's office who recalls: "It was the first and only time I have seen him cry; this defamatory article was that upsetting." In his diary Hofmann record-ed: "A misleading, poor article by *STERN's* reporter Axmann. *Cave!* (Beware!)[196] Once and for all time. It says, 'Thousands of narcotics victims do not bother him (A.H.)!"[197]

After that, Hofmann sometimes demanded a fee for interviews, not for the money, but because he hoped to discourage journalists with this requirement. To his great surprise, some paid the amount demanded without objection. He gave his last interview one week before his death to a reporter with the German tabloid *Bild*.

Plants of the Gods

After having corresponded with each other for several years about botanical and other scientific questions, Albert Hofmann and the American Richard Evans Schultes, founder of ethnobotany, met for the first time in Berlin in May 1964 at a meeting of the Society for Pharmaceutical Plant Research. Schultes' dry humor, his sense of reality, work ethic, and dependability reminded Hofmann of the characteristics of his Swiss compatriots. Dick, as Hofmann called him, explained that it was no accident, since his ancestors were members of the old, established Schulthess family of Zurich.

Long before their meeting, Hofmann had been working on two projects based on ethnobotanical discoveries made by Schultes. With two articles (Schultes 1939 and 1940), Schultes had initiated the botanical identification of sacred mushrooms; his publication about ololiuqui (Schultes 1941) served Hofmann as the basis for his research on morning glory seeds.

I know of no culture in the world at present or any time in the past that has not been heavily involved with one or more psychoactive substances.

Andrew Weil

287

Richard E. Schultes, Albert Hofmann, Boston, end of the 1970s

Richard E. Schultes, Gordon Wasson, Albert Hofmann

Schultes remained associated with Harvard University throughout his life. Every spring on Commencement Day, Harvard celebrates the awarding of academic degrees. Even today, the graduates wear robes and flat caps with tassels to the ceremonies. During one of Hofmann's visits, Schultes obliged his friend to join in the festivities incognito, wearing the traditional black and red robe of professors. For Hofmann his appearance as a Harvard professor remained as unforgettable as the informative tour Schultes gave him of the famous Botanical Museum of which Schultes became director in 1970.

Hofmann was impressed with Schultes' ability as an ethnobotanical researcher and his excellent nose. After a conference in Mexico City in 1981, he accompanied his friend to the south of Mexico where Schultes wanted to help a student searching for a particular tree. The aromatic blossoms of this rare tree were used as an ingredient in the preparation of chocolate. Hofmann vividly recalls how Schultes was led solely by his sense of smell to the blossoms they sought at an open air market in Oaxaca.[198]

Hofmann did not take the special relationship with his colleague for granted: "When scientific collaboration is combined with friendship, it becomes both much more pleasurable and fruitful. My relationship with Dick Schultes is an example of such an experience."[199] Their wives, Anita and Dorothy, became friends as well. The two couples visited each other regularly into the 1990s.

Their rewarding relationship resulted in the chemist and the ethnobotanist co-authoring two books. Their first, *The Botany and Chemistry of Hallucinogens* (Schultes, Hofmann 1973), was aimed at academics and appeared in 1973. Six years later, *Plants of the Gods* (Schultes, Hofmann 1979) appeared, intended for

Commencement Day at Harvard University,
(l. to r.) Richard E. Schultes, Elizabeth Coughlin,
George R. Morgan, Michael Balik, Albert Hofmann

a wider audience; the German edition *Pflanzen der Götter* (Schultes, Hofmann 1980) appeared one year later. The large format volume systematically documents the sacred use of hallucinogenic drugs in diverse cultures. It is richly illustrated with hundreds of photos, many published for the first time. The general introduction to the chemistry, distribution, and use of hallucinogens is followed by fourteen chapters, each giving a comprehensive description of one important plant, its history and use. The authors stress their importance for research on the human psyche. A "plant encyclopedia" in the center section describes ninety-one psychoactive plants and mushrooms. It was a groundbreaking work for those times.

When it was time for a new edition, the authors realized that the book needed to be revised as some entries were obsolete or required supplementing. Hofmann recognized that age prevented him from bringing the information up to date and wished to find a younger expert to step in. Hamburg ethnologist, Christian Rätsch, considered it a great honor for Hofmann to request that he update *Pflanzen der Götter*, provide it with new illustrations and augment it wherever necessary. The newly revised edition appeared in German in 1998 and in English in 2001, including new chapters on ayahuasca analogues,[200] the *Salvia divinorum* plant, and the Australian pituri plant.

Wisdom of the Greeks

Classical Greece was a lifelong and inexhaustible source of inspiration for Albert Hofmann, to the extent that he sometimes wondered if his fascination stemmed from a past life experienced in that era. From a young age, he had been stirred by Greek myths and the world of the gods; he read the Homeric epics, the Iliad and the Odyssey, studied the great philosophers, admired the Greek scientists, and examined their cults.

He was particularly intrigued by the legendary mysteries of Eleusis, their practices and significance, written about by innumerable researchers of antiquity. Each year for nearly two thousand years, secret ceremonies were observed at Eleusis, about twelve miles west of Athens. Participation was open to all free citizens except those whose hands "bore the blood of an unexpiated victim." Sophocles, playwright of tragedies,

> Adventures happen only to those incapable of planning an expedition.
>
> *Richard E. Schultes*

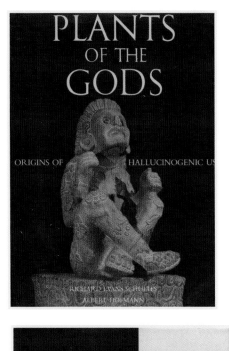

effused: "Thrice blessed are those of mortals, who having seen those rites depart for Hades. For to them alone is granted to have a true life there." Distinctions are made between the great and the lesser mysteries. The lesser mysteries were celebrated in spring. The great mysteries, the *teletai*, took place in September and lasted nine days. They were inaugurated by a procession bearing the sacred articles from Eleusis to a temple near the Acropolis in Athens. The ceremonies began with the ritual washing of the priest in the sea and the sacrifice of a young pig. Two days later, the procession started back to Eleusis. Once there, nothing more could be eaten. Fasting was broken with the consumption of the ritual drink "kykeon." After that, the initiates entered the hall, the Telesterion. What happened there remained secret under threat of death. In the evening, a joyful feast with dancing followed and lasted through the night. In the early morning a bull was sacrificed.

Gordon Wasson, Albert Hofmann, and antiquities researcher Carl Ruck devoted themselves to the mystery and believe they found a solution "nearly 2,000 years after the last rites were conducted and approximately 4,000 years after the first." They saw in kykeon an ergot potion closely related to LSD. They summarized their findings and conclusions, which questioned the previous literature about Eleusis and its associated cultic practices in their book *The Road to Eleusis: Unveiling the Secret of the Mysteries* in 1978.

The impetus for this new theory came from Gordon Wasson who was seeking a fresh challenge after his elucidation of the Mexican mushroom cult. While studying Greek cults, he discovered great similarities

Albert Hofmann and Gordon Wasson, 1976

between his experiences in Mexico and the descriptions of the Eleusinian mysteries. With this knowledge, Wasson turned to mythologist Carl Ruck. After extensive studies of texts and references, Ruck confirmed that "the probability was clearly in favor of the hypothesis that rye ergot was the psychotropic ingredient of the Eleusinian potion." When Hofmann visited Wasson in Danbury, Connecticut in 1975, Wasson asked the chemist whether he thought it plausible that a method had been discovered in ancient Greece to isolate a hallucinogen from ergot with action comparable to that of LSD. Hofmann promised to look into the matter. As a potential hallucinogenic substance, he chose ergonovine,[201] the placenta strengthening element of ergot that also was present in ololiuqui. He supposed that its hallucinogenic properties had not been discovered because it is used in such extremely low doses to stop postpartum bleeding. Having already encountered such problems several times over the course of his career, he knew that only a self-experiment could bring clarity. At noon on April 1, 1976, Hofmann took 1.5 mg of ergonovine—six to fifteen times the therapeutic dose customarily used. The drink had a clearly detectable effect and proved to Hofmann that "ergonovine has a mildly hallucinogenic effect if taken in a quantity equivalent to an effective dose of lysergic acid amide, the main component of ololiuqui." Hofmann had ergot varieties from different host grasses analyzed in Sandoz labs for their chemical composition. An important discovery was made that supported Wasson's theory: The ergot that grew on *Paspalum distichum*, a wild grass, contained the same hallucinogenic components as ololiuqui.

Paspalum is found throughout the Mediterranean region and is frequently infested with ergot. The hallucinogenic ergot alkaloids are water soluble, in contrast to those that are non-psychoactive and used medicinally. Hence, it was not particularly difficult for the ancient Greeks to gain a pure extract from the wild grass that was psychedelically active. Hofmann considered the suitability of different hosts for ergot which, depending on its location and host grass, differed considerably in its composition. He came to the conclusion that it is impossible to determine the composition of the ergot on rye or wheat that was raised thousands of years earlier. He did see an indication of some connection between grass varieties with the

> The enjoyment of hallucinogenic plants has been a part of human life for thousands of years; however, recognition of the degree to which these plants have shaped the history of the indigenous and more developed cultures is more recent in Europe and the United States.
>
> *Richard Evans Schultes and Albert Hofmann*

291

Eleusinian mysteries in the fact that the Greeks associated the mysteries with Demeter and Kore, the mythical ancestors of the wheat and rye grain cultivated at the time.

Two years after the inquiry, Hofmann made his formal report, summarized his research, and confirmed that the Greeks most certainly could have produced a hallucinogen from ergot: "This conclusion is based on the assumption that those schooled in the knowledge of herbs in ancient Greece were just as expert as those in Mexico before the conquest." From our contemporary perspective, the fact that Hofmann was able to submit various ergot samples to Sandoz for extensive chemical and pharmacological analysis five years *after* his retirement is a remarkable accommodation on the part of his former employer.

Scholarly Dialogue

Twelve years before Wasson's inquiry, the topic of the Eleusinian mysteries first figured prominently in Hofmann's life when the eminent religious scholar Karl Kerényi wrote to him with pharmacological questions related to Eleusis. A lively correspondence and exchange of ideas ensued and extended over the next two years.

Kerényi was born in Temesvár, then in Austro-Hungary, today in western Romania, and traveled extensively after finishing his studies. His doctorate in

> There is a kernel of truth in the fact that in Schiller's hymn "Ode to Joy," "daughter of Elysium" is popularly sung as "daughter in delirium;" indeed, it was in an extraordinary state that the delirious daughters and sons of the Western world experienced the Eleusinian ritual for nearly two thousand years.
>
> *Mathias Bröckers*

Budapest was on Plato and Longinus. In 1936 he was appointed professor for classical philo-logy and ancient history at the University of Pécs. (Pest) During WWII he immigrated to Switzerland, became a lecturer in Hungarian language and literature at the University of Basel and guest professor at universities in Bonn, Oslo, Rome and Genoa. A Swiss citizen since 1962, Kerényi lived until his death in 1973 in Kilchberg near Zurich. He was a co-founder and research director of the C.G. Jung Institute in Zurich for nearly twenty years. C.G. Jung, who had grown up in Basel, was the founder of analytic psychology. Both considered their collaborative work to be fruitful. Kerényi conducted a more than twenty-year correspondence with German writer Thomas Mann and also with Hermann Hesse. Kerényi considered the world of the Greek gods to be an expression of genuine human experience and found great resonance for this idea outside the guild of historians of religion.

The first letter from Karl Kerényi to Albert Hofmann dates from November 12, 1963; the last known response from Hofmann to Kerényi is dated August 30, 1965. Kerényi initiated contact because he wished to know from Hofmann whether information was available about psychotropic effects of *Mentha pulegium*. He suspected that this plant could have played a significant role in Greek mysteries. He knew Hofmann's work on LSD and ololiuqui and had read in *Psychedelic Review* of the effects of *Salvia divinorum,* which belongs to the same family as *Mentha pulegium*. He asked Hofmann whether it might be that "*Mentha pulegium* which was clearly mentioned in religious and non-religious contexts, but the function of which remained unclear, belonged to the psychoactive plants Lewin called 'phantastica.'"

Hofmann thanked him for his letter and answered that he had visited Kerényi's evening lectures on Greek mythology in Basel some time ago and that it was a pleasure to be contacted "about a topic that has long interested me, namely the possible significance of certain drugs in Greek religious history." He mentioned that Wasson had considered other plant-based drugs in addition to mushrooms, such as different arbutus species which belonged to the family of *Ericaceae* and were found in the Mediterranean region. According to the phytochemical literature, the fruit of *Arbutus unedo*, the strawberry tree, is said to have a narcotic effect.[202] Hofmann knew nothing of reports regarding psychotropic properties of *Mentha pulegium*. However, in his first letter, he refers to the mushroom theory of Gordon Wasson, who predicted that the solution to the puzzle of the Eleusinian Mysteries was to be found in indole compounds. Wasson based this assumption, which he himself deemed "daring speculation," on the identity of the syllable *my* both in *mykes,* Greek for mushroom, and in *mysteria*. Kerényi considered this purely linguistic accident: "I believe that the layman's assumption that mushrooms could have played a role in Greek mysteries is entirely without substance." Contradicting this clear statement, he continued that "the name of so important a city as Mycenae derives from Mycenae, a goddess or heroine, and linguistically both names could clearly derive from *mykes*, mushrooms." To that

Karl Kerényi

point, he cites the legend of the founding of Mycenae passed down by Pausanias which says that Perseus, suffering from thirst, picked a mushroom whereupon a spring opened up and Perseus drank and joyfully founded the city. Kerényi adds: "To my knowledge, the only one, but a remarkably unique piece of evidence." He described the nine days of preparatory fasting, the course of events at the mysteries of Eleusis, and included an illustration of a goddess sitting beneath a strawberry tree as she offers poppy seed capsules to approaching devotees; for him, proof that the strawberry tree and poppy were used as intoxicants.

In his answer, Hofmann delved into the preparatory fasting: "The natural scientific explanation of the visions and hallucinations of the desert holy men, e.g. Saint Antonius, and of the condition itself, is to be found in the practice of fasting." He added: "Regretfully, for a scientific explanation of the *epopteia* phenomena the factors you have already cited suffice. It is not necessary to postulate any other specific, highly potent psychotropic drug.... From my personal chemical and pharmacological viewpoint, I would say: 'unfortunately, it is not necessary.'"

Although Hofmann found no convincing evidence of psychoactive properties in *Mentha pulegium*, he wanted to analyze them chemically. He pointed out that he could no longer demonstrate a psychotropic effect from

> I think I am the reincarnation of a classical Greek. Greek sculpture always fascinated me as a child. For Greeks, beauty, not love, was always the highest ideal.
>
> *Albert Hofmann*

the pressed juice of *Salvia divinorum* which he had gathered on his Mexico expedition. As with the Salvia, the active ingredients of *Mentha* might also be unstable. He concluded with the remark: "You inspire me to look into problems that are much closer to my interests than the magic drugs of Mexico."

In a further letter, Kerényi described in detail the legends related to the strawberry tree which he had explored in conversations with many local farmers and scholars in Greece. He cited Aristotle's claim that a strong alcoholic beverage could interrupt the state of intoxication produced by diluted wine. Hofmann answered characteristically: "This statement should be verified experimentally, neither a difficult nor an unpleasant task, before anyone attempts to explain it."

In November 1964, Kerényi arranged for berries and branches of Arbutus species to be sent to Hofmann. Before submitting them for chemical analysis, he tested their presumed psychoactive properties himself. "The fruit was in good condition and quite fresh, so I immediately undertook two self-experiments. I ate 167 g of the splendid yellow-red *Arbutus unedo* fruit which had a sweetish, bland taste. This is the amount of this unusual food that can be eaten before it becomes disagreeable. I managed to eat 114 g of the small wild Arbutus and felt no effects from any of these trials. Hence, a chemical analysis would be superfluous. So, I wonder how this finding matches up with your report from Samothrace (letter of May 28, 1964) according to which the raw fruit is intoxicating when eaten."

Hofmann and Kerényi conducted a truly scholarly exchange. Their letters were never

inconsequential, but consistently show substantial debates on various aspects of religious studies, on psychoactive substances in general and the contents of the plants Kerényi suspected to be kykeon in particular. However, neither the effect of *Mentha pulegium* nor that of the strawberry tree was conclusive. Nevertheless, Kerényi gave a lecture in Strasbourg with the title "Preconditions for Initiation in Eleusis—kykeon with *Mentha pulegium*." He was the more eager correspondent and often answered Hofmann's letter on the same day. During the entire exchange and even after a personal meeting in Basel, they still called each other Sie, the respectful form of address in German, and in contrast with most of Hofmann's other correspondents, all private questions and remarks were left out.

Lay readers found both the theory of Wasson who supposed ergot alkaloids to be the active principle of kykeon, and that of Kerényi questionable and unconvincing. It remains puzzling why neither Wasson, nor Hofmann nor Kerényi himself pursued the reference to the quote from Pausanias: "That Perseus, suffering from thirst, picked a mushroom whereupon a spring opened up with which he refreshed himself and founded the city." That mushroom could not have contained ergot because it was not known or identified in ancient Greece as a mushroom. It was also true that the mystery of Eleusis was of Mycenaean origin and Kerényi wrote in his letter: "To my knowledge, the only proof, but unique proof" for the use of magic mushrooms in ancient Greece.

Eleusis became for Hofmann a symbol and model for the kind of ceremonial initiation ritual that he wished for his LSD

(Back row, l. to r.) Agnes Tschudin, Anupama Grell, Roger Liggenstorfer, Albert Hofmann, Christian Rätsch, Jonathan Ott, (front) Claudia Müller-Ebeling, Babak Samareh

Lost in contemplation at Eleusis, 2000

in the future because "the mysteries contributed significantly to healing and overcoming the cleavage between mankind and nature, one could also say removing the separation between Creator and creation. The cultural historical impact can scarcely be over-estimated. Here the Greeks, who were suffering from dissension and their rational tendency to objectify, found healing through mystic experience of wholeness that brought belief in immortality in eternal existence."[203]

At Eleusis

At the invitation of his friend and publisher Roger Liggenstorfer, Hofmann traveled in September 2000 on his first and only trip to the places of worship southwest of Athens. The diverse group of tourists,

which also included ethnologist and art historian Claudia Müller-Ebeling, Christian Rätsch and Jonathan Ott, visited Delphi, Mykonos, and Athens in addition to Eleusis during a one week trip. "Albert Hofmann was deeply moved as we sat between the foundation walls of the Telesterion, the ancient initiation hall of the Eleusinian mysteries and imagined how for two thousand years initiates drank psychedelic kykeon here and experienced divine revelations. He was also quite touched as we entered the innermost shrine at Delphi in which the Pythia sat, intoxicated by smoke, and spoke her oracles," reports Christian Rätsch. Roger Liggenstorfer recalls: "The visit to Eleusis was like a homecoming for Hofmann. He felt a strong connection; I have never before or since seen him so withdrawn into himself."

295

Insights and Outlooks

> He who understands nothing but chemistry, does not really understand even that.
> *Georg Christoph Lichtenberg*

A Good Question

The friendship between Albert Hofmann and Dieter Hagenbach, founder of Sphinx Verlag in Basel, began in 1977 with the publication of an interview with Hofmann in *Sphinx* magazine. From then on, Hagenbach visited Albert and Anita Hofmann at various intervals, often remaining long into the night. Their conversations were always inspiring and, of course, centered on his most famous discovery. However, the things they mostly talked about were aspects and questions that an LSD experience brings to the forefront of consciousness: the meaning and purpose of our existence, the beauty of nature, the magnificence of creation, the origin and evolution of the universe; themes which we can barely approach with our limited minds and knowledge. Their conversations about anything and everything dealt with the insights granted by LSD and the outlooks to be gained from it.

During one of his visits, Hagenbach happened to casually inquire as to whether Hofmann had written anything else besides his autobiographical work about the discovery of LSD. "Yes, yes," he answered, "For years I have been summarizing various thoughts on science and philosophy which seemed important to me in essays. Would you like to read them?" Of course, Hagenbach very much wanted to read them. He was impressed by the essays and, although Hofmann had not planned to publish them, Hagenbach was able to convince him to do so.

The little book, entitled *Einsichten Ausblicke (Insight Outlook)*, appeared in the fall of 1986 and was immediately well received. Hofmann was excited by his renewed success as a writer and registered with satisfaction that there were apparently readers interested in him and his work who had not read *LSD - My Problem Child*. More often than after the publication of his first book, he began to be invited by

Robert Williams, *In the Land of Retinal Delights*, oil on canvas, 137.8 x 110.5 cm, 1968. Robert Williams is one of the better known underground artists of the 1960s. Born in 1943, still a prolific artist, he belongs to the Zap Comix Collective in San Francisco, where he began as a cartoonist and went on to painting large-scale oils. Among his collectors are Timothy Leary, Nicholas Cage and Leonardo DiCaprio

various organizations and institutions to give readings, lectures, and to participate in round-table discussions. With his remarks about the transmitter and receiver principle, his thoughts about security in the natural scientific-philosophical view of life, his examination of the concept of possession of property, and with two shorter essays, on the dying of the

Albert Hofmann with Dieter Hagenbach before and after discussing Hofmann's book, *Einsichten Ausblicke (Insight Outlook)*

forests and the sun as a nuclear power plant, he gained up a new circle of topics and readers. To Albert Hofmann, this book contained the "core of my philosophy of life."

After the original German edition of this collection of essays dedicated to his grandchildren quickly sold and went out of print, a new edition appeared from Nachtschatten Verlag on April 16, 2003, the sixtieth anniversary of the discovery of LSD. The following month, the revised edition was presented at the *Buch Basel* trade show with a reading by the author. His essay on the death of the forests was replaced by a chapter called "Thoughts and Images" and a collection of his poems and aphorisms were added.

A Model of Reality

> While there is only one outer space, there are as many inner spaces as there are humans.
>
> *Albert Hofmann*

In the longest essay in the book, Hofmann deals with the question "What is reality?"

He sees it as the outcome of the interrelationship between the inner mental world and the outer material world. In his view, the exterior world comprises the entire material and energetic universe, which includes our own corporeality. He describes the inner world of human consciousness as that which goes beyond a scientific definition, because consciousness is required to define the term. Hofmann postulates that only a single external world exists, whereas there are as many interior worlds as there are individuals.

He uses the term "reality" for the world we experience through our senses. Reality is inconceivable without an "I" to experience it as its subject. Reality is the result of the interaction between material and energetic signals originating from the outer world and the consciousness that receives them. If either transmitter or receiver is lacking, then no reality is created. Hofmann emphasizes that our senses can only perceive a small portion of the signals emanating from the outer world. Our eyes, for instance, process only a very limited segment of the electromagnetic spectrum—from 0.4 to 0.7 thousandths of a millimeter. Within this narrow band which we perceive as light, we distinguish different colors. It is important to remember that no colors exist in the exterior world, only waves of different lengths. We designate waves 0.7 microns long as "red," those that are 0.4 microns as "blue." However, there is no way to determine whether other people have the same color experience because color perception is an event in our inner space. This same limitation applies equally to our other sensory perceptions, be they auditory, gustatory, olfactory or tactile. How signals received from the outer world are transformed into the dimension of mental sensibility remains an unsolved mystery and a fundamental gap in our cognitive capacity. Fundamentally characteristic of this reality is its delimitation by the narrow band of impulses to which our receptors respond. Hofmann illustrates his thoughts with examples: If our eyes reacted to long waves in the radio range, we could see into other countries; if they reacted to short wave X-rays, solid objects would become transparent. Consequently, our seemingly objective picture of the outside world is, in reality, a subjective one. If everyone has their own picture of reality, the question arises regarding the truth of these individual realities. Hofmann says that since these all represent individual realities they are, therefore, all "true" but not in any absolute, objective sense. Humans

and animals share the scientifically inexplicable capacity to transform impulses from energy and matter into the inner experience of a living picture. This image of the exterior world first becomes human reality when we factor in the "noosphere," the domain of human thought. Objectively, the outer world only consists of matter and energy, mental symbols in the form of sound waves, that is, spoken words and music, and of material in the form of books, paintings, and buildings. The mental world exists in the outer sphere exclusively in the form of symbols, which only become reality in the mental sphere thanks to the ability of humans to decipher them.

The transmitter-receiver metaphor reveals the fact that reality is created anew in every moment and is a dynamic process, the result of continuous decoding of external signals into inner experiences. The experience of reality, the main objective of mysticism, thus arises only in the here and now. Reality as process creates time: Without reality, there would be no time and not the other way around. The participation of the receiver in forming reality gives the

> The most beautiful thing we can experience is the mysterious.
> *Albert Einstein*

> We are a process of perceiving, just as the universe we experience is a process of perceiving. Inner and outer perceptions are one. Consciousness is all there is.
> *Peter Lemesurier*

individual the possibility of consciousness. Each person is the creator of his or her own world. Hence, the responsibility and freedom of each person is based on this capacity to create one's own world. Just as each person is the receiver of messages from fellow humans, so too, each functions as a transmitter that can only convey feelings to fellow humans via matter and energy, i.e. words and gestures.

Even our own bodies, which we can see and sense, belong to the external world as do our sensory organs, neural pathways and brains. The electrical currents and impulses conducting signals from the exterior world are measurable, and as such, objectified; hence they can be attributed to the transmitter. The great gap in science is the transition from the material- energy event to the immaterial, subjective perception and experience; it represents the interface between transmitter and receiver where they coalesce into the wholeness of life.

This picture of reality is dualistic, whereby the duality merges into a transcendental reality if we track the evolution of humans back to their origins. Our body results from the merging of an ovum and a sperm which come from our parents. Hence, conception involves a material transfer. Clearly, an unbroken link exists with all ancestors back to the origin of living matter, the primal cell. This concept conveys that on a material level, we are related to all living organisms. The primal cell came into being from inanimate matter at the dawn of evolution by spontaneous generation. The line between lifeless matter and the first living cells forms the boundary between our knowledge and the realm of imagination and faith.

For him "every living organism embodies the realization, the transformation of the plan, for a new idea into a reality." The more differentiated and developed the form of a creation, the more intellectual content it can express. "The human brain, with its fourteen billion nerve cells, each of which is connected to six hundred thousand other nerve cells, is the most complicated, highly organized form of life in the known universe. The spiritual element which even manifests the spirit of its creator...." As a scientist, Hofmann finds it inconceivable that so highly organized an entity as a cell would have arisen by chance. He is firmly convinced that the genesis of the primal cell followed a plan which resulted from an idea, which in turn came from the spirit. Nor could Hofmann imagine that the component materials out of which the primal cell was made were due to chance, since even atoms are highly organized structures, virtual microcosms. The atom, as the smallest unit of lifeless matter, and the cell as the smallest unit of all living organisms, have similar blueprints. Both consist of a nucleus and a shell and for both, the nucleus is the more important element; the atomic nucleus features matter, mass, and gravity, while the cell's nucleus carries the genetic code and genes. Hofmann employs the metaphor of a cathedral: Even if the requisite construction materials, technical devices and necessary energy are all present, without the idea and plan of an architect, a cathedral will never be built. If the random genesis

> Exploring the universe showed me that the existence of matter is a miracle that requires a supernatural explanation.
>
> *Allan Sandage, astronomer*

of a single cell is inconceivable, how much more so does this apply to life forms of much greater complexity. For Hofmann, "every new living organism embodies the realization, the transformation of the plan, of a new idea into reality." The divine element that embodies the spirit of its creator has reached its greatest degree of perfection in the human brain and enables humans to be self-aware. In Hofmann's metaphor, the brain is part of the material universe and hence of the sender. But the blueprint of the brain has developed the capacity that Hofmann defined as "receiver." Consequently, matter and spirit, transmitter and receiver are melded in the human brain.

On another occasion, Hofmann placed his concept within the context of his discovery: "LSD is the most immediate, the closest and the most mysterious junction between the material and the mental and spiritual world. An almost invisible trace of LSD matter might, in the mental and spiritual world, within the human consciousness, rouse heaven or hell."[204]

Dualism does not exist in reality but is only a construct that Hofmann used to understand considerations of how reality is created. Every form created in the outer realm, from atoms to galaxies, from the cell to the myriad forms of life, represents the realization of an idea; the question about the origin of the idea is the question of the source of life. For Hofmann, a divine idea is the origin and support of the creation. This manifestation of the divine idea continuously transmits the message of the Creator. However, as we rarely open our senses to the message of the infinity of the starry heavens and the

beauty of our earth with its innumerable creatures, we remain encapsulated in our narrow and egocentric world view. We forget that we are part of creation, and that there are no barriers between subject and object, that dualism is only a construction of our minds.

In Hofmann's opinion, mere intellectual comprehension of such thoughts does not lead to an understanding strong enough to fundamentally alter our worldview. Therefore, it is necessary to experience these truths in a mystical state, existentially. In a state of expanded or cosmic consciousness, when the receiver is attuned to the whole breadth of perception, boundaries between subject and object, ego and outer world dissolve and merge. "In such an ecstatic condition, the transmitter and the receiver, the outer material and the inner spiritual world, the outer and inner space are fused together, they are united in the consciousness; thus, we must develop a notion of the original idea, the idea out of which the world was born, the idea that already was with God." (Hofmann 1986, 55)

Philosophy and Ecology

All states of well-being depend upon a sense of security, whether within the family or larger communities. Conversely, for Hofmann unhappiness is usually connected with a sense of being both separated and alone. The relationship between security and happiness applies not only to the fate of an

> If the study of natural science and the miracles of creation doesn't turn you into a mystic, then you are not a natural scientist.
>
> *Albert Hofmann*

individual but to whole cultural epochs. In the second essay from *Insight Outlook*, "Security in the Natural Scientific-Philosophical View of Life," Hofmann describes the transformation of worldviews down through the course of history with respect to their relationship to the creation and to living nature. He believes that current problems are due to the dysfunctional relationship between people and nature, and that the prevailing, one-sided materialist, purely scientific worldview cannot offer people a sense of security. Looking for the causes of this alienation from nature, he sees its beginnings in seventeenth-century Europe in the emergence of measurement-oriented scientific exploration of nature, which succeeded in explaining the physical and chemical laws of the material world. He views this biased, materialism as the myth, the faith of our time, and considers its adoption to be a fateful error. While its contents are correct, this view is incomplete and represents only one side of the coin. What is at stake is to recognize the grotesque tunnel vision of this perspective. Hofmann describes his mystical experience of nature as a child as one of

Albert Hofmann's article "The Sun, a Nuclear Power Plant—An appeal by a natural scientist", appeared April 9, 1977 in the daily newspaper *Basler Zeitung*, in 1986 as an essay in *Einsichten Ausblicke (Insight Outlook)*. Hofmann liked the illustration by Basel artist Mario Grasso so much that Hofmann's son Dieter, a friend of Grasso's, gave him the original for his birthday.

the main reasons he decided to take up the profession of chemist, wishing to learn and understand the mysterious processes of nature. He sharply criticizes the materialist vision of Nobel Prize winner Jacques Monod "who with his book, *Chance and Necessity*, which is unscientific and arrogant, has wrought great damage to those who are semi-educated in natural sciences." Hofmann's subsequent reflections show that his scientific knowledge had opened a view which brought him a sense of security. As a chemist, what he sees in a plant is not only that which the non-chemist sees, but beyond to its inner structure and chemical and physical processes. He vividly describes how many generations of chemists it took to decipher these complex processes and how much work and research lay behind the synthesis of each of the many substances that constitute a plant. "Every little blade of grass is capable of this effort. It produces these materials [which] the work of hundreds of chemists for many years would not be sufficient to synthesize, quietly and humbly with light as its only source of energy. A chemist has to marvel at this."

The third essay is a meditation on the concepts "possession" (Besitz) and "ownership." (Eigentum) In German, the word "Besitz" comes from "besitzen" which describes the act of sitting on something,

> We are creatures of light—that is not just a mystical experience to which the word enlightenment and the significance of light in many religions points, but rather also a discovery of natural science.
>
> *Albert Hofmann*

as on a chair. Earlier, "Besitz" only referred to that which one could use personally. Over the course of time, "Besitz" took on a more comprehensive and symbolic meaning. Since the legal concept of ownership (Eigentum) developed, it is possible to possess more than one can personally use. Hofmann sees in this possibility the seed of a significant part of the human tragedy. Since ownership comprises the right to control property's disposal, the accumulation of possessions results in the accumulation of power and control. Hofmann believes this power based on ownership is detrimental to human happiness. Much discord and dissatisfaction would vanish if people were aware of this difference and "we were to concentrate more on real possessions and less on property. A Chinese aphorism underlines the meaning of this in the most succinct way: 'The master said: My garden… his gardener smiled.'"

At the edge of the forest near Hofmann's house stands an old boundary stone. "On one side it displays the coat of arms of the neighboring monastery Mariastein, for several centuries the owner of the forest glade on which our house is located. On the other side, looking out over France, a bas-relief still clearly shows the arms belonging to none less than the great French statesman Jules Mazarin (1602–1661), who was given these properties by Louis XIV, in recognition of his outstanding services." Driven by greed the statesman, who was considered one of the richest men in Europe, died without ever having set foot on his Alsatian holdings. This is a prime example of the illusory nature of ownership which is only property but not possession. "The vagabond who wandered around that lovely area owned the land in reality while the rich man in Paris owned it only on paper."

In the two shorter essays in *Insight Outlook*, Hofmann addresses topics in ecology that were of particular interest in the 1980s. One involved "Botanical Reflections on the Death of the Forests." In the second, "The Sun, a Nuclear Power Plant," he expounded on the workings of the sun, a mighty power plant to which all on earth owe life. He demonstrated that the sun, an "extraterrestrial nuclear reactor," is the origin of all earthly energy sources, including wood, coal, petroleum, natural gas, and hydropower. He is vehemently opposed to "igniting solar fire," i.e., building nuclear fusion or atomic power stations on earth because he believes the contamination of the earth with life threatening radioactivity is a danger that could scarcely be contained. The use of atomic energy is not simply a further development of earlier technologies of gaining energy, but something completely new,

> The highest which man can attain is astonishment.
> *Johann Wolfgang von Goethe*

namely an encroachment into the heart of matter. Hofmann admired Austrian-American biochemist Erwin Chargaff for his statement that mankind should "neither touch nor alter" either the atomic nucleus or the cell nucleus. Although Hofmann spoke out for the freedom to do research, he feared that manipulation of atomic and cell nuclei would bring more disadvantages than benefits. To him, the production of genetically modified species was "playing with fire" since these alterations cannot be undone.

The essay was a plea for the sun as the ideal energy source of the future because "It has been calculated that the amount of energy reaching the earth on one single day in the shape of the sun's rays would be sufficient to meet our present energy requirements for several hundred years."

Honors and Awards

For his research and discoveries, Albert Hofmann received great recognition and numerous honors from scientific quarters. In May 1963, Hofmann was named a member of the World Academy of Art and Science. The daily *Basler Nachrichten* headlined an article—*Basel Chemist Honored*: "The World Academy of Art and Science named Dr. Albert Hofmann, deputy director of the chemical-pharmaceutical division of Sandoz AG, as a Fellow Member. The World Academy of Art and Science, which comprises some 150 scientists, writers, and artists from around the world, is a transnational institution that treats vital problems of humankind at the highest scientific and ethical levels. The honorable appointment of Dr. Hofmann follows in appreciation of his groundbreaking dis-

coveries in psychotropic drugs." His director, Arthur Stoll, congratulated him effusively on this honor and was pleased with the gain in prestige for Sandoz.

Hofmann received his first honorary doctorate, Dr. Pharm. h.c., from the Royal Pharmaceutical Institute of Sweden alongside the King of Sweden in Stockholm on May 31, 1966. His second honorary doctorate was the Dr. sc. Nat. h.c. Zurich, the highest Swiss scientific distinction, awarded him by the prestigious Swiss Federal Institute of Technology (ETH) in Zurich.[205]

In Sweden once more in 1971, he received the Scheele Medal named after the German surgeon Karl Scheele (1884–1966). The American Society of Pharmacognosy awarded him honorable membership in 1975. In September 1977, he became an honorable member of the Society for Medicinal Plant and Natural Product in Zurich. A delighted Hofmann wrote to his friend Finn Sandberg, "So a little something is still happening in my later years." A third honorary doctorate, Dr. rer. Nat. h.c. in pharmacy, was awarded to Hofmann by the Free University of Berlin in December 1988 "for his fundamental contributions to the isolation, structural clarification, and total synthesis of the active ingredients of important medicinal plants, for his ground-breaking work in developing specific pharmaceuticals by partially synthetic modification of natural ergot alkaloids, for his successful phytochemical investigation of Mexican magic mushrooms, for the discovery of the unique psychoactive properties of LSD, and for critical analysis of the consequences of this discovery." Since 1979, the Society for Toxicological and Forensic Chemistry has awarded the Jean-Servais Stas Medal, named after the Belgian chemist,

Principal Pierre E. Marmier of the Swiss Federal Institute of Technology (ETH), Zurich, confers the Dr. sc. Nat. h.c. degree to Albert Hofmann, 1966

As ostentatious as the founding of the Albert Hofmann Foundation in Los Angeles in 1988 was, it had to discontinue its activities a few years later, despite repeated backing from prominent donors, much to the chagrin of its name giver.

for "service in forensic human sciences;" in 1995, they honored Hofmann with this distinction in Mosbach, Germany.

However, the most distinguished prize, the Nobel Prize for Chemistry, eluded him. In the mid-1960s, he was visited by representatives of the Nobel Prize committee during a period in which the mass media was causing a furor by describing LSD as a "demonic drug." Hofmann, and his scientist friends, believed that this adverse publicity cost him the Nobel Prize because the Academy was afraid of sending out the wrong signals.

Stimulus and Impetus

Let us guard against the greatest danger before us—that we take life for granted. *Ernst Jünger*

A Belgian in Burg

To coincide with the investiture of the new principal of the Swiss Federal Institute of Technology in Zurich whose inaugural speech was on the subject of an imminent paradigm shift, the International New Age Symposium co-organized by Dieter Hagenbach and Susanne Seiler, was held in November of 1984 on the theme of "Pathways into Our Future." About a thousand attendees listened to speakers who addressed the challenges of urgently needed changes in social, cultural and political assumptions. Along with American journalist Marilyn Ferguson, author of the bestseller *The Aquarian Conspiracy,* the attentive audience heard philosopher of religion Arnold Keyserling, psychologist and parapsychologist Stanley Krippner, mythology researcher Sergius Golowin, theologian and sociologist Hilarion Petzold, economist Hans A. Pestalozzi, physicist Fritz-Albert Popp, and Albert Hofmann with a talk about expansion of consciousness.

Looking back, it is striking that press coverage scarcely mentioned Albert Hofmann.

Only Nicolas Broccard from the *St. Galler Tagblatt* recognized Hofmann's remarks as "an important concern of the New Age movement: Each person should be responsible for himself and take charge of his life. According to Hofmann's transmitter-receiver concept, all people have the capacity for expanding their consciousness and, in other words, for experiencing reality more comprehensively."[206] He quotes from Hofmann's lecture: "Since reality only arises in each individual, reality or the world can only be changed within the individual. That means each person must try to perfect himself as a receiver to change the world, to reshape it, which is so urgently needed."[207]

Hofmann showed himself to be receptive to the charm of Marilyn Ferguson who invited him to visit her in Los Angeles on his next journey to America. Hofmann gladly accepted her invitation on his following trip to California and with her, experienced the empathic opening of the heart on MDMA in the hills above the City of Angels.

Albert Hofmann practicing Tai Chi with his Ling Chi on his 80th birthday

Joël Vandroogenbroeck

A second encounter that had consequences took place in Zurich. The group *Brainticket* was playing a midnight concert during a symposium event on the congress hall stage. The founder of this experimental rock band in 1968, Joël Vandroogenbroeck, was a Belgian multi-instrumentalist living in Basel. *Brainticket* became world famous in 1971 with their *Cottonwoodhill* album, a musical setting of both the heavenly and the hellish aspects of an LSD trip. A year later, they produced *Psychonaut*, which conveys the lovely aspects of a trip. Both albums have long since been regarded classics of psychedelic music. Although a devotee of Mozart, Hofmann's curiosity prompted him to listen to the unfamiliar electronic sounds and learn what influence his LSD was having on the work of young musicians.

As chance or fate would have it, Vandroogenbroeck's daughter Nathalie also lived in the small village of Burg where the Hofmanns resided. When her father took a break from touring in 1989, she invited him to stay with her. Shortly thereafter, at a village festival, her father asked her if she knew the older gentleman sitting at a table near them whom he thought he recognized. She was astonished and asked: "You don't know him? That's Doctor Hofmann. He lives here up on the hill." The pleasure at their unexpected reunion was genuine, as both remembered their brief encounter in Zurich. When Vandroogenbroeck's wife returned to Switzerland and both thought of settling in the area, it happened that the Hofmanns were looking for a new tenant for the separate apartment in the front section of their house. They met to discuss it and Hofmann explained: "We are old folks and not twenty anymore. We live in a beautiful setting but it is pretty remote here along the border. That is why we like to have younger people nearby who can keep an eye on the house when we are on vacation or traveling to a conference; and we like having creative artists around us." The two couples came to an agreement within a few days, and became friendly neighbors for the next two years.

Whenever the Hofmanns went on a journey, the Vandroogenbroecks looked after the entire house, watered the flowers, and set the alarm system. When the musician played the piano or flute, the Hofmanns gladly listened. One day, the musician accompanied the chemist on the daily walk he always took at the same hour. Hofmann asked him: "Do you know why I became a chemist? Well, just look how wonderful nature is! I've always been curious to discover what was behind all of that. I always wanted to understand the laws of nature. Why? How? What are the secrets of life? What drives all of this along? I understand some of it, but there is still so much to learn and so little time remaining." Vandroogenbroeck could only say that he had already accomplished so much in his life, whereupon Albert Hofmann once again told him the story of his discovery.

Visitors From Around the World

The eminent German physician Wilhelm Hufeland (1762–1836) wrote of a man who, in his opinion, had a good chance to live a long life: "He is cheerful, loquacious, and sympathetic, open to joy, love and hope, but closed to feelings of hate, anger and envy. His passions will never be violent and rapacious."[208] Hufeland's description characterizes Hofmann very well. Just as he always liked to travel and become acquainted with new and remote regions, so too he was happy to receive visitors and make new acquaintances, particularly with people who had achieved something special in their lives and fields. "Despite our great seclusion, we never feel alone or lonely. The children came and often come to us in the countryside, and later on the grandchildren as well. We have celebrated many joyful family events together

at the Rittimatte and we often receive visits from friends who also love this beautiful place." Anita and Albert Hofmann always welcomed their guests and large circle of friends with open arms and hearts. Among them were Mareile Wolff and several couples, the von Kreuzigers, the Werthmüllers and the Hagenbuchs. Hofmann also maintained friendly ties after retirement with a few of his former colleagues. Since their expedition to Mexico, Gordon Wasson was a good family friend and visited the Hofmanns regularly. He would stay up to three weeks and "shuffled around the house in large slippers," recalls Hofmann's son Andreas. Other guests from abroad who were frequent and welcome guests were the ethnobotanist Richard Schultes and his wife Dorothy.

Basel art dealer Carl Laszlo and translator and publisher Udo Breger were fans of American Beat literati. When Laszlo learned that Breger was personally acquainted with writer William S. Burroughs and artist Brion Gysin, concrete plans soon developed to invite the two to Basel. Breger got in touch with Brion Gysin, and Carl Laszlo arranged the exhibition "Dreamachine" with his friend, Basel gallery owner Miklos von Bartha. For the vernissage in June 1979, he flew Burroughs in from New York. Also in attendance was Albert Hofmann, accompanied by Gordon Wasson who was staying with the Hofmanns at the time. Hofmann took the opportunity to spontaneously invite Burroughs, Gysin, and Breger to the Rittimatte. The following day they were driven up to Burg by Dieter Hagenbach. The beaming couple received their guests. The weather was at its best and they enjoyed themselves around the well-laid table. Over coffee, cake and homemade brandy, talk was restricted to a cultivated exchange of pleasantries but there were no intellectual conversations matching the potential of those present. Nonetheless, there was the obligatory short walk up to the legendary bench where, pointing out the boundary stone from Napoleonic times, Hofmann explained to his astonished guests that part of his estate lay in France. The foreign artists expressed amazement that such a stone, hidden in the forest, was the only thing to indicate an international frontier.

In one of his novels, bestselling Swiss author Martin Suter described an edifying trip on magic mushrooms so aptly and knowledgeably that it motivated Hofmann to personally meet with the writer. When the author, who lived on Ibiza and in Guatemala, returned to his native Switzerland for a while in the summer of 1994, the two met for conversation at Hofmann's home on the Rittimatte. As Martin Suter recalls: "Albert Hofmann had just read my novel *Die dunkle Seite des Mondes (The Dark Side of the Moon)*,[209] the story of a business lawyer who was so changed by a mushroom trip, that he withdrew into the forests of a nearby recreation area. And he liked the description of the forest, the world of the managers, and the depiction of the psilocybin trip. I was especially pleased by this last comment because, on that point, I had been uncertain until now; I had, and here I reveal an especially well kept author's secret, no personal experience with psilocybin. These words of praise from the mouth of Dr. Hofmann were as if Johann Gutenberg had told me that my book was especially well printed. I admit it, I am one of those authors who while writing, sometimes imagines the reader, but I did not expect the scientist who isolated and synthesized psilocybin as a reader; otherwise I wouldn't have been able to describe that passage so freely. My wife and I first visited the Hofmanns that summer and spent a stimulating, entertaining and inspiring afternoon. We drank tea and a glass of mind-

(l. to r.) Gordon Wasson, Albert Hofmann, Udo Breger, William S. Burroughs in front of a Dreamachine, Galerie von Bartha, Basel, June 7, 1979

(l. to r.) William S. Burroughs, Gordon Wasson, Brion Gysin, Albert Hofmann, Rittimatte 1979

(l. to r.) Margrith Nay Suter, Albert Hofmann, Martin Suter

(l. to r.) Stanislav Grof, Martina Hoffmann, Albert Hofmann, Robert Venosa, Christina Grof

(l. to r.) Albert Hofmann, Mark Geyer, David E. Nichols, Franz X. Vollenweider, at the restaurant Schwanen in Wolschwiller, Alsace in summer 1998

expanding plum brandy in front of the great windows in the living room." The two became friends and they stayed in touch. For his next work, Martin Suter anticipated Albert Hofmann to be one of its readers so surely "that I dedicated my novel to him."[210] Hofmann also maintained good connections with other Swiss writers, among them Eveline Hasler, Ernst Jaeckle, Maria Modena and Walter Vogt.

Gallery owner, art dealer and museum founder Ernst Beyeler, himself highly trained in the appreciation of art and a nature lover, was extremely impressed with Albert Hofmann's relationship to nature and the observations he expressed so personally in his book *Lob des Schauens (In Praise of Observing)*. Beyeler was fascinated by the beauty of the and visited the Hofmanns several times to discuss art and nature.

Prominent LSD researchers and experts also came to the Rittimatte to pay Hofmann their respects: Günter Amendt, Mathias Bröckers, Rick Doblin, Amanda Feilding with her husband Lord Jamie Neidpath, Sergius Golowin, Stanislav Grof, Joan Halifax, Jon Hanna, Michael Horowitz, Stanley Krippner, Timothy Leary, John C. Lilly, Ralph Metzner, Claudia Müller-Ebeling, Jeremy Narby, David E. Nichols, Jonathan Ott, Vanja Palmers, Christian Rätsch, Andrew Sewell, Ann and Alexander Shulgin, Rolf Verres, Franz X. Vollenweider and many others.

Unannounced, and from all over the world, many people came to the Rittimatte to see the "father of LSD." Hippies, dropouts, epicureans, and artists; some wished to thank him and brought presents, others wanted to share their experiences or wished to be photographed with him. Quite a few

311

of these uninvited guests were met at the door late in the evening by Hofmann himself, who asked them in to his house, spoke with them and offered hospitality. Hofmann remarked: "Whenever it was possible, I received these visitors or went to an agreed upon appointment. I considered it a responsibility that came with my role in the history of LSD and have attempted to be a source of information and advice."

Border Crosser

Albert Hofmann exemplifies a border crosser in the truest sense: On the Rittimatte, he was between Switzerland and France; intellectually, between science and mysticism; in attitudes, between conventionality and nonconformity. Inwardly, he remained socially conservative, his milieu is bourgeois. From childhood on, he was extremely disciplined. An educated middle class citizen. Well into his old age, he learned poems by heart and was pleased to have appropriate opportunities to recite them. Invitations to concerts of classical music at his home were part of his world. Hofmann put great value on a well-groomed appearance, both for himself and others. He did not appreciate it when guests dressed sloppily, spoke crudely, ate without manners, or drank excessively. He was less than impressed when, after giving a lecture in Basel, a well-known English psychiatrist visited him strongly inebriated. Nevertheless, the Hofmanns showed remarkable poise when guests behaved badly, such as the occasion when an anthropologist during her visit to the Rittimatte, scarcely bothered to conceal herself when shooting up with a syringe.

Albert Hofmann with Christian Rätsch and Alex Grey, Amsterdam 1998

Hofmann's greatest admirers were, for the most part, unconventional people. Their high regard, even veneration, of his person led him to be increasingly more tolerant in his attitude towards non-conformists. Hofmann was not an opportunist but simply naturally open towards new acquaintances. Not until his later years did he gradually lose his reserve and begin to enjoy his excursions into the wide world of psychedelic culture, at times even taking a toke on a joint. At the 1998 Psychoactivity Conference in Amsterdam, Hofmann received a standing ovation after his lecture. He then enjoyed dancing with several young women at the conference's exuberant techno party at the "in" spot, the Melkweg. Despite his ninety-two years and the exotic music, he amazed those present with his dexterity on the dance floor. He was last seen at three in the morning with a dance partner barely a third his age.

Speakers at the Psychoactivity Conference, Amsterdam 1998

As a researcher, he was curious about all consciousness-altering substances and techniques and wished to try their effects on his own body and mind. Despite the overwhelming experience of his first self-experiment in 1943, Hofmann carried out countless further tests: In the 1940s with different lysergic acid derivatives, at the end of the 1950s with magic mushrooms and psilocybin, with the lysergic acid alkaloids of morning glories, in Mexico with *Salvia divinorum*, and near the end of his professional career with fly agaric (*Amanita muscaria*) from Siberia that Finn Sandberg sent him upon his request; after retirement, to verify Wasson's Eleusis hypothesis he took ergonovine, and at the suggestion of Karl Kerényi, he ingested the fruit of the strawberry tree.

Well into very advanced age, Hofmann occasionally experimented with low doses of LSD which he took instead of Hydergine® to increase blood flow in his brain. He considered doses of about 20 micrograms of LSD to be mentally stimulating, a type of "psycho-vitamin" and

mood elevator. At over ninety years old, he experienced an intensive trip with fifty micrograms of LSD. To him, his LSD was unique and not comparable with other substances. He justified its special status from its potency alone. He was incensed when Basil Gelpke showed a therapy session with MDMA in his film *Albert Hofmann—LSD and its Discoverer*. This was in spite of the fact that he had spoken positively of MDMA which he had tried a few times with, among others, Ralph Metzner, to whom he wrote that "Anita would like it." Privately, in the company of close friends, Hofmann smoked the strongly psychoactive dried mucus of the Colorado toad (*Bufo alvarius*), which contains 5-Meo-DMT, and he reported afterwards an exhilarating feeling of intimacy with nature.

The Tank and the Deep Self

Throughout his whole life, John Cunningham Lilly remained true to one of his basic principles: "Thou shalt not bore

313

God," which he called the "eleventh commandment." Born January 6, 1915 in St. Paul, Minnesota, Lilly studied medicine, neurology, physics, biology, psychology and biophysics.

During the Second World War, Lilly devised new techniques for monitoring respiration at high altitude in Air Force fighter pilots. At the National Institute for Mental Health, he researched aspects of human sensors. Until then, the prevailing doctrine among neurophysiologists was that the brain depended upon exterior stimuli to remain awake and active. Lilly's idea for testing that hypothesis was to isolate the brain from all exterior influences. This led him to develop a light-and-sound insulated "isolation tank," later also called "Samadhi tank" or "floatation tank;" with an ambient temperature conforming to that of human skin. It was half-full of a strong salt water solution kept at body temperature. This environment provided the person lying in it with the sensation of floating and effected the highest possible sensory deprivation in which the body's boundaries dissolve, resulting in a feeling of weightlessness in infinite space. As it turns out, thought processes neither slow nor stop during this state—quite the opposite proves to be true.

Lilly's first encounter with LSD came early in the 1960s, under the knowledgeable guidance of a colleague at the National Institute of Mental Health, and with a dose of 100 micrograms of "pure Sandoz." He immediately recognized the potential of the substance. Especially in combination with the isolation tank, he saw undreamt of possibilities for delving into the depths of the brain and into the vastness of the universe.

He described his experiences with LSD in the isolation tank in his book *The Center of the Cyclone*. (Lilly 1972) On his first trip, shortly after the LSD began to take effect, he remarked: "Every psychiatrist, every psychoanalyst should be forced to take LSD in order to know what is over here" and added: "The usual things happened that had been well written about in the literature by Aldous Huxley and many others. The sudden enhancement and deepening of all color and form, the transparency of real objects, the apparent living nature of material matter, all appeared immediately." After a second trip he recalled that: "I traveled through my brain, watching the neurons and their activities." He subsequently undertook experiments with doses of 300 micrograms of LSD during which he remained in the tank for up to twenty-four hours He was able to recall "on demand," daydreams and hallucinations, set in motion events of inner reality of such brilliance and truth that they could easily be mistaken for events in the external world. After ten years of work with the isolation tank, he summed up: "In the province of the mind, what one believes to be true, either is true or becomes true within certain limits. These limits are to be found experientially and experimentally. When the limits are determined, it is found that they are further beliefs to be transcended. The body imposes definite limits." (Lilly, 1977)

Lilly developed a complex model of the human brain as a bio-computer consisting of neuronal circuits equipped with

> LSD allowed me to befriend the alien part of my nature. That allowed me to befriend the alien parts in others.
>
> *Christian Rätsch*

John C. Lilly with Albert Hofmann, Solar System
Conference, November 13-16, 1981, Institute of
Ecotechnics, Aix-en-Provence

Albert Hofmann, John C. Lilly in Lugano in November 1993
at the scientific conference organized by Sandoz for the
50th anniversary of the discovery of the effect of LSD

John C. Lilly with Albert Hofmann at the Rittimatte, 1991

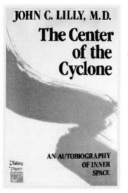

countless different properties. "The "human bio-computer" is guided by inherited and acquired programs that are constantly adapting to inner and outer conditions and the requirements of life. Lilly was primarily interested in "programming and metapro-gramming the human bio-computer." In his book by that name (Lilly 1987), he describes different techniques for exploring consciousness and controlling or "metapro-gramming" its functions.

Lilly gradually moved away from main-stream science. He compared humankind's current condition to Plato's Allegory of the Cave, in which from birth, humans are so tightly bound to their cave, that they con-stantly turn their backs to the light and can see only a poorly lit cave wall. Everything that happens behind them casts a shadow on the wall. Since they perceive nothing more, they take these shadow images to be real things. This remains the case even after one of them is untied, returns from outside the cave and attempts to tell them the true nature of things.

His magnetic personality brought Lilly in contact with scientists, artists and prominent persons, some of whom accepted his invitation to enter the tank: Richard Alpert, Richard Feynman, Buckminster Fuller, Aldous Huxley, Oscar Ichazo, Grace Jones, R.D. Laing, Timothy Leary, Burgess Meredith, Fritz Perls, Alan Watts and Robin Williams.

The first meeting between Albert Hofmann and John Lilly took place in 1977 in Santa

315

Cruz, California, at the colloquium "*LSD—A Generation Later.*" Hofmann was pleased to meet Lilly and told him: "I have read your book *Center of the Cyclone*, and we have had very parallel experiences!" Lilly met with Hofmann at various occasions several times during the 1990s: In Lugano in 1993 at the scientific conference held upon the fiftieth anniversary of the discovery of the effects of LSD, and several times at the Rittimatte. In 1996, Hofmann sent Lilly a photo with the greeting: "To my dear friend John Lilly: Pioneer Companion in Modern Consciousness Research." The two spirited researchers met for the last time in 1999 over lunch at the Hotel Drei Könige in Basel.

The Indian from Hamburg

As a student in the early 1980s, Christian Rätsch read *LSD - My Problem Child* and was impressed. He wished "to shake the hand of this marvelous man some day and to thank him for discovering LSD," but thought it improbable that he would ever meet the famous chemist. While doing field research in southern Mexico's rain forest among the Lacandon Mayan tribe in 1982, he was introduced to entheogenic Balché tree bark (*Lonchocarpus violaceus*). He took this as an opportunity to contact Albert Hofmann to ask what he knew about this plant. Several months later, when a native brought him the mail that had come to San Cristobal, it contained a letter from Hofmann who wrote that he had not answered immediately because he had first wished to speak with his friend Richard Schultes. Neither of them knew anything about the tree or its bark with hallucinogenic

effect but hoped to learn more about it from the young ethnologist. It was typical of Hofmann when he received questions, even from students with whom he was not acquainted, that he did not simply ignore them or respond with just a few cursory words but would consult a friend with a world reputation in order to give an adequate answer.

Two years later, at Stanislav Grof's invitation, Christian Rätsch gave a talk at Esalen about the Lacandon tribe and the use of their psychoactive drink. On the morning of his arrival, he unexpectedly ran into Albert Hofmann who was invited as a guest of honor. "I made an effort and introduced myself. I told him how happy I was to receive his letter in the rain forest. Albert Hofmann remembered and asked me about my experiences there. Our first conversation lasted nearly two hours. Albert Hofmann was incredibly gracious." Later, Rätsch learned that on the previous evening, Hofmann had taken MDMA for the first time and truly enjoyed the experience, not to mention the attention of lovely young women in the stone tubs fed from a hot spring with a view of the Pacific Ocean.

Hofmann invited Rätsch to visit on the Rittimatte to continue their conversation and to get to know each other better. "I very gladly took the revered Swiss chemist up on his generous invitation. With pounding heart, I stood at his door and pressed the doorbell. A small youngster opened, looked at me, and called into the house: 'Grandpa, there's an Amerindian at the door!' The boy was Simon Duttwyler, Albert Hofmann's grandson who was interested in chemistry. That is how Christian Rätsch got the nickname with which Albert and Anita Hofmann

Albert Hofmann, Claudia Müller-Ebeling, Christian Rätsch with a photo of grandson Simon holding his essay on his grandfather up to the camera

Albert Hofmann, Christian Rätsch, Roger Liggenstorfer holding a photo of Simon in his "lab"

Albert Hofmann and Timothy Leary in the studio of German TV channel Premiere on July 16, 1993, for a program on the fiftieth anniversary of the discovery of LSD

At a private party at Christian Rätsch's, his father Paul Rätsch brought his legendary green soup and lets Timothy Leary try a taste. July 1993

affectionately addressed him from then on. The two researchers became good friends and this was the first of their many conversations on the Rittimatte. During several visits to Hamburg, Hofmann came to know and appreciate Rätsch's parents. He particularly liked the motto Rätsch's father had carved into the roof beam of their garage: Liebe das Leben (Love life).

In July 1993, Rätsch organized a television program in Hamburg with Albert Hofmann and Timothy Leary, marking the 50th anniversary of LSD. As they climbed into a taxi together on the way to the studio, Rätsch asked the driver to drive carefully because he was carrying valuable cargo. When the irritated driver looked in the rear view mirror, he said: "Can this be true? Have I Timothy Leary and Albert Hofmann on board? And I know who you are, too." Afterwards, Rätsch organized a party in a private suite where the two men solemnly renewed their friendship.

317

For Rätsch, Albert Hofmann was not just a friend but a mentor who opened doors for him and supplied forewords to several of his books, including his magnum opus, which became the standard reference book for advanced study in the field: *The Encyclopedia of Psychoactive Plants.* (Rätsch 1998)

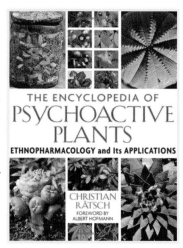

THE ENCYCLOPEDIA OF
PSYCHOACTIVE PLANTS
ETHNOPHARMACOLOGY and Its APPLICATIONS

CHRISTIAN RÄTSCH
FOREWORD BY ALBERT HOFMANN

The Trip Advisor

During the 1980s, Roger Liggenstorfer traveled Switzerland as a market vendor. At his stand, the educated merchant sold literature about the counterculture scene and books on hemp and hemp growing. This resulted in an indictment for "encouraging drug consumption." The High Court upheld a first time verdict of three weeks in prison, to be served on parole and further ordered the books to be burned. Liggenstorfer, however, refused to be discouraged. He founded the Nachtschatten Verlag in Solothurn in 1984, which focused on drug education. Up to the present, he has published more than one hundred titles by authors like Albert Hofmann, Christian Rätsch, and Ralph Metzner. Liggenstorfer's credo is that only someone who has the necessary information about an individual drug, can assess its risks and possibly avoid taking it. A year later, he founded a bookstore in Solothurn called Dogon, which became a meeting place of the scene. When the bookstore changed location in 1991, Liggenstorfer didn't need a moving van. A human chain of friends and customers handed the books from one person to another over a stretch of at least three hundred meters (one thousand feet) to the new shop. He became active in political bodies such as the municipal drug commission and the National Association on Addiction Policy, also serving for many years as president of *Eve & Rave Schweiz*, "an independent organization close to the scene which promotes risk awareness and personal responsibility concerning drug use."

In January 1984, Liggenstorfer invited Albert Hofmann to give a lecture. Hofmann spontaneously agreed, asking for no fee but merely his travel expenses, and said that he wished to speak about more than just LSD, namely, the relationship between inner and outer space and the current issue of the time, the dying forests. Ten years later, on the occasion of the fiftieth anniversary of LSD, Liggenstorfer organized a celebration and party in Basel. Hofmann did not come in person, because "he still feared damaging his reputation by making appearances in that context." At the ninetieth birthday celebration that Liggenstorfer organized for Hofmann in the Restaurant Teufelhof in Basel, the publisher presented him with a copy of the book *Maria Sabina— Botin der heiligen Pilze (Maria Sabina— Messenger of the Sacred Mushrooms)* (Liggenstorfer, Rätsch 1996) dedicated to Hofmann. For dessert, the guests were served a "sacred mushroom" on their plate, which all consumed.

Liggenstorfer co-edited the anthology *Die berauschte Schweiz* (Intoxicated Switzerland).[211]

In front of the Restaurant Teufelhof, Basel 1996

More than a hundred people and media representatives attended its launch, which is where Hofmann met Emilie Lieberherr, the politically active *grande dame* of Swiss drug policy. Among the greatest achievements of this Zurich city councilor who died in 2011, besides her involvement in setting policy for the elderly and youth, was the authorization of medical prescription and controlled distribution of heroin. "Emilie Lieberherr distributes heroin, cocaine and all currently used drugs free to junkies and doesn't get punished. Emilie Lieberherr is the head of the Zurich Social Welfare Office. On behalf of drug addicts, she consciously breaks the Swiss Controlled Substances Law," is how the German magazine *Focus* described her work in 1994. The

chemist and the politician were delighted to meet and had a lively discussion.

In conjunction with the premiere of director Peter Mettler's film *Gambling, Gods and LSD*, Hofmann and Liggenstorfer spent three days together in the spring of 2002 at the film festival *Vision du Réel* in Nyon, Switzerland on Lake Geneva. They were an unlikely pair, the ninety-some year old scientist and the long-haired drug activist, too young to pass for Hofmann's son. In the lobby, they met Swiss Federal Councilor Ruth Dreifuss. Hofmann introduced the young man as his bodyguard. Liggenstorfer recalls that "Albert enjoyed this trip together like a school boy. He enjoyed feeling young again in my presence, staying up all hours,

319

In conversation with Federal Councilor Ruth Dreifuss (r.)

Peter Mettler, director of the film *Gambling, Gods and LSD*, Albert Hofmann, Roger Liggenstorfer, Nyon, spring 2002

Sergius Golowin in conversation with Albert Hofmann at the birthday party

dancing, flirting and getting carried away without regard for convention."

Nachtschatten Verlag issued a new edition of Hofmann's *Die Mutterkornal-kaloide (The Ergot Alkaloids)* (Hofmann 2000) and two years later a new edition of his privately printed *Lob des Schauens* (*In Praise of Observing*). (Hofmann 2002) On April 19, 2003, the publishing house invited the Hofmanns and nearly two dozen of their friends to a leisurely luncheon to celebrate "60 Years of LSD," again at the Teufel-hof. Two weeks later, Nachtschatten presented the new edition of *Einsichten*

Ausblicke with a reading by Albert Hofmann at the *Buch Basel* fair. The Hofmanns attended the annual meetings of the publishing house several times. On his frequent visits to the Rittimatte, Liggenstorfer often brought along with him interesting people from all over the world.

On August 1, 2000, the Swiss National holiday, Lars Rudin, a.k.a. DJ Olowanpi, organized a Goa Party in Kleinlützel, not far from the Rittimatte. Liggenstorfer asked Hofmann if he would like to have a look. Hofmann accepted and was well rested and ready to go on Sunday morning at nine o'clock, without telling his wife. Once at the location, he told Rudin that he loved that place, and that he enjoyed many wonderful LSD experiences there, and was pleased how the party was influenced by his discovery.

Exactly a year later, on August 1, 2001, another Goa Party took place at the same location, during which Nina Hagen also gave a performance. Once again, Albert Hofmann showed up on Sunday morning. He greeted the bleary-eyed party goers

Albert Hofmann enjoys a joint at the Goa Party

Ariane, Albert Hofmann, Goa Gil

Albert Hofmann, Goa Gil

Albert Hofmann, Peter Hess, Ralph Metzner
at the Rittimatte, September 1996

who could hardly believe it when they saw the famous chemist there. He then joined musician and DJ Goa Gil onstage and danced a few steps. Besides the unfamiliar music, he was irritated that everyone danced by themselves rather than in pairs, as Hofmann was accustomed to in his generation. Noticeably relaxed he sat down, took a few whiffs from the circling joints and signed some LSD blotters.

His last contact with Liggenstorfer was three days prior to his death. Hofmann called his publisher and friend and casually asked whether good quality LSD was still available on the market. He was reassured by the answer and, unsolicited, delivered some tips for its safe storage.

(l. to r.) Roger Liggenstorfer, Beatrix Nabholz-Hofmann, Gaby Duttwyler-Hofmann, Andreas and Ruth Hofmann-Fleig at the group exhibit *Psychonautic Map 2*, Galerie Incontro, Zurich 2003

The Third Member

After having met Richard Alpert in 1962 in Basel and Timothy Leary in 1971 in Lausanne, Hofmann met Ralph Metzner, the third member of the one-time Harvard group, for the first time in October of 1977 at a conference on hallucinogenic mushrooms held in San Francisco. At their second meeting at Esalen in 1984, the two became friends and corresponded regularly with each other from then on. After founding his Green Earth Foundation in 1988, Metzner asked if he might list Hofmann as an advisor to the foundation. Hofmann's response indicates the degree of his sympathy for the foundation's mission of harmonizing the relationship of humans to the earth: "I am ready and willing to serve as a member of the Board of Advisors; it is greatly to be hoped that the network of efforts to rescue life on earth spreads quickly and becomes a decisive political power."

In August 1989, Hofmann expressed his compliments and thanks to Metzner for his book *Hineingehen—Wegmarken für die Transformation (Opening to Inner Light - The Transformation of Human Nature and Consciousness)*. (Metzner 1986) "How did the Babylonian confusion of tongues that led to the splintering of consciousness come about? I believe that this fundamental question can be answered if one recalls that the elemental archetypes, the basic metaphors, are already symbols grasped in words for the underlying structures of reality, but are not the reality itself. There is only *one objective* reality.... There is hope in that ever more people are seeking direct access to the

(l. to r.) Ralph Metzner, Michael Horowitz, Albert Hofmann, at a reception, Fitz Hugh Ludlow Memorial Library, San Francisco 1977

source, to first hand revelation. That must lead to the unity of humankind's awareness of reality, to a cosmic consciousness in two senses." In another letter in March 1990 in which Hofmann thanks Metzner for his contribution to the commemorative publication *Gateway to Inner Space* (Rätsch, 1990), he stressed that: "It is probably not necessary for me to emphasize in detail how much I agree with your thoughts and opinions. We have both drunk from the same source."

From then on, they met more frequently at international conferences and at the Rittimatte. Their conversations and letters deal with chemistry and alchemy, revolving around the differences between pure ingredients and plant-based compounds, and discuss the advantages and disadvantages of synthetic substances in comparison to those occurring naturally. Metzner wrote to Hofmann in 1999: "As Paracelsus once said, the difference between medicine and poison is a matter of dosage. Maybe plants are safer because the dosage is lower and the concentrations are more effective because the dosage is higher. Then safety and effectiveness would depend more on

Albert Hofmann with Ralph Metzner at the Rittimatte, July 2007

the experience cannot be psychologically integrated and results in mental disturbance which leads to catastrophic behavior. Despite a very great therapeutic range, the proper dosage is also crucial for LSD."

Metzner's contribution on alchemy as a spiritual path for the book *Albert Hofmann und die Entdeckung des LSD* (Bröckers, Liggenstorfer 2006) closes with the words: "I am *not* saying that LSD or any other psychoactive molecule *is* the legendary Philosopher's Stone. I am saying that through the discovery of psychedelic substances, and in particular LSD (with its extreme potency), and with his immediate recognition of its spiritual significance,

setting, awareness and usage." Hofmann's response was: "The difference between pure substances and plant-based compounds (entire plants or extracts) is that that the former can be dosed more precisely than herbal preparations. This is extremely important for highly active substances with low therapeutic range (the ratio of a dose of moderate effect to a dose that is fatal). For heroin, the therapeutic range is very narrow, namely 1:3, i.e., if one took three times as much as for a normal dosage, it is fatal; hence the high number of heroin deaths. For LSD, the therapeutic range is very broad. An exact value is not established since no LSD fatalities are known in which death was due to the physical toxicity of LSD. The danger of LSD consists in the depth of its psychological effect, if

Ralph Metzner 2008

Albert Hofmann has re-connected the broken thread of the West's alchemical wisdom tradition. With his published contributions to scientific chemistry and medicine, at the time and the place in which he found himself, he provided all present and future seekers a wonderful aid in their quest for that most precious water-stone of wisdom, and a key to liberating self-knowledge. For that, I bow to Albert Hofmann, from the depths of my soul, with the most profound gratitude." When they next met in the summer of 2006 at the Rittimatte, Hofmann greeted him warmly with the words: "Instead of bowing, allow me to embrace you."

Wisdom of Years

Plants give us nourishment, they give us healing remedies, and they give us medicaments for consciousness. From sunlight, plants produce our food and the air we breathe. And our consciousness is ultimately nothing other than the highest transformation of this solar energy. We are children of the sun! *Albert Hofmann*

Reflections on Nature

On the Rittimatte, Albert Hofmann found the childhood paradise he had lost. It reminded him of the place "where I was happy as a lad, the Jura meadows with the same flowers and the same broad view into the distance." As a boy, he had promised himself that one day he "would again live in a countryside like the Jura." On his ninetieth birthday, he presented his relatives and friends with the illustrated book *Lob des Schauens* which he'd had privately printed in a limited edition. In the text, he pays homage to experiencing and appreciating nature by looking intently at things; the image section comprises twenty-five photographs of butterflies, all of which Rittimatte. He explains that as a child he did not wish to grow any older than thirty-five because he found "people who were older than that were no longer beautiful." He later revised his view, "but the love for all things beautiful has never left me. So a desire grew within to make something beautiful in honor of such a lofty birthday, now that one is not so beautiful anymore, and to somehow combine that with thoughts and insights which have come with age." He wanted to reactivate his artistic talent and to make pencil sketches or water colors of the landscape and record his thoughts on the subject of beauty. However, when he saw a publication by his former colleague Werner Huber with photos of butterflies, he changed his mind and asked Huber whether he would contribute the image section to his anniversary edition. Huber was delighted to oblige since he had been researching the microfauna of Jura meadows in his free time for years and was the perfect choice for this task. At different seasons of the year, Werner Huber would roam the Rittimatte with his camera.

LOB DES SCHAUENS

Albert Hofmann

The real magic of discovery lies not in seeking new landscapes, but in having new eyes.

Marcel Proust

Illustration of Albert Hofmann by Jakob Krattiger, 2004

Gaby Duttwyler-Hofmann, Andreas Hofmann, Beatrix Nabholz-Hofmann at Lake Lucerne on their parents' diamond wedding anniversary, 1995

The oldest and youngest residents of Burg

Hofmann recalls, "Sometimes I went with him on his stalking trips. These were special adventures: In the midday heat of summer we watched butterflies soaring in the tall fragrant grass; or in springtime we searched along the edge of the forest for the first lemon-yellow brimstone butterfly." Collaboration with the adroit photographer was a great pleasure and brought back memories of earlier days when his hobby was taking pictures and developing them in his own darkroom. Hofmann's *Lob des Schauens* ends with the conclusion that love is the highest level of seeing: "The scientific view of vision makes us aware of the wonderful, fundamental fact that each person creates his own image of the world within. That is true for the higher animals as well, but only humans are able to interpret and understand the spiritual message this image conveys—the wordless revelation of the CREATOR. In this way, by means of thinking, seeing becomes observing. All knowledge, and hence our entire humanity, is based on observing. Observing enhances our awareness of the wonder of creation and of our own creaturehood. Since the evolution of humankind parallels the expansion of consciousness, the perfection of seeing in order to observe is of the greatest significance.

There are different levels of development in the progression from seeing to observing. Mere perception of an object without its arousing our interest is the first level. In the second, the object stimulates our interest.

At the third level, the object is considered in more detail and examined, which is the beginning of thought and scientific exploration. The highest level of seeing and relating to an object is reached when the boundaries between subject and object, between observer and observed, between

> A scientific world-view which does not profoundly come to terms with the problem of conscious minds can have no serious pretensions of completeness.
>
> *Sir Roger Penrose*

> To recognize the action of nature and to recognize in what way human action should relate to nature: That is the goal.
>
> *Zhuangzi*

On his 90th birthday, Albert Hofmann invited the residents of Burg to an aperitif and light fare in the village Ackermann restaurant, January 1996

my consciousness and the outside world have been removed: When I am one with the world and its spiritual foundation. That is the state of love.

The highest level of seeing is love. The converse is also true: Love can be defined as the highest level of seeing. No higher praise can be rendered to seeing than that it has been elevated to observing."

Secrets of A Long Life

Hofmann maintained his daily routine and self-discipline into his old age. Nearly every morning he wrote in his diary and answered letters. In the afternoon he and his wife often received friends and guests who were served elegantly prepared cakes and tea. And as a rule, they were offered one or two small glasses of kirsch, greengage or mirabelle plum brandy which he had distilled from his own garden. Their children and the growing number of grandchildren were frequent visitors, as were Albert's sister Anni and his brother Walter. Sometimes the Hofmanns became pensive

and sad that because of their old age, they had already lost so many friends.

After he'd caused a small fender-bender in his early nineties, Hofmann decided to give up driving a car. Whenever the Hofmanns had to leave the Rittimatte, they called a taxi from a neighboring village. Hofmann took a daily walk. He liked to sunbathe. A woman friend recalled: "I came to pick him up one hot summer day. He wasn't ready yet and still had to dress after he had lain naked for a half hour each on his stomach and his back in the blazing sun."

When asked for the secret to his vigor at such an advanced age, Hofmann mentioned several reasons of which the first was the daily morning swim which the fit and active couple continued into their later years. Mareile Wolff was amazed when they vacationed together on the Greek Isle of Samos that the couple, even though they were over ninety, swam in the sea before breakfast.

Hofmann considered it healthy to eat raw eggs because they contained everything

327

Kenya 1974

In the Dordogne, 1990

Ling Chi, the Chinese mushroom
of immortality, on Albert
Hofmann's shelf

a creature needed. His breakfast consisted of *muesli* (raw grains, fruits and nuts) with two, sometimes three, beaten raw eggs. That cholesterol should be a problem he found absurd. For lunch he usually prepared himself an oatmeal soup enriched with a goodly portion of cream. Hofmann did daily exercise for his health, since, at his age, he had already lost many so many friends and acquaintances. It was important to him to regularly stimulate blood circulation in his brain. In their daily fitness program, the Hofmanns hung upside down, using a set of rings installed outside the house. This activity so worried their children that they bought them a professional inversion device. That Hofmann trained regularly can be seen from his diary: "Finished the daily gymnastic exercises feeling totally fit, lifted barbells, suspension by the feet with head below, sprinting on the mowed meadow behind the house, barefoot, this time, a complete gymnast."[212]

Lastly, Hofmann's positive attitude towards life and the ability to be present and enjoy every moment contributed to his vitality. Whenever you called him and he got out

his agenda to check his appointment calendar, he could usually be heard whistling happily to himself. Nor did he allow others' expectations to pressure him. If requests exceeded his capacity and he felt overloaded, he merely said: "After all, I'm not ninety anymore!"

Hofmann survived a severe crisis in 2002. On Pentecost, he fell at home and had to have a hip replacement surgery. After the operation, he developed complications because his physicians told him to become active much too early. His fear of a second procedure was so great that he told a number of persons close to him that he would prefer not to live any longer. The medical professor in charge, however, was able to calm him. The second surgery proceeded satisfactorily, but required a longer hospital stay and several weeks in a rehabilitation clinic in Rheinfelden near Basel.

For the Hofmanns to smoothly manage their daily routine in their seclusion, they had to rely on support. Their children helped a great deal, especially their son Andreas, who lived nearby and assisted them in all matters. Hofmann preferred receiving help from a trusted person rather than hiring strangers, which sometimes led to friction. For the most part, an unusually cordial relationship reigned within the entire family.

Frontier Areas

Albert Hofmann believed that a scientist who studied the wonder of creation and did not thereby become a mystic was not a natural scientist. Simon Duttwyler described his grandfather's attitude as being open to all empirical observations and that he "never said that anything could not be, rather, 'keeping in perspective, it exists but we simply don't yet know how it works.'"[213] With this approach, he shows an openness toward paranormal phenomena, a topic that always was touched upon in his conversations with Lucius Werthmüller due to the nature of the latter's work. Anthropologist and professor of parapsychology, Stanley Krippner was also among Hofmann's good friends. Hofmann corresponded extensively with the exceptional Irish medium Eileen J. Garrett, founder of the well-known Parapsychology Foundation, with whom

he met at her conferences in Southern France. He was interested in her plans for investigating whether the use of psychedelics favored the appearance of paranormal phenomena. For Hofmann, paranormal phenomena such as telepathy and telekinesis were easily conceivable; the empirical observations that suggest their existence convinced him.

He was likewise open to the notion of spiritual healing methods. When his oldest son Dieter in his teenaged years suffered from a knee problem that resisted therapy, Hofmann sent him to a healer recommended to him by an acquaintance and scheduled a series of treatment sessions. Although the young man thought the healer's methods were strange, he had to admit that, contrary to his expectation, the problem gradually disappeared and never bothered him again. Hofmann harbored no doubt about a life after death. His friend Mareile Wolff remembers: "We often spoke about dying and death. He said that he had absolutely no fear of death because he was one-hundred percent certain that death was only a transformation,

Albert Hofmann greets the Dalai Lama at the conference of the International Transpersonal Association 1983 in Davos

Albert Hofmann, Greg Dugan (m.) R. Buckminster Fuller at the Institute of Ecotechnics Conference, France, 1982

329

Galactic Conference, September 17 to 20, 1982, Institute of Ecotechnics, Aix-en-Provence. (front, l. to r.) R. Buckminster Fuller, Lynn Margulis, Albert Hofmann, Mark Nelson, David Malin, Krafft Ehricke, Phil Hawes, Roy Walford (rear, l. to r.) Richard Dawkins, Graham Leonard, William Dempster, Ben Epperson, Victor Clube, Robert Hahn

a transition into a different form of existence. Therefore, he was curious and looked forward to the life hereafter."

Art and Ability

Hofmann was happy when he was actively creating: He drew, painted, sculpted and photographed. In his understanding, art always had to do with beauty. Competence in craftsmanship was a prerequisite for him to qualify a work as art. He could appreciate art up to the classical moderns; he loved Picasso's work in all its phases. On the other hand, he could not relate to contemporary art: Installations, performance and action art left him cold, as did the paintings of Jackson Pollock. He'd even considered Joseph Beuys a charlatan, until he had studied his drawings, whereupon he amended his judgment.

Although neither he nor his wife played an instrument, Hofmann retained a close relationship with classical music. He wanted to learn to play the piano but soon gave it up. "He wished to make us do what he himself could not. He had us learn instruments; for me it took a whip. Dieter played clarinet, Gaby the piano, and I, flute and guitar. Whenever we had company, she and I always had to play, Gaby on the piano, and I on the flute. For me it was no fun,"Andreas recalls.[214] Hofmann's favorite composers were Schubert, Beethoven and Wolfgang Amadeus Mozart whom he loved above all others. As with modern art, Hofmann did not appreciate modern music. Through his son Andreas he developed an understanding of jazz: "I played jazz, and he was always up for that. He found a connection through us, not to modern jazz, but to Dixieland. As a flautist, I played cool jazz, which he found interesting."

Rilke, Goethe and Schiller were among his favorite authors. He was especially fond of Goethe's philosophy of nature. He also read twentieth century literature, in particular the works of Huxley and Jünger whom he highly esteemed as writers and as friends.

Hofmann found no opposition or contradiction between art, faith and science: They simply represented different forms of contemplation. He admired the painters, composers and writers whose works he loved and marveled: "How can a person create something out of nothing?" That was for him the distinction between an artist, a genuine creator, and a chemist, who builds upon something that already exists

Drawings from Albert Hofmann's travel diaries

Handwriting Analysis for Albert Hofmann

For the analysis of the handwriting of Albert Hofmann, four samples of his script were used: Three in his original hand from the years 1966, 1975 and 2006 and the fourth, a copy of an entry from a lab journal made in 1943 on the occasion of his first self-experiment with LSD. The originals were written when Albert Hofmann was sixty, seventy-four, and one-hundred years old. The journal entry was made when he was thirty-seven. Whether that entry from 1943 was made while he was under the influence of LSD is not known. Below, the sample from when Hofmann was thirty-seven years old is described and psychologically interpreted, independent of the conditions under which it was made. It is striking how concentrated, disciplined, precise and small the writing is and how attention was paid to clearly place the letters in the space. As a writing instrument, a pointed pen was most likely used. In contrast with the upstrokes, the broad downward strokes indicate strong pressure. Moreover, the writer strove to write legibly. Legibility largely stems from paying attention to the patterns taught in school, avoiding separated letters, and moving in a continuous line. The writing appears to have required great effort which also led to crowding.

Movement, shape, use of space and the nature of the strokes are the elements of handwriting that make it possible to comment about personality.

One must assume that the sample from 1943 reflects the scientist's "professional writing," seeking to communicate his findings clearly and unambiguously. This sample contains little personal expression.

The writing movement is controlled. With several of the ascenders or descenders, it is somewhat more expansive. Motion constraint shows that volition and intellect prevail and emotional impulses remain under control. This need not lead to an emotionally neutral appearance. Increased writing pressure and excessive strokes here and there point to temperament and intensity. While impulsiveness seems to be controlled, it may subliminally "bubble up."

To interpret the tense, and in many instances sensitive and sharp strokes, one must assume that the writer is also sensitive and irritable. One could speak of controlled affect and driven dynamism.

Will and discipline are shown in the precise form of the letters. He must have been a tenacious, persistent, sometimes even stubborn negotiator. The writing indicates astute analytic thinking and an aggressive problem- solving style. The placement of the letters indicates planning, structured action, organization and the need for clear and regulated procedures.

This writing sample suggests a person strongly guided by willpower and rationality who is a precise, and systematic thinker, and man of principle with endurance, a strong work ethic, but also with the tendency to demand much of himself, to put pressure on himself while keeping emotions under control.

The later, more spontaneously written samples corroborate the impression that the handwriting from 1943 was strongly shaped by professional influence that barely allowed for the expression of temperament, drive and feelings.

The sample from 1966 similarly shows discipline, precision, toughness, and the capacity to persist. The writing is here more relaxed and spontaneous. The writer displays more vitality, spontaneity, and naturalness. Here and there, a sense of humor even shows itself, through will and self-control should not be overlooked—also vitality and strong drive, with a constitution showing great psychic vitality.

The handwriting from 1975 shows much more dynamism than the others. Self-confidence, poise, openness and immediacy can be seen. The personality seems more harmonious and open in contrast with earlier when will and reason were more dominant. Élan, verve, receptivity and emotional vigor, but also impulsiveness, are directly expressed. In a playful way vanities and self-expression also come across.

This personality values recognition and admiration and hardly would hide its light under a bushel.

Zest for action, joy of living, spontaneous interest, curiosity, motivation and spontaneity, sometimes with overbearing features, are characteristics that have manifested themselves to those about him.

These features are also found in the sample from the one-hundred year old writer. The writing does show some aspects of aging. The vitality shown in the hand of the sixty-four year old has lost some of its verve and expansiveness. Qualities such as clarity, orderliness, stability and uniformity come to the fore while volition and self-control have gained in significance.

As in the first sample where discipline served more to dominate the dynamic energy, this control increasingly serves to use resources optimally. Despite a more placid and balanced rhythm, openness, spontaneous interest and emo-tional responsiveness, as well as still-youthful confidence are not lost—even though the earlier excess in energy of younger years no longer was available.

Fritz Gassner, Graphologist SGG, Zurich

A Grandson Remembers

An atmospheric and vivid picture of Anita and Albert Hofmann in old age is portrayed by their grandson Simon Duttwyler, who followed in the chemist's footsteps, studying at the University of Zurich like his grandfather where he obtained his doctorate in 2010: "Whenever I think of my grandparents, I always see the two of them together. My earliest memories are of family reunions, such as my grandfather's eightieth birthday. From primary school and up until their deaths, I regularly spent a week to ten days with my grandparents during vacation. These visits were always very interesting. As a child I couldn't imagine anything better than to be in this house, surrounded by nature. I was free to do what I wished and felt at home. My grandparents often had visitors, intellectuals and artists. I especially remember the

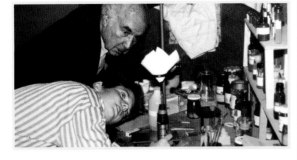

The chemistry set turns into a veritable laboratory; time for a consultation from the expert

Simon Duttwyler in conversation with the authors in Basel, 2010

Cherry harvest

warmth of their hospitality towards all guests. What I miss most today is the feeling of security that they gave me. My grandfather had more time for me than he'd had for my mother and her siblings.

I especially treasure memories of the times we spent together outdoors, of grandfather's genuine reverence for plants and animals. He knew all the plants, which impresses me to this day because I still can't name them. He would rhapsodize over anything beautiful, such as gemstones. He could sit in front of his work place at seven in the morning meditating on dewdrops on the grass and say: 'See how beautiful that is.' He noticed and observed so many tiny, inconspicuous things which most people passed by without a thought. He took nothing for granted, rather he always asked himself anew: How can a tree grow out of such a small seed? To him it was a mystery and he passed along this mindset to me. Pausing

and asking: Is that simply so or is there something more to it? He questioned much that others regarded as trivial. An important factor in his success as a chemist was that he didn't allow himself to be influenced by preconceived notions, but approached every task with an open mind. He had very deep insight into existing scientific knowledge. He often said there was still something miraculous behind things. You can't simply dismiss this statement as ignorance. I have the same attitude today: There are things we can investigate, but never fully explain. My world view was decisively influenced by my grandparents.

My grandfather looked at things seriously: "When I see all that works together so that life may function, I must assume that there is an ingenious plan behind it." He thought it unscientific to suppose that everything could be explained without some higher power. When he spoke of the creator, he didn't concretize the concept. When I was a child there was a prayer before going to sleep. Despite that, grandfather wasn't devoutly religious, and we were never together in a church.

In retrospect, I am amazed at how readily comprehensible his writings are. One of his great achievements was that he could write simply and clearly about complicated and complex topics.

When I was about eleven years old, he showed me how to grow crystals by adding a seed crystal to a sugar or table salt solution. That fascinated me and we then bought chemicals with which to grow colored crystals. That aroused my interest in further chemical experiments. For Christmas, my parents gave me a chemistry set which I took along to the Rittimatte on vacations. My grandfather never tried to steer me in the direction of chemistry and never spoke of my possibly studying chemistry; during my studies, we seldom talked shop about chemical issues. Indirectly, however, his ongoing palpable fascination made the difference for me. My grandfather followed developments in chemistry well into his advanced years. He wanted to see my text books and was enthused when he browsed through them. He thought whatever I mentioned about my studies was marvelous and that he was happy for me. Never did he say that in the old days things used to be better."[215]

Albert Hofmann Turns One Hundred

Still mentally and physically fit, the "old man of the mountain" celebrated his centenary on January 11, 2006. He invited the entire village for cocktails and snacks that evening in the village tavern, Restaurant Ackermann. A few days later, the villagers gave him a photo album of all the pictures taken at the event. The commune presented him with a new bench above the Rittimatte with the inscription: "For the 100th Birthday of Albert Hofmann." The whole family and many friends were invited to a private birthday celebration held the following Saturday at the moated castle in Bottmingen. His three surviving children reviewed and commented on their father's long life and also showed numerous slides—Andreas took the first third, his sisters Gaby and Beatrix the following parts of his life. Hans Hagenbuch, the eldest son of Hofmann's boyhood friend Werner Hagenbuch, and Richard Stadler entertained the guests with anecdotes from his past. Martin Vosseler, a committed environmental activist and a friend of the jubilarian for several years, brought some episodes of Hofmann's life alive in poetic form which made the audience smile.

The Gaia Media Foundation organized an official ceremony that was held in the packed auditorium of the Basel Museum der Kulturen on the morning of January 11. Among the two-hundred invited guests were many scheduled to speak at the symposium planned for the following weekend who had arrived several days in advance to join the tribute. Even being in poor health could not prevent Anita Hofmann from attending. Stanislav Grof made a special trip from the USA but, because of conflicts in his agenda, he regretted that he could not participate in the symposium. Print journalists, radio stations and television channels were well repre-

Albert Hofmann at one hundred years on his bench, a present of the commune
on his milestone birthday

Albert Hofmann and his guests at his private celebration on Saturday
January 14th, 2006 at the Restaurant Schloss Bottmingen

Anita and Albert Hofmann

The family celebrates the centenarien

Albert Hofmann-Rain in Bottmingen

(l. to r.) Chris Heidrich, Wolfang Maria Ohlhäuser, Albert Hofmann, Roger Liggenstorfer

The von Kreuziger couple congratulates the jubilarian

sented at the ceremony. Hofmann was honored by brief speeches from Basel government councilor, Christoph Eymann, director of research at Novartis, Paul Herrling, philosopher Hans Saner, gallery owner and art dealer Ernst Beyeler, writer Martin Suter, and Dieter Hagenbach of the Gaia Media Foundation. At Hofmann's request, the laudation was given by his longtime friend Rolf Verres. Interludes of music by the well-known violinist Volker Biesenbender played in between the speeches. Afterwards, a reception with cocktails was held at the museum's restaurant, Rollerhof, where Hofmann received warm congratulations.

Swiss Television broadcast three segments on Hofmann's birthday, including one on the main evening news. The local television station, Telebasel, made Hofmann's milestone birthday its evening news feature story. The national radio station DRS 1 devoted a special two-hour program while DRS 3 dedicated an entire day to the event. The *New York Times* honored him as did dozens of media channels throughout the world. Swiss Federal President Moritz Leuenberger congratulated him with a personal letter:

336

Christoph Eymann   Paul Herrling   Ernst Beyeler   Hans Saner   Martin Suter

Albert Hofmann addresses the audience and the media at the end of the LSD Symposium

Dear Doctor Hofmann,

It is a privilege and gives me great pleasure to congratulate you on your one hundredth birthday!

If there were, in Switzerland, a council of the wise, you most certainly belong to it. (To avoid any misunderstanding, I do not mean this council is supposed to be the Federal Council....) I know, you modestly wave to decline. You do not seek out the spotlight and are not eager to always be asked your opinion. Even so, you are among those whose words carry some weight and have an impact. You are a great researcher of human consciousness.

In your writings you raise questions that concern us all: How do we perceive our environment? How real is that which we experience as reality?

I must confess that I, being active in politics, sometimes immensely yearn for objectivity or at least wish for it to be a hope....

However, I can console myself with your insights: You recognized, very early on, that rational knowledge reaches limits and that not everything can be objectified. Therefore, you have spoken out on behalf of subjective experience as also belonging to the realm of science. Mysticism as the highest form of subjective knowledge does not contradict reason; on the contrary,

337

Albert Hofmann signs the petition, Promotion of Scientific Research of Psychoactive Substances

(l. to r.) H.R. Giger, Albert Hofmann, Stanislav Grof, at the reception following the official celebration

it extends reason. There is not only one reality and one view of things, rather there are unlimited possibilities of perception.

You thus represent a fundamental concern of the Enlightenment. It would be fatal to banish every subjective understanding from science, since that would mean, in the final analysis, excluding human consciousness itself from science.

Through your research and writings, Dr. Hofmann, you have helped keep artistic, philosophical and religious questions alive in scientific discussions.

I thank you for your inspiring and equally beneficial thoughts and wish you all the best for your birthday.

Sincerely,
Moritz Leuenberger

Hofmann's delight in receiving the Federal President's thoughts can be seen in his letter of thanks.

Dear Mr. Leuenberger,

Of all the good wishes and tributes bestowed upon me on my centenary, your letter has given me the greatest pleasure and honor. For this most valuable gift, I thank you from my heart.

If all citizens and representatives of the media were as well informed about political issues as you are about philosophy and natural science, the Federal Council could more easily carry out the measures it deems necessary.

It would be my wish that more politicians develop keener environmental awareness and deeper insight into the big picture of the cycles in nature.

Let us hope that the symposium in Basel has contributed to an expansion of consciousness in this direction.

If ever-increasing numbers of people were to realize the natural richness, beauty, and wonder of creation, this expanded awareness could preserve nature before it is destroyed and could save humanity from extinction.

With warm regards,
Albert Hofmann

Rolf Verres   Ralph Metzner   Christian Rätsch   David E. Nichols   Günter Amendt

Concert by the band Guru Guru

The Old Man and His Child

As related above, on the occasion of Albert Hofmann's one-hundredth birthday, the Gaia Media Foundation presented the international symposium "LSD - Problem Child and Wonder Drug" in Basel.[216] However, there was one big obstacle to preparations that had to be faced. The Congress Center had already been booked for that birthday weekend on behalf of their annual earnings press conference by Novartis, the successor company to Sandoz for which Albert Hofmann had worked his entire professional life. It took perseverance to convince the global corporation's management to yield the space to Gaia Media for the desired date, but yield they did. The symposium took place from January 13 to 15 under the sponsorship of such eminent institutions as: The Beckley Foundation which advises the British government and the United Nations on drug issues; the Society for Medicinal Plant Research of which Hofmann was an honorary member; the European Collegium for Consciousness Studies, founded

> I think that it has never been as necessary in human evolution to have this substance, LSD. It is just a tool to turn us into what we are supposed to be.
>
> *Albert Hofmann*

Lucius Werthmüller in conversation with Albert Hofmann at the LSD Symposium

THE SPIRIT OF BASEL

LSD

Problem Child and Wonder Drug

International Symposium
on the Occasion of the 100th Birthday
of Albert Hofmann

January 13th – 15th 2006
Convention Center Basel, Switzerland

Lectures • Panels • Seminars • Workshops
Exhibitions • Multimedia • Concerts • Parties
www.LSD.info

by his friend Hanscarl Leuner; the Swiss Medical Society for Psycholytic Therapy; the American drug documentation organization Erowid, and the Multidisciplinary Association for Psychedelic Studies. The Heffter Research Center at the Psychiatric Clinic of the University of Zurich and the Heffter Research Institute of Santa Fe, New Mexico, provided overall patronage for the scientific parts of the conference.

Almost sixty years after Hofmann's momentous discovery, more than eighty scientists, consciousness researchers, therapists, artists and witnesses from around the world illuminated the phenomenon of LSD from all perspectives and discussed its history, spread, potential, dangers and effects in more than sixty informative lectures, presentations, seminars and panel discussions.

On the first day of the congress, the history of the drug was featured under the title: From the Plants of the Gods to LSD. On Saturday, The Ecstatic Adventure covered the broad spectrum of its uses and effects.

On Sunday, contributions focused on New Dimensions of Consciousness, visions of a new way to deal with LSD. The symposium drew the elite of international consciousness researchers, among others: psychiatrists Charles S. Grob and Ralph Metzner, pharmacologist David E. Nichols, Alexander and Ann Shulgin from the USA; sociologist and drug expert Günter Amendt, ethnologist Christian Rätsch, and brain researcher Franz Vollenweider from Europe. Prominent artists such as Alex Grey and eyewitnesses such as Barry Miles came to Basel to speak of their personal experiences with LSD and its influence on art and culture. There was great interest in the remarks of the venerable chemist Alexander T. Shulgin, who had created hundreds of psychedelic substances in the previous fifty years.

Without a doubt, the highest points of the event were the appearances by Albert Hofmann whose life work was recognized in a tribute by Rolf Verres and in several lectures. In two conversations with Lucius Werthmüller, the mentally alert guest of honor related the dramatic story of his

Michael Horowitz   Alexander Shulgin   Juraj Styk   Jeremy Narby   Barry Miles

famous discovery and articulated his visions and hopes for his "problem child" and its potential to become a "wonder drug." Several times he expressed the wish that this symposium might provide impetus for a new way of thinking. He was greeted with a storm of flashbulbs from dozens of photographers and appreciated with a standing ovation from the international audience.

In the lobby of the Congress Center several exhibits were to be seen, including a photo documentary of "100 Years of Albert Hofmann." There were wall panels displaying correspondence and documents from Hofmann's personal archives as well as many historical documents and objects on the subject of LSD. In addition to the conference, a broad spectrum of cultural programs was offered, including concerts and parties. More than two thousand people participated in the symposium coming from every continent and over thirty-five countries. Hofmann was the first to sign a petition to the responsible authorities in Bern and Brussels calling for a new, impartial policy concerning the use of LSD and related substances and requesting that LSD be made available again for scientific

research. Nearly all the speakers signed below the signature of the birthday celebrant. In the closing event, Hofmann was moved to express his feeling that his "problem child has definitely become a wonder child." The future-oriented conference was for him "my biggest birthday gift." As the two authors (Hagenbach and Werthmüller) accompanied him to his taxi Sunday evening to take leave, Albert Hofmann had tears of joy in his eyes. He embraced them and said: "Now we are like the 'three confederates'" (referring to founders of Switzerland in 1291).

The Congress Center is attached to a five-star hotel where the speakers were staying. The hotel's director was a woman who had known one of Hofmann's daughters since their teens. She provided a room at no cost for Hofmann for the duration of the conference so that he could rest from his exertions now and again. To give her employees an idea of what significant occasion this congress marked, she asked us to prepare an information sheet on LSD. The hotel lobby was a place where different worlds met. An Indonesian government official on state

John "Hoppy" Hopkins,
John Dunbar

At the speaker's reception:
Franz X. Vollenweider, Mark A.
Geyer, David E. Nichols

(l. to r.) Bettina Werthmüller, Dieter Hagenbach, Albert Hofmann, Lucius Werthmüller,
Sabin Sütterlin

Demonstration by the International Society for Human Rights outside the forum

business in Switzerland wondered about the unconventional, colorful mix of guests and the sweet smell that hung in the air. When the International Society for Human Rights, a group close to the Church of Scientology, requested permission from city authorities to hold a demonstration against the event, the Basel police ensured the group's organizers of their protection in case any problems might arise.

The congress promoted general acceptance of psychedelic research. Some two-hundred journalists and film crews from around the globe followed the symposium. Worldwide media coverage was huge, largely positive and characterized by objectivity.

Yet Another Tribute

Hofmann regarded the marriage of Sandoz with Ciba-Geigy in 1986 with suspicion. After its announcement, he wrote Richard Schultes: "Perhaps you have heard that Sandoz and Ciba have merged into a giant new company with the name Novartis. The rise in the stock price was sensational and 10,000 people lost their jobs. A pure crime!" Nonetheless, Hofmann accepted an invitation to lunch on his ninety-fifth birthday with Daniel Vasella, board president until 2013 and, from 1996 to 2010, CEO of Novartis. Vasella arranged for him to be picked

Daniel Vasella congratulates Albert Hofmann

on ergot alkaloids and gives a historical survey of the company's natural product research department. This is followed by a contribution from Werner Huber, the photographer who contributed the pictures in *Lob des Schauens*, and, longer personal statements by his friends Rolf Verres and Volker Biesenbender on philosophical aspects of Hofmann's work. The final piece from Engel is about St. Anthony's fire in the art of the Middle Ages.

The speech was delivered by Daniel Vasella. The celebration was enriched with songs from Richard Strauss, Robert Schumann and Johannes Brahms. Volker Biesenbender and his trio, Avodah, played a medley of art and folk music from five centuries. Hofmann, accompanied by his wife and children, enjoyed the music and the tribute on the site of his former workplace which, thirty-five years after his retirement, was scarcely recognizable.

up at the Rittimatte and chauffeured home afterwards.

Novartis invited around two hundred guests to a celebration on February 7, 2006 in their auditorium to honor Hofmann's one hundredth birthday. Former Sandoz employee, Günter Engel gave an overview of Hofmann's accomplishments and presented him with a commemorative publication, *Grenzgänge—Albert Hofmann zum 100. Geburtstag* (Engel, Herrling 2006), that he and research director Paul Herrling had prepared. The book opens with an introduction to Hofmann's work

Without a doubt, merthergin helped save thousands of lives, but its worldwide fame was due to another substance, namely the synthesis of LSD. The path from ergot to LSD shows that this was no chance discovery, but rather the result of systematic research activity carried out tenaciously over years.

Your contribution to pharmaceutical chemistry not only led to the success of your former company Sandoz and hence to that of Novartis afterwards, but it also earned you great distinction in the pharmaceutical and medical world, which led to numerous honorary doctorates and awards.

Daniel Vasella's address honoring Albert Hofmann on February 7, 2006, Novartis, Basel

Between Earth and Heaven

Everything ends in mystery. Heraclitus

Connections with the Whole World

Until the end of his life, Albert Hofmann maintained ties with his countless friends. He corresponded with them and wanted to know how they were doing. He carefully and personally answered inquiries received from people around the world even those whom he did not know. He wrote his letters by hand, seldom using a typewriter. Fascinated by the possibilities offered by computers, he marveled at the speed of modern communication modes. However, he had strong reservations about these innovations and followed the advance of technology in the world with a critical eye. His voluminous correspondence recurrently demonstrates Hofmann's kindness and sympathy as well as his comprehensive knowledge. It is amazing how few corrections he ever made in his handwriting. In the tradition of Goethe, whom he admired, the process of answering correspondence was part of Hofmann's daily ritual.

On his one-hundredth birthday, he received bushels of letters, birthday cards and presents, including many from visitors to the LSD Symposium. Even though the authors assured him that the congratulants did not expect a personal answer, he could not be dissuaded. During the next months, he undertook to send handwritten thank-you notes for every single gift and greeting card.

Although his address and telephone number were listed in all directories, the authors continuously received inquiries from journalists around the world wishing to know how they could get in touch with Hofmann. As a rule, he always answered the phone himself. Even if guests were present, he would pick it up as soon as it rang.

The Albert Hofmann Medal

Since 2007 the University of Zurich has been awarding the Albert Hofmann Medal every one or two years for outstanding achievement in organic chemistry. Simon Duttwyler described how the idea for this prestigious award came about: "During my studies I never mentioned that Albert Hofmann

is my grandfather because of the unforeseeable and diverse reactions. Surprisingly, many conservative people often react with openness while supposedly liberal people close down. After I had completed my studies, my grandfather was giving a lecture in Zurich. I casually mentioned to my professor, Jay Siegal, that the discoverer of LSD was giving a lecture because I wanted to see his reaction. His great interest led me to tell him that he was my grandfather and to request that he please handle this information confidentially. Soon thereafter, we drove to the Rittimatte and visited my grandparents. Jay Siegal was impressed with them. Since 1959 the University of Zurich has awarded the Karrer Medal, one of the most prestigious distinctions in chemistry, whose winners often subsequently receive the Nobel Prize. Siegel wanted to establish a similar prize in my grandfather's name. He was of the opinion that this was appropriate, given his achievements and renown and he promptly set things in motion." An independent committee awards the prize. The first to be so honored was Princess Chulabhorn Walailak, a Thai chemist who had founded an institute for researching traditional Thai herbal remedies in Bangkok, "where research similar to what Hofmann did at Sandoz sixty years earlier is undertaken." Albert Hofmann was present at the ceremony and was very impressed by the attractive princess and her research.

> I believe that psychedelics used wisely would enable us as individuals and collectively as a society to develop a sense of core identity that transcends divisive distinctions based on national origin, religion, race, gender, class and political orientation.
>
> *Rick Doblin*

From Problem Child to Wonder Drug

After a survey of 4,000 British citizens carried out in 2007 by *The Telegraph*, Hofmann was selected by a jury of six experts as the most important living genius. He shared first place with British computer scientist Tim Berners-Lee, who founded the World Wide Web at CERN in Geneva. In third place came George Soros, the American investor, and not until seventh place was the name of physicist Stephen Hawking to be found. Hofmann reacted to this great honor with the words: "Not I, LSD was chosen."[217]

There is sound and magic to those three letters which have an impact even seventy years after LSD's discovery. The story of LSD and the counterculture has long since become a subject of historians. Psychedelic substances are being newly evaluated and a more objective tone can be discerned. Even if LSD is an extraordinary substance, it remains a mystery as to why it made such waves compared to mescaline, which has similar effects and has long been known but has never attracted such great attention. The success and renown of the substance have to do with the personality of its discoverer. Although he did not receive the Nobel Prize, Hofmann is the best known chemist of the twentieth century. His name will forever be inextricably linked to the discovery that made him world-famous. Whereas, only experts know which chemists discovered such successful medicines and substances as the birth control pill, valium or even morphine and vitamin C.

Albert Hofmann is the only chemist known to a wide public. In his old age, he had the status of a pop star, and not just in California, as the reaction of the public clearly showed when he appeared at the LSD Symposium in Basel.

Back to the Future

In February 2005 *New Scientist* reported a detailed account of a revival of psychedelic medicine, based upon several studies with psychedelics. Organizations such as MAPS, with its energetic driving force, Rick Doblin, are successfully campaigning for the authorization of studies in the USA, Israel, the Netherlands and Switzerland.

At the LSD Symposium in 2006 in Basel, the organizers sent an appeal to the departments of health of various countries to once again allow LSD research. The Swiss minister of the Federal Department of Home Affairs, Pascal Couchepin, in charge for health issues, indicated in his response that, provided there was compliance with the appropriate scientific and ethical stan-

dards, nothing should stand in the way of research projects with LSD.

This was the starting point for a project to study the effects of LSD in the context of psychotherapy. On January 11, 2007, Albert Hofmann's 101st birthday, Peter Gasser, a psychotherapist and physician from Solothurn, Switzerland, submitted a study protocol to the ethics commission of the canton of Aargau for a "LSD-Assisted Psychotherapy for Anxiety Associated with Life-Threatening Illness." The same day, at the invitation of the Gaia Media Foundation, Gasser and other members of the Swiss Medical Society for Psycholytic Therapy, Rick Doblin and representatives of the Multidisciplinary Association for Psychedelic Studies, which is funding the study, and foundation board members Michael Gasser, Dieter Hagenbach and Lucius Werthmüller met in Basel to toast the person of honor. Unfortunately, Hofmann had to cancel his participation at the last minute. In his letter of regret, he thanked all involved and expressed his joy that "my problem child

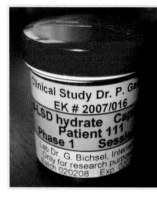

LSD for the study

Peter Gasser with Rick Doblin

Peter Gasser

will finally become a wonder child after all." In November 2007, Peter Gasser received permission from the Swiss Federal Office of Health for his pilot study. After 35 years of forced interruption, it has once again become possible to carry out psychotherapy with LSD.

For Hofmann, who had always highly valued LSD's therapeutic potential, it was a late but significant satisfaction for him to witness the resumption of research into LSD as a tool in psychotherapy. He had long hoped that LSD would be accorded the place it deserved in medicine and spoke of the approval as the "fulfillment of a heart's desire." The path could be long and difficult in Gasser's opinion, "yet a great step towards acceptance has been taken to let both the public and the professional world regard LSD as a medicine." This breakthrough has been reported internationally in the media and subsequently comparable studies are in preparation in various countries.

Gasser's study builds upon work done earlier by Stanislav Grof, Eric Kast and others. According to Gasser, the preliminary results show "that LSD is quite suitable to touch the existential dimension of such people. Confronted with the possibility of impending and premature death as well as suffering pain and helplessness, people with serious, potentially fatal, illnesses are open and ready for an existential experience such as LSD can provide." The study concluded at the end of May 2011 with the final therapy session. Peter Gasser considered an important result to be "that no appreciable side effects or challenging incidents, such as uncontrollable anxiety states (bad trips) or other psychological

crises, arose. On the contrary, all patients reported that they had profited from the treatment. A final statistical analysis will provide more accurate data; however, the finding that LSD psychotherapy is a safe and effective treatment is an important result for such a small pilot study."

The huge media response to this study should not obscure the fact that only a very small minority of physicians and psychiatrists are interested in the medical-therapeutic use of psychedelics. It could take a long time before psychedelic research is as far along as it was forty years ago and the approval of psychedelic substances as adjuncts to therapy and self-exploration is considered normal, not just for study purposes, let alone the fulfillment of Hofmann's wish for a modern Eleusis involving sacred drugs.

Behind Every Strong Man

During marriage, Anita Hofmann, as an independent and determined woman, was responsible for the smooth running of the daily routine, for the household, and for cohesion in the family. She put her own interests and needs last, quietly took care of many things, and protected her husband from intrusions on his privacy and contemplative time. Like many women of her generation, she did not complain about her situation. She was pragmatic and practical by nature; her husband was trusting and seldom imagined anything bad in people. Sometimes she had to discourage him from taking on too many obligations. Like her spouse, she was a good listener, communicative, providing hospitality to every visitor, and was a perfect hostess. Even in her advanced years, she encouraged friends and guests to stay for dinner.

When it was clear that they would soon be moving to their remote new home in 1967, she clandestinely learned how to drive and, after having passed the driver's test, held up her license before the eyes of her astonished family. Anita Hofmann was a plant lover with a green thumb. She liked to talk with her friends Heidi Werthmüller and Mareile Wolff about gardening; they exchanged tips, seeds, cuttings and seedlings.

In the mid-1960s, Anita Hofmann fell ill with Guillain Barré syndrome. She was paralyzed and could not move for several weeks, but her iron will enabled her to exercise and recover much faster than her doctors had predicted. In advanced years, she required hip replacement surgery and was stricken by nearly fatal blood poisoning. In her last years, she suffered almost constantly from pain which she managed without saying much about it.

In front of the family portrait by Basel artist
Irène Zurkinden, June 2006

In the shadow of her famous husband, she accepted the traditional woman's role as a matter of course. At her eightieth birthday celebration she gave a moving talk. Her husband interrupted to correct her about something whereupon she reso-lutely said: "Albert, I am speaking now!"

Farewell and Mourning

Anita Hofmann died at home on December 20, 2007 at the age of ninety-four in the presence of her husband and their daughter Beatrix. Her death did not come as a surprise; she had suffered for years from severe arthritis and required medication to make it bearable. She had arrived at the point where she no longer desired to live. On the eve before her death, the brother of Hedy Brodbeck, the woman renting the apartment in the front of the house, came to visit and gave a little private concert for her on his flute. She could barely speak but through her gestures and facial expressions let him understand how happy it made her. Beatrix Nabholz and Andreas Hofmann were with her as often as possible. Anita Hofmann too believed in "a soul that can fly away when we die," but she did not go into detail and spoke little of the idea of an afterlife.

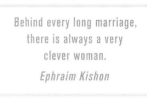

Behind every long marriage, there is always a very clever woman.
Ephraim Kishon

A family can develop only with a loving woman as its core.
Friedrich Schlegel

It was a wrenching loss for her husband, to whom she was married for almost seventy-five years and for whom she had always been a mainstay. A few months earlier, the two had absorbed a heavy stroke of fate, the death of their daughter Gaby.

Albert did not speak much about Anita's death. However, their grandson Simon recalls moments when he "sat in her room and seemed extremely sad." He did not wish to show his pain and grief. "We can't expect him to show the same emotions as people of my generation if you consider the time in which he grew up." But Hofmann knew that, "soon I will go, too, and see Anita again." About a year before his death he mentioned that, similar to an out-of-body experience, he sometimes felt his consciousness was no longer in this world but looking down on himself from outside and in these moments was unsure whether he was still alive at all. He was of the firm conviction that death was a transition into another life and we would see our relatives in the hereafter.

The funeral service for Anita Hofmann was held in the idyllic St. Margarethen church on a small hill overlooking Basel. An incident at Anita's burial which their friend Mareile Wolff recounted was characteristic of Hofmann's nature and his empathy. As she consoled him in front of the chapel, he quickly changed the subject and asked her about her recently published volume of poetry, congratulated her, and emphasized how much he liked her poems.

Anita Hofmann

Echo of a Life's Work

On the occasion of his fiftieth birthday in 1993, Dieter Hagenbach founded the Gaia Media Foundation. Among the guests attending the festivities were Albert and Anita Hofmann, H.R. Giger, Claudia Müller-Ebeling and Christian Rätsch. After the LSD Symposium of 2006, Albert Hofmann expressed the wish to somehow contribute to the foundation's success and he joined its board. On Easter 2008, the Gaia Foundation organized a follow-up event, the World Psychedelic Forum.[218]

More than eighty well-known scientists, drug experts, artists and observers from around the world reported on and discussed aspects of all psychedelic substances from many divergent points of view, including their histories, their effects, and their potentials. The theme of the first day of the congress was Psychedelic Experience: The Gates of Perception Open, while on Saturday the focus was on The Legacy of the Shamans: Old Traditions and New Dimensions. On Sunday, the theme was Transformation of Consciousness: The Challenge of the 21st Century. Among the presenters were Mathias Bröckers, Rick Doblin, Stanislav Grof, Jon Hanna, Kathleen Harrison, Michael Horowitz, Dennis McKenna, Ralph Metzner, Jeremy Narby, Nana Nauwald, Vanja Palmers, Torsten Passie, Dale Pendell, Daniel Pinchbeck, Christian Rätsch, Thomas B. Roberts, Manuel Schoch and Wolf-Dieter Storl. Prominent artists and contemporaries, such as Carolyn Garcia, filmmaker Jan Kounen, art historian Claudia Müller-Ebeling, visionary artist Alex Grey, sadhu Baba Rampuri from

India and shaman Kajuyali Tsamani from Colombia, also came to Basel to describe their personal experiences with psychedelics and their influence on culture and art. The World Psychedelic Forum again was widely reported in the media and attracted some two-thousand participants from thirty-seven countries. A highlight holding great promise for the future was the *Rising Researchers* lectures and discussions, organized and coordinated by Thomas B. Roberts, now retired professor of Educational Psychology. During the three day forum, more than thirty young researchers from different specialties reported on their work.

The Gaia Media Foundation launched two resolutions, signed by presenters and visitors, requesting political and governing bodies of Switzerland and the UN to do everything within their power to adapt regulations regarding the handling of consciousness expanding substances to

---

RESOLUTION

The undersigned speakers of the *World Psychedelic Forum* of Mach 24, 2008 encourage legislators and international policy bodies to reconsider their attitude towards hallucinogenic substances and to take into account modern research findings and societal change.

They are of the opinion that the current prohibition and criminalization policy, expressed in particular in the Convention of Psychotropic Substances of February 21, 1971 (Art. 7 et seq. and Schedule I) and the UN Convention against Illicit Traffic in Narcotic Drugs and Psychotropic Substances of December 20, 1988.

- considerably impedes scientific research on hallucinogenic substances,
- pushes the therapeutic use of such substances into illegality,
- renders a quality control of products sold on already existing markets impossible, criminalizes in particular responsible, also low risk of such substances. Rather, the undersigned speakers and participants of the *World Psychedelic Forum* are convinced,
- that the current equation of hallucinogenic substances (like LSD, Mescaline, Psilocybin) with Heroin and Cocaine does not reflect the true risks involved in their use nor their societal significance,
- that there is no evidence that hallucinogenic substances create dependency,
- that by far, most of the users are able to control the risks involved in their use,
- that prohibition and criminalization are not able to suppress consumption.

The speakers of the *World Psychedelic Forum* maintain that the human right to self-determination of the grown-up and responsible citizen should allow him or her to be the sole judge of what he or she regards as dangerous or unreasonable.

Regulation should be limited to situations where juveniles or handicapped are in need of support or where third parties are put at risk. Administrative regulation is sufficient to address such unwanted risk. Administrative sanctions should be limited to a minimum.

In the spirit of an open and liberal society the undersigned speakers and participants of the *World Psychedelic Forum* appeal to legislators and policy bodies worldwide to reconsider the current simplistic and harmful attitude to hallucinogenic substances.

Rick Doblin   Daniel Pinchbeck   Claudia Müller-Ebeling   Manuel Schoch   Kathleen Harrison

Bia Labate   Wolf-Dieter Storl   Baba Rampuri   Carolyn Garcia   Thomas B. Roberts

accommodate recent scientific findings and changes in society. The text was drafted by the authors with the assistance of several prominent jurists and law experts, like world renowned professor Mark Pieth from the University of Basel. Albert Hofmann was among the signatories, which included most of the presenters, physicians, scientists, drug specialists and several hundred of the participants in the conference. The German language resolution requests the political authorities in Switzerland incorporate the following perspectives into law in keeping with the 2005 expert report published by the Swiss Federal Commission on Drug Issues. The English language resolution relates to internationally applied UN conventions and was sent to the relevant institutions in Vienna, the United Nations Office on Drugs and Crime in Brussels, Washington, and Berlin:

During the preparatory phase of the conference, we asked Albert Hofmann if we might list him in the program as guest of honor. He answered decisively: "If I come, I also want to say something." He was looking forward to a brief appearance but to his regret had to cancel due to health reasons. His presence was sorely missed by all presenters and visitors, but his spirit could be felt during the entire conference. His grandson Simon Duttwyler spent Easter week with him on the Rittimatte. Albert Hofmann asked him to convey a message of greeting to all.

His grandson recalled: "During the time before the conference, he was unsure what his role would be. On good days, he was

Dennis McKenna   Stanislav Grof

convinced that he would take part, on bad days he said he certainly did not want to expose himself to all that hubbub. After he had decided to stay home, we sat at the table and I asked him: 'What would you want to say to them if you were there?' My grandfather formulated his message of greeting in very little time, and I wrote it down for him. He regrets his absence, since he was very impressed by the earlier symposium."

The World Psychedelic Forum did not result in a "clash of civilizations" as it had two years earlier, but again different worlds did meet in the large and busy hotel lobby. The Swiss National Soccer Team checked into the hotel the same time as Forum attendees. Many television crews were present, some for the conference, but most for the soccer. It was not too difficult for the journalists to tell the difference between the two teams.

A number of speakers used the opportunity to visit Hofmann at his home, among them Stanislav Grof and Carolyn Garcia, a former member of the Merry Pranksters who presented him with an Acid Test "certificate." Other visitors during these last days were Roger Liggenstorfer and his partner Chris Heidrich, Günter Amendt, Juraj Styk, Mathias

Bröckers, Carmen and H.R. Giger. Although he did not let it show, the visits took their toll. In the nights after lengthy visits, he slept poorly and "often was dizzy and had difficulties with his balance. He fell repeatedly, but like a child, very relaxed, and has gone beyond hurt," as the tenant and caretaker Hedy Brodbeck recalled.

The Ultimate Journey

Early on the morning of April 29, 2008, Albert Hofmann died of a heart attack at the age of one hundred and two in his house on the Rittimatte. Three days earlier, a musician offered a harp concert as thanks for the experiences he'd had with Hofmann's discovery. His daughter Beatrix Nabholz found the concert "very moving and a final bouquet, even though my mother is sorely missed." Two days before his death on Sunday afternoon, Hofmann was still able to visit his neighbor Margrit Diem on foot. Simon Duttwyler telephoned him the evening before his death. Nothing indicated that the end was coming: "He was lively and in good spirits and wanted to organize another house concert. That later consoled me. I learned of his death through a phone call from one of my brothers. I felt sad, but also relieved. My grandfather had reached one hundred and two years, he didn't have to suffer, and could not have had a more beautiful morning to leave on his great journey."

Hedy Brodbeck had been constantly linked to the Hofmanns' home via mobile intercom. Since Anita's death, she visited Albert Hofmann more frequently. "We often ate dinner together. On the evening before his death, we sat for a long time and talked about anything and everything. Around ten o'clock, I said that it was probably time for sleep and helped him as usual to go to bed. On this night, however, he hardly wanted to let me leave. When we reached his bedroom, he wanted to know how my father had died. I told him that he simply went to sleep in my arms. He thought that was very beautiful." The next morning he called her at half past seven and said: "I'm so cold." She went over immediately and he told her: "Now I have to die." He asked her to phone his son, but she couldn't reach him. Andreas Hofmann called back shortly to say he was not in the area and couldn't get there that fast. She telephoned the doctor who advised her to give him two diuretic tablets. Meanwhile, the housekeeper had arrived. "About one hour later, around half past eight, he died in my arms with a smile on his face," Hedy Brodbeck remembered. A few minutes later, son Andreas arrived, and an hour later, daughter Beatrix, who had phoned her father almost daily, reached the Rittimatte.

Albert Hofmann had never feared death. He would say that he did not believe in a life after death, but knew about it. He was quite sure that death was merely a transition to another life. He even was curious about the afterlife and looked forward to meeting his loved ones again.

In his last interview one week before his death, he confirmed his opinions: "Meanwhile, LSD no longer is a problem child. I am proud of this wonder drug that opens the doors of perception. LSD has brought happiness to many people. I don't think that I need LSD to die; I can face death with joy. I am looking forward to seeing my relatives and friends again. And when we die, we won't enter a void; we won't be lost. There is just a transformation." To the final question on the meaning of life, he replied: "To rejoice over creation. The beauty of creation is the best drug in the world," and he sent the reporter off with the question: "Do you hear the silence"?

Even before all the family members had been informed, the news of his death spread on American websites and could be read in his Wikipedia entry. It remains unclear how the news found its way so quickly across the ocean, although none have come forth to admit they posted it. Albert Hofmann was survived by his children Andreas and Beatrix, ten grandchildren, and as many great-grandchildren.

This funeral service was also held at the peaceful St. Margarethen church. His son Andreas read the summation of his life that his father had written himself. Hofmann's colleague from work, Jürg Rutschmann, with whom he had become friends shortly before retiring, paid tribute to his achievements and closed with a conversation he'd had with his friend: "When I was bringing Albert Hofmann home to his mountain paradise Rittimatte after a get-together with Sandoz friends, we sat for a while and looked out into Alsace and talked about everything under the sun, as one so lightly puts it. He summed things up by saying that despite the incredible progress of science, particularly in our lifetime, a sensible and honest scientist would have to conclude that the mysteries of the world, of the cosmos, of life and of human nature have not gotten any smaller or less challenging. We are left with a stance that could be rendered by the lovely word *Mirari*, suggesting we look, be amazed, and marvel. Albert

At the last visit by the authors in April 2008

Hofmann has now ceased working to advance science, he has stopped looking. May his amazement at the fragile beauty and miracle of the world live on in us and in those who follow to advance the natural sciences." Organ music from Bach and the sounds of Volker Biesenbender's violin opened and closed the ceremony.

The chapel was full. Many relatives, friends, colleagues from work, acquaintances and residents of Burg were among the mourners. The family invited them to come to Bottmingen Castle afterwards.

Their children, Andreas Hofmann and Beatrix Nabholz, planted two trees on the Rittimatte, a field maple for their father and only few feet away, a linden, which was their mother's favorite; and buried their parents' ashes beneath them. Daughter Beatrix explained: "In their later years, they often spoke of Philemon and Baucis, and hoped that like them they too would die together.

This wish was almost granted. That is why Andreas and I planted the trees at their graves so the two can continue to talk with each other, as in the Greek myth."[219]

The authors visited Hofmann a few days before his death, reporting in detail on the World Psychedelic Forum and brought him greetings from many presenters and visitors. Even in his last days, he was able to walk unaided but for a cane. As so often before, he led us around the house and rejoiced over the blossoming plants and fresh spring green of the trees and meadows. Until his last breath, he was living full of joy, vital energy and with an alert mind. Even though Albert Hofmann is no longer with us, his LSD will never again vanish from our world; of this, its discoverer was certain. We share his hope and wish that LSD will once more be authorized for meaningful and safe use, that it may contribute to expanding human consciousness and making the world a better place. The summary Albert Hofmann wrote ends with the words: "Nature, the creation, was described by Paracelsus as the 'book written by the finger of God.' In my life I was fortunate to have this profoundly uplifting and comforting experience: To whomever understands how to read this book, not only with scientific curiosity but with wondering, loving eyes, will be revealed a deeper, more marvelous reality in which we are all secure and forever united."

355

Appendix

Retrospective on a Researcher's Life

The year after Albert Hofmann's death, Baden's Historical Museum dedicated a special exhibition to its world-famous citizen. The splendid show, that ran from October 23, 2009, to March 7, 2010, was organized by museum director Barbara Welter and exhibit curator Beat Gugger, and documented Hofmann's life, his research, his love of nature, and his holistic worldview. It was based on records and objects from Hofmann's estate which his heirs had made available, along with their many valuable suggestions, on writings and information of the researcher from friends like Dieter Hagenbach, Lucius Werthmüller and Roger Liggenstorfer, as well as items lent by private collections, the Gaia Media Foundation, the company archives of Novartis and the Pharmacy Museum Basel.

Acknowledgments

The authors wish to thank the Hofmann family, particularly Andreas Hofmann, Beatrix Nabholz-Hofmann and Simon Duttwyler, for their trust and support; Stanislav Grof for the foreword; Sabin Sütterlin, Andrea Werffeli, Jean Willi and Felix Bächlin for revision of the manuscript; Walter Dettwiler and Carol Billod from the Novartis company archives for their cooperation, Barbara Welter from the Baden Historical Museum and curator Beat Gugger for their inspiring communication; Fritz Gassner for his graphological analysis.

Further thanks go to Philip Hansen Bailey, John Barth Beresford, Virginia Beresford, Udo Breger, Ron Brettin, Hedy Brodbeck, the people of Burg, Rick Doblin, Christina Engelbart, Earth and Fire Erowid, James Fadiman, Robert Forte, David Goldstein, Jon Hanna, Michael Horowitz, Pierre Joset, Roger Liggenstorfer, Connie Littlefield, Dieter Merz, Ralph Metzner, Claudia Müller-Ebeling, Jonathan Ott, Christian Rätsch, Jürg Rutschmann, Nick Sand, Helen Sandmeier, Susanne G. Seiler, Joël Vandroogenbroeck, Martin Witz, Mareile Wolff, the photographers, artists, galleries, collectors and many others who have enriched our book considerably with valuable information, suggestions and illustrations.

Finally, we thank the entire team at Synergetic Press for their cooperation, especially director Deborah Parrish Snyder for making this edition possible, William Geuss for translation, Linda Sperling for translating and editing, John Cole for book design, Lakshmi Narayan at Awake Media for cover design, and Jim Mafchir for production assistance.

Notes

1 Golowin, S. *Lustige Eid-Genossen: Aus die phantastische Geschichte der freien Schweiz.* Zurich, 1972.

2 Jaun, R. *Amerikanisierung and Rationalisierung der Arbeitsverhält-nisse in der Schweiz 1873–1959.* Zurich, 1986.

3 Justus von Liebig, German chemist, 1803–1873.

4 Hofmann, A. "LSD – Seine Geschichte und Stellung in der Mutter-kornforschung." Lecture at Sandoz Forum, June 14, 1988.

5 Hofmann, A. "Vermag Einsicht in naturwissenschaftliche Wahrheit psychotherapeutisch zu wirken?" Lecture at European College for the Study of Consciousness (ECSC), held in Freiburg im Breisgau, 1989.

6 Fraction: Subgroup of chemical substances in a mixture of substances independent of their physical state.

7 Hofmann, A. "LSD – Seine Geschichte and Stellung in der Mutter-kornforschung." Lecture at Sandoz Forum, June 14, 1988.

8 Hofmann, A. "LSD ganz persönlich." Lecture at a session of the ECSC, Heidelberg, February 22–25, 1996.

9 Hofmann, A. "Halluzinogene in alten Kulturen und heute." Lecture at the Forum of the Disentis Monastery School, May 31, 1990.

10 "Discovery" is not the right word, since the substance is not found in nature, but rather was first synthesized by Hofmann. On the other hand, Hofmann was the one who discovered its effects. "Discovery" is seldom applied to chemical substances. "Made" or "produced" are more fitting terms, but we use "created" below because it is the term most commonly used.

11 Hofmann, A. "LSD ganz persönlich," op. cit.

12 Details supplied by Susanne G. Seiler from conversations with Albert Hofmann and Susi Weber Ramstein, Fall of 2006.

13 Acromegaly denotes a pronounced enlargement of body extremities (hands, feet, chin and lower jaw, ears, nose and eyebrow ridges and genitals). It is caused by uncontrolled production of a growth hormone.

14 The terms used are the most common. In addition, we used: Eidetics, illusinogens, mysticomimetics, psychodysleptics, psycholytics. In this book we use the terms hallucinogens and psychedelics.

15 Lewin's original classifications were: *Inebriantia*, inebriants such as alcohol or ether; *Exitantia*, stimulants like khat or amphetamine; *Euphorica, narcotics,* such as morphium and heroin; *Hypnotica,* tranquilizers, such as kava; *Phantastica,* such as peyote or ayahuasca.

16 Delirantia are psychoactive substances which, like hallucinogens, change visual, acoustic or tactile perception. Different from the hallucinogens, recall of experience is unclear because deliriants cause additional symptoms such as mental confusion, memory loss and strong disorientation. Scopolamine and hyoscyamine, alkaloids of the nightshade plants, are among the most important deliriants. Dissociatives is the collective term for drugs that isolate the cortex from the limbic system. In a complete state of dissociation, the brain stops receiving signals from the body and vice-versa. The best known substances in this class are ketamine, laughing gas and salvinorin A, the active ingredient in *Salvia divinorum.* Oneirogenics (Greek: *oneiros,* the dream) are substances that evoke dream-like experience with drowsiness. In this state, interior images are perceived as genuine so that the dream-world and the real world are indistinguishable. The best known oneirogenic plant is harmaline which is found in the seeds of the Syrian rue *(Peganum harmala),* among others.

17 According to neuroscientist Franz Vollenweider, LSD acts as follows: It mainly affects the brain's serotonin receptors. Twelve of these docking sites are known; LSD primarily stimulates subtype 2A. Simultaneously, dopamine-receptors are also activated. One consequence is the stimulation of the brain's thalamus region which processes, filters, and relays exterior and interior sensory stimuli to the cerebrum. Hallucinogens cause the thalamus to lose this filter action and appears to lead to exaggerated awareness of sensory impressions which can cause hallucinations. Glutamate floods the frontal lobe. Brain regions that normally do not communicate begin to react in synchrony. Perception of one's surroundings changes and sensory impressions may overlay one another. Vollenweider says, "We notice that different brain functions–the neuronal correlates of consciousness–are altered." How consciousness itself arises, we simply do not know.

18 N,N-Dimethyltryptamine, or DMT, is a tryptamine-alkaloid hallucinogen.

19 Timothy Leary, Interview in *Playboy,* September 1966.

20 Lilly J.C. "Dolphin-Human Relation and LSD-25," *The Use of LSD in Psychotherapy and Alcoholism,* edited by Harold A. Abramson, M.D., 1967, pp.47-52.

21 The reference to the novel *Alice in Wonderland* relates to the potion Alice drinks in the White Rabbit's house and her subsequent change of size. This reference to Carroll's novel recurs many times in the history of LSD, most notably in the Jefferson Airplane song "White Rabbit" from their 1967 album *Surrealistic Pillow.*

22 Gehlen, R. *Der Dienst: Erinnerungen 1942–1971,* Munich, 1971.

23 The Food and Drug Administration (FDA), which is part of the U.S. Department of Health and Human Services, oversees food and drug safety in the United States.

24 Hornblum, A.M. *Acres of Skin: Human Experiments at Holmesburg Prison: A Story of Abuse and Exploitation in the Name of Medical Science.* New York, 1998.

25 Klein, Naomi. *The Shock Doctrine: The Rise of Disaster Capitalism.* New York, 2007.

26 Available on YouTube, search term: Porton Down LSD.

27 *Mengeles Erben: Menschenexperimente im Kalten Krieg.* Documentary film by Dirk Pohlmann, Germany 2009.

28 *Zeit-Fragen, Zurich,* No. 10, October 1997.

29 NBC stands for: Nuclear, Biological, Chemical.

30 Letter from Colonel H. Gessner, Swiss Federal Laboratories for Materials Testing and Research for Industry, Construction and Commerce, (EMPA), Zurich, dated March 15, 1962.

31 *Carrefour* No. 363, August 29, 1951; 'Point de Vue' – *Images du Monde*, Paris, September 6, 1951; *Paris Match*, Paris, October 27, 1951.

32 Hofmann, A. "Informationen über die Brotvergiftungen in Pont-St. Esprit," Basel, November 11, 1951; Stoll W. A. "Informationen über die Brotvergiftungen in Pont-St. Esprit, Solothurn," November 27, 1951; Hofmann, A. Diary entries from November 3-9, 1951.

33 Colorimetry (also known as absorption photometry or spectrophotometry) is a means of determining the concentration of a light-absorbing substance in a liquid, solid or gaseous phase by comparative measurement of a sample of known concentration. From: Brockhaus ABC Chemie, Leipzig 1965.

34 *Le Figaro* No. 3099, August 26, 1954.

35 Frank Olson Legacy Project, www.frankolsonproject.org

36 Letter to John Beresford from March 5, 1973.

37 Blas Pablo Reko thought that teonanácatl was a subspecies of the fly agaric mushroom *(Amanita muscaria)* and thereby spread another false conjecture (Reko 1936).

38 Johnson, J.B. "The Elements of Mazatec Witchcraft," *Ethnologiska Studier*, No. 9, pp. 128–150, Gothenburg, 1939.

39 www.imaginaria.org/wasson/life.htm

40 In *LSD – Mein Sorgenkind,* Hofmann wrote of 32 mushrooms being collected, whereas in his handwritten experimental protocol he wrote 30.

41 Among Hofmann's co-workers were Dr. A.J. Frey, Dr. H. Ott, Dr. Th. Petrzilka and Dr. F. Troxler.

42 Letter from Osmond to Hofmann, August 1963.

43 Letter from Hofmann to Osmond, April 18, 1968.

44 International Union of Pure and Applied Chemistry (IUPAC).

45 The American chemist and pharmacologist of Russian origin, Alexander Shulgin, is known for his decades of work in systematic designs of hallucinogens, largely from the structural classes of phenethylamine and tryptamine. Shulgin has synthesized and tested hundreds of psychoactive compounds in self tests; hence he is one of the persons with the greatest amount of practical experience with psychedelics. He too reports of occasionally sensing the spirit of the new molecule being created during the procedure. (Shulgin 1991)

46 Ortega, Alfredo. Journal of the Chemical Society. Perkin Transactions. 1, 2505, 1982.

47 Valdes, L.J. Journal of Organic Chemistry 47, 16, 1984.

48 Interview with Maria Sabina in *Magazin L'Europe*, Milan 1971.

49 Guzmán, G., J.W. Allen & J. Gartz. "A worldwide geographical distribution of the neurotropic fungi, an analysis and discussion." *Annali del Museo Civico di Rovereto*: Sezione Archeologia, Storia, *Scienze Naturali* 14: 189–280, Rovereto, Italy, 1998.

50 Andreas Hofmann in a conversation with the authors.

51 Werthmüller, H. *Der Weltprozess und die Farben – Grundriss eines integralen Analogiesystems.* Stuttgart, 1950.

52 Hofmann, A. "Rudolf Gelpke und der Hanf-Rausch." Lecture given at the 7th Symposium of the ECSC. Hamburg, May 26-28, 1995.

53 Thalidomide was a drug sold by Grünenthal pharmaceuticals as a sleeping pills and tranquilizer under the brand names Contergan and Softenon. At the end of the 1950s through the early 1960s, they resulted in severe defects in many unborn children and the Contergan scandal. At the end of the 1950s, and at first unexplained clustering of congenital deformities occurred. It was independently confirmed in Germany, Great Britain and Australia that the fetal damage was due to the agent thalidomide. Grünenthal did not react at first to the warnings. Although the manufacturer already had received 1,600 reports of malformations observed in newborns by 1961, it continued to sell Contergan. Only after a newspaper article in *Welt am Sonntag* on November 26, 1961 did Grünenthal finally stop marketing Contergan. According to the German Federal Association of Contergan Victims, some 5,000 children were born malformed. Other sources speak of 10,000 cases world-wide, of which 4,000 are in Germany. In addition, there were an unknown number of miscarriages.

54 "Sauser," the new wine, is fermenting grape juice that is lightly alcoholic.

55 Hans Werthmüller obituary in the *Basler National Zeitung*, January 17, 1972.

56 Armin Mohler, born 1920 in Basel, was a Swiss publicist, writer and journalist. He is known as an apologist for the so-called conservative revolution. Writer Ernst Jünger first noticed Mohler when he saw Mohler's positive article about him in 1946 in *Weltwoche*. From 1949 to 1953 Mohler was Jünger's private secretary. As Jünger revised some of his earlier writings for new editions, reworking them to de-emphasize national revolutionary points of view, Mohler was disappointed and distanced himself from Jünger; they remained estranged. Armin Mohler died in 2003 in Munich.

57 Hofmann, A. "Drogen und Rausch im Leben und Werk von Ernst Jünger." Lecture at 2nd Jünger Symposium, March 31, 2000.

58 Donald Eric Broadbent (1926–1993) was a British psychologist who focused on attention and memory. His filter model of attention in particular (1958) achieved importance. It postulated an early bottleneck in a processing system of limited capacity with strictly serial processing: Of stimuli which simultaneously arrive in sensory memory storage, certain ones would be made available for further processing on the basis of their physical features and be forwarded on an all-or-nothing basis. According to Broadbent, unprocessed stimuli would remain in the sensory memory for a certain period for eventual later accessing.

59 Diary entry of August 22, 1961.

60 Letter from Osmond to Hofmann on March 26, 1964.

61 Hofmann, A. "Drogen und Rausch im Leben und Werk von Ernst Jünger," op cit.

62 Letter from Osmond to Hofmann, August 1963.

63 William James, 1842–1910, was an American author, professor of psychology and philosophy at Harvard University from 1876 to 1907.

64 James, William. *The Will to Believe and Other Essays in Popular Philosophy*. New York, 1897.

65 James, William. *The Varieties of Religious Experience*. New York, 1897.

66 Ralph Metzner, in *Birth of a Psychedelic Culture* by Ram Dass, Ralph Metzner and Gary Bravo, Santa Fe, New Mexico, 2010, 17.

67 Ibid, 18.

68 The version of the story mentioned by Hollingshead in his autobiography (Hollingshead 1973), which was widely disseminated by several authors on the Internet, must be considered a legend. In fact, a normal teaspoon holds four grams of sugar corresponding to one sugar cube. Five thousand teaspoons of powdered sugar correspond

to around 20 kilograms, which would not fit into any commonly available mayonnaise jar. If we take the usual container holding 500 grams as a basis, a single spoonful corresponds to only 100 milligrams of sugar–not a very efficient approach. How he combined powdered sugar with water into a paste also remains a puzzle. Research and questioning of Hollingshead's contemporaries and acquaintances have shed no light on the matter.

69 Leary, T. "How to Change Behavior," *Clinical Psychology, XIV International Congress of Applied Psychology*, Vol. 4, edited by S. Nielsen, Copenhagen 1962, 58, 50–68.

70 Diary entry of August 23, 1961. The Donati is one of the better restaurants in Basel.

71 *Newsweek*, June 10, 1963.

72 *Boston Globe*, September 1, 1977.

73 Leary 1986, 169; Leary, Metzner, Alpert 1971.

74 Baier, K. "Lesen als spirituelle Praxis in der Gegenwartskultur," *Religionen nach der Säkularisierung: Festschrift für Johann Figl zum 65. Geburtstag*, Münster 2011, 243-278.

75 The original correspondence which was placed at the authors' disposal states "100 grams of LSD."

76 The official dismissal did not occur until May 6, 1963.

77 Hofmann writes 500 grams, although the orders were each 100 grams.

78 Burleigh, Nina. *A Very Private Woman: The Life and Unsolved Murder of Presidential Mistress Mary Meyer*. New York, 1998, 212.

79 Heymann, C. David. *The Georgetown Ladies' Social Club: Power, Passion, and Politics in the Nation's Capital*. New York, 2003.

80 Hermann Hesse, in a letter to Rudolf Pannwitz, January 1955, *Briefe*. Frankfurt am Main, 1951.

81 The book of the same name appeared in 1967; the title is due to a misprint. A typesetter took the intended word "message" to be "massage", which McLuhan enjoyed immensely. His famous slogan "the medium is the message" had become a cliché; now he had the opportunity to alter it ironically and lend it new meaning (Klett-Cotta, Stuttgart, 2011).

82 Braunstein P. & M.W. Doyle. *Imagine Nation*. London, New York, 2002.

83 Acid is the street name for LSD.

84 Grateful Dead Magazine *The Golden Road*, No. 10, N.p., n.d.

85 Huxley, Aldous. "A Treatise on Drugs," *Chicago Herald and Examiner,* October 10, 1931.

86 Horowitz, M. "The Antidote to Everything." Symposium Lecture, *LSD – Problem Child and Wonder Drug*, Basel, January 14, 2006.

87 "Upbeat," "beatific," and "being on the beat" are associations that resonate with Kerouac's label.

88 Allen Ginsberg's *Howl* (1956), Jack Kerouac's *On the Road* (1957), William S. Burroughs' *Naked Lunch* (1959).

89 Eisner, B. "LSD Purity – Cleanliness is next to godliness." *High Times*, January 1977.

90 Hunter's Joycean cascade of words was left in the German edition as "untranslatable."

91 Grateful Dead Magazine *The Golden Road*, op. cit.

92 Leland, John. *Hip, the history*, New York, 2004, 4–10.

93 Fallon, M. "A New Haven for Beatniks," *San Francisco Examiner*, September 5, 1965.

94 Logemann, E. "Impressionen vom Internationalen Symposium" *LSD – Sorgenkind und Wunderdroge* (January 13–15, 2006, Congress Center Basel), Text + Kritik, 73 (1): 21, 2006.

95 Marcuse, H. *Ideen zu einer kritischen Theorie der Gesellschaft*. Frankfurt am Main, 1969.

96 Ibid.

97 2,5-Dimethoxy-4-methylamphetamine (DOM, also known as STP) and 3,4-Methylendioxyamphetamine (MDA) are synthetic hallucinogens and chemically belong to the phenethylamine group.

98 The conversation is found on the DVD as well as in the German version broadcast by ARTE on January 21, 2011.

99 In an interview with Martin Witz in the spring of 2009 for his film *The Substance*, Zurich 2011.

100 Ginsberg, Allen, with G. Ball. *Allen Verbatim: Lectures on Poetry, Politics, Consciousness*. New York: MWBooks, 1974, 28.

101 Thompson, Hunter S. *Fear and Loathing in Las Vegas*. New York, 1971.

102 "A cultivated binge: Plato and drug culture in ancient Greece," Michael A. Rinella in an interview with Jörg auf dem Hövel about ecstasy and philosophy in ancient Greece, and Plato as a progenitor of drug politics. *Telepolis*, April 28, 2010.

103 Zimmermann, G. "Minnesang und Rockmusik." INST: Institut zur Erforschung und Förderung regionaler und transnationaler Kulturprozesse. www.inst.at/trans/17Nr/1-13/1-13_zimmermann17.htm

104 Hicks, Michael. *Sixties Rock: Garage, Psychedelic, and Other Satisfactions*. Urbana, Illinois: University of Illinois Press, 1999, 59.

105 Aldous Huxley also chose part of a sentence from Blake as the title for his essay *The Doors of Perception* about his first mescaline experience. (Huxley 1954)

106 Nisenson, Eric. *Ascension: John Coltrane and His Quest*. New York: St. Martin's Press, 1993.

107 Quiring, B. "Psychokraut," *Der Freitag*, February 19, 2011.

108 Miles, B. *Paul McCartney: Many Years from Now*. London: Henry Holt & Co., 1997.

109 Santana, Carlos. "Live ist Trumpf, von Woodstock bis heute," interview with Bavarian Radio online, November 20, 2007.

110 Depending on the source, this quote is attributed to actor Robin Williams, musician David Crosby or Hog Farmer Wavy Gravy.

111 Murray, C.S. *Crosstown Traffic: Jimi Hendrix & the Post-war Rock 'n' Roll Revolution*. New York: St. Martin's Press, 1989.

112 Jackson, Blair. *Garcia: an American life*. New York: Penguin, 1999.

113 Boyd, Joe. *White Bicycles: Making Music in the 1960s*. London: Serpent's Tail, 2006.

114 Hänni, P. *Bern 68. Ein Quantensprung im Bewusstsein*, recorded by M. Hofer, Baden, 2008.

115 Leary, T. *Start Your Own Religion*. Millbrook, New York, 1967.

116 *Rolling Stone* 124, December 21, 1972.

117 *TIME*, March 1966.

118 *LIFE*, March 25, 1966.

119 Memorandum of the Management Board Meeting of August 10, 1965.

120 Communications Office of Sandoz AG, Publicity Department, Basel, April 18, 1966.

121 Statement of Karen P. Tandy, Administrator, Drug Enforcement Administration, before the Subcommittee for the Departments of Commerce, Justice, State, the Judiciary and Related Agencies, March 24, 2004.

122 The United States Sentencing Commission is an independent judicial authority of the USA. Its purpose is to establish sentencing policies and practices for the federal courts.

123 Letter to John Beresford from July 1, 1993.

124 Letter from John Beresford from July 14, 1993.

125 Letter to John Beresford from March 31, 1996.

126 From letters in May 1996.

127 An allusion to the novel *Through the Looking Glass* by Lewis Carroll.

128 Unger, Sanford M. "Mescaline, LSD, Psilocybin and Personality Change. A Review," *Psychiatry: Journal for the Study of Interpersonal Processes*, Volume 26, Number 2, 1963.

129 Grof, S. "Psycholytic and psychedelic therapy with LSD: Toward an integration of approaches." Address to the Conference of the European Association for Psycholytic Therapy, Frankfurt, October 1969.

130 In contrast with the positive results in Maryland and with Osmond's earlier trials in Saskatchewan, Canada, the results from an extensive controlled study at Mendota State Hospital showed no significant positive influences. The study was done at Mendota State Hospital in Madison, Wisconsin at the end of the 1960s. The investigators randomly divided 176 alcoholics who had volunteered for the project into four groups. The first received psychedelic therapy with LSD, the second one treatment with LSD in which hypnosis was also employed (hypnodelic treatment), the third only LSD without therapy, and the fourth a general milieu therapy. Half of each group was given Antabuse, a drug used to treat alcohol dependence, at the end of the experiment. The results of this study were negative. The investigators found no significant differences between the four groups; the rate of improvement was extremely low. After six months, 70 to 80 percent of the patients of all categories still drank, after one year 80 to 90 percent. The prescription of Antabuse also showed no effect. (Ludwig, A.M., J. Levine, L.H. Stark. *LSD and Alcoholism: A Clinical Study of Treatment Efficacy.* Springfield, 1970).

In the 1950s, several studies using LSD in treating alcoholics showed a success rate of 50 percent. Some of the earlier studies, however, exhibited methodological weaknesses. Mariavittoria Mangini reexamined the earlier studies and concluded in her article published in 1998 that the question of the efficacy of LSD in the treatment of alcoholism remained an open question (Mangini, M. "Treatment of alcoholism using psychedelic drugs: a review of the program of research" *Journal of Psychoactive Drugs*, 30, No. 4, 1998, pp. 381–418).

131 Abraham Harold Maslow, born on April 1, 1908, was the oldest of seven children of Jewish Russian immigrants. He received his doctorate in psychology and received a professorship in 1937 at City University of New York; in 1951 he went to Brandeis University in Boston. Maslow was honored as "Humanist of the Year" in 1967. He died of a heart attack on June 8, 1980.

132 The therapy approaches of Viktor E. Frankl's logotherapy, Erich Fromm's humanistic psychoanalysis, and Fritz Perls' gestalt therapy all resemble humanistic psychology.

133 The five levels are from bottom to top: physiologic needs; safety needs; social needs; individual needs; need for self-actualization.

134 Holotropic from the Greek *holos* "whole" and *trepein* "to turn or direct towards a thing."

135 "Rebirthing" is a therapy method for self experience developed by Leonhard Orr in the 1960s. It enables one to re-experience one's own birth and bring repressed emotions and experiences to the surface. The most important element of rebirthing is circular breathing, deep inbreathe and exhalation without pause.

136 Ralph Metzner in a communication to the authors, 2010.

137 Letter from November 2, 1964.

138 Ibid.

139 *Tricycle* No. 21, Summer 1996.

140 Coleman, James William. *The New Buddhism: The Western Transformation of an Ancient Tradition.* Oxford, 2001, 201.

141 Halifax, J. "Being With Dying. Contemplative Care of Dying People," a talk at the University of Virginia Medical Center, October 21, 1998, transcribed by Shell Halley.

142 *Mönch und Millionär,* Context 12, November 24, 2008.

143 Ibid.

144 Govinda, Lama Anagarika. *Buddhistische Reflexionen.* Munich 1983 (published in English as: *Buddhist Reflections.* York Beach, Maine, 1991).

145 Kornfield, J. "Psychedelic Experience and Spiritual Practice. A Buddhist Perspective," Interview with Jack Kornfield by Robert Forte (available online at www.lycaeum.org/~sputnik/Misc/buddhism.html).

146 *Du*, October 14, 1994.

147 Müller-Ebeling, C. and Rätsch C. *Zauberpflanze Alraune.* Solothurn, 2004.

148 *True Visions*, Bologna 2006, 33.

149 It was by chance that a Kachina doll was involved. One of Janiger's first subjects noticed it in his office and insisted on painting it during his LSD trip. Janiger decided to conduct all of the experiments using the same object.

150 Fax to Dieter Hagenbach on January 12, 2006.

151 The American perception researcher H. Klüver described the patterns which informed hallucinations from mescaline as: "a) grid, mesh. meander pattern, filigree, honeycomb pattern, chess board pattern; b) spider webs; c) tunnels, funnels, alley, cones, sleeves, spirals" (Vergoossen, M. "Halluzinatorische Formkonstanten in der europäischen Malerei," Seminar, Dresden 2007.)

152 Müller-Ebeling, C. "Künstlerkontakte mit Albert Hofmann," Lecture, *Transition*, Berlin, January 25, 2002.

153 www.viceland.com, 200

154 In a conversation with Dieter Hagenbach, December 2010.

155 Albert Hofmann to Dieter Hagenbach.

156 McCloud, S. *Comics richtig lessen.* Hamburg, 1994.

157 Eisner, Will. *Mit Bildern erzählen: Comics & Sequential Art.* Wimmelbach, Germany, 1995.

158 The expression "Damascus experience" describes an experience that gives a person decisive self-knowledge and changes their outlook and behavior for the better. The term originally referred to the

encounter with Jesus Christ that happened to Paul of Tarsus on the road to Damascus which changed him from a persecutor of early Christians into an apostle, who became St. Paul.

159 *The Paris Review*, Issue 193, Summer 2010.

160 Guthrie, Lee. *The Life and Loves of Cary Grant*. New York, 1977.

161 *Lexikon des Internationalen Films*. Marburg, 2001.

162 Interview with Rick Doblin, in *MAPS*, Vol. XIII, 1, Spring 2003.

163 CNN Interview on the Joy Behar Show, July 16, 2010.

164 Fahey, Todd Brendan. "The Original Captain Trips - Who Was 'Captain' Al Hubbard?" rense.com/general28/dshwo.htm

165 Campbell, Joseph. *Changing Images of Man*, (Systems science and world order library), New York, 1981.

166 Stolaroff, M. "Tribute to Dr. Albert Hofmann," *Albert Hofmann und die Entdeckung des LSD* by Mathias Bröckers and Roger Liggenstorfer, Baden, 2006.

167 *MAPS,* Vol. XVIII, 1, Spring 2008.

168 *Wired*, January 16, 2006.

169 Müller, D. "LSD als Treibstoff der Computerbranche?" ZDNet.de | Alle Seiten der IT. www.zdnet.de/2045968/lsd-als-treibstoff-der-computerbranche/

170 Bill Gates Interview in *Playboy*, December 8, 1994.

171 Brand, S. "Spacewar," *Rolling Stone*, December 1972.

172 Turner, F. *From Counterculture to Cyberculture: Stewart Brand, the Whole Earth Network, and the Rise of Digital Utopianism*. Chicago: Univ. of Chicago Press, 2006, based on interview with Brand on July 17, 2001.

173 Wikipedia.

174 Barbrook, R. & A. Cameron. "The Californian Ideology," *Telepolis*, 5. April 1997.

175 A term coined by Buckminster Fuller in the early 1960s.

176 Vindheim, J.B. Green Papers, February 4, 2009.

177 Grober, U. "Modewort mit tiefen Wurzeln...," *Jahrbuch Ökologie* 2003, Munich 2002, pp. 167–175.

178 Harrison, K. "Treat her Right. Lessons from a Medicine Walk," *MAPS Bulletin*, Volume XIX, 1, 2009.

179 On a walk with Dieter Hagenbach, during which he also explained that photosynthesis only required one particular form of leaf, it remained an incomprehensible miracle of creation that from the beginning, the leaves of every kind of bush and tree in the entire world differ from each other, just as no two snowflakes are alike.

180 Harvey, G. *Animism: Respecting the Living World*. London, New York, 2005, 128.

181 Metzner, R. "Consciousness Expansion and Counterculture in the 1960s and Beyond," *MAPS* , Vol. XIX, 1, 2009.

182 Ibid.

183 Rees, A. "Nobel Prize genius Crick was high on LSD when he discovered the secret of life," *Mail on Sunday*, London, August 8, 2004.

184 Press conference of the Symposium *LSD – Problem Child and Wonder Drug,* Basel, January 13-15, 2006.

185 Abraham, Ralph, Rupert Sheldrake & Terence K. McKenna. *Trialogues at the Edge of the West: Chaos, Creativity, and the Resacralization of the World*. Santa Fe, New Mexico: Bear & Co., 1992.

186 *GQ* magazine, July 1991.

187 Ghamari-Tabrizi, Sharon. *The Worlds of Herman Kahn: The Intuitive Science of Thermonuclear War*. Cambridge, Massachusetts, 2006, 70, 75.

188 Macey, David. *The Lives of Michel Foucault: A Biography*. New York: Pantheon, 1994.

189 Dock Ellis in a radio interview with Donnell Alexander and Neille Ilel, summer 2008.

190 We heard this anecdote from Hofmann and others in various versions.

191 Application for the building permit was made on December 21, 1966, the permit was received on May 23, 1967. The family moved at the end of October 1968; on November 2nd, they registered with the commune of Burg as residents.

192 Hofmann, A., "Was mich bewogen hat, dieses Buch zu schreiben," Lecture at book presentation for *LSD – Mein Sorgenkind,* Basel, September 18, 1979.

193 Diary entries from September 18 and 20, 1979.

194 Diary entry from April 16, 1983.

195 2nd International Conference on Hallucinogenic Mushrooms, Port Townsend, Washington, October 27–30, 1977.

196 Latin: Be careful!

197 Diary entry from September 20, 1979.

198 "A Fruitful Friendship between an Ethnobotanist and a Chemist," Lecture by Albert Hofmann, translated and given by Jonathan Ott at the Ethnobotany Conference, San Francisco, October 18–20, 1996.

199 Ibid.

200 The active ingredients for preparing a potion with action analogous to Ayahuasca are to be found in plants which grow outside the South American rain forest; such plants also thrive in more easily accessible regions, including Europe.

201 Ergonovine, also known as ergometrine or ergobasine, is a naturally occurring chemical compound in the ergot alkaloid group. The active ingredient of Methergine®, methylergometrine, also known as methylergonovine or methylergobasine, is a semisynthetic pharmaceutical produced from ergonovine.

202 *Arbutus unedo* is not mentioned in Christian Rätsch's *Enzyklopädie der psychoaktiven Pflanzen*, a standard work on the subject; however, *Arbutus parviflora* from South America is mentioned.

203 Hofmann, A. "Die Botschaften der Mysterien von Eleusis an die heutige Welt," lecture manuscript 1993.

204 Letter to Julio Santo Domingo from March 4, 2005.

205 "With this certificate, the Federal Institute of Technology (ETH) awards Dr. Albert Hofmann in Zurich an Honorary Doctor of Science in recognition of his successful scientific pharmaceutical research, in particular the isolation, elucidation of the constitution and chemical modification of Scilla-glycosides, alkaloids and hallucinogenic Psilocybe and Ipomoea-compounds, findings that led to the development of important pharmaceuticals," Zurich, November 15, 1969.

206 Broccard, N. "Hoffnung auf die Sterne," *St. Galler Tagblatt*, November 30, 1984.

207 Hofmann, A. "Bewusstseinserweiterung," Lecture, International New Age Symposium, Zurich, November 17, 1984.

208 Hufeland, Christoph Wilhelm. *Makrobiotik oder Die Kunst, das menschliche Leben zu verlängern*. Jena, 1796.

209 Suter, M. *Die dunkle Seite des Mondes*. Zurich, 2000.

210 Martin Suter in his speech at the tribute to Albert Hofmann on his 100th birthday on January 11, 2006, Basel.

211 Liggenstorfer R., C. Rätsch & A. Tschudin. *Die berauschte Schweiz*. Solothurn, 1998.

212 Diary entry from June 18, 1985.

213 Simon Duttwyler in conversation with the authors, Summer 2010.

214 Andreas Hofmann in a conversation with the authors, 2010.

215 Excerpts by the authors from a conversation with Simon Duttwyler in the summer of 2010.

216 www.lsd.info

217 The list of the 100 greatest living geniuses was composed for the British newspaper *Daily Telegraph* by six experts on creativity and innovation from Creators Synectics, a global consulting firm. They conducted a poll of 4,000 persons who could nominate up to ten living persons they considered to be geniuses. The 100 most frequently mentioned who satisfied the standards were ranked according to several criteria. These comprised among others, how significantly the candidate's contribution challenged and turned conventional thinking upside down, their effect on the public, their intellectual substance, their achievements and their cultural impact.

218 http://www.psychedelik.info

219 In his Metamorphoses the Roman poet Ovid tells the story of Philemon and his wife Baucis: Jupiter and his son Mercury were traveling disguised as humans to avoid recognition as gods. As they sought quarters for the night, no one wished to offer the two wanderers shelter until an elderly couple, Philemon and Baucis, took them in and generously fed them. The gods rewarded Philemon and Baucis for their hospitality by transforming their hut into a golden temple. In addition, they were granted one wish. The couple, bound by their love, wished to serve as priests in the temple and to die at the same moment. At the end of their lives, the gods changed them into two trees that stood alongside each other. Philemon became an oak tree, Baucis a linden and Jupiter turned the town with the hard-hearted people into a lake. This motif was later taken up by numerous writers, Jean de la Fontaine, Johann Wolfgang von Goethe, Kurt Tucholsky, Max Frisch and Patrick Süskind among others.

Bibliography

Aaronson, Bernard Seymour, and Humphry Osmond. *Psychedelics: the Uses and Implications of Hallucinogenic Drugs*. Garden City, New York: Anchor Books, 1970.

Abramson, Harold A. "The Use of LSD in Psychotherapy and Alcoholism." Paper presented at the International Conference on the Use of LSD in Psychotherapy Alcoholism, Indianapolis, Indiana, 1967.

Abramson, Harold A. "The Use of LSD in Psychotherapy - Transactions." Paper presented at the Conference on d-Lysergic Acid, Diethylamide, New York, New York, 1960.

Allen, John W. and R. Gordon Wasson. *Wasson's First Voyage: The Rediscovery of Entheogenic Mushrooms*. Seattle, Washington: Psilly Publications and Raver Books, 1997.

Allyn, David. *Make Love, Not War: The Sexual Revolution, an Unfettered History*. Boston, Massachusetts: Little, Brown, 2000.

Amendt, Günter. *Die Legende vom LSD*. Frankfurt am Main: Zweitausendeins, 2008.

Artaud, Antonin. *The Peyote Dance*. New York, New York: Farrar, Straus and Giroux, 1976.

Badiner, Allan Hunt, and Alex Grey. *Zig Zag Zen: Buddhism on Psychedelics*. San Francisco, California: Chronicle Books, 2002.

Barritt, Brian. *The Road of Excess: A Psychedelic Autobiography*. London: PSI, 1998.

Barron, Frank, Richard C. DeBold, and Russell C. Leaf, eds. *LSD, Man & Society*. Middletown, Connecticut: Weslyan University Press, 1967.

Baur, M. and S. Baur. *Die Beatles und die Philosophie*. Klett-Cotta Verlag, 2010.

Beringer, K. *Der Meskalinrausch: Seine Geschichte und Erscheinungsweise*. Berlin: Springer, 1927.

Biderman, A.D. and H. Zimmer. *The Manipulation of Human Behavior*. New York, London: Wiley, 1961.

Bigwood, Jeremy and Jonathan Ott. "Teonanácatl: Hallucinogenic Mushrooms of North America." Extracts from the Second International Conference on Hallucinogenic Mushrooms, held October 27-30, 1977, near Port Townsend, Washington.

Bishop, Malden Grange. *The Discovery of Love: A Psychedelic Experience with LSD-25*. New York, New York: Dodd, Mead, 1963.

Black, David. *Acid: The Secret History of LSD*. 1998.

Blum, Richard H. *Utopiates: The Use and Users of LSD-25*. Palo Alto, California: Atherton Press, 1964.

Boon, Marcus. *The Road of Excess: A History of Writers On Drugs*. Cambridge: Harvard University Press, 2002.

Bové, Frank James. *The Story of Ergot*. New York: S, Karger, 1970.

Bower, Tom. *The Paperclip Conspiracy: The Hunt for the Nazi Scientists*. New York, 1988.

Braden, William. *The Private Sea: LSD & the Search for God*. Chicago, 1967.

Brand, Stewart. "We Owe it All to the Hippies." *TIME*, March 1, 1995.

Braunstein, Peter, and Michael W. Doyle. *Imagine Nation: The American Counterculture of the 1960s and '70s*. London, New York: Routledge, 2002.

Brewer, Tony. "LSD." *St. James Encyclopedia of Pop Culture*. Farmington Hills, Michigan, 2002.

Bröckers, Mathias. *Trans Psychedelischer Express: Eleusis – Basel – Babylon – und weiter*. Solothurn: Nachtschatten Verlag, 2002.

Bröckers, Mathias, Albert Hofmann, and Roger Liggenstorfer. *Albert Hofmann und die Entdeckung des LSD: Auf dem Weg nach Eleusis*. Baden: AT Verlag, 2006.

Busch, Anthony K., and Walter C. Johnson. "LSD- 25 As an Aid in Psychotherapy, (Preliminary Report of a New Drug)." Diseases of the nervous system 11(8) (1950): 241-243.

Caldwell, W.V. *LSD Psychotherapy: An Exploration of Psychedelic and Psycholytic Therapy*. New York: Grove Press, 1969.

Carroll, Elizabeth. "The Answer to the Atom Bomb, Rhetoric, Identification, and the Grateful Dead." *Americana: The Journal of American Popular Culture (1900-Present)*. Volume 6, Issue 1, 2007.

Cashman, John. *LSD die Wunderdroge*. Berlin, 1967.

Chandler, A.L. and M.A. Hartman. "Lysergic acid diethylamide (LSD-25) as a facilitating agent in psychotherapy," *Archives of General Psychiatry*, 2:286-299, 1960.

Cheek, F.E., H. Osmond, M. Sarett, and R.S. Albahary. "Observations regarding the use of LSD-25 in the treatment of alcoholism," *Journal of Psychopharmacology*, 1: 56–74, 1966.

Chilton, W.S. et al. "Psilocin, bufotenine and serotonin. Historical and biosynthetic observations," *Journal of Psychedelic Drugs,* 11 (1–2): 61–69, 1979

Christensen, M. *Acid Christ: Ken Kesey, LSD and the Politics of Ecstasy*. Tucson, Arizona, 2010.

Clark, W.H. *Chemical Ecstasy. Psychedelic Drugs and Religion*. New York, 1969.

Cloud, C. *Acid Trips and Chemistry*. Berkeley, 1999.

Cockburn, Alexander and Jeffrey St. Clair. *Whiteout: The CIA, Drugs, and the Press*. London, New York, 1998.

Cohen, Sidney. *The Beyond Within: The LSD Story*. New York, 1966.

Conners, Peter H. *White Hand Society: The Psychedelic Partnership of Timothy Leary and Allen Ginsberg*. San Francisco, 2010.

Cousto, H. *Vom Urkult zur Kultur: Drogen und Techno*. Solothurn, 1995.

DeBold, Richard C. and Russell C. Leaf, eds. *LSD, Man & Society*. Middletown, Connecticut, 1967.

DeKorne, J. *Psychedelischer Neo-Schamanismus*. Löhrbach, 1995.

De-Nurs, Yehiel. *Shivitti: A Vision by Ka-tzetnik*. San Francisco: Harper & Row, 1989.

De Ropp, R. *Drugs and the Mind.* New York, 1960.

Devereux, P. *The Long Trip. The Prehistory of Psychedelia*. London, 1997.

Dobkin de Rios M. and O. Janiger. *LSD, Spirituality and the Creative Process*. Rochester, Vermont 2003.

Doblin, R. "Pahnke's 'Good Friday Experiment.' A long-term follow-up and methodological critique," *Journal of Transpersonal Psychology*, 23: 1–28, 1991.

Doblin, R. "Dr. Leary's Concord Prison Experiment. A 34-Year Follow-up Study," *Journal of Psychoactive Drugs*, Oct-Dec 1998.

Dunlap, J. (Pseud. Davis A.). *Exploring Inner Space. Personal Experiences Under LSD-25*. New York, 1961.

Dyck, E. "Flashback. Psychiatric Experimentation with LSD in Historical Perspective," *The Canadian Journal of Psychiatry*. 50: 381–388, 2005.

Dyck, E. *Psychedelic Psychiatry: LSD from Clinic to Campus*. Baltimore, Maryland, 2008.

Edwards, Gavin. *Do You Want To Know A Secret die grossten Geheimniss, Mythen und Geruchte der Rockwelt*. Berlin: Schwarzkopf, 2009.

Eliade, Mircea. *Schamanismus und archaische Ekstasetechnik*. Zurich, 1955.

Emboden, William A. *Narcotic Plants*. 1972. Second Revised and Enlarged Edition, New York, 1980.

Engel, Günter and P. Herring, eds. *Grenzgänge: Albert Hofmann zum 100 Geburtstag*. Basel, 2006.

Estrada, Alvaro. *Maria Sabina: Her Life and Chants*. Santa Barbara, California, 1981.

Fadiman, James. *The Psychedelic Explorer's Guide: Safe, Therapeutic and Sacred Journeys*. Rochester, Vermont 2011.

Feilding, Amanda. *Hofmann's Elixir: LSD and the New Eleusis*. Oxford, 2008.

Forte, Robert, ed. *Timothy Leary: Outside Looking In*. Rochester, Vermont, 1999.

Forte, Robert, ed. *Entheogens and the Future of Religion*. San Francisco, 1997.

Frederking, W. "Über die Verwendung von Rauschdrogen (Meskalin und Lysergsaurediäthylamid) in der Psychotherapie," *Psyche*. 54: 7: 342, 1953.

Fuller, John G. *The Day of St. Anthony's Fire*. New York, 1968.

Furst, Peter T. *Flesh of the Gods*. New York, 1972.

Furst, Peter T. *Hallucinogens and Culture*. San Francisco, 1976.

Furst, Peter E. *Encyclopedia of Psychoactive Drugs, Mushrooms; Psychedelic Fungi*. New York, 1986.

Gartz, Jochen. *Narrenschwämme*. Solothurn, 1999.

Gartz, Jochen. "Teonanácatl." Lecture at symposium *LSD – Sorgenkind und Wunderdroge*. 2006.

Gasser, Peter. "Die Psycholytische Therapie in der Schweiz von 1988–1993," *Schweizer Archiv Neurologische Psychologie* 147(2): 59–65, 1966.

Gasser, Peter. "Die Psycholytische Psychotherapie aus der Sicht der Patienten," *Eine katamnestische Erhebung, Kantonale Psychiatrische Klinik*. 1994.

Gelpke, Rudolph. "Von Fahrten in den Weltraum der Seele. Berichte über Selbstversuche mit Delysid (LSD) und Psilocybin (CY)," *Antaios*, Vol. III No. 5., 393–411, 1962.

Gelpke, Rudolph. *Vom Rausch im Orient und Okzident*. Stuttgart, 1966

Giger, H.R. *H.R. Giger's Necronomicon*. Basel, 1977.

Golas, Thaddeus. *Der Erleuchtung ist es egal, wie du sie erlangst*. Basel, 1979.

Goldsmith, Neal M. *Psychedelic Healing. The Promise of Entheogens for Psychotherapy and Spiritual Development*. Rochester, Vermont, 2010.

Golowin, Sergius. *Die Magie der verbotenen Märchen: Von Hexendrogen und Feenkräutern*. Hamburg, 1973.

Golowin, Sergius. *Das Reich des Schamanen: Der Eurasische Weg der Weisheit*. Basel, 1982.

Gordon, Alastair. Spaced Out. *Radical Environments of the Psychedelic Sixties*. New York, 2008.

Gray, Christopher. *The Acid Diaries: A Psychonaut's Guide to the History and Use of LSD*. Rochester, Vermont, 2010.

Grey, Alex. *Sacred Mirrors: The Visionary Art of Alex Grey*. Rochester, Vermont, 1990.

Grey, Alex. *Transfigurations*. 1990.

Griffiths, R.R., W. A. Richards, U. McCann, and R. Jesse. "Psilocybin can occasion mystical experiences having substantial and sustained personal meaning and spiritual significance." *Journal of Psycho-Pharmacology* 187 (2006): 268-283.

Griffiths R.R., M.W. Johnson, W.A. Richards, U. McCann and B.D. Richards. "Mystical-type experiences occasioned by psilocybin mediate the attribution of personal meaning and spiritual significance 14 months later," *Journal of Psychopharmacology* 22.6 (2008): 621-632.

Grim, Ryan. *This Is Your Country on Drugs: The Secret History of Getting High in America*. Hoboken, New Jersey, 2009.

Grinspoon L. and J.B. Bakalar, eds. *Psychedelic Reflections*. New York, 1983.

Grinspoon L. and J.B. Bakalar. *Psychedelic Drugs Reconsidered*. New York, 1997.

Grob, Charles. *Hallucinogens: A Reader*. New York, 2002.

Grof, Stanislav. "LSD and the Cosmic Game. Outline of Psychedelic Cosmology and Ontology," *Journal for the Study of Consciousness* 5.165 (1972–3).

Grof, Stanislav. *LSD Psychotherapy: Exploring the Frontiers of the Hidden Mind*. Alameda, California, 1980.

Grof, Stanislav. *The Psychology of the Future*. New York, 1980, 2000.

Grof, Stanislav. *Realms of the Human Unconscious: Observations from LSD Research*. New York, 1976.

Grof, Stanislav. *The Ultimate Journey: Consciousness and the Mystery of Death*. Sarasota, Florida, 2006.

Grof, Stanislav. *When the Impossible Happens: Adventures in Non-Ordinary Realities*. Louisville, Colorado, 2006.

Grof, S. and H.Z. Bennett. *Die Welt der Psyche. Die neuen Erkenntnisse der Bewusstseinsforschung*. Hamburg, 1997.

Grof, S., L.E. Goodman, W.A. Richards and A.A. Kurland. "LSD-assisted psychotherapy with terminal cancer," *International Pharmaco Psychiatry*. 8(1973): 129-144.

Grof, Stanislav and C. Grof. *Spirituelle Krisen*. Munich, 1990.

Grof, Stanislav and J. Halifax. *The Human Encounter with Death*. New York, 1977.

Grunenberg, Christoph and Jonathan Harris. *Summer of Love: Psychedelic Art, Social Crisis and Counterculture in the 1960s*. Liverpool University Press, 2005.

Guggisberg, Hans. *Mutterkorn: Vom Gift zum Heilstoff*. Basel, 1954.

Guzmán, Gaston. "The Genus Psilocybe. A Systematic Revision of the Known Species Including the History, Distribution and Chemistry of the Hallucinogenic Species," *Beihefte zur Nova Hedwigia*. 74 (1983).

Harman, W.W. and H. Rheingold. *Higher Creativity. Liberating the Unconscious for Breakthrough Insights*. Los Angeles, California, 1984.

Harman, W.W. et al. "Psychedelic Agents in Creative Problem-Solving. A Pilot Study," *Psychological Reports*. 19.1 (1966): 211–2.

Harner, Michael J., ed. *Hallucinogens and Shamanism*. London, 1973.

Harpignies, J.P., ed. *Visionary Plant Consciousness: The Shamanic Teachings of the Plant World*. Rochester, Vermont, 2007.

Hartmann, R.P. *Malerei aus Bereichen des Unbewussten. Künstler experimentieren unter LSD*. Cologne, 1974.

Hayes, Charles. *Tripping: An Anthology of True-Life Psychedelic Adventures*. New York, 2000.

Heim, Roger. "Nouvelle investigations sur les champignons hallucinogènes," *Editions du Museum Nationale d'Histoire Naturelle*. Paris, 1967.

Heim, Roger. *Les champignons toxiques et hallucinogens*. Paris, 1963.

Heim, Roger, and R.G. Wasson. "Les champignons hallucinogènes du Mexique," *Editions du Museum Nationale d' Histoire Naturelle*. Paris, 1958.

Heinrich, Clark. *Die Magie der Pilze: Psychoaktive Pilze in Mythos, Alchemie und Religion*. Munich, 1998.

Hesse, Hermann. *Der Steppenwolf*. Berlin: S. Fischer, 1927.

Higgs, John. *I Have America Surrounded: The Life of Timothy Leary*. Fort Lee, New Jersey, Barricade Books, 2006.

Hintzen, Annelie and Torsten Passie. *The Pharmacology of LSD: A Critical Review*. Oxford, New York: Oxford University Press in collaboration with Beckley Foundation Press, 2010.

Hoffer, Abram, and Humphry Osmond. *The Hallucinogens*. New York: Academic Press, 1967.

Hofmann, A., and H. Tscherter. "Isolierung von Lysergsäure-Alkaloiden aus der mexikanischen Zauberdroge Ololiuqui (Rivea Corymbosa (L.) Hall. F.)." *Experientia* 16, no. 9 (1960/09/01 1960): 414-14.

Höhle, Sigi, and C. von Sehrwald. *Rausch und Erkenntnis: Das Wilde in der Kultur*. Munich, Knaur, 1986.

Hollingshead, Michael. *The Man Who Turned on the World*. New York: Abelard-Schuman, 1974.

Hunt, Linda. *Secret Agenda: The United States Government, Nazi Scientists, and Project Paperclip, 1945 to 1990*. New York: St. Martin's Press, 1991.

Huxley, Aldous. *The Doors of Perception*. New York: Harper, 1954.

Huxley, Aldous. *Heaven and Hell*. New York: Harper, 1956.

Huxley, Aldous. *Island: A Novel*. New York: Harper, 1962.

Huxley, Aldous. *The Perennial Philosophy*. New York; London: Harper & Brothers, 1945.

Huxley, Aldous, Michael Horowitz, and Cynthia Palmer. *Moksha: Writings on Psychedelics and the Visionary Experience (1931-1963)*. New York: Stonehill, 1977.

Huxley, Laura Archera. *This Timeless Moment: A Personal View of Aldous Huxley*. New York: Farrar, Straus & Giroux, 1968.

Inglis, Brian. *The Forbidden Game: A Social History of Drugs*. New York: Scribner, 1975.

Janzing, Gereon. *Psychoaktive Drogen weltweit: Zu Ethnologie und Kulturgeschichte, Schamanismus und Hexerei*. Löhrbach: Pieper & The Grüne Kraft, 2000.

Johnson, Ken. *Are You Experienced? How Psychedelic Consciousness Transformed Modern Art*. Munich; New York: Prestel Verlag, 2011.

Josuttis, Manfred, and Hanscarl Leuner. *Religion und die Droge: Ein Symposion über religiöse Erfahrungen unter Einfluss von Halluzinogenen*. Stuttgart: W. Kohlhammer, 1972.

Jungaberle, Henrik. *Therapie mit Psychoaktiven Substanzen: Praxis und Kritik der Psychotherapie mit LSD, Psilocybin und MDMA*. Bern: Huber, 2008.

Jünger, Ernst. *Annäherungen: Drogen und Rausch*. Stuttgart: Klett Verlag, 1970.

Jütte, Robert. *Medizin und Nationalsozialismus: Bilanz und Perspektiven der Forschung*. Göttingen: Wallstein Verlag, 2011.

Kaiser, David. *How the Hippies Saved Physics: Science, Counterculture, and the Quantum Revival*. New York: W.W. Norton, 2011.

Kaplan, Steven Laurence. *Le pain maudit : Retour sur la France des annees oubliees, 1945-1958*. Paris: Fayard, 2008.

Kast, E.C., and V.J. Collins. "Study of Lysergic Acid Diethylamide as an Analgesic Agent." *Anesthesia and Analgesia* 43 (1964).

Kent, James L. *Psychedelic Information Theory: Shamanism in the Age of Reason*. Seattle, Washington: PIT Press / Supermassive, LLC, 2010.

Kerényi, Karl. *Die Mysterien von Eleusis*. Zurich, 1962.

Kesey, Ken. *One Flew Over the Cuckoo's Nest*. New York: Viking Press, 1962.

Ketchum, James S. *Chemical Warfare Secrets Almost Forgotten: A Personal Story of Medical Testing of Army Volunteers with Incapacitating Chemical Agents during the Cold War (1955-1975)*. Santa Rosa, California, 2006.

Kleps, Art. *Millbrook: The True Story of the Early Years of the Psychedelic Revolution*. Oakland, California: Bench Press, 1977.

Klüver, Heinrich. *Mescal, and Mechanisms of Hallucinations*. Chicago: University of Chicago Press, 1966.

Klüver, Heinrich. *Mescal: The "Divine" Plant and Its Psychological Effects*. London: Paul, Trench, Trubner, 1928.

Koch, Egmont R., and Michael Wech. *Deckname Artischocke: Die geheimen Menschenversuche der CIA*. Munich, 2003.

Kosel, Margret. *Gammler, Beatniks, Provos. Die schleichende Revolution*. Frankfurt: Bärmeier & Nikel, 1967.

Krippner, S. "Psychedelic Drugs and Creativity." *Journal of Psychoactive Drugs* 17, no. 4 (1985).

Krippner, S., and M. Winkelman. "Maria Sabina: Wise Lady of the Mushrooms." *Journal of Psychoactive Drugs* 15, no. 3 (1983).

Kupfer, Alexander. *Göttliche Gifte: Kleine Kulturgeschichte des Rausches seit dem Garten Eden*. Stuttgart: Verlag J.B. Metzler, 1996.

Kurland, A.A., C. Savage, W.N. Pahnke, S. Grof, and J.E. Olsson. "LSD in the Treatment of Alcoholics." *Pharmacopsychiatry* 4, no. 02 (1971): 83-94.

La Barre, Weston. *The Peyote Cult*. New Haven, Connecticut, 1938, New York, 1969.

Lattin, Don. *The Harvard Psychedelic Club: How Timothy Leary, Ram Dass, Huston Smith, and Andrew Weil Killed the Fifties and Ushered in a New Age for America*. New York: HarperOne, 2010.

Leary, T.F. "A Program of Research with Consciousness-Altering Substances." Harvard University, 1961.

Leary T.F., Metzner R., Presnell M., Weil G., Schwitzgebel R., Kinne S. "A New Behavior Change Program for Adult Offenders Using Psilocybin." *Psychotherapy, Therapy, Research and Practice* 2, no. 2 (July 1965).

Leary, Timothy. *Changing My Mind, Among Others: Lifetime Writings*. Englewood Cliffs, New Jersey: Prentice-Hall, 1982.

Leary, Timothy. *Chaos & Cyberculture*. Berkeley, 1994.

Leary, Timothy. *Flashbacks: An Autobiography*. Los Angeles; Boston: J.P. Tarcher, 1983.

Leary, Timothy. *Interpersonal Diagnosis of Personality; a Functional Theory and Methodology for Personality Evaluation*. New York: Ronald Press, 1957.

Leary, Timothy, Ralph Metzner and Richard Alpert. *The Psychedelic Experience: A Manual Based on the Tibetan Book of the Dead*. New York: University Books, 1964.

Leary, Timothy. "Use of Psychedelic Drugs in Prisoner Rehabilitation." *British Journal of Social Psychiatry*, v. 2 (1968) 27–51.

Leary, Timothy, George A. Koopman and Robert Anton Wilson. *Neuropolitik: Die Soziobiologie der menschlichen Metamorphose*. Basel: Sphinx Verlag, 1981.

Leary, Timothy, George H. Litwin, and Ralph Metzner. *Reactions to Psilocybin Administered in a Supportive Environment*. Maryland: The Williams & Wilkins Co., 1963.

Leary, Timothy, Hassan I. Sirius, and R.U. Sirius. *Leary on Drugs: Writing and Lectures from Timothy Leary (1970-1996)*. Berkeley, California: Re/Search Publications, 2008.

Leary, Timothy. *Exo-Psychologie: Handbuch für den Gebrauch des menschlichen Nervensystems gemäss den Anweisungen der Hersteller*. Basel: Sphinx Verlag, 1981.

Lee, Martin A., and Bruce Shlain. *Acid Dreams: The CIA, LSD, and the Sixties Rebellion*. New York: Grove Press, 1985.

Letcher, A. *Shroom: A Cultural History of the Magic Mushroom*. HarperCollins, 2008.

Leuner, H. "Die psycholytische Therapie. klinische Psychotherapie mit Hilfe von LSD-25 und verwandten Substanzen." *Zeitschrift für psychotherapeutische medizinische Psychologie* 13 (1963): 57-64.

Leuner, H. "Psychotherapie mit Hilfe von Halluzinogenen." *Arzneimittel-Forschung* 16, no. 2 (1966): 253-5.

Leuner, Hanscarl. *Die experimentelle Psychose*. Berlin; Göttingen; Heidelberg: Springer, 1962.

Leuner, Hanscarl. *Halluzinogene: Psychische Grenzzustände in Forschung und Psychotherapie*. Bern: Verlag Hans Huber, 1981.

Leuner, Hanscarl. *Katathymes Bilderleben, Grundstufe: Einführung in die Psychotherapie mit der Tagtraumtechnik. Ein Seminar*. Stuttgart; New York: Thieme, 1981.

Leuner, Hanscarl. *Psychotherapie und religiöses Erleben: Ein Symposion über religiöse Erfahrungen unter Einfluss von Halluzinogenen*. Berlin: VWB - Verlag für Wissenschaft und Bildung, 1996.

Lewin, Louis. *Phantastica*. Berlin: George Stilke, 1927.

Lidz, T., and A. Rothenberg. "Psychedelismus: Die Wiedergeburt des Dionysos." *Psyche* 24, no. 5 (1970): 359-74.

Liggenstorfer, Roger, Christian Rätsch, Betty G. Eisner, Álvaro Estrada, and Jochen Gartz. *María Sabina - Botin der heiligen Pilze: Vom traditionellen Schamanentum zur weltweiten Pilzkultur*. Aarau: AT-Verlag, 1998.

Lilly, John C. *The Center of the Cyclone; an Autobiography of Inner Space*. New York: Julian Press, 1972.

Lilly, John C. *Communication Between Man and Dolphin: The Possibilities of Talking with Other Species*. New York: Julian Press, 1978, 1987.

Lilly, John C. *The Deep Self*. New York, 1977.

Lilly, John C. *Man and Dolphin: Adventures of a New Scientific Frontier*. New York: Doubleday, 1961.

Lilly, John C. *The Mind of the Dolphin: A Nonhuman Intelligence*. New York: Doubleday, 1967.

Lilly, John C. *Programming and Metaprogramming in the Human Biocomputer: Theory and Experiments*. New York: Communication Research Institute, 1968.

Lilly, John C. *The Scientist: A Novel Autobiography*. Philadelphia: Lippincott, 1978. Ronin, 1996.

Lilly, John C. *Simulations of God: The Science of Belief*. New York: Simon and Schuster, 1975.

Ludwig, A.M. "Altered States of Consciousness." *Archives of General Psychiatry* 15 (1966): 225-34.

McCoy, Alfred W. *The Hidden History of CIA Torture: America's Road to Abu Ghraib*. New York, 2004.

Metzner, Ralph. *Der Brunnen der Erinnerung: Von den mythologischen Wurzeln unserer Kultur*. Braunschweig: Aurum-Verlag, 1994.

Metzner, Ralph. *The Expansion of Consciousness*. Berkeley, California: Regent Press, 2008.

Metzner, Ralph. "Reflections on the Concord Prison Project and the Follow-up Study." *Journal of Psychoactive Drugs* 30, no. 4 (1998).

Metzner, Ralph, and Diane Darling. *Sacred Mushroom of Visions: Teonanácatl: A Sourcebook on the Psilocybin Mushroom*. Rochester, Vermont: Park Street Press, 2005.

Metzner, Ralph, and Foundation Green Earth. *Mind, Space, and Time Stream: Understanding and Navigating Your States of Consciousness*. Berkeley, California: Regent Press, 2009.

Metzner, Ralph. *The Unfolding Self: Varieties of Transformative Experience*. Novato, California: Origin Press, 1998.

Michels, Volker, and Hermann Hesse. *Materialien zu Hermann Hesses "Der Steppenwolf."* Frankfurt am Main: Suhrkamp, 1972.

Miles, Barry. *In the Sixties*. London: Jonathan Cape, 2002.

Miles, Barry. *Hippie*. New York, New York: Sterling, 2004.

Mithoefer, M.C. "The Safety and Efficacy of ±3,4-Methylenedioxy-Methamphetamine-Assisted Psychotherapy in Subjects with Chronic Treatment-Resistant Posttraumatic Stress Disorder. The First Randomized Controlled Pilot Study." *Journal of Psychopharmacology* 25, no. 4 (2010): 439-52.

Mullen, S. "Captain Al' Hubbard. An Appreciation." *Agoravox* 27 (October 2009).

Mullis, Kary B. *Dancing Naked in the Mind Field*. New York: Pantheon Books, 1998.

Mylonas, George E. *Eleusis and the Eleusinian Mysteries*. Princeton, New Jersey: Princeton University Press, 1961.

Naranjo, Claudio. *The Healing Journey: New Approaches to Consciousness.* New York: Pantheon Books, 1974.

Narby, Jeremy. *The Cosmic Serpent: DNA and the Origins of Knowledge.* New York: J.P. Tarcher/Putnam, 1998.

Newland, Constance A. *Abenteuer im Unbewußten: Das Experiment einer Frau mit der Droge LSD.* Munich: Szczesny, 1964.

Nichols, D.E. "Hallucinogens." *Pharmacology & Therapeutics* 101 (2004): 131-81.

Nutt, D., L.A. King, W. Saulsbury, and C. Blakemore. "Development of a Rational Scale to Assess the Harm of Drugs of Potential Misuse." *Lancet* 369, no. 9566 (2007): 1047-53.

Olvedi, Ulli. *LSD-Report.* Frankfurt am Main: Suhrkamp, 1972.

Osmond, Humphrey. "Ololiuqui: The ancient Aztec narcotic. Effects of Rivea corymbosa." *British Journal of Psychiatry,* 101, 526-537, 1955.

Ott, Jonathan. *The Age of Entheogens & the Angel's Dictionary.* Kennewick, Washington: Natural Products Co., 1995.

Ott, Jonathan. *Hallucinogenic Plants of North America.* Berkeley, California: Wingbow Press, 1976.

Ott, Jonathan. *Pharmacotheon: Entheogenic Drugs, Their Plant Sources and History.* Kennewick, Washington: Natural Products Co., 1993.

Otto, Steve. *Can You Pass the Acid Test?: A History of the Drug and Sex Counterculture and Its Censorship in the 20th Century.* Frederic, Maryland: Publish America, 2007.

Pahnke, W.N., A.A. Kurland, S. Unger, C. Savage, and S. Grof. "The Experimental Use of Psychedelic (LSD) Psychotherapy." *JAMA: the Journal of the American Medical Association* 212, no. 11 (1970): 1856-63.

Pahnke, Walter N., Albert A. Kurland, Sanford Unger, Charles Savage, Sidney Wolf, and Louis E. Goodman. "Psychedelic Therapy (Utilizing LSD) with Cancer Patients." *Journal of Psychoactive Drugs* 3, no. 1 (1970): 63-75.

Pahnke, Walter N., and William A. Richards. "Implications of LSD and Experimental Mysticism." *Journal of Religion and Health* 5, no. 3 (1966): 175-208.

Pahnke, Walter Norman. *Drugs and Mysticism: An Analysis of the Relationship between Psychedelic Drugs and the Mystical Consciousness.* A Thesis presented to the Committee on Higher Degrees in History and Philosophy of Religion, Harvard University, June 1963.

Pellerin, Cheryl. *Trips: Wie Halluzinogene wirken.* Aarau: AT Verlag, 2001.

Perry, Charles. *The Haight-Ashbury: A History.* New York: Random House, 1984.

Pinchbeck, Daniel. *Breaking Open the Head: A Psychedelic Journey into the Heart of Contemporary Shamanism.* New York: Broadway Books, 2002.

Pletscher, A. and D. Ladewig. *50 Years of LSD: Current Status and Perspectives of Hallucinogens: A Symposium of the Swiss Academy of Medical Sciences.* (Lugano-Agno, Switzerland, October 21 and 22, 1993.) New York: Parthenon, 1994.

Puharich, Andrija. *The Sacred Mushroom: Key to the Door of Eternity.* Garden City, New Jersey, 1959.

Ram Dass. *The Only Dance There Is: Talks Given at the Menninger Foundation, Topeka, Kansas, 1970, and at Spring Grove Hospital, Spring Grove, Maryland, 1972.* Garden City, New York: Anchor Press, 1974.

Ram Dass. *Remember: Be Here Now.* San Cristobal, N.M.: s.n., 1971.

Ram Dass, and Rameshwar Das. *Be Love Now: The Path of the Heart.* New York: HarperOne, 2010.

Ram Dass, and Stephen Levine. *Grist for the Mill.* Santa Cruz, California: Unity Press, 1977.

Ram Dass, Ralph Metzner, and Gary Bravo. *Birth of a Psychedelic Culture: Conversations About Leary, the Harvard Experiments, Millbrook and the Sixties.* Santa Fe, New Mexico: Synergetic Press, 2010.

Rätsch, Christian. *50 Jahre LSD-Erfahrung: Eine Jubiläumsschrift.* Solothurn; Löhrbach: Nachtschatten-Verlag, 1994.

Rätsch, Christian. *Enzyklopädie der psychoaktiven Pflanzen: Botanik, Ethnopharmakologie und Anwendung.* Aarau: AT Verlag, 1998.

Rätsch, Christian. *Pilze und Menschen: Gebrauch, Wirkung und Bedeutung der Pilze in der Kultur.* Aarau; Munich: AT Verlag, 2010.

Rätsch, Christian, ed. *Das Tor zu inneren Räumen: Heilige Pflanzen und psychedelische Substanzen als Quelle spiritueller Inspiration: Eine Festschrift zu Ehren von Albert Hofmann.* Südergellersen: Verlag Bruno Martin, 1992.

Reavis, Edward. *Rauschgiftesser erzählen: Eine Dokumentation.* Frankfurt am Main: Bärmeier u. Nikel, 1967.

Reko, Victor A. *Magische Gifte. Rausch- und Betäubungsmitteld der neuen Welt.* Stuttgart, 1936.

Richards, W., S. Grof, L. Goodman and A.A. Kurland. "LSD-Assisted Psychotherapy and the Human Encounter with Death." *Journal of Transpersonal Psychology* 4, no. 2 (1972): 121-50.

Riedlinger, T.J. and T. Leary. "Strong Medicine for Prisoner Reform. The Concord Prison Experiment." *MAPS Bulletin* 4, no. 4 (1994): 22-25.

Rinella, Michael A. *Pharmakon: Plato, Drug Culture, and Identity in Ancient Athens.* Lanham, Maryland: Lexington Books, 2010.

Roberts, Andy. *Albion Dreaming: A Popular History of LSD in Britain.* London: Marshall Cavendish, 2008.

Roberts, Thomas B. *Psychedelic Horizons.* Charlottesville, Virginia; Exeter, UK, 2006.

Rom, Tom, and Pascal Querner. *GOA—20 Years of Psychedelic Trance.* Solothurn: Nachtschatten Verlag, 2010.

Ross, Colin A. *Bluebird: Deliberate Creation of Multiple Personality by Psychiatrists.* Richardson, Texas: Manitou Communications, 2000.

Roszak, Theodore. *From Satori to Silicon Valley: San Francisco and the American Counterculture.* San Francisco, California: Don't Call It Frisco Press, 1986.

Roszak, Theodore. *The Making of a Counter Culture: Reflections on the Technocratic Society and Its Youthful Opposition.* New York: Doubleday, 1969.

Rubin, David S., ed. *Psychedelic: Optical and Visionary Art since the 1960s.* San Antonio, TX; Cambridge, Massachusetts: San Antonio Museum of Art in association with the MIT Press, 2010.

Ruck, Carl A.P. *Sacred Mushrooms of the Goddess and the Secrets of Eleusis.* Berkeley, California: Ronin, 2006.

Ruck, Carl A.P. "Wasson and the Psychedelic Revolution." www.brain-waving.com.

Sahagún, Bernardino de. *Historia general de las cosas de Nueva España.* 1569-1585. Mexico 1938, Madrid 1905, Mexico, 1986.

Samorini, Giorgio. *Halluzinogene im Mythos: Erzählungen vom Ursprung der psychoaktiven Pflanzen.* Solothurn: Nachtschatten Verlag, 1998.

Sandford, Jeremy. *In Search of the Magic Mushroom: A Journey Through Mexico.* New York: 1973.

Sankar, D.V. Siva. *LSD: A Total Study.* Westbury, New York: PJD Publications, 1975.

Santesson, Carl Gustaf. *Einige mexikanische Rauschdrogen.* Stockholm: Almqvist & Wiksell, 1939.

Saunders, Nicholas, Anja Saunders, and Michelle Pauli. *In Search of the Ultimate High: Spiritual Experience from Psychoactives.* London: Rider, 2000.

Savage, C. "Lysergic Acid Diethylamide (LSD-25). A Clinical-Psychological Study." *American Journal of Psychiatry* 108 (1952): 898.

Schmidbauer, Wolfgang. "Halluzinogene in Eleusis?" *Antaois* 10, no. 18 (1969).

Schmidbauer, Wolfgang, and Jürgen VomScheidt. *Handbuch der Rauschdrogen.* Frankfurt am Main: Fischer Taschenbuch Verlag, 2003. W.,

Schou, Nick. *Orange Sunshine: The Brotherhood of Eternal Love and Its Quest to Spread Peace, Love, and Acid to the World.* New York: Thomas Dunne Books, 2010.

Schultes, Richard Evans. *A Contribution to Our Knowledge of Rivea Corymbosa, the Narcotic Ololiqui of the Aztecs.* Cambridge, Massachusetts: Botanical Museum of Harvard University, 1941.

Schultes, Richard Evans. *The Identification of Teonanacatl. A Narcotic Basidiomycete of the Aztecs.* Botanical Museum Leaflets of Harvard, Vol. 7(3):32–54, February 21, 1939.

Schultes, Richard Evans. "Teonanacatl: The Narcotic Mushroom of the Aztecs." *American Anthropologist* 42, no. 3 (1940): 429-43.

Schultes, Richard Evans, and Albert Hofmann. *The Botany and Chemistry of Hallucinogens.* Springfield, Illinois: Thomas, 1973.

Schultes, Richard Evans, and Albert Hofmann. *Plants of the Gods: Origins of Hallucinogenic Use.* New York: McGraw-Hill, 1979.

Schultes, Richard Evans, and Elmer W. Smith. *Hallucinogenic Plants.* New York: Golden Press, 1976.

Selvoin, J. *Summer of Love.* London: Dutton/Penguin, 1994.

Sessa, B. "Can Psychedelics Have a Role in Psychiatry Once Again?" *The British Journal of Psychiatry,* June (2005): 457-58.

Sewell, R.A., J.H. Halpern, and H.G. Pope, Jr. "Response of Cluster Headache to Psilocybin and LSD." *Neurology* 66, no. 12 (2006): 1920-2.

Sewell R.A. and J.H. Halpern. "The Effects of Psilocybin and LSD on Cluster Headache. A Series of 53 Cases." Abstract. Presented to the National Headache Foundation's Annual Headache Research Summit. February, 2006.

Shafy, S. "Ein Schubs in der Not." *Der Spiegel* 30, no. 20, July 2009.

Sherwood, J.N., M.J. Stolaroff, and W.W. Harman. "The Psychedelic Experience: A New Concept in Psychotherapy." *Journal of Neuropsychiatry* 4 (1962).

Shulgin, Alexander T., and Ann Shulgin. *Pihkal: A Chemical Love Story.* Berkeley, California: Transform Press, 1992.

Shulgin, Alexander T., and Ann Shulgin. *Tihkal: The Continuation.* Berkeley, California: Transform Press, 1997.

Simpson, C. *Blowback: America's Recruitment of Nazis and Its Effects on the Cold War.* New York: Collier Books, 1989.

Singer, Rolf. "Mycological Investigations on Teonanácatl, the Mexican hallucinogenic mushrooms. Part I. The history of Teonanácatl, field work and culture." *Mycologia* 50, no. 2 (1958): 239-61.

Singer, Rolf, and Alexander H. Smith. "Mycological Investigations on Teonanácatl, the Mexican hallucinogenic mushrooms. Part II. A taxonomic monograph of Psilocybe, section Caerulescentes." *Mycologia* 50, no. 2 (1958): 262-303.

Slotkin, James Sydney. *The Peyote Religion: A Study in Indian-White Relations.* Glencoe, Illinois: Free Press, 1956.

Smith, Huston. *Cleansing the Doors of Perception: The Religious Significance of Entheogenic Plants and Chemicals.* New York: Jeremy P. Tarcher/Putnam, 2000.

Snelders, S. "The LSD Therapy Career of Jan Bastiaans, M.D." *MAPS Bulletin* 8 (1998): 18-20.

Snyder, Solomon H. *Drugs and the Brain.* New York: Scientific American Books, 1986.

Solomon, David, ed. *LSD: The Consciousness-Expanding Drug.* New York: G.P. Putnam's Sons, 1966.

Stafford, P. *Psychedelic Encyclopedia.* Berkeley, California, 1977.

Stafford, Peter G., and B.H. Golightly. *LSD: The Problem-Solving Psychedelic.* New York: Award Books, 1967.

Stamets, Paul. *Psilocybin Mushrooms of the World: An Identification Guide.* Berkeley, California: Ten Speed Press, 1996.

Steckel, Ronald. *Bewusstseinserweiternde Drogen: Eine Aufforderung zur Diskussion.* Berlin: Edition Voltaire, 1969.

Stevens, Jay. *Storming Heaven: LSD and the American Dream.* New York: Atlantic Monthly Press, 1987.

Stockings, G.T. "A clinical study of the mescaline psychosis, with special reference to the mechanism of the genesis of schizophrenic and other psychotic states." *The British Journal of Psychiatry* 86, no. 360 (1940): 29-47.

Stolaroff, Myron J. *Thanatos to Eros: Thirty-Five Years of Psychedelic Exploration.* Berlin: VWB - Verlag für Wissenschaft und Bildung, 1994.

Stolaroff, Myron J. *The Secret Chief: Conversations with a Pioneer of the Underground Psychedelic Movement.* Charlotte, North Carolina: MAPS, 1997.

Stolaroff, Myron J. *The Secret Chief Revealed: Conversations with Leo Zeff, A Pioneer of the Underground Psychedelic Therapy Movement.* Sarasota, Florida: MAPS, 2004.

Stoll, W.A. "Ein Neues, in sehr kleinen Mengen wirksames Phantastikum." *Schweizer Archiv für Neurologie und Psychiatrie* 64 (1949): 483.

Stoll, W.A. "LSD, ein Phantastikum aus der Mutterkorngruppe." *Schweizer Archiv für Neurologie und Psychiatrie* 60 (1947): 279.

Stratton, R. "Altered States of America. The CIA's Covert LSD Experiments." *SPIN* magazine, March 1994.

Straumann L., Wildmann D. Schweizer Chemieunternehmen im "Dritten Reich," Veröffentlichung der Unabhängigen Expertenkommission Schweiz – Zweiter Weltkrieg, Zurich 2002.

Stresser-Péan, G. "Hippies Flocking to México for Mushroom Trips." *New York Times*, 23, July 1970.

Taeger, Hans Hinrich. *Spiritualität und Drogen: Interpersonelle Zusammenhänge von Psychedelika und religiös-mystischen Aspekten in der Gegenkultur der 70er Jahre.* Markt Erlbach: Martin, 1988.

Tarnas, Richard. "LSD Psychotherapy: Theoretical Implications for the Study of Psychology." A Thesis, Humanistic Psychology Institute, San Francisco, 1976.

Tart, Charles T. *Altered States of Consciousness: A Book of Readings.* New York: Wiley, 1969.

Tendler, Stewart, and David May. *The Brotherhood of Eternal Love: From Flower Power to Hippie Mafia: The Story of the LSD Counterculture.* London: Cyan, 2007.

Thomas, Gordon. *Journey into Madness: The True Story of Secret CIA Mind Control and Medical Abuse.* New York: Bantam Books, 1989.

Thomas, Klaus. *Die künstlich gesteuerte Seele.* Stuttgart: Enke, 1970.

Tonkinson, Carole. *Big Sky Mind: Buddhism and the Beat Generation.* New York: Riverhead Books, 1995.

Torgoff, Martin. *Can't Find My Way Home: America in the Great Stoned Age, 1945-2000.* New York: Simon & Schuster, 2004.

Trachsel, Daniel, and Nicolas Richard. *Psychedelische Chemie.* Solothurn: Nachtschatten Verlag, 2000.

Troxler, F., F. Seemann, and A. Hofmann. "Abwandlungsprodukte von Psilocybin und Psilocin. 2. Mitteilung über synthetische Indolverbindungen." *Helvetica Chimica Acta* 42, no. 6 (1959): 2073-103.

Turner, Fred. *From Counterculture to Cyberculture: Stewart Brand, the Whole Earth Network, and the Rise of Digital Utopianism.* Chicago: University of Chicago Press, 2006.

Turner, Steve. *The Gospel According to the Beatles.* Louisville, Kentucky; Westminster, UK: John Knox, 2006.

Villoldo, Alberto, and Stanley Krippner. *Healing States.* New York: Simon & Schuster, 1987.

Vollenweider, F.X., and M. Kometer. "The Neurobiology of Psychedelic Drugs: Implications for the Treatment of Mood Disorders." *Nature Reviews Neuroscience* 11, no. 9 (2010): 642-51.

Wallraff, Günter, with illustrations by Jens Jensen. *Meskalin: Ein Selbstversuch.* Berlin, 1968.

Walsh, Roger N., and Charles S. Grob. *Higher Wisdom: Eminent Elders Explore the Continuing Impact of Psychedelics.* State University of New York Press, 2005.

Wasson, R.G. "The Divine Mushroom: Primitive Religion and Hallucinatory Agents." *Proceedings of the American Philosophical Society* 102, no. 3 (1958): 221-23.

Wasson, R.G. "The Mushroom Rites of Mexico." Harvard Review 1 (1963): 7-17.

Wasson R.G. "The Hallucinogenic Mushrooms of Mexico. An Adventure in Ethnomycological Exploration." *Transactions of the New York Academy of Sciences* 21:325–339, 1959

Wasson, R.G. *Persephone's Quest: Entheogens and the Origins of Religion.* New Haven: Yale University Press, 1986.

Wasson, R.G. "Seeking the Magic Mushroom." *LIFE* magazine, May 13, 1957.

Wasson, R.G. *Soma: Divine Mushroom of Immortality.* New York: Harcourt, Brace & World, 1968.

Wasson, R.G. *The Wondrous Mushroom: Mycolatry in Mesoamerica.* New York: McGraw-Hill, 1980.

Wasson, R.G., Albert Hofmann, and Carl A.P. Ruck. *The Road to Eleusis: Unveiling the Secret of the Mysteries.* New York: Harcourt, Brace, Jovanovich, 1978.

Wasson R.G. *The Hallucinogenic Fungi of Mexico. An Inquiry into the Origins of the Religious Idea Among Primitive Peoples.* Botanical Museum Leaflets of Harvard 19(7): 137–162, 1961, Originally given on August 30, 1960 as the annual lecture of the Mycological Society of America in Stillwater, Oklahoma 1960.

Wasson, R.G., and Thomas J. Riedlinger. *The Sacred Mushroom Seeker: Essays for R. Gordon Wasson.* Portland, Oregon: Dioscorides Press, 1990.

Wasson, R.G. *The Hallucinogenic Mushrooms of Mexico and Psilocybin: A Bibliography.* Botanical Museum, Harvard University, 1963.

Wasson, Valentina Pavlovna, and R. G. Wasson. *Mushrooms, Russia and History.* New York: Pantheon Books, 1957.

Watts, Alan. *The Joyous Cosmology: Adventures in the Chemistry of Consciousness.* New York: Pantheon Books, 1962.

Weil, Andrew. "Drugs and the Mind." *Harvard Review* 1, no. 4, Summer 1963: 1-3.

Weil, Andrew. *The Natural Mind: A New Way of Looking at Drugs and the Higher Consciousness*. Boston: Houghton Mifflin, 1972.

Weil, Andrew. "The Strange Case of the Harvard Drug Scandal." *LOOK* magazine, November 5, 1963.

Weil, Gunther M., Ralph Metzner, and Timothy Leary, eds. *The Psychedelic Reader: Selected from the Psychedelic Review*. Secaucus, New Jersey: Carol Publishing Group, 1993.

Weinreich, Wulf Mirko. *Integrale Psychotherapie: Ein umfassendes Therapiemodell auf der Grundlage der Integralen Philosophie nach Ken Wilber*. Leipzig: Araki, 2005.

Wilber, Ken. *The Spectrum of Consciousness*. Wheaton, Illinois: Theosophical Publishing House, 1993.

Winkelman, Michael, and Thomas B. Roberts. *Psychedelic Medicine: New Evidence for Hallucinogenic Substances as Treatments*. Westport, Connecticut: Praeger Publishers, 2007.

Witt, Peter Nikolaus. *Die Wirkung von Substanzen auf den Netzbau der Spinne als biologischer Test*. Berlin: Springer, 1956.

Wolfe, Tom. *The Electric Kool-Aid Acid Test*. New York: Bantam Books, 1999.

Yensen, Richard, and D. Dryer. "Thirty Years of Psychedelic Research: The Spring Grove Experiment and Its Sequels." *Yearbook of the European College for the Study of Consciousness (ECBS) 1993–1994*, 1995, 73-101. Berlin: VWB - Verlag für Wissenschaft und Bildung.

Yensen, Richard. "Vom Mysterium zum Paradigma. Die Reise des Menschen von heiligen Pflanzen zu psychedelischen Drogen." See: *Das Tor zu inneren Räumen* (1992) under Rätsch, Christian, op. cit.

Zehentbauer, Josef. *Körpereigene Drogen: Die ungenutzten Fähigkeiten unseres Gehirns*. Munich: Artemis & Winkler, 1992.

Zinberg, Norman Earl. *Drug, Set, and Setting: The Basis for Controlled Intoxicant Use*. New Haven, Connecticut: Yale University Press, 1984.

Zinberg, Norman Earl. *Alternate States of Consciousness: Multiple Perspectives on the Study of Consciousness*. New York: The Free Press; London: Collier Macmillan, 1977.

The final resting place of Albert and Anita Hofmann

Publications by Albert Hofmann

Books

Hofmann, Albert. *Die Mutterkornalkaloide: Vom Mutterkorn zum LSD - die Chemie der Mutterkornalkaloide.* Stuttgart, 1964. Reprint of Original. Solothurn, 2000.

Hofmann, Albert. *LSD – Mein Sorgenkind.* Stuttgart,1979, München, 1999. English: *LSD – My Problem Child.* New York, 1980; *LSD – My Problem Child. Reflections on Sacred Drugs, Mysticism and Science.* Los Angeles, 1983. French: *Mon Enfant Terrible.* Montpellier, 1983. Spanish: *LSD – Como descubrí el ácido y que pasó después en el mundo.* Barcelona, 1980. Italian: *LSD – il mio bambino difficile.* Milano, 1995.

Hofmann, Albert. *Einsichten Ausblicke.* Basel: Sphinx, 1986. Revised and expanded edition, Solothurn, 2003. English: *Insight Outlook*, Atlanta, Georgia, 1989.

Hofmann, Albert, and Werner Huber. *Lob des Schauens.* 1996. Reprint, Solothurn: Nachtschatten-Verlag, 2002.

Wasson, R.G., Albert Hofmann, and Carl A.P. Ruck. *The Road to Eleusis: Unveiling the Secret of the Mysteries.* 1978. Reprint, Berkeley, California: 2008. *Der Weg nach Eleusis. Das Geheimnis der Mysterien*, Frankfurt,1984. *El camino a Eleusis. Una solución al enigma de los Misterios*, México, 1980.

Schultes, Richard Evans, and Albert Hofmann. *Plants of the Gods: Origins of hallucinogenic use.* 1979. Reprint, Rochester, 2001. *Pflanzen der Götter. Die magischen Kräfte der Rausch und Giftgewächse*, Bern, Stuttgart: Hallwag, 1980. *Überarbeitete und ergänzte Neuauflage.* Aarau : AT Verlag, 1998. *Les plantes des dieux. Les plantes hallucinogènes, botanique et ethnologie.* Paris, 1993. *Plantas de los dioses: orígenes del uso de los alucinógenos.* México, 2002.

Schultes, Richard Evans, and Albert Hofmann. *The Botany and Chemistry of Hallucinogens.* Rev. and enl. 2d ed. Springfield, Illinois: Thomas, 1980.

Scientific Papers and Articles

Baldwin, M., and A. Hofmann. "Hallucinations." *Handbook of Clinical Neurology* 4 (1969): 327-39.

Bhattacharji, S., A.J. Birch, A. Brack, A. Hofmann, H. Kobel, D.C.C. Smith, Herchel Smith, and J. Winter. "79 Studies in Relation to Biosynthesis. Part XXVII. The Biosynthesis of Ergot Alkaloids." *Journal of the Chemical Society* (1962): 421-25.

Brack, A., A. Hofmann, F. Kalberer, H. Kobel, and J. Rutschmann. "Tryptophan aus biogenetischer Vorstufe des Psilocybins." *Archiv der Pharmazie* 294 (1961): 230-34.

Cerletti, A., and A. Hofmann. "Mushrooms and Toadstools." *Lancet* 1, no. 7271 (1963): 58-9.

Fehr, T., P.A. Stadler, and A. Hofmann. "Demethylierung des Lysergsäuregerüstes." *Helvetica Chimica Acta* 53, no. 8 (1970): 2197-201.

Goutarel, R., A. Hofmann, M.M. Janot, A. Le Hir, and N. Neuss. "Identité de l'iso-rau-himbine et de la 3-épi-a-yohimbine." *Helvetica Chimica Acta* 40 (1957): 156-60.

Heim, R., A. Brack, H. Kobel, A. Hofmann, and R. Cailleux. "Déterminisme de la formation des carpophores et des sclérotes dans la culture du psilocybe mexicana Heim, Agaric hallucinogéne du Mexique, et mise en évidence de la psilocybine et de la psilocine." *Comptes rendus hebdomadaires des séances de l'Académie des Sciences* 246 (1958): 1346-51.

Heim, R., A. Hofmann, and H. Tscherter. "Sur une Intoxication collective à syndrome psilocybien causée en France par un Copelandia." *Comptes rendus hebdomadaires des séances de l'Académie des Sciences. Série D: Sciences naturelles* 262, no. 4 (1966): 519-23.

Heim, R., and A. Hofmann. "Isolement de la psilocybine à partir du Stropharia cubensis Earle et d'autres espèces de champignons hallucinogènes mexicains appartenant au genre Psilocybe." *Comptes rendus hebdomadaires des séances de l'Académie des Sciences* 247 (1958): 557-61.

Hofmann, A., A.J. Frey, and H. Ott. "Die Totalsynthese des Ergotamins." *Experientia* 17, no. 5 (1961): 206-07.

Hofmann, A., R. Heim, A. Brack, H. Kobel, A.J. Frey, H. Ott, Th. Petrzilka, and F. Troxler. "Psilocybin und Psilocin, zwei psychotrope Wirkstoffe aus mexikanischen Rauschpilzen." *Helvetica Chimica Acta* 42, no. 5 (1959): 1557-72.

Hofmann, A., H. Ott, R. Griot, P.A. Stadler, and A.J. Frey. "Die Synthese und Stereochemie des Ergotamins. (58. Mitteilung über Mutterkornalkaloide." *Helvetica Chimica Acta* 46, no. 6 (1963): 2306-28.

Hofmann, Albert. "The Active Principles of the Seeds of Rivea Corymbosa and Ipomoea Violacea." *Psychedelic Review* 1 (1963): 302-16.

Hofmann, A. Alcaloïdes indoliques isolés de plantes hallucinogènes et narcotiques du Mexique, Phytochemie et plantes medicinales des terres du Pacifique, Nouméa (Nouvelle-Calédonie) 28 (1966): 223-41.

Hofmann, A. "Arzneimittel pflanzlicher Herkunft." *Kontakt* 15 (Juli 1962).

Hofmann, A. "b-Yohimbin aus den Wurzeln von Rauwolfia canescens L." *Helvetica Chimica Acta* 38 (1955).

Hofmann, A. "Chemical aspects of psilocybin, the psychotropic principle from the Mexican fungus, Psilocybe mexicana Heim." *Neuro-Psychopharmacology* (1959): 446-48.

Hofmann, A. "Chemical, pharmacological and medical aspects of psychotomimetics." *Journal of Experimental Medical Sciences* 5 (1961): 31-51.

Hofmann, A. "Das Geheimnis der mexikanischen Zauberpilze gelüftet." *Schweizer Radio-Zeitung* 4 (1960): 7-10.

Hofmann, A. "Die Chemie der Mutterkorn-Alkaloide." *Planta Medica* 6 (1958): 381-94.

Hofmann, A. "Die Chemie der Rauwolfia-Alkaloide unter Berücksichtigung neuester Ergebnisse." *Planta Medica* 5 (1957): 145-56.

Hofmann, A. "Die Erforschung der mexikanischen Zauberpilze." *Schweizer Zeitschrift für Pilzkunde* 1 (1961): 1-10.

Hofmann, A. "Die Erforschung der mexikanischen Zauberpilze und das Problem ihrer Wirkstoffe." *Basler Stadtbuch* 1964 (1964): 141–56.

Hofmann, A. "Die Geschichte des LSD 25." *Triangel, Sandoz-Zeitschrift für medizinische Wissenschaft* 2 (1955): 117-24.

Hofmann, A. "Die heiligen Pilze in der Heilbehandlung der Maria Sabina." *Ethnopsychotherapie, Psychotherapie mittels außergewöhnlicher Bewusstseinszustände in westlichen und indigenen Kulturen*, edited by A. Dittrich and C. Scharfetter. Stuttgart: 1987.

Hofmann, A. "Die Isolierung weiterer Alkaloide aus Rauwolfia serpentina Benth. 3. Mitteilung über Rauwolfia-Alkaloide." *Helvetica Chimica Acta* 37, no. 3 (1954): 849-65.

Hofmann, A. "Die kulturhistorische Bedeutung halluzinogener Drogen." Lecture given at the Internationalen Pharmaziehistorischen Kongress, Basel 1979; *Sphinx Magazin* 16 (1981), 12-13.

Hofmann, A. "Die neuesten Ergebnisse auf dem Gebiet der Mutterkornalkaloide." *Dansk Tidskrift for Farmaci* 37 (1963): 181-200.

Hofmann, A. "Die psychotropen Wirkstoffe der mexikanischen Zauberpilze." *Chimia* 14 (1960): 309-18.

Hofmann, A. "Die psychotropen Wirkstoffe der mexikanischen Zauberpilze." *Verh. Naturforschung Gesellschaft* 71 (1960): 239-56.

Hofmann, A. "Die psychotropen Wirkstoffe der mexikanischen Zauberpilze." *Chemistry Letters* 383 (1965): 156-64.

Hofmann, A. "Die Wechselbeziehung von innerem und äußerem Raum, Das Sender-Empfänger-Konzept der Wirklichkeit." *Sphinx Magazin* 25 (1984).

Hofmann, A. "Die Wirkstoffe der mexikanischen Zauberdroge Ololiuqui." *Planta Medica* 9, no. 04 (1961): 354-67.

Hofmann, A. "Discovery of D-Lysergic Acid Diethylamide – LSD." *Excerpta Sandoz* 1 (1955): 3-4.

Hofmann, A. "The discovery of LSD and subsequent investigations on naturally occurring hallucinogens." *Discoveries in Biological Psychiatry*, edited by F.J. Ayd, Jr. and B. Blackwell, 91-106. Philadelphia, Pennsylvania: Lippincott, 1970.

Hofmann, A. "Drugs originating from plant sources." *Contact* 15 (July 1962): 4-6.

Hofmann, A. "Einsichten Ausblicke. Geborgenheit im Naturwissenschaftlich-philosophischen Weltbild." *Entheogene Blätter* 2 (2003): 160-72.

Hofmann, A. "Gehaltsbestimmung und Pharmakologie des Mutterkorns und seiner Zubereitungen." *Pharmaceutisch Weekblad* 100, no. 44 (1965): 1261-83.

Hofmann, A. "Gli allucinogeni." *Panorama medico Sandoz* 1 (1971): 4-10.

Hofmann, A. "Historia de las investigaciones químicas básicas sobre los hongos sagrados de México." In *Teonanácatl: Hongos alucinógenos de Europa y América del Norte*, edited by J. Ott and J. Bigwood, 55-68. El Escorial: Swan, 1985.

Hofmann, A. "History of the Basic Chemical Investigations on the Sacred Mushrooms of Mexico." In *Teonanácatl, Hallucinogenic Mushrooms of North America*, edited by J. Ott and J. Bigwood, 47-61. Seattle: Madrona, 1978.

Hofmann, A. "How LSD originated." *Journal of Psychedelic Drugs* 11, no. 1-2 (1979).

Hofmann, A. "Investigaciones sobre los hongos alucinógenos mexicanos y la importancia que tienen en la medicina sus substancias activas." *Artes de México* 16 (1969): 23-31. (Includes English translation)

Hofmann, A. "La constitución de los alcaloides del cornezuelo." *Farmacognosia* 13 (1954) 333-356.

Hofmann, A. "La estructura del ácido lisérgico." *Farmacognosia* 13 (1954): 311–332.

Hofmann, A. "Le teonanácatl el l'ololiuqui, deux anciennes drogues magiques du Mexique." *Bulletin des stupéfiants* 23 (1971): 3-14.

Hofmann, A. "Les hallucinogènes." *La recherche* 1 (1970): 239-57.

Hofmann, A. "Los alcaloides con núcleo indólico." *Farmacognosia* 13 (1954): 293–310.

Hofmann, A. "Mexikanische Zauberdrogen und ihre Wirkstoffe." *Planta Medica* 12, no. 03 (1964): 341-52.

Hofmann, A. Naturwissenschaft und mystische Weltanschauung, als "Laienpredigt." *Nicht Fisch, Nicht Vogel*, edited by T. Pfeifer and H.R. Felix. Basel 1994.

Hofmann, A. "Neuere Entwicklungen auf dem Gebiet der Mutterkornalkaloide." *Pharmazeutische Zeitung* 110 (1965): 1371-78.

Hofmann, A. "Notes and documents concerning the discovery of LSD." *Agents and Actions* 1, no. 3 (1970): 148-50.

Hofmann, A. "Oxytocics." *Journal of Experimental Medical Sciences* 4 (1961): 105-25.

Hofmann, A. "Pilzgifte als Halluzinogene." *Selecta* 7 (1965): 2146.

Hofmann, A. "Planned research and chance discovery." *International Sandoz Gazette* 23, no. 3 (1979).

Hofmann, A. "Planned research and chance discovery in pharmaceutical development." *Clinical Research and Regulatory Affairs* 16, no. 4 (1999): 139-56.

Hofmann, A. "Psychoaktive Drogen als Berührungspunkt naturwissenschaftlicher Forschung mit modernem Mystizismus." *Neue Zürcher Zeitung* 4 (March 1970): 27-29.

Hofmann, A. "Psychoaktive Stoffe aus Pflanzen." *Die Therapie Woche* 17 (1967): 1739-46.

Hofmann, A. "Psychotomimetic Agents." Burger A., ed. *Chemical Constitution and Pharmacodynamic Action*, Vol. II, *Drugs Affecting the Central Nervous System*. New York: M. Dekker (1968), pp. 169–235.

Hofmann, A. "Psychotomimetic drugs: chemical and pharmacological aspects." *Acta Physiologica et Pharmacologica Neerlandica* 8 (1959): 240–258.

Hofmann, A. "Psychotomimetic Substances." *The Indian Journal of Pharmacy* 25 (1963): 245-56.

Hofmann, A. "Psychotomimetics, chemical, pharmacological and clinical aspects." *The Indian Practitioner* 14 (1961): 195-197.

Hofmann, A. "Rauhimbin und Isorauhimbin, zwei neue Alkaloide aus Rauwolfia serpentina Benth. 2. Mitteilung über Rauwolfia-Alkaloide." *Helvetica Chimica Acta* 37, no. 1 (1954): 314-20.

Hofmann, A. "Recent developments in ergot alkaloids." *The Australasian Journal of Pharmacy (*30 January 1961).

Hofmann, A. "Recherches sur des alcaloïdes peptidiques d'ergot semi-synthétiques." *Bulletin de chimie thérapeutique* 5 (1968): 367-55.

Hofmann, A. "Relationship between spatial arrangement and mental effects." Rinkel, M., and H.C.B. Denber, eds. *Chemical Concepts of Psychosis.* New York: McDowell, Obolensky (1958). 85-90.

Hofmann, A. "Ride through the Sierra Mazateca in Search of the Magic Plant Ska 'Maria Pastora.'" *The Sacred Mushroom Seeker. Essays for R. Gordon Wasson*, edited by T.J. Riedlinger, 115-27. Portland, Oregon, 1990.

Hofmann, A. "Rudolf Gelpke und der Hanf-Rausch." *Die berauschte Schweiz*, edited by R. Liggenstorfer, C. Rätsch and A. Tschudin. Solothurn 1998.

Hofmann, A. "Struktur und Synthese der Halluzinogene." *Journal Mondiale de Pharmacie* 13 (1970): 187-205.

Hofmann, A. "Teonanácatl and ololiuqui, two ancient magic drugs of Mexico." *Bulletin on Narcotics* 23 (1971): 3-10.

Hofmann, A. "The transmitter-receiver concept of reality." *ReVision: The Journal of Consciousness and Change* 10 (1988): 5-11.

Hofmann, A. "Über den Curtius'schen Abbau der isomeren Lysergsäuren und Dihydro-Lysergsäuren. (12. Mitteilung über Mutterkornalkaloide." *Helvetica Chimica Acta* 30, no. 1 (1947): 44-51.

Hofmann, A. *Über den enzymatischen Abbau des Chitins und Chitosans.* Inaugural dissertation, University of Zürich, 1929.

Hofmann, A., and A. Cerletti. "Die Wirkstoffe der dritten aztekischen Zauberdroge oder die Lösung des 'Ololiuqui'-Rätsels." *Deutsche medizinische Wochenschrift* 86 (1961): 885-93.

Hofmann, A., and A. Cerletti. "Los principios activos de la tercera droga mágica azteca o la solución del enigma "Ololiuqui." *Medicina Alemana* 11 (1961): 228-32.

Hofmann, A., and A. Cerletti. "Ololiuqui – die dritte aztekische "Zauberdroge." *Panorama* 8 (March 1961).

Hofmann, A., and A. Cerletti. "Ololiuqui – the third Aztec "wonder drug." *Panorama* 7 (July 1961).

Hofmann, A., A. Frey, H. Ott, T. Petrzilka, and F. Troxler. "Konstitutionsaufklärung und Synthese von Psilocybin." *Experientia* 14 (1958): 397-401.

Hofmann, A., R. Heim, A. Brack, and H. Kobel. "Psilocybin, ein psychotroper Wirkstoff aus dem mexikanischen Rauschpilz Psilocybe mexicana Heim." *Experientia* 14 (1958): 107-12.

Hofmann, A., Roger Heim, and Hans Tscherter. *Présence de la psilocybine dans une espèce européenne d'Agaric, Le Psilocybe semilanceata.* Paris: Gauthier-Villars], 1963.

Hofmann, A., and F. Troxler. "Identifizierung von Psilocin." *Experientia* 15 (1959): 101-04.

Hofmann, A., and H. Tscherter. "Isolierung von Lysergsäure-Alkaloiden aus der mexikanischen Zauberdroge Ololiuqui (Rivea corymbosa [L.] Hall)." *Experientia* 16 (1960): 414-16.

Le Hir, A., R. Goutarel, M.M. Janot, and A. Hofmann. "Sur la constitution de l'isorauhimbine." *Helvetica Chimica Acta* 37, no. 7 (1954): 2161-65.

Ott, H., A.J. Frey, and A. Hofmann. "The Stereospecific Cyclization of N-(a-Hydroxyacyl)-Phenylalanylproline Lactams." *Tetrahedron* 19 (1963): 1675-84.

Ott, H., A. Hofmann, and A.J. Frey. "Acid-catalyzed isomerization in the peptide part of ergot alkaloids." *Journal of the American Chemical Society* 88, no. 6 (1966): 1251-6.

Schlientz, W., R. Brunner, and A. Hofmann. "d-Lysergyl-L-valin-methylester, ein neues, natürliches Mutterkornalkaloid." *Experientia* 19 (1963): 397-98.

Schlientz, W., R. Brunner, A. Hofmann, B. Berde, and E. Stürmer. "Umlagerung von Mutterkornalkaloid-Präparaten in schwach sauren Lösungen. Pharmakologische Wirkungen der Isomerisierungsprodukte." *Pharmaceutica Acta Helvetiae* 36 (1961): 472-88.

Schlientz, W., R. Brunner, A. Rüegger, B. Berde, E. Stürmer, and A. Hofmann. "b-Ergokryptine, ein neues Alakloid der Ergotoxin-Gruppe." *Pharmaceutica Acta Helvetiae* 43 (1968): 497-509.

Schlientz, W., R. Brunner, A. Rüegger, B. Berde, E. Stürmer, and A. Hofman. "Beta-Ergokryptine, a New Alkaloid of the Ergotoxine Group." *Experientia* 23, no. 12 (1967): 991-2.

Schlientz, W., R. Brunner, P.A. Stadler, A.J. Frey, H. Ott, and A. Hofmann. "Isolierung und Synthese des Ergostins, eines neuen Mutterkorn-Alkaloids. 62. Mitteilung über Mutterkornalkaloide." *Helvetica Chimica Acta* 47, no. 7 (1964): 1921-33.

Schlientz, W., R. Brunner, F. Thudium, and A. Hofmann. "Eine neue Isomerisierungsreaktion der Mutterkornalkaloide vom Peptid-Typus." *Experientia* 17 (1961): 108-09.

Stadler, P.A., A.J. Frey, and A. Hofmann. "Herstellung der optisch aktiven Methyl-benzyloxy-malonsäurehalbester und Bestimmung ihrer absoluten Konfiguration. 57. Mitteilung über Mutterkornalkaloide." *Helvetica Chimica Acta* 46, no. 6 (1963): 2300-05.

Stadler, P.A., S. Guttmann, H. Hauth, R.L. Huguenin, E. Sandrin, G. Wersin, H. Willems, and A. Hofmann. "Die Synthese der Alkaloide der Ergotoxin-Gruppe. 70. Mitteilung über Mutterkornalkaloide." *Helvetica Chimica Acta* 52, no. 6 (1969): 1549-64.

Stadler, P.A., and A. Hofmann. "Chemische Bestimmung der absoluten Konfiguration der Lysergsäure. Mitteilung über Mutterkornalkaloide." *Helvetica Chimica Acta* 45, no. 6 (1962): 2005-11.

Stadler, P.A., A.J. Frey, F. Troxler, and A. Hofmann. "Selektive Reduktions- und Oxydationsreaktionen an Lysergsäure-Derivaten. 2,3-Dihydro- und 12-Hydroxy-lysergsäure-amide." *Helvetica Chimica Acta* 47 (1964): 756-69.

Stauffacher, D., P. Niklaus, H. Tscherter, H.P. Weber, and A. Hofmann. "Cycloclavin, ein neues Alkaloid aus Ipomoea hildebrandtii Vatke. 71. Mutterkornalkaloide." *Tetrahedron* 25, no. 24 (1969): 5879-87.

Stauffacher, D., H. Tscherter, and A. Hofmann. "Isolierung von Ergosin und Ergosinin neben Agroclavin aus den Samen von Ipomoea argyrophylla VATKE (Convolvulaceae)." *Helvetica Chimica Acta* 48, no. 6 (1965): 1379-80.

Stoll, A. "Die herzaktiven Substanzen der Meerzwiebel: Scillaren A." *Helvetica Chimica Acta* 16 (1933): 703-33.

Stoll, A., A. Brack, H. Kobel, A. Hofmann, and R. Brunner. "Die Alkaloide eines Mutterkornpilzes von Pennisetum typhoideum Rich und deren Bildung in saprophytischer Kultur. 36. Mitteilung über Mutterkornalkaloide." *Helvetica Chimica Acta* 37, no. 6 (1954): 1815-25.

Stoll, A., and A. Hofmann. "Amide der stereoisomeren Lysergsäuren und Dihydro-Lysergsäuren. 38. Mitteilung über Mutterkornalkaloide." *Helvetica Chimica Acta* 38, no. 2 (1955): 421-33.

Stoll, A., and A. Hofmann. "Canescine and pseudoyohimbine from the roots of Rauwolfia canescens L.1." *Journal of the American Chemical Society* 77, no. 3 (1955/02/01 1955): 820-21.

Stoll, A., and A. Hofmann. "Die Alkaloide der Ergotoxingruppe: Ergocristin, Ergokryptin und Ergocornin. (7. Mitteilung über Mutterkornalkaloide)." *Helvetica Chimica Acta* 26, no. 5 (1943): 1570-601.

Stoll, A., and A. Hofmann. "Die Dihydroderivate der natürlichen linksdrehenden Mutterkornalkaloide. (9. Mitteilung über Mutterkornalkaloide)." *Helvetica Chimica Acta* 26, no. 6 (1943): 2070-81.

Stoll, A., and A. Hofmann. "Die Hydrierung des Scillarens A und die physiologische Prüfung einiger Scillanderivate, 10. Mitteilung über Herzglucoside." *Helvetica Chimica Acta* 18, no. 1 (1935): 401-19.

Stoll, A., and A. Hofmann. "Die optisch aktiven Hydrazide der Lysergsäure und der Isolysergsäure. (4. Mitteilung über Mutterkornalkaloide)." *Helvetica Chimica Acta* 26, no. 3 (1943): 922-28.

Stoll, A., and A. Hofmann. "The Ergot Alkaloids." *The Alkaloids*, Vol. 8, 725-783. New York: Academic Press, 1965.

Stoll, A., and A. Hofmann. "Partialsynthese von Alkaloiden vom Typus des Ergobasins. (6. Mitteilung über Mutterkornalkaloide)." *Helvetica Chimica Acta* 26, no. 3 (1943): 944-65.

Stoll, A., and A. Hofmann. "Sarpagin, ein neues Alkaloid aus Rauwolfia serpentina Benth." *Helvetica Chimica Acta* 36, no. 5 (1953): 1143-47.

Stoll, A., and A. Hofmann. "Umsetzungsprodukte von Scillaren A (8. Mitteilung über Herzglucoside)." *Helvetica Chimica Acta* 18, no. 1 (1935): 82-95.

Stoll, A., and A. Hofmann. "Zur Kenntnis des Polypeptidteils der Mutterkornalkaloide Ii. (Partielle Alkalische Hydrolyse der Mutterkornalkaloide). 20. Mitteilung über Mutterkornalkaloide." *Helvetica Chimica Acta* 33, no. 6 (1950): 1705-11.

Stoll, A., A. Hofmann, and B. Becker. "Die Spaltstücke von Ergocristin, Ergokryptin und Ergocornin. (8. Mitteilung über Mutterkornalkaloide)." *Helvetica Chimica Acta* 26, no. 5 (1943): 1602-13.

Stoll, A., A. Hofmann, and R. Brunner. "Alkaloide aus den Blättern von Rauwolfia canescens L. 4. Mitteilung über Rauwolfia-Alkaloide." *Helvetica Chimica Acta* 38, no. 1 (1955): 270-83.

Stoll, A., A. Hofmann, and A. Helfenstein. "Die Identität der A-Scillansäure mit Allocholansäure. 11. Mitteilung über Herzglucoside." *Helvetica Chimica Acta* 18, no. 1 (1935): 644-59.

Stoll, A., A. Hofmann, and A. Helfenstein. "Die Natur der Sauerstoffatome im Scillaridin A. (6. Mitteilung über Herzglucoside)." *Helvetica Chimica Acta* 17, no. 1 (1934): 641-64.

Stoll, A., A. Hofmann, E. Jucker, Th. Petrzilka, J. Rutschmann, and F. Troxler. "Peptide der isomeren Lysergsäuren und Dihydrolysergsäuren. 18. Mitteilung über Mutterkornalkaloide." *Helvetica Chimica Acta* 33, no. 1 (1950): 108-16.

Stoll, A., A. Hofmann, and W. Kreis. "Die Doppelbindungen des Scillaridins A. (7. Mitteilung über Herzglucoside)." *Helvetica Chimica Acta* 17, no. 1 (1934): 1334-54.

Stoll, A., A. Hofmann, and W. Kreis. "Über glucosidspaltende Enzyme der Digitalisblätter. (12. Mitteilung über Herzglucoside)." *Hoppe-Seyler's Zeitschrift für physiologische Chemie*, 249, 1935.

Stoll, A., A. Hofmann, and Th. Petrzilka. "Die Dihydroderivate der rechtsdrehenden Mutterkornalkaloide (11. Mitteilung über Mutterkornalkaloide)." *Helvetica Chimica Acta* 29, no. 3 (1946): 635-53.

Stoll, A., A. Hofmann, and Th. Petrzilka. "Die Konstitution der Mutterkornalkaloide. Struktur des Peptidteils. Iii. 24. Mitteilung über Mutterkornalkaloide." *Helvetica Chimica Acta* 34, no. 5 (1951): 1544-76.

Stoll, A., A. Hofmann, and J. Peyer. "Die Bruttoformeln des Scillaridins A und seiner Derivate (13. Mitteilung über Herzglucoside)." *Helvetica Chimica Acta* 18, no. 1 (1935): 1247-51.

Stoll, A., A. Hofmann, and W. Schlientz. "Die stereoisomeren Lysergole und Dihydro-lysergole. 15. Mitteilung über Mutterkornalkaloide." *Helvetica Chimica Acta* 32, no. 6 (1949): 1947-56.

Stoll, A., A. Hofmann, and F. Troxler. "Über die Isomerie von Lysergsäure und Isolysergsäure. 14. Mitteilung über Mutterkornalkaloide." *Helvetica Chimica Acta* 32, no. 2 (1949): 506-21.

Stoll, A., and A. Hofmann. "Alkaloids from the leaves and roots of Rauwolfia canescens L." *Society of Biological Chemists, India, Souvenir* (1955): 248-58.

Stoll, A., and A. Hofmann. "The Chemistry of the Ergot Alkaloids." *Chemistry of the Alkaloids*, edited by S.W. Pelletier, 267-300, 1970.

Stoll, A., A. Hofmann, and R. Brunner. "Über ein neues Alkaloid vom Typus der Mutterkornalkaloide." *Chimia* 8 (1954): 265-66.

Stoll, A., A. Hofmann, H.G. Leemann, H. Ott, and H.R. Schenk. "Synthese der sauren Peptidreste und der thermischen Spaltprodukte von Mutterkornalkaloiden." *Helvetica Chimica Acta* 39 (1956).

Stoll, A., W. Kreis, and A. Hofmann. "Über Scillarenase. *Hoppe-Seyler's Zeitschrift für physiologische Chemie*, 24, 1933.

Stoll, A., Th. Petrzilka, J. Rutschmann, A. Hofmann, and H. Günthard. "Über die Stereochemie der Lysergsäuren und der Dihydrolysergsäuren. 37. Mitteilung über Mutterkornalkaloide." *Helvetica Chimica Acta* 37, no. 7 (1954): 2039-57.

Stoll, A., J. Peyer, and A. Hofmann. "Synthese von optisch Aktiven a-Amino-alkoholen. 5. Mitteilung über Mutterkornalkaloide." *Helvetica Chimica Acta* 26, no. 3 (1943): 929-43.

Stoll, A., J. Rutschmann, and A. Hofmann. "Über Die Synthese von 14c-Diäthylamin und 14c-Lysergsäurediäthylamid." *Helvetica Chimica Acta* (1954): 820–24.

Stoll, A., F. Troxler, Albert Hofmann, and J. Peyer. "Eine neue Synthese von Bufotenin und verwandten Oxytryptaminen." *Helvetica Chimica Acta* 38 (1955): 1452–72.

Stoll, A., F. Troxler, and A. Hofmann. "Über die Umwandlung von 6-Methyl-8-amino-ergolin in 6-Methyl-8-oxy-ergolin. 29. Mitteilung Über Mutterkornalkaloide." *Helvetica Chimica Acta* 35, no. 4 (1952): 1259-63.

Stoll, Arthur, and Albert Hofmann. "Racemische Lysergsäure und ihre Auflösung in die optischen Antipoden." *Hoppe-Seyler's Zeitschrift für physiologische Chemie*, 7, 1937.

Stütz, P., P.A. Stadler, and A. Hofmann. "Synthese von Ergonin und Ergoptin, zweier Mutterkornalkaloid-Analoga der Ergoxin-Gruppe". *Helvetica Chimica Acta* 53, no. 6 (1970): 1278-85.

Taylor, W.I., A.J. Frey, and A. Hofmann. "Vomilenin und seine Umwandlung in Perakin." *Helvetica Chimica Acta* 45, no. 2 (1962): 611-14.

Troxler, F., and A. Hofmann. "Oxydation von Lysergsäure-Derivaten in 2,3-Stellung. 47. Mitteilung über Mutterkornalkaloide." *Helvetica Chimica Acta* 42, no. 3 (1959): 793-802.

Troxler, F., and A. Hofmann. "Substitutionen am Ringsystem der Lysergsäure I. Substitutionen am Indolstickstoff." *Helvetica Chimica Acta* 40 (1957): 1706-20, 21-32.

Troxler, F., and A. Hofmann. "Substitutionen am Ringsystem der Lysergsäure. II. Halogenierung." *Helvetica Chimica Acta* 40 (1957): 2160-70.

Troxler, F., F. Seemann, and A. Hofmann. "Abwandlungprodukte von Psilocybin und Psilocin. 2. Mitteilung über Synthetische Indolverbindungen." *Helvetica Chimica Acta* 42, no. 6 (1959): 2073-103.

Compiled by Jonathan Ott with the support of Lilly Brown, Albert Hofmann's secretary while at Sandoz, and Albert Hofmann; expanded by Dieter Hagenbach.

Photo Credits

Hofmann family collection: Pages xxii, 4, 5 bottom and top, 6, 7, 9, 10, 12 bottom, 13, 14 left and right, 15, 16, 17, 26, 28 middle, left, and right, 29 left and right, 30 left and right, 31 left and right, 32 top, 33 top left, bottom left and right, 34, left and right, 35 left and right, 47 bottom right, 68, 85 right, 87, 91 Top, 107 top, bottom left and right, 109, 111 left and right, 116 left and right, 117, 123 left and right, 127 (bottom left photo: Sanford Roth) 132, 133, 238 left, 266 right, 268, 269 left and right, 285 left and right, 286, 288 left and right, 289, 291, 305 top left, 325, 328 left, 331 (drawings), 329 left, 333 top left and right, 335 bottom left and right, 336

Collection Lucius Werthmüller: Pages x, 52 right, 60 top, 99 top and bottom, 108, 113 top and bottom right, 119, 120, 168 right, 187, 201 middle, 238 right, 277, 291, 328 top middle, 333 bottom left, 339 bottom and top row except first, 341 top row, 342 middle and top row left and middle, 347 middle

Novartis company archives: Pages 18, 21 top and bottom, 22 bottom right, top left and right, 23, 24, 25 top, bottom left and right, 37, 38 left and right, 39 top, bottom left and right, 40 left and right, 41, 43, 49, 45, 47, 51 left and right, 63 left and middle, 89, 95, 97, 98 left, 102, 103, 270, 271 left and right, 272, 343

Collection Roger Liggenstorfer: Pages 245 middle, 259 right, 297 left and right, 312, 317 top left and right (right photo: Claudia Müller-Ebeling), 319, 320 bottom left, 320 top left and right, 321 bottom right, top row and second row left

Collection Stanislav Grof: Pages xi, xv, xvi, xviii, xx, 199, 208, 209, 213 left, 220, 223 right, 311 middle

Collection Dieter Hagenbach: Pages 54, 183 middle, 246 top, 255 right, 290 bottom

Collection Virginia Beresford: Pages 194 left and right (Photo: Werner Pieper), 195 (photo: Lee Harris)

ABB Switzerland Historical Archive: Pages 3, 11, 12 middle

Isaac Abrams: Page 233

© Robert Altman: Page 159

Michael Ansler: Page 76

Baden Historical Museum: Pages 2, 356

Philip Hansen Bailey: Pages 63 right, 315 middle and bottom

Udo Breger: Pages 298 left, 299, 303, 310 right, 315 top left

Bernd Curmudgeon: Page 196

Clayton Call, © Getty Images: Page 165 top left

© Dean Chamberlain: Page vii-ix

Jack Coddington: Page 191

© Robert Crumb: Pages 243 left, 245 top row

DEA Museum, Washington, D. C: page 52 middle. (Photo: Erowid.org 2011)

Rick Doblin: Page 215 right

The Doug Engelbart Institute: Page 252 right

Simon Duttwyler: Pages 340 right, 342 top right, 336 bottom

Gene Erowid Center's Stolaroff Collection: Page 250 (photo: Erowid.org 2011)

Jennifer Esperanza: Page 113 bottom left

James Fadiman: Page 252 left

freeleonardpickard.org: Page 192

Peter Gasser: Page 347 right

© Alex Grey: Page 227, 231

Beat Gugger: Pages 266 left, 267

Matteo Guarnaccia and Galleria Antonio Colombo Arte Contemporanea, Milano: Page 241

Jon Hanna, © Erowid.org 2011: Page 345

Robert "Rio" Hahn: Page 258

Marie Harding, Institute of Ecotechnics: Page 330, 329 right

Lee Harris: Page 195

Naomi Harris: Pages 335 top, 349

Kathleen Harrison: 229 top and middle, 260

Andreas Hofmann: Pages 355, 371

© Martina Hofmann: Page 240 bottom

Michael Horowitz Collection: Pages 263, 277, 278

Intermedia Foundation: Page 154

Graham Keen: Page 182 left

Klarwein Family: Page 237

Jakob Krattiger: Page 325

Hugo Jäggi: Page 326

© François Lagarde: Cover photo, Pages 104, 115, 310 left, 328 right, 372-373

© Lisa Law: Pages 157, 163 top right, middle, 180 left and right, 234

Timothy Leary Futique Trust: Page 146 left, 147 left

Tobias Madörin: Page 239

Magliabecchiano Codex, National Library Florence: Page 91 middle

MAPS: Page 347 left

Mark McCloud Collection: Pages 245 right, middle bottom, 246 bottom right

Rosie McGee: Page 164 top

Collection of Ralph Metzner: Page 321 middle right, 323 top left

Claudia Müller-Ebeling: Page 236 top, 317 right, 355 top

NASA: Page 257 left

National Film Board of Canada: Page 223 left (Photo: Kent Martin)

Wolfgang Maria Ohlhäuser: Page 249

Frank Olson Project: Page 85 top

Vanja Palmers: Page 221 right

© Gordon Peters/Corbis, Page 184

Eva Presenhuber: Page 297

Pascal Querner: Page 176-177

Ram Dass personal archive: Page 135, 143, 147 (Photo: Peter Gould)

Collection Christian Rätsch: Page 317 middle left and bottom, 307

Hansjörg Sahli: Page 230, 337 top row, 339 top row first photo on the left, 338, 340 top left, 342 bottom right

Nick Sand: Page 168 top left

Nick Sand, Gene Bernofsky, Glamour 1970: Page 168 middle

© Gilbert Shelton: Page 243 top right, 245 bottom left

Swiss International Air Lines Ltd.: Page 183 bottom

© Richard Toelanie: Cover and title page psychedelic graphic

© Robert Venosa, collection Jody Polishchuk, Toronto: Page 59

© Robert Venosa, collection Miguel Bose, Madrid: Page 210

Peter Vogel: Page 322

Wikimedia Commons: Page 240

Robert Williams and Tony Shafrazi Gallery, New York: Page 297

Marianne Wohlleb: Page 283 left

Some images the photographer or artist was not able to be identified. Please contact the publisher if your credit was missed.

Index of Names

At the last visit by the authors April, 2008

382

About the Authors

Dieter Hagenbach

Lucius Werthmüller

Dieter Hagenbach was born 1943 in Basel, Switzerland. He studied architecture and the arts at the Academy of Fine Arts, Düsseldorf, Germany. In 1975 he founded Sphinx publishing house, with works by Joseph Campbell, H.R. Giger, George Gurdjieff, Jean Houston, Timothy Leary, John Lilly, Terence McKenna, Alan Watts, Robert Anton Wilson, among others. From 1977–1986 he was editor of *Sphinx* magazine and the German language edition of the *Brain/Mind Bulletin*.

Dieter Hagenbach met Albert Hofmann in the mid-1970s and remained his friend until his death. In 1986 he published Albert Hofmann's book *Einsichten Ausblicke (Insight Outlook)*. From 1990–2005 Hagenbach acted as a literary agent. In 1993 he launched the Gaia Media Foundation. He was initiator and program manager of the international symposium "LSD – Problem Child and Wonder Drug" in Basel, 2006, on the occasion of Albert Hofmann's 100th birthday, and was in charge of the program for the 2008 "World Psychedelic Forum" in Basel. Since 2002 Dieter Hagenbach has been the editor of the Gaia Media Foundation website and the monthly electronic *GoodNewsLetter*.

Lucius Werthmüller was born 1958 in Basel, Switzerland. He is a consciousness researcher and parapsychologist. Since 1991 he has been president of the Basel Psi Association with over 1,200 members, the largest organization in the field of the paranormal and the spiritual in Switzerland, and is editor of the *Psi-Info* magazine. In 2000 he was awarded the "Swiss Foundation for Parapsychology" prize. For eight years Lucius was project manager of the "Basel Psi-Days," a congress with the reputation as the most important public congress on "border areas" of science worldwide. Since 1992 he has run an antique bookshop specializing in parapsychology and spirituality.

Lucius is a founding board member of the Gaia Media Foundation. He was project manager of the international symposium "LSD – Problem Child and Wonder Drug" in 2006 on the occasion of the 100th birthday of Albert Hofmann in Basel, and of the "World Psychedelic Forum" held in 2008. Lucius met Albert Hofmann, who was a good friend of his parents, as a child and remained close to him until the end of his life. Lucius has three adult sons and lives with his partner, Sabin, in Basel.

Other Books from Synergetic Press

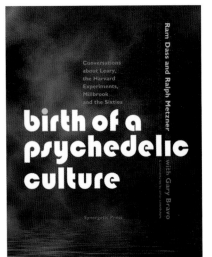

Birth of a Psychedelic Culture: Conversations about Leary, the Harvard Experiments, Millbrook and the Sixties

By Ram Dass and Ralph Metzner with Gary Bravo

Birth of a Psychedelic Culture shines a bright light on the emergence of the sixties culture and the experiments with mind-altering substances undertaken by Professors Timothy Leary, Richard Alpert (Ram Dass) and then-Harvard graduate student Ralph Metzner. Based on a series of conversations between Metzner and Ram Dass and recorded by psychiatrist and author Gary Bravo, this book describes their initial experiments at Harvard, the experiments after they were dismissed from Harvard, their journeys to India and their reflections on that transformative era.

ISBN: 978-0-907791-38-6 / Paperback / 264 pages / 8x10 inches / Illustrated / $29.95

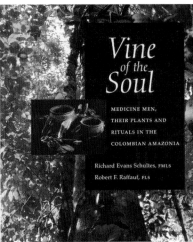

Vine of The Soul: Medicine Men, Their Plants and Rituals in the Colombian Amazonia

By Richard Evans Schultes, Robert Raffauf

Vine of the Soul is a collection of essays and photographs depicting life in the Amazon rainforest during the years that Schultes lived there. While Schultes, who proved to have a great eye for lighting, composition and subject matter, took the photos himself, the essays are co-authored by botanist extraordinaire Robert F. Raffauf. As plants are a priority for the indigenous peoples of the rainforest – just as they are for Schultes and Raffauf – plants and the people who use them (particularly medicine men, or payés) constitute much of the subject matter.

ISBN: 978-0-907791-31-7 / Paperback / 290 pages / 160 B&W photos / 8x10 inches / $29.95

Ayahuasca Reader: Encounters with the Amazon's Sacred Vine

By Luis Eduardo Luna, Steven F. White

The most comprehensive collection of authoritative writings on the subject ever published. A panorama of texts translated from nearly a dozen languages on the ayahuasca experience. These include indigenous mythic narratives and testimonies, religious hymns, as well as narratives related by western travelers, scientists, and writers who have had contact with ayahuasa in different contexts. Some of the material in this Reader has been published before in difficult to find journals and books in a variety of languages.

ISBN: 978-0-907791-32-4 / Paperback / 264 pages / 8.5x11 inches / Illustrated / $29.95

**Full list of titles at
www.synergeticpress.com**